QuickBase: The Missing Manual

QuickBase: The Missing Manual

Nancy Conner

O'REILLY®

Beijing · Cambridge · Farnham · Köln · Sebastopol · Tokyo

QuickBase: The Missing Manual

by Nancy Conner

Copyright © 2007 O'Reilly Media. All rights reserved.
Printed in the United States of America.

Published by O'Reilly Media, Inc., 1005 Gravenstein Highway North, Sebastopol, CA 95472.

O'Reilly books may be purchased for educational, business, or sales promotional use. Online editions are also available for most titles (*http://safari.oreilly.com*). For more information, contact our corporate/institutional sales department: (800) 998-9938 or *corporate@oreilly.com*.

Printing History:

February 2007:   First Edition.

ISBN: 978-0-596-52960-4
1300713031
[SAR 11/09]

[LSI]   2011-03-25

Table of Contents

Introduction

It's two a.m., and suddenly you sit bolt upright in bed, wondering whether you remembered to email everyone the agenda for your eight-o'clock meeting. Or you've been working for three days now trying to merge a dozen versions of the same spreadsheet. You're at the point where you have to sit on your hands to keep from strangling the next unfortunate soul who wanders past your desk. Or you can't get the IT brainiacs to see why their self-described "brilliant" solution doesn't fit so well with your workflow —and your forehead is getting sore from pounding it against the wall.

There's got to be a better way—and thanks to QuickBase, there is. QuickBase is a Web-based, workgroup-friendly, data-sharing program that puts *you* in control of your work. No more trying to coordinate your team via a blizzard of emails, or playing frustrating games of "guess which document is the right one." QuickBase lets you capture, modify, share, and manage data and documents—quickly and easily.

What You Can Do with QuickBase

QuickBase saves your organization time and money, letting you manage and share the information that makes your business tick: sales figures, project timelines, drafts of documents, purchase or work requests—whatever information you need to keep business flowing smoothly. Use QuickBase to perform any of these chores:

- **Capture and modify data.** Whatever kind of data you need to store—sales leads, catalog listings, project milestones, workflow checklists, or whatever—you can use QuickBase's forms to record and organize that data in a way that makes sense to you. And changing records is a cinch—whether one at a time or en masse.

- **Filter, sort, and group data.** Just because you capture a ton of information doesn't mean you want to see it all at once. Easily find the records that match your criteria, and then sort those records into groups that make their relationships clear.

- **Display your data online.** QuickBase uses reports (Chapter 2) to let you display and summarize data. Choose from six main report styles: Table, Grid Edit, Summary/Crosstab, Calendar, Chart, and Timeline. And switching between reports is easy—you can take the tasks listed in a table, for example, and display them as a timeline with just a couple of mouse clicks.

- **Create printed reports.** Print out a hard copy, embed QuickBase charts in the annual report, or email this month's sales numbers.

QuickBase comes packed with some particularly cool features, making it a great cure for your worst business headaches:

- **Prebuilt applications.** You don't have to go back to school to learn how to design a QuickBase *application* (QuickBase's term for the mini-databases you use to work on each project). QuickBase supplies dozens of ready-made applications for a wide range of purposes—sales and customer management, back-office tasks, project management, issue tracking, and many more. Within minutes, you can create and start using a new application. (Of course, if you've got just a bit of gumption, you can build your own app from scratch; see the bullet point on customization, below.)

- **User access controls.** In QuickBase, you can assign people different roles within your application; each role has a different level of access built in. For example, most applications come with three predefined roles: viewer, participant, and administrator. Viewers can look at the application's data but can't change it; participants can work with the data in various ways (such as adding records); and administrators have full control of the database. These built-in roles are a handy starting place for defining levels of access, but you're not stuck with them; you can customize any role or create a new one to meet your application's precise needs.

- **Email notifications.** You can tell QuickBase to send out automatic notifications to a list of users you select whenever an important record changes. So when someone uploads the latest version of a document or when the boss assigns you a new task, you're never in the dark.

- **Customization.** Gertrude Stein wrote, "A rose is a rose is a rose." But QuickBase is not QuickBase is *not* QuickBase. The QuickBase applications your team uses probably look very different from the ones they're using in another company, because you can tweak—or overhaul—QuickBase applications to get them just so. Customize any application—even prebuilt ones—to meet your organization's exact needs. Add or remove fields, shuffle their order, change a text box to a multiple-choice drop-down menu, even add your own text or logo to an application. Does your company talk about "tickets" or "work requests" instead of "work orders?" No problem. You don't have to change company lingo—you can change the name of the records in QuickBase. It's so flexible, you'll think the program was custom designed just for you.

- **Accessibility.** Because it's Web-based, you can access QuickBase anytime, from anywhere you have an Internet connection (for browser requirements, see "Browser Requirements" on page xv). Time zones and business travel will never again interfere with your team's ability to work together.

- **Reliability.** QuickBase is a product of Intuit, the same folks who make TurboTax, Quicken, and QuickBooks. With more than 20 years' experience focusing on business and financial management, Intuit offers the experience and dependability your firm needs when sharing the data that powers your business.

- **Flexibility.** Ever wait through one or two presidential administrations for Microsoft to release a new version of its software? QuickBase *won't* leave you wondering who'll be in the Oval Office by the time the next upgrade comes out. Because QuickBase is a Web-based program, Intuit can (and does) frequently roll out new features. So you get the benefits of the latest technology, user suggestions, and ways to make your life easier—all on a regular basis. And here's more good news: This *Missing Manual* is continuously updated to reflect any major QuickBase changes that Intuit releases.

What You Need to Get Started

When you say QuickBase, emphasize the *quick*—because it takes just a few minutes to create an account and start uploading your data. (Chapter 1 gives you details about how to get started with QuickBase and takes you for a spin around the site.) The following section covers the very basics of what you need to use QuickBase.

A QuickBase Account

Each person using QuickBase needs an account to use the service. Intuit offers several different plans, depending on how many users and how much storage space you need. You can even try QuickBase free for 30 days: Go to www.quickbase.com (*http://www .quickbase.com*), look for the Free Trial section, and click the link that says, "Click here to get started." Once you've created an account ("Creating an Account" on page 2), QuickBase starts your free 30-day trial. If you decide you like QuickBase, it's easy to switch over to a billing program. Just click the "subscribe now" link at the bottom of your My QuickBase page.

TIP

You might get invited to join someone *else's* QuickBase setup, even if you're not yet a QuickBase user. In that case, you don't need to worry about who created (or pays for) the billing account. All you have to do to accept the invitation is register with QuickBase; see "Managing Your Account Information" on page 19 for details.

Browser Requirements

QuickBase comes packed with lots of modern Web page controls. To get the most out of your QuickBase experience you need to use one of the following Web browsers:

- Internet Explorer 5.5 or later (on Windows PCs).

- Any browser, Windows or Mac, based on Mozilla 1.6 or later, including Netscape 7.1, Firefox 1.6, and others.

TIP

To find out which version of a Web browser you're using, open your browser and, on its menu bar, click Help→About.

If you've got the right browser, you're nine-tenths of the way there. Just a few other things to check for:

- **Make sure you've got JavaScript enabled.** JavaScript lets your browser run programming code, making Web pages more interactive. (If you're not sure whether your browser has JavaScript enabled, see the box in "When Java(Script) and Cookies Don't Mean a Coffee Break" on page xvi.)

- **Make sure that your Web browser accepts cookies.** Cookies are small text files that a remote Web site downloads to your computer, which helps to customize your visits to the site. (The box in "When Java(Script) and Cookies Don't Mean a Coffee Break" on page xvi tells you how to set your browser to accept cookies.)

- **Check that your browser is SSL-compliant (it almost definitely is).** SSL is all about security; it stands for *secure sockets layer*, and it means your browser can send and receive sensitive information over the Internet without giving away your secrets to anyone else. With SSL, data is encrypted (scrambled) and authenticated (unscrambled) using a secret key. That sounds like something out of a suspense novel, but all it means is that your information is secure. If you've ever bought anything from an online store, you've probably experienced SSL. To make sure that you've got a secure connection to QuickBase, make sure that the address in your browser's address bar begins with *https,* not just *http* (the *s* stands for *secure*). You can also check for a little picture of a closed padlock in the lower-right corner of your browser; a locked padlock means the connection is secure.

NOTE

If you're a Mac fan, QuickBase works best if you use Mozilla/Firefox as your Web browser. Right now, QuickBase doesn't support Internet Explorer or Safari browsers on the Macintosh.

UP TO SPEED

When Java(Script) and Cookies Don't Mean a Coffee Break

To use QuickBase, you need to have both JavaScript and cookies enabled in your Web browser. Your browser probably came with both activated, but if you're having trouble using QuickBase, it's worth checking to make sure your browser's settings are correct.

To flick on JavaScript in Internet Explorer version 5.5 or higher, follow these steps:

1. Select Tools→Internet Options.

   The Internet Options box opens.

2. Click the Security tab. In the "Security level for this zone" section, click the Custom Level button.

   A Security Settings box opens. This box has a long list of options.

3. Scroll down the list to the Scripting section. Under "Active scripting", make sure that Enable is turned on. If it's not, turn it on. Click OK.

   If you changed "Active scripting" from Disable or Prompt to Enable, Internet Explorer asks if you really want to change its security settings. (If you didn't make any changes, you won't see this confirmation box.)

4. Click Yes.

IE takes you back to the Internet Options box. Click OK to close the box and return to what you were doing. Now you've got JavaScript working for you.

In Mozilla, you enable or disable JavaScript starting with Edit on the menu bar:

1. Select Edit→Preferences.

   The Preferences box opens.

2. In the left-hand Category menu, click the plus sign next to Advanced, and then click Scripts & Plug-ins.

   The Scripts & Plug-ins pane appears.

3. Under "Enable JavaScript for", make sure that the checkbox next to Navigator is turned on. If it isn't, click the box to insert a checkmark and then click OK.

You've enabled JavaScript.

Now for the cookies. Internet Explorer 5 handles these a little different from IE 6. If you're working with IE 5.5, follow steps 1 and 2 above for opening the Internet Explorer Security Settings box. In the Security Settings list (step 3), scroll down to Cookies. For "Allow cookies that are stored on your computer," make sure Enable is turned on. Then continue with step 4.

For IE 6 or later, here's how to turn on cookies:

1. Select Tools→Internet Options.

   The Internet Options box appears.

2. Click the Privacy tab. In the middle of the box is a slider that corresponds to your browser's cookie settings. Make sure the slider is at Medium; if it's not, move the slider to the Medium setting. (This setting allows your computer to accept cookies from QuickBase while protecting it from third-party cookies, which marketers often use to collect information about your Web-surfing habits.) Click OK.

IE saves your settings and returns you to the Web page you were looking at.

In Mozilla, you manage cookies using the aptly named Cookie Manager. First, surf over to www.quickbase.com (*http://www.quickbase.com*). Then, in Mozilla, select

Tools→Cookie Manager→"Allow Cookies from this Site." That's it. How much easier could it possibly get?

About This Book

If you're the type who thinks designing a database solution for your business needs sounds about as fun and easy as a do-it-yourself root canal, prepare to have your mind changed. The best way to learn QuickBase is to jump in and start playing with it; this book will show you where to dive in and how to get started. Before you know it, you'll want to use QuickBase for everything from managing sales leads to organizing your grandmother's recipe collection.

If, on the other hand, you've been managing information and designing databases ever since you first got bored with coloring books and nursery rhymes—if you dream in rows and columns—this book will elevate you to QuickBase guru, helping you use the site to its full potential.

Novice or expert, here's a taste of what you'll find in the following pages:

- Get your database solution up and running in minutes—not days—using one of QuickBase's dozens of prebuilt applications (Chapter 6).

- Create a report (Chapter 2) to display your data in the way that best gets your point across. Filter out irrelevant records, group records into categories, and customize column layout. From pie charts ("Chart Reports" on page 56) to stoplight reports ("Color My World" on page 76), QuickBase offers reports that display your data in useful ways.

- Control who has access to your data—and what they can do with it—using customizable roles ("Adjusting What Roles Can See and Do" on page 364).

- Use formulas to make QuickBase do the math for you—performing calculations using a specific field or fields ("Creating a Formula Field" on page 421)—to create a custom column ("Using Formulas to Design Reports" on page 435), or design a custom query ("Choosing Which Columns Appear in an Embedded Table" on page 483). Excel and Access whizzes will feel right at home with these tools.

- Create relationships to link different tables (a *relationship* populates a field in one table with a record from another table), even tables in different applications. Chapter 10 tells you all about table relationships.

- Embed a QuickBase table in your company's Web page ("Inserting a Table of Detail Records" on page 482).

- Create a survey that anyone on the Internet can respond to ("Project Management" on page 197).

- Browse through a library containing hundreds of applications ("A Tour of Quick-Base's Application Templates" on page 195)—some designed by QuickBase, some by other QuickBase users—where you can hunt for ideas, get inspired, or steal (er, borrow) a trick or two.

About the Outline

QuickBase: The Missing Manual is divided into three parts, each containing several chapters:

- **Chapters 1 through 4** start you off with the nuts and bolts of using QuickBase. You might be invited to join an existing application and have no clue what to expect when you get there. These chapters get you up to speed fast, starting with a quick tour of the site and explaining the different ways QuickBase lets you view, filter, display, and share data and documents. In no time you'll be creating new records, importing and modifying data, working with documents, and generating reports and automatic emails—all like the pro that you are.

- **Chapters 5 through 9** show you how to set up your own QuickBase application. This section starts off with some suggestions to help you plan your QuickBase solution before you even sign in to the site: define the problem, explore your work-flow, track information, and keep your team working together. When you're ready to take your QuickBase solution live, you can use one of QuickBase's prebuilt applications as a launchpad or create your own application from scratch—both these approaches get a chapter apiece. Getting your application up and running is one thing—keeping it running *smoothly* is another. Learn tips and techniques for customizing your application, inviting users and controlling their access, working with tables within an application, and much, much more.

- **Chapters 10 through 12** offer advanced application management tools. These chapters take you from merely working with QuickBase to ruling it—elevating you to King or Queen of All Things QuickBase. Take charge of your applications: master table relationships, formulas, and advanced fields; and create sophisticated reports using exact forms. And even if you think API stands for Annual Precipitation Index or the American Potato Institute, by the time you finish this section, you'll know that QuickBase's API (it stands for Application Program Interface, by the way), lets developers interact with QuickBase behind the scenes.

The Very Basics

You'll find very little jargon or nerd terminology in this book. You will, however, run across a few terms and concepts that you'll encounter frequently in your computing life:

- **Clicking.** This book gives you three kinds of instructions that require you to use your computer's mouse or trackpad. To *click* means to point the arrow cursor at something on the screen and then—without moving the cursor at all—to press and release the clicker button on the left side of the mouse (or laptop trackpad). To *right-click* means to point the cursor and click the button on the right side of the mouse (or trackpad); Mac users with only one mouse button can replicate this maneuver by hitting the Control key while they're clicking. And to *drag* means to move the cursor while pressing the button continuously.

- **Menus.** The *menus* are the words at the top of your browser: File, Edit, and so on. Click one to make a list of commands appear, as though they're written on a window shade you've just pulled down.

  Some people click and release the mouse button to open a menu and then, after reading the menu command choices, click again on the one they want. Other people like to hold down the mouse button continuously after the initial click on the menu title, drag down the list to the desired command, and only then release the mouse button. Either method works fine.

- **Keyboard shortcuts.** Every time you take your hand off the keyboard to move the mouse, you lose time and potentially disrupt your workflow. That's why many experienced computer fans use *keystroke combinations* instead of menu commands whenever possible. Ctrl+B (⌘-B on a Mac), for example, is a keyboard shortcut for boldface type in most word-processing programs.

  When you see a shortcut like Ctrl+Shift (⌘-Shift) (which lets you select a range of options from a list), it's telling you to hold down the Ctrl or ⌘ key, and, while it's down, press the Shift key, and then release both keys.

About→These→Arrows

Throughout this book, and throughout the Missing Manual series, you'll find sentences like this one: "Select Customize→Create a new→Table." That's shorthand for a much longer instruction that directs you to open three nested commands in sequence, like this: "On the QuickBase page, you'll find a menu item called Customize. Select that. On the Customize menu is an option called "Create a new"; click it. On *that* menu is yet another option called Table. Click it to open a page that allows you to create a new table." This kind of arrow shorthand helps to simplify the business of choosing commands in menus, as shown in Figure I-1.

Safari® Books Online

When you see a Safari® Books Online icon on the cover of your favorite technology book, that means the book is available online through the O'Reilly Network Safari Bookshelf.

Safari offers a solution that's better than e-Books. It's a virtual library that lets you easily search thousands of top tech books, cut and paste code samples, download chapters, and find quick answers when you need the most accurate, current information. Try it free at http://my.safaribooksonline.com (*http://safari.oreilly.com*).

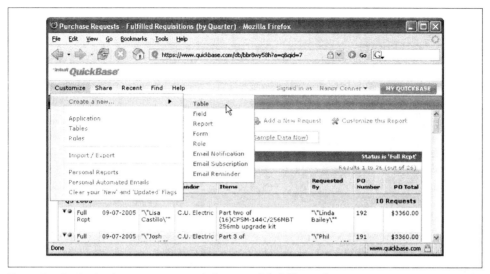

Figure I-1. In this book, arrow notations help to simplify folder and menu instructions. For example, "Select Customize→Create a new→Table" explains the actions shown here: Click the Customize menu, then select the "Create a new" menu item. From the flyout menu that appears, select Table.

CHAPTER 1

Signing Up and Taking a Quick Tour

The hardest challenge you'll ever face with QuickBase is quickly describing what it is. A highly customizable database? A workflow management system? A Web site that can make your working life a whole heckuva lot easier? Yes, yes, and yes.

Because it helps with so many different tasks, QuickBase doesn't fit neatly into the program categories we're used to talking about—database or spreadsheet programs, contact managers, or project management applications, for instance. But whatever you want to call it, at heart, QuickBase is an amazingly powerful and endlessly customizable database, whose greatest tools are offered up to you, lucky QuickBase user, even as you're shielded from some of the highly technical underpinnings that power everything it can do.

Whatever information your business relies on, QuickBase lets you share it easily with those who need it. QuickBase provides a secure, centralized place to store, work with, and share data: reports, specifications, spreadsheets, price lists, client information, work orders, invoices, purchase orders—any kind of data your organization uses. So wherever your team members are, they can get on the Internet, sign in to QuickBase, and view, add, and edit data. They can submit billable hours, track leads, share documents, submit and prioritize change requests—whatever. QuickBase's flexibility lets you create forms that work for your business and display your data in a variety of different ways, using charts, tables, timelines, and more.

Half your mental investment in QuickBase is made just getting acquainted with all the various virtual levers, switches, boxes, and forms that you have at your disposal. That's what this book is designed to do. In this chapter you'll take your kickoff tour so you know your way around this machine. Specifically, you'll learn how to:

- Register to use QuickBase
- Respond to an invitation to join a QuickBase application
- Use your My QuickBase page, your home page inside QuickBase
- Set your preferences and manage your account information
- Get started with an application

• Use an application's Dashboard page

NOTE

You'll see the term *application* used everywhere within QuickBase. An application is simply QuickBase-speak for a database that stores and organizes your information. You might be invited to join someone else's application, or you can create your own.

Creating an Account

Think of a QuickBase account as your nametag that lets you roam the halls of a giant data storage warehouse, crammed full of all kinds of interesting tidbits. The account gives you access to names and contact info, requests from fellow QuickBase users, and a timeline of who's doing what on a project—everything you need to know to get your job done, all in one place. It's all essential stuff. But you can't peek at it if you're not registered. Registering takes only a few seconds—and then you're good to go.

To register with QuickBase, you take one of two routes:

• **Create a brand-new account.** When you've got information you want to organize —client lists, expense reports, inventory spreadsheets, your vintage baseball card collection—open a new account to get started. The first 30 days are free.

• **Accept an invitation.** When someone has information they want to share with you—you've just joined a new project management team or a client wants your opinion on a report—that person sends you an email invitation to join their application.

Either way, you'll be up and running on QuickBase in no time.

Creating a New Account

If you want to create a new account to sniff around QuickBase and try out its features, you can do so for free with a 30-day trial. (When you're ready to pull the trigger and pay for an account, just click the "Subscribe now" link in the bottom-left part of your My QuickBase page—that's the first page you see when you sign in to the site.) Head over to the QuickBase home page at *www.quickbase.com* (Figure 1-1), and then follow these steps:

1. In the upper-right corner, click the "Sign in" link.

   The Sign In page, shown in Figure 1-2, opens.

2. Click the "Create a log-in" link.

   The Register page, shown in Figure 1-3, opens. Registration requires three steps: Register, Verify, and Sign In. Get the process started by typing in your email address. Then choose a password (it has to be at least eight characters long), confirm

---

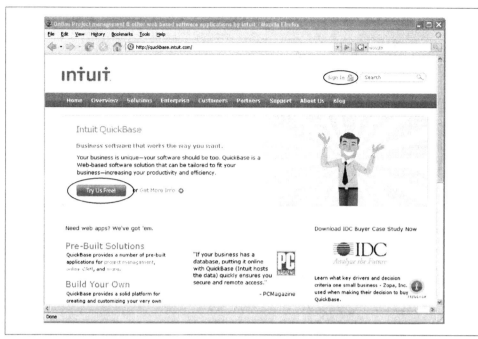

Figure 1-1. To register with QuickBase (or to sign in once you've registered), click the Sign In link (circled; if you don't have an account yet, you can create one on the next page). If you're interested in trying QuickBase free for a month, click the Try Us Free! button (also circled). You can even search QuickBase's Help files before you give the program a try—type any term into the upper-right Search box (next to the Sign In link), and then click the magnifying glass.

the password, and type in your first and last names. QuickBase also requires some information about your company and your role in it, so fill that in, too. Read QuickBase's terms of service (if you're into that sort of thing) by clicking on whatever country you live in. Turn on the checkbox to indicate you agree to the terms, and then click the Register button.

NOTE

Currently, QuickBase accounts are available only to residents of the United States, Canada, the United Kingdom, and Japan.

Figure 1-2. QuickBase's Sign In screen. When registering for a new account, click the "Create a log-in" link. (If you type in your email address and then click "Create a log-in," the box that pops up has your email address all filled in.) If you've already got a QuickBase account, enter your email address and password here to gain access to the site. If you have an account and you've forgotten your password, clicking the "Forgot your password for QuickBase?" link lets you reset it—just make sure the new password is one you'll remember!

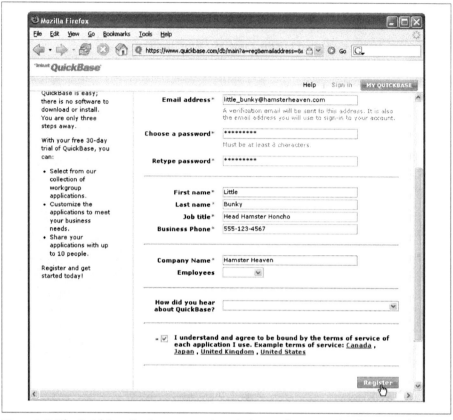

Figure 1-3. The QuickBase Register page gathers the basic information QuickBase needs to open your account.

3. Check your email for a message about your QuickBase registration. In the email, click the "click here" link.

   You're whisked back to QuickBase for the next step.

4. Sign in to QuickBase for the very first time. QuickBase has already filled in your email address; all you need to do is type in the password you chose back in step 2, and then click the "Sign in" button.

   Presto! You're registered.

NOTE

If for some reason the "click here" link in your verification email doesn't work, scroll to the bottom of the email for further instructions. There's a link you can copy and paste into your Web browser to finish the registration process.

Help! I Didn't Get My Verification Email

As soon as you click Register in step 2 of the registration process, QuickBase's verification email wings its way through cyberspace to your email inbox. But what if you go through the registration steps, fill in all the needed info, click Register—and then sit back to wait for an email that never appears?

The likely culprit? Your spam filter—an overzealous junk-mail catcher that probably nabbed the QuickBase verification email before you even saw it. To find the email, try one of these strategies:

- Check your email program's Junk folder.
- Add the following address to your email program's address book: *corp-sales@quickbase.com*.
- Try signing in to QuickBase. If your account is unverified, QuickBase's Unverified Account page appears. This page lists the email address you used to register; double-check that address to make sure you didn't make a mistake typing it in. If your email address looks OK, click the Resend Verification Email button to try again.
- If all else fails, talk to your network administrator to make sure that your network's settings aren't filtering emails that come from QuickBase.

You can't use QuickBase until you've got a verified account, so getting that verification email is an absolute must!

Accepting an Invitation

If someone with a QuickBase account wants you to start using one of their QuickBase applications, you'll get an email invitation to join QuickBase. The email has the name of the application and the words "QuickBase Invitation" in the subject line.

The body of the email contains a link to a page within QuickBase; click that link to go to the Register page, which tells you that QuickBase has started to create an account for you. The Register page is identical to the one shown in Figure 1-3. Enter your name and a password, and QuickBase takes you straight to the application's Dashboard page ("Getting Started with Applications" on page 36). From there, you can work with the application in whatever capacity the administrator who invited you has assigned.

If you're invited to work with someone else's QuickBase application, you may or may not have the ability to create your *own* applications. It depends on the permissions (usage rights) that you've been granted. If you don't see a Create a New Application button in the upper-right part of your My QuickBase page, you don't have permission to create applications. Permission levels range from viewer—a role that lets you look at an application but not play with it—to billing account administrator, who's the Great Grand Pooh-bah of a QuickBase billing account. (A billing account is the umbrella that gathers together all the applications of one paying customer—for example, your company might have just one billing account, but many applications within that account.)

For any given account, the billing account administrator has the power to decide who can create applications, who can manage them, and who can't have access to the account at all. If you're missing that Create a New Application button and you want to create your own applications, talk to the person who invited you and ask them to give you "create applications" permission.

Signing In

After you have a QuickBase account, you can sign in from any of the public pages on the site. Just look in the upper-right corner for the "Sign in" link. This whisks you right to the Sign In page shown back in Figure 1-2. Type in your email address or your QuickBase screen name ("Edit user information" on page 20) if you have one, enter your password, and then click the "Sign in" button. If it's all correct, QuickBase takes you right to your My QuickBase page ("Using Your My QuickBase Page" on page 8).

If you don't share a computer with anyone else, you can save yourself some typing by staying permanently signed in to QuickBase. On the Sign In page, just turn on the checkbox that says, "Keep me signed in on this computer unless I sign out." If you choose this option, it's still a good idea to sign out at the end of the day or if you're going to be away from your computer for a while—you don't want someone else messing with your business while you're at lunch or in a meeting.

Forgot your password?

It happens to the best of us. When you registered with QuickBase you selected a password that would be easy to remember and tough for anyone else to crack—only now, you can't for the life of you remember what it was. To get back into the QuickBase Kingdom, just follow these steps:

On the Sign In page (glance back to Figure 1-2), type in your email address, and then click the "Forgot your password for QuickBase?" link. (Or you can just click the link and then fill in the email address on the next page.) This opens the "Forgotten Password —Step 1" page. Verify that the email address is the one you used to register for QuickBase and then click Next.

For obvious security reasons, QuickBase needs to verify that you are who you say you are. So it sends a verification email to the address you entered. When that email arrives in your inbox, you have 90 minutes to respond. (If you don't respond in that time, your old password remains in effect.) The verification email contains a link; clicking it takes you to the "Forgotten Password—Step 2" page, where you choose a new password. Type it in twice and click OK. This takes you back to the Sign In page, where you can sign in using your brand-new password.

Signing out

All good things must come to an end, even a session of working in QuickBase. To sign out of QuickBase, look in the upper-right corner of any QuickBase page, where you'll see the words "Signed in as" and your name. Next to your name is a little drop-down arrow. Clicking the arrow gives you a couple of options: Sign Out and Edit User profile —bet you can guess which one signs you out. When you click Sign Out, the page that opens lets you sign in again or jump over to the QuickBase home page.

Using Your My QuickBase Page

Your My QuickBase page (Figure 1-4) is your home within QuickBase. It's the page you see when you first sign in, your command center, your bird's-eye view of everything in your QuickBase account. From it, you can work with existing applications or create new ones (if you've got permission to do so; see the Note in "Accepting an Invitation" on page 6). You can take a look at the reports (ways of displaying your data) you work with most often. And you can manage your account information, search for an application, create and manage groups of folks who'll work on an application—whatever you want to do with QuickBase, this page is your starting point.

TIP

When you're signed in to QuickBase, you're never more than a click away from your My QuickBase page. Whatever page you're on, just look in the upper-right corner for the bright orange My QuickBase button. Click it to zip back to your My QuickBase page.

Viewing and Organizing Your Applications

QuickBase *applications* are databases that let you and your team tackle projects—like tracking sales figures, managing spreadsheets of customer accounts, developing re-

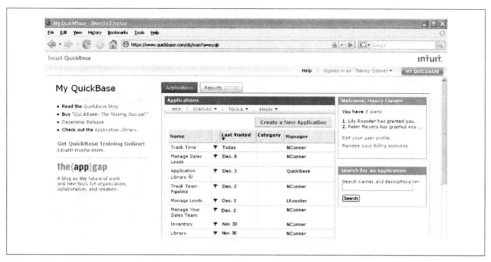

Figure 1-4. My QuickBase is the page you see when you sign into QuickBase. The Applications tab, shown here, displays a list of the applications you've opened most recently. This tab also offers a Search box so you can find a particular application. The Home tab shows up to 10 items: up to six reports, which you choose from all your applications, as well as text boxes for to-do lists, reminders, links to other Web pages, and more.

quirements specifications, and so on. The rest of the chapters in this book show you everything you need to know about the different types of applications and how to work with them. But before you focus on those details, it's worth taking a brief look at how to manage the applications on your My QuickBase page. Your starting point is the Applications table, which shows every application you have access to.

TIP

As the number of your applications grows, it can get just a wee bit harder to find the specific application you want. So QuickBase helps you out. To find a particular application, look at the menu options in the bar just above the Applications display; click Tools→Search for an application. A search box opens. Type in any word or phrase, and QuickBase hunts through the names and descriptions of all your applications. Once your QuickBase account has 20 or more applications, QuickBase makes searching even easier by making the search box a permanent feature on the right-hand side of your My QuickBase page. So when your list of applications grows as long as your arm, shift your eyes to the right to find the "Search for an Application" box.

You can display your My QuickBase applications in either Icons format (little database symbols with application names) or in Details format (a table that tells you all about who manages an application, when you last opened it, and more). To switch from Icons format to Details format—or vice versa—click Display just above the list of applications, and then select either Icons or Details.

What Those Icons Mean

When you scan the detailed list of your QuickBase applications, you'll probably notice a bunch of icons next to many application names. Here's what they mean.

Icon	What It Means
⊜	Anyone with Internet access can see this application.
▼	This application has changed; someone has modified existing records (data) or added new records since you last cleared the change flag.
NEW!	This is a new application.
UPDT	You won't see this icon on your My QuickBase page, but it shows up in your applications. Like the change flag, it means that someone has modified this application (or record).

Not everyone likes to see a hundred little flags waving all over the place. The quick 'n' easy way to clear the update icons is to look just under the blue bar that says Applications for the Tools button, then click Tools→"Clear flags". A box appears, asking you to confirm. Click OK, and wave goodbye to the flags.

Clearing flags means that you remove all the New and Updated flags from all your applications. But it doesn't affect anyone else's flags. So if you clear the flags from your My QuickBase page, you don't have to worry about George in the Peoria office missing an important update when he gets back from his vacation.

You can sort the information in your detailed Applications table in a number of different ways:

- **By application name.** Just click the Name header to sort applications alphabetically by name, in either ascending or descending order. If the triangle next to the Name is pointing up, the names are in ascending order; if it's pointing down, they're descending.

- **By when you last worked with an application.** Click Last Visited to find applications you worked with most recently or those you haven't worked with in a long time. (This is QuickBase's standard way of organizing your applications: the ones you visited most recently appear at the top of the list.)

- **By category.** If you've created a category and assigned some applications to it, you can sort applications by category so that all applications belonging to a certain category appear together; click Category to sort applications in this way. (Read on to learn how to create a category.)

- **By manager.** Click the Manager header to sort alphabetically by manager name in ascending or descending order. In QuickBase, a *manager* is the person who has administrative rights to control an application.

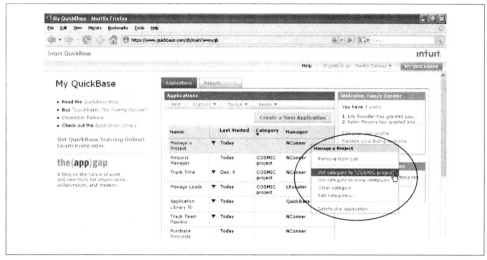

Figure 1-5. In the Applications table, right-click any row for quick help in organizing your applications. You can remove an application from your personal list, permanently delete an application you created, or create a category to fine-tune how your Applications list is organized.

If things get crowded, you can reorganize, hide, or permanently delete one or more of your applications. In Details display (see above), right-click any application in the Applications table (don't right-click the application's name; click the row that it's in). The menu that appears (Figure 1-5) lets you manage your applications in the following ways:

- **Hide this application.** This action doesn't delete an application—it just removes it from the list on your personal My QuickBase page.

TIP

If you've hidden an application and then have a change of heart, you can find it again and restore it to your Applications list. Search for it by clicking Applications→Search for an application. In the Search box that appears, you can search for all applications you have access to; find the banished application, and then click Add to bring it home to My QuickBase.

- **Set, clear, or edit category.** Categories help you organize your applications. A *category* simply groups similar applications to make it easy to find them. See "Using categories to organize your applications" on page 12 for the lowdown on creating and using categories.

- **Delete this application.** If you created an application, you can delete it using this menu. Deleting an application removes it entirely from QuickBase. Only the manager of an application or the administrator of a corporate account can delete an application.

Using categories to organize your applications

As your list of applications grows, you'll want a quick and easy way to organize your applications so you can find the info you need when you need it.

The best way to do this is with categories, which work like a filing system. You simply create the categories that make sense to you, and then organize applications into those categories. Because you're the one creating the categories and sorting applications into those categories, your organization reflects the way you work and think. Your categories appear only on your My QuickBase page; no one else sees them. So you can't mess up anyone else's categories—and they can't mess with yours.

Here's how to create a category and put an application into it:

1. Start from your My QuickBase page. Make sure it's set to Details display rather than Icons display.

   What's the difference? Icons display merely lists the names of your applications, along with little pictures of databases. Details display shows you a table that lists your applications and gives you some information about each one (when you last visited the application, who manages it, and any category you've assigned the application to). If you're in Icons display, look above all those icons for the Display button and click Display→Details.

2. In the detailed list of applications, find an application you want to categorize and right-click its row.

   A shortcut menu pops up, listing the application's name at its top.

3. Click "Assign a category to this application".

   The New Categories box appears, asking you to name the new category. You can categorize your applications however you like; the categories affect only your own My QuickBase page. So you might categorize applications by project name, by office location, by people you like working with—whatever works for you.

4. Type in the name of your new category, and then click OK.

   The new category's name appears in the Category column of the application. QuickBase also adds the category you just created to the menu that pops up when you right-click an application, making it easy to add other applications to that category. After you've created at least one category, you can sort applications by category: just click the Category header to sort in ascending or descending alphabetical order.

TIP

A quick way to add a new category to the pop-up menu is to use the Tools menu (just above the applications list). Click Tools→Edit categories. The Edit Categories box lets you edit (or delete) existing categories or create new ones.

After you've created and assigned some categories, you can tweak them in a few different ways:

- **Edit a category.** To change the name of a category (maybe you misspelled Project *Cosmic* as Project *Comic* and want to fix the typo—no matter how appropriate the misspelled name is), click Tools→Edit categories. The Edit Categories box displays all your existing categories, each in a text box. Click the category name you want to change, and then edit away. Click OK when you're done.

- **Delete a category.** When you don't need a category anymore—maybe your sunblock company closed its Anchorage sales office and there's no longer a need for an Alaska category—click Tools→Edit categories. In the box that pops up, find the category you want to get rid of, highlight it, and then press the Delete key. Click OK, and the category is history.

NOTE

When you delete a category, you don't delete the applications associated with that category. Instead, they become uncategorized.

- **Uncategorize an application.** If you want to remove an application from a category without deleting the category itself, go to your My QuickBase page's Application list (make sure you're looking at a table of applications in Details display), find the application you want, and right-click it. From the pop-up menu that appears, select "Clear category". You've set the application free.

- **Reassign an application from one category to another.** This isn't like divorce and remarriage—you don't have to unhitch an application from its previous category before you can assign it to a new one. Reassigning an application takes one short step. From the Details display of applications in My QuickBase, right-click the application you want; from the pop-up menu, select the name of the new category. Out with the old, in with the new.

TIP

To reduce clutter, you can display applications from one particular category. After you've created at least one category, new options appear on the Show menu above the Applications table: "Show all categories" (this is the default setting) and "Show [category name]"—for example, if you've created a category called Northeast Region, this option will say Show Northeast Region. To show applications in a specific category, click Show and then select the category you want to display. Applications that belong to other categories (or that haven't been categorized) magically disappear. (To get them back, use the same menu to choose a different category or show all categories.)

Hiding an application from My QuickBase

When you don't need a particular application anymore—it's obsolete or expired, for example—you don't need it cluttering up your My QuickBase page. When you still want just-in-case access to an old application's data, it's easy to remove a single application from your Applications list: Start in Details display and right-click the application's row. When the shortcut menu pops up, select "Remove from List". The application still exists and you still have access to it, but it's no longer on the list of applications on your My QuickBase page.

Restoring an application you've hidden

Oops—you hid an application from the list and you need it back—*now*. Luckily, you can find the application and get it back on your list without much trouble. Just take these steps:

1. Find the AWOL application: From your My QuickBase page, click Tools→Search for an application.

   The "Search for an Application" box appears.

2. In the text box, type in the name of the application you're looking for (or some part of it), and then click Search.

   A list of applications appears.

3. Find the one you want, and click Add. Or you can click the name of an application to open it and verify that it's the one you want.

   Either way, the application is back in your Applications list when you return to My QuickBase.

TIP

When you've got more than 20 applications in your Applications list, the "Search for an Application box" appears on the right-hand side of your My QuickBase page. Save yourself a step in the search process by typing your search terms directly into this box.

What if you're drawing a complete blank on the application's name? You can still get it back. In step two above, leave the text box blank and click Search. Doing so brings up the "Search for an Application" page, which offers you these choices:

- Search for text in the name or description of an application. (This option is the same as the one you get with the regular quick Search, but it's not much help if you can't remember anything about the application's name.)
- List all applications to which I have been granted access.
- List all applications that I manage.
- List all applications that are accessible by the group (you type in the name of a QuickBase group).

Choose one and click Search. By scanning the list of applications that you have access to, or that a group you belong to can access, you can easily find the missing application.

WARNING

Don't confuse removing an application with deleting it. When you remove an application from your My QuickBase, the application still exists, but it no longer appears in your Applications list. When you delete an application, you get rid of the application (and all its data) completely. It's gone, kaput, kablooey—and you can't get it back.

Keeping Tabs on Your Data: Using the Home Tab

Your My QuickBase page has a customizable tab called the Home tab, where you can select and display reports from your QuickBase applications. In QuickBase, a *report* is a way of showing your application's data. You can take all or part of a table's data and display it in a graphic format like a pie chart or a line chart. You can also create crosstab reports, summary tables, and timelines. (Chapter 2 tells you all about reports.) After you've created some reports for different applications, you can gather together the reports you view most often right on your My QuickBase page. The Home tab lets you display up to six reports, chosen from all of your applications. In addition, you can create text boxes for the Home tab and fill them with whatever information you want —a task list, notes to yourself, whatever. As you'll see, you can even embed a link to another Web page. It's your Home tab; what you do with it is up to you.

The Home tab can hold a maximum of 10 items, including up to six reports. So if you have five reports, for example, you can also have up to five text boxes. If you have three reports, you can have up to seven text boxes, and so on.

NOTE

The Home tab is still in beta, which means that QuickBase's developers are still testing it—and they want your feedback. After you've tried out the Home tab, let the good folks at Intuit know what you think. Open the Home tab and click its upper-right Send Beta Feedback link. A dialog box opens; type in your praise, suggestions, complaints—whatever—then click Submit to send your thoughts to QuickBase's developers.

Adding a Report to the Home Tab

The first time you click the Home tab on your My QuickBase page, you see a page like the one in Figure 1-6, which displays placeholders for your reports and text boxes. To add a report, follow these steps:

1. In the upper-left corner of the placeholder you want to replace with a report, click Add→Report.

Figure 1-6. The Home tab lets you choose reports from your applications and gather them together in one place. Click Add Report (circled) to choose a report to display here.

The Add Report dialog box appears, which lists all the applications in your account in alphabetical order.

2. **In the dialog box, turn on the radio button for the application that contains the report you want, and then click Next.**

The Add Report dialog box changes to show a list of the tables in that application.

3. **Turn on the radio button of the table whose data the report displays, and then click Next.**

The dialog box displays a list of the reports associated with that table.

4. **Turn on the radio button of the report you want and click Add.**

QuickBase displays the report you chose on the Home tab. As the data changes in the table that generates the report, the report changes, as well.

To add another report, simply repeat those steps (you can have up to six reports on the Home tab). When you're finished adding reports, click Done. The page changes to show just your reports, without their frames, as shown in Figure 1-7.

NOTE

If you try to add a new report when you've already got six on the Home tab, QuickBase displays a dialog box telling you that you already have the maximum number of reports on the tab. If you want, you can delete a report from the tab ("Working with Elements on the Home Tab" on page 18) and then add a new one.

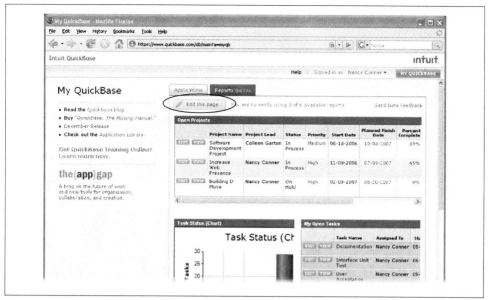

Figure 1-7. This is what the Home tab looks like after you've added a couple of reports to it. To add another report or a text box, edit text, move elements around, or delete an element from the tab, click "Edit this page" (circled).

TIP

If you want to edit or view a particular record in the report, click the record's Edit or View button (as appropriate). QuickBase opens that record, ready for you to work with it.

Adding a Text Box to the Home Tab

In addition to reports, you can also add text boxes to the Home tab to store and display reminders, a list of phone numbers, links to sites and online documents, or whatever you'd find helpful to see on your My QuickBase page. To add a text box, you first open a text editor and then use that editor to enter the info you want. Here's how:

1. On your My QuickBase page's Home tab, click the upper-left "Edit this page" button.

   The page changes to show a frame around each existing element on the page. (If you haven't yet added any elements to the Home tab—that is, if the tab looks like Figure 1-6—you won't see an "Edit this page" button. In that case, skip ahead to step 2.)

2. Click Add→Text Editor.

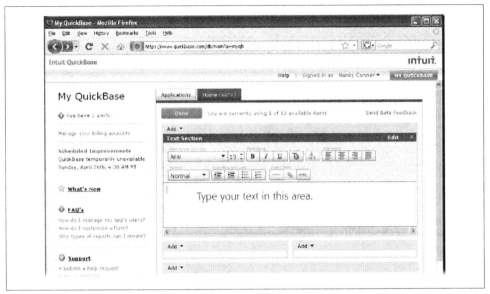

Figure 1-8. Use this simple text editor to add a text section to your Home tab.

QuickBase opens a text editor, right on the Home Tab, as shown in Figure 1-8. This text editor has formatting buttons similar to those found in your favorite word-processing program, such as font size, bold, italic, and so on.

3. Type in the text area and use the various buttons to format your text. When you're finished typing, click the Home tab's upper-left Done button.

QuickBase closes the text editor and displays your text in its own box.

Working with Elements on the Home Tab

After you've added some reports and text to the Home tab, you can work with those elements in various ways. To do so, click the Home tab and then click "Edit this page". The tab changes to show each element inside a frame. When it does, you can do the following:

- **Add a new report.** Click Add→Report where you want the report to appear, and then follow the steps for adding a report (see page xx).

- **Edit text.** If you need to change or edit the contents of an existing text box, just click the "Edit this page" button. When you do, all the text boxes on the page magically turn into text editors. Just click the text editor you want and make your changes. Click Done when you're finished.

- **Insert a link into text.** To insert a hyperlink that whisks you off to another Web page, click "Edit this page" to open the Home tab's text boxes as text editors. Select the text you want to hold the link and then, on the formatting toolbar, click the Link button, which looks like some links of chain. The Link Options dialog box opens. In this box, type or paste in the Web address of the page you're linking to. If you want the link to open in a new window, turn on the "Open in a new window" checkbox. You can add an description of the page you're linking to, if you like (it's optional). (This description appears when you hover your cursor over the link.) When you're finished, click outside the Link Options box to close it.

- **Remove a link from text.** If you want to get rid of a link in some text, click "Edit this page" and select the text that has the link you're deleting. Click the Link button to open the Link Options box. At the bottom of the box, click "Remove link from text". QuickBase removes the link and closes the dialog box.

- **Move an element.** To move a report or text box to a different spot on the Home tab, click the blue bar at the top of the report, and then drag the element to its new location. Let go of the mouse button to drop the element into place.

- **Delete an element.** In the blue bar at the top of the report or text box, click the right-hand X and QuickBase removes the element from the Home tab. QuickBase doesn't ask you to confirm the deletion and there's no Undo button, so make sure you really want to delete the element. This is especially important for text boxes, because you lose your text when you delete a text box.

NOTE

Deleting a report from the Home tab doesn't affect the report itself or the application where the report lives. If you accidentally delete a report, simply add the same report again.

Managing Your Account Information

My QuickBase is the place to go when you need to change or manage information about your QuickBase account. To get started, look on the right-hand side of your My Quick-Base page and click your "Signed in as" name, then select Edit User Profile. (To zip over to your User Profile page even faster, you can simply click the "Edit your user profile" link in the upper-right Welcome box.) This takes you to the User Profile page, shown in Figure 1-9.

On the left-hand side of the User Profile page is a box with four links. These let you edit or otherwise manage your account.

NOTE

When you manage your account information, the clock is ticking. For security, QuickBase gives you up to 60 minutes to make changes—but that's all. When those 60 minutes are up, the page expires and you lose any work you haven't saved. So if you're making extensive changes to your account information, be sure to save frequently.

Figure 1-9. The User Profile page displays your QuickBase account information and lists any groups you belong to. From here, you can edit your personal information, change your user preferences or password, and—if you have more than one account associated with an email address—manage those accounts.

Edit user information

You can change your first name, last name, or email address. (If you type in a new email address, you'll have to verify it by responding to an email.) You can also create a screen name. The main advantage of having a screen name is that it hides your email address; when someone looks you up through the User Picker, they see your screen name, first and last name, and the word *private* instead of an email address. (They can still send you email through QuickBase, but your address isn't visible.) So if you're the super-secret type, a screen name is a good idea. If you've got a screen name, you can also use it (instead of your email address) to sign in to QuickBase, saving yourself a couple of keystrokes.

NOTE

Individuals control their own user information. Application managers and billing account administrators can't touch it.

Edit user preferences

They say no two snowflakes are alike, and QuickBase users have just as much variety. This section lets you manage some aspects of how you see and experience QuickBase:

- **Icon style.** When you look at a QuickBase table, you see a series of rows and columns. Each row represents a *record*—a purchase request, a client's contact information, a work order, and so on. Each column represents a *field*, a piece of information within that record, such as the purchase request number, item description, estimated cost, and so on. At the beginning of each row in a table are two small buttons labeled EDIT and VIEW. To view or work with a record—to see a purchase request, for example, or to update the number of boxes of copier paper listed in the request—you click one of those buttons.

  If you don't want the labeled buttons cluttering up your table, you can change them to letters that take up less space: E for editing and V for viewing (makes sense, huh?). When setting your preference, select Descriptive if you want the labeled buttons or Small if you want the symbols.

- **Newsletter.** QuickBase sends out an occasional newsletter with news and info. If you want to receive it, turn on the checkbox. If you change your mind, come back and uncheck the box.

- **Edit contact preferences.** Click the link at the bottom of the User Preferences box to limit how much promotional contact you have with QuickBase. You can turn on checkboxes to indicate that you don't want promotional phone calls, email, or postal mail from QuickBase. (You'll still get messages related to your QuickBase account, such as service messages and renewal notices).

Change password

You can change your QuickBase password whenever you like. (For security, it's not a bad idea to change your account password every few months.) Just type in your current password, and then type in the new one and confirm it. Click Save Changes and you've got yourself a new password.

Manage user accounts

QuickBase lets you have several different accounts all associated with the same email address. (These are really several different screen names linked to one email address. QuickBase treats each screen name like a separate account.) Why would you want to do this? One reason is if you're a manager setting up roles ("Creating a Brand-New Role" on page 356) for an application. To see what the different roles can do, you can create several different accounts tied to your own email address, assign different roles to each account, and then see how the restrictions associated with a role affect users in that role.

To create multiple accounts (each using a different screen name) for your email address, follow these steps:

1. From your My QuickBase page, click your "Signed in as" name→Manage User Accounts.

   This opens the Multiple User Accounts page, shown in Figure 1-10.

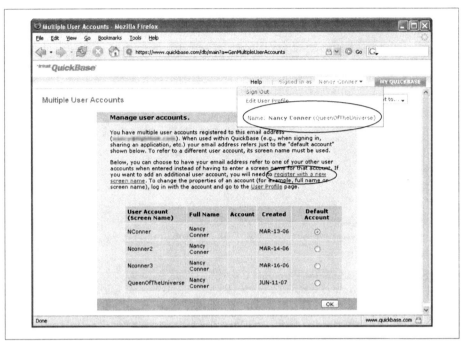

Figure 1-10. To create a new account with a new screen name for your email address, click the "register with a new screen name" link (circled). As you can see in the upper-right corner, your new screen name is linked to the name you used to open your original QuickBase account.

2. Click "register with a new screen name".

   The Register page opens, with your email address already filled in.

3. Type in the screen name and password for the new account, turn on the Terms of Service agreement checkbox, and then click Register.

   QuickBase sends a verification email to your registered email address.

4. Check your email. When the verification email arrives from QuickBase (it'll probably show up within a couple of minutes, but could take up to an hour), open it and then click the verification link.

   As soon as you respond to the email from QuickBase, your new account is ready. The new screen name is linked to the name and email address you first used to open your QuickBase account.

When you have more than one account associated with your email address, you need to let QuickBase know which screen name represents your main account, which QuickBase calls your *default account*. (This is the account you use most. If you're creating a new screen name to test permission levels, for example, you don't want to make the test screen name your default account. To select or change your default account, start from My QuickBase and select "Edit your user profile"→Manage User Accounts. Turn on the radio button next to the screen name you want as your main account, and then click OK.

To sign in with an alternate account, use that account's screen name on the Sign In page.

Need to change your name in your QuickBase account? Maybe you got married or divorced, had a religious conversion, or woke up convinced you'd be much happier going by Twinkle Starshine from now on. To change your name in QuickBase, start from your My QuickBase page. On the right-hand side, select "Edit your user profile". Alternatively, click the arrow next to your "Signed in as" name, and then click Edit User Profile. Either route gets you to the User Profile page, where you'll see a box called My User Information. In that box, click the Edit button. In the User Information box that opens, type in your new name, and then click Save Changes.

Manage application tokens

Application tokens add another layer of security to your QuickBase applications by making sure that only authorized API calls have access to your application. Use this link to create an application token. (Chapter 8 gives you step-by-step details for working with tokens.)

Managing Your Billing Account

If you're the first person in your organization to create a QuickBase account, then you're also the proud parent of a *billing account,* which is how Intuit keeps track of how many people in your company are using QuickBase (that number's important, since subscriptions come in 10-, 100-, 500-, 2,000-user varieties). Fortunately, you don't have to worry about any of these money or subscriber-count issues unless you're the billing account administrator. (You can figure this out by looking at the left-hand side of your My QuickBase page: if there's no link that says "Manage your billing account," skip ahead to "Alert! Alert!" on page 35 and thank the bean counters that someone else is footing the bill.) If you're still reading, that means you need to know how QuickBase billing works.

When you open a new account, you can create applications and invite others to join them (and those folks, in turn, can invite *other* people to join). This means that many

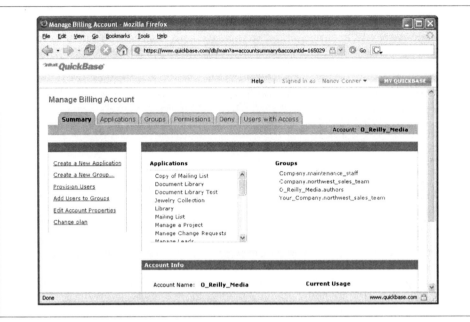

Figure 1-11. If you're the billing account administrator for your organization's QuickBase account, you carry out your high-level account management duties on this page. Click one of the six tabs along the top of the page to (from left to right) get a snapshot of the account, manage applications, manage groups, manage users by setting their privileges, deny certain users access to certain applications, or see which applications a particular user has access to. Each tab has a left-hand menu that lets you select among common actions related to that tab.

QuickBase users can be associated with one billing account. If you start with a free 30-day trial of QuickBase, for example, up to 10 people can use that one billing account —or more than 10 if you subscribe to a QuickBase service plan at the end of those 30 days. Regardless of how many people are associated with your billing account, you'll want to know your way around the Manage Billing Account page, which is where you, oh generous bill payer, can keep tabs on where your money is going. To get started, on your My QuickBase page, click the "Manage your billing account" link, which takes you to the Manage Billing Account page, shown in Figure 1-11. This page has six tabs —Summary, Applications, Groups, Permissions, Deny, and Users with Access—each of which are discussed in the sections that follow.

NOTE

The billing account administrator doesn't control user access to applications (that's the application manager's job), but a billing account administrator does have the power to deny a user access to the entire account—and therefore any application within it.

Want a receipt for the payment you make each month to QuickBase? If you pay by credit card, you can get a receipt each time you pay, but you need to set this up with Intuit by contacting the QuickBase support team: On your My QuickBase page, look for the left-hand Support section and click the "Submit a help request" link. This opens the Contact QuickBase page. (You can also get to the Support page by clicking Help→Help & Support and then selecting the right-hand Submit Support Case link.) Then just tell QuickBase support that you'd like to receive a monthly receipt, and they'll take care of the rest. Once everything's all set, you'll get an email each month with a link to that month's receipt. You can view the receipt, bookmark it, or print it from your Web browser.

Billing Account Administration

If I'm the billing account administrator, what are my rights and responsibilities regarding the account?

If you're the one who opened the billing account—the umbrella account that your organization pays for and your coworkers use for their QuickBase applications—you're automatically the billing account administrator. In this role, you can create applications, create other administrators, and grant high-level permissions for creating applications or denying account access.

Here's what billing account administrators can do:

- **Manage other users.** Being the billing account administrator does *not* give you godlike power over everyone else who uses the account. This is a good thing. After all, you want application managers to be the ones who control their applications —so, for example, they're the ones who can add or invite new users and control access rights (like who can view or edit an application) for the applications they create and manage. As billing account administrator, though, here's what you can do: view everyone who has access to the account, give people the ability to create applications, and remove people from the account. "Managing Your Billing Account" on page 23 teaches you how to do these things.

- **Manage applications.** As billing account administrator, you can delete applications, change an application's ownership, and keep people who use your account from letting anyone with Internet access have access to an application; in other words, you can force your people to limit application access to other QuickBase account holders. (See "Users with Access tab" on page 32 for details.)

- **Manage the billing account.** As billing account administrator, you also have some responsibilities. It's your job to keep the QuickBase billing info up to date, keep an eye on things so that users don't exceed the limits of your service plan, and upgrade or downgrade your service plan if necessary.

If all that power and responsibility gets to be a bit much to handle, you can share billing account administrator status—or even transfer the job to someone else. To do so, start on your My QuickBase page and click "Manage your billing account". Then click the Permissions tab to share or transfer your account administration privileges. (See "Permissions tab" on page 31 for more on this.)

Summary tab

The Summary tab gives you information about your account, including applications, service plan and usage statistics, time zone, and company information.

TIP

Click the name of your plan (QuickBase Trial Plan, QuickBase 100+ Monthly Plan, and so on) for a quick reminder of that plan's limits: number of users, space for applications, and space for files. Compare those figures with the Current Usage stats to see whether you need to upgrade your service plan. Details on each plan are shown in Table 1-1.

Use the left-hand menu to perform these actions:

- **Create a New Application.** Chapter 6 and Chapter 7 tell you everything you ever wanted to know about creating applications, whether you want to use a QuickBase-provided template or start from scratch.

- **Create a New Group.** Creating a *group* helps you organize your users: it's simply a set of users you gather together into a named entity. You can also create a new group from the Groups tab ("Groups tab" on page 30 discusses groups in more detail).

- **Provision Users.** Imagine you're dealing with a new consultant or employee, and you want this person to have access to some of your account's applications—but not others. Before an application manager even invites a new user to join, you—or anyone with full management privileges—can *provision* that user. Provisioning a user means you assign him to a group that you choose. Then, when an application manager invites that new user to join an application, the new guy's permissions are already set, according to the group you added him to.

- **Add Users to Groups.** Clicking this link whisks you over to the Groups tab, where you can find users and add them to your groups.

- **Edit Account Properties.** Here, you can do the following:
  - Edit the name of your organization's QuickBase account: You can name your account whatever you like, just make sure that the name is at least four characters and does *not* include any spaces.
  - Grant (or take away) permission to make applications available to anyone on the Internet: Turn on the checkbox if you want to allow anyone (even non-

QuickBase users) accessible to your applications; make sure the box is clear if you don't.

— Change the email address for your billing account.

— Change your account's time zone: The time zone you select is the one that determines the dates and times for all applications in the account.

— Review the QuickBase terms of service.

- **Change plan.** If you're on the 30-day free trial, you can subscribe to one of Quick-Base's four service plans shown in Table 1-1. Whichever level of plan you choose, you can pay either monthly or annually.

Table 1-1. QuickBase Service Plan Comparison

Plan	Price per Month/Year	Number of Users	Applications (Maximum Size)	Attached Files (Maximum Size)
QuickBase	$249/$2,988	10	5 MB	15 MB
QuickBase 100+	$500/$6,000	100	15 MB	250 MB
QuickBase 500+	$1,500/$18,000	500	55 MB	1 GB
QuickBase 2000+	$5,000/$60,000	2,000	250 MB	4.9 GB

NOTE

Annual plans simplify paying for your QuickBase account, but there are a few things you should know about paying annually. If you choose to pay once a year, you've signed up for a full year of service. That means if you decide to cancel or downgrade your QuickBase account, you *don't* get a refund or credit. And if you sign up for an annual account, you *can't* switch to a monthly account. But here's the good news: You can upgrade at any time. So as the number of QuickBase users in your organization grows, so can your service plan.

POWER USERS' CLINIC

QuickBase Enterprise Edition

In a large organization, the number of QuickBase accounts can multiply faster than rabbits in April. But unlike those pesky rabbits, multiple QuickBase accounts are easy to manage. QuickBase Enterprise Edition gives you centralized control of multiple QuickBase accounts.

Here's how it works: When you buy the Enterprise Edition, your organization gets its very own QuickBase *realm*. A realm is an umbrella account that groups multiple QuickBase accounts together for one-stop administration. The structure gives you centralized, high-level control over who's using QuickBase—and how they're using it. You can keep an eye on usage and costs for all QuickBase accounts in your realm. You also get control of password policies and users in those accounts. For example, if you're security-conscious, you can make sure all users change their passwords on a regular basis—and you can control the number of passwords QuickBase stores so folks don't keep switching back and forth between just a couple of passwords. You can also require a minimum length or a combination of characters (such as mixing upper- and lowercase or letters and numbers).

Similarly, for applications that hold sensitive data, you can use the Enterprise Edition's *IP filtering* feature to control the locations from which users can access those applications. (An *IP address*, or Internet Protocol address, is the unique address of a computer on the Internet.) IP filtering simply means that you can specify the IP addresses of the computers that can access a particular application. So you don't have to worry about who's looking over Joe's shoulder as he works on sensitive data—because Joe will only be able to access that data from the office.

Later, if Joe leaves your organization, you can make sure Joe also leaves behind his ability to see your data, by denying him access to all accounts in your realm in one fell swoop—faster, easier, and more thorough than trying to hunt down the accounts he worked with one at a time.

Another benefit of the Enterprise Edition is that it lets you keep your company brand and presence consistent. For example, you can create a custom Web address where peple go to use your QuickBase applications, rather than sending them to at www.quickbase.com (*http://www.quickbase.com/p/home.asp*). This is super-handy if you have applications that customers can access. So a company named Wonderful Widgets Galore could make www.WonderfulWidgetsGalore.quickbase.com the starting point for all its QuickBase applications. And the company could also put its Wally the Widget Weasel logo at the top of every page of every application, making its branding consistent.

The QuickBase Enterprise Edition lets you be the master of your own realm, controlling access, policies, and users across many accounts and applications. In fact, you can be the master of several realms, because your organization can set up more than one. To find out more, flip to "Using QuickBase Enterprise Edition" on page 332 or visit www.quickbase.com (*http://www.quickbase.com/p/home.asp*) and click the Enterprise link.

Applications tab

This tab shows you a list of all the applications in your account, and displays the following info:

- Application name
- Number of users of that application
- Application size in KB
- Size of any attached files, also in KB

As billing account administrator, it's part of your job to keep an eye on the size of the applications in your billing account. Each billing plan allows only so much space for your applications and attachments, as explained in Table 1-1, so it's up to you to rein in any application managers who are hogging all the space. (If you're not sure which plan your company has or what its limitations are, you can easily find out. From My QuickBase, click "Manage your billing account". On the Summary tab of the Manage Billing Account page, look in the Account Info section for Plan. Click the name of your plan to get a pop-up window that spells out how much space your plan has for applications and attachments, and also the number of users.)

- Number of tables
- Application manager's name
- Notes
- Date someone last modified the application

If you want to email an application's manager, click the manager's name. In the box that opens, click Send Mail, type in your subject and message, and then click Send.

The fastest way to delete an application is to turn on the checkbox to the left of the application's name, and then hit the Delete Selected button in the very top or very bottom row of the Applications table. You can select and delete a bunch of applications at once.

A busy organization is likely to have tons of applications showing up on this page. You don't have to scroll through them all to find the one you want. Above the table of applications is the Find Applications box. Type in the name of the application you want (or some part of it), and then click Find. The table shrinks down to display only those applications that have your search term in the name.

Click the name of any application to get more detailed information about the application or to perform one of these actions:

- **Show application stats.** This repeats some of the information from the main Applications tab, but adds details like creation date, number of records or documents in the application, and how many times someone's visited that application: both the total number of hits and today's hits. (QuickBase shows you the hit count for all users; it *doesn't* break that number down to tell you that Gilbert Allen has opened the application 15 times today while Sue Caldwell hasn't looked at it since last Tuesday.)

- **Delete application.** This is how you remove an application from QuickBase—permanently. To make sure you don't delete an application by mistake, you have to confirm your decision to get rid of the application.

- **Transfer application.** To switch management of an application from one user to another, click this link, and then type in the screen name or email address of the person you want to take over the application. The person you transfer to has the option to accept or reject the transfer.

NOTE

When you transfer an application, you can transfer the application's management, its ownership, or both. What's the difference? Money, mostly. An application's *manager* is its main administrator, but the manager doesn't incur any billing obligations. An application's owner represents the account to which that application is billed.

- **View users.** This link shows you a list of folks who have access to the application. Click it to change a user's role, add existing users, invite new users to the application, or remove a user from the application.

Groups tab

Groups are a convenient way to organize users. For example, say you're gathering the business requirements for a Web site you're thinking about launching. You need to be able to share drafts of your evolving specifications with a wide range of people: your requirements-gathering team, end-users, managers, corporate sponsors, and developers. (Marketing and Legal are going to want a peek at them, too.) Even though you need to give all those people access to your draft specification, you don't want just *anybody* jumping in and making changes to the document. So you can sort people into groups, and then assign each group its own role ("Assign a group a role" on page 381). You might have a group called *viewers* who can read documents (but not edit them) and another group called *team members*, who can add new documents and edit existing ones. That way you don't have to worry about who's getting their thumbprints all over your spec.

If you can create and share an application, you can also create a group. What makes groups especially useful is that they let you invite users and assign roles en masse.

NOTE

For the whole story on creating and working with groups, check out Chapter 9.

The main page of the Groups tab shows you the names of any groups you've created and how many users are in each group. Click a group's name to go to the Manage Group

---

page, where you can find more information about that group: the group's description, who's in it, each person's permission level (member, manager, or both), and the billing account the group belongs to.

The Manage Group page's left-hand menu also lets you do these nifty things:

- Add users to the group, one at a time or en masse. You can even add a whole group to another group.
- Copy the group.
- Delete the group.
- Edit the group's properties: Change the group's name or description, associate it with a different billing account, or let other managers help out with group management.
- List applications accessible to this group.

Permissions tab

This tab shows you a list of users who have your permission to create and manage applications within your account. From here, you can email those users, change their level of management (the options are full management, support level, and no management), bestow or take away the ability to create applications, and add or remove users who have management privileges.

What do the different management levels entail? Full management means that a user can delete any application or group in the account, view an application's permissions list, edit the membership of any group in the account, and grant a user account-management permission. In other words, dole these privileges out with caution: Full managers have the same powers as the billing account administrator ("Managing Your Billing Account" on page 23).

Support-level management is more limited—these managers can't, for example, edit group membership or delete an application managed by someone else. They also lack the power to change the billing plan and set administrative rights like the ones discussed in this section. What these managers can do is manage applications: create new ones, create and assign roles, invite and manage users, and all the neat stuff described from Chapter 6 onward.

NOTE

The names listed on the Account Permissions page belong to people who have permission to create or manage applications. If a person's not on the list, she may still be able to *use* the applications in your account, she just can't create or manage them. You can add people to this list, though. If you want to grant account-management powers to someone, add the person to this list and then set permissions.

Deny tab

This tab lets you deny any user access to all applications in your account. It's handy when, for example, an employee leaves your organization and you don't want that person to come back and fiddle with your data.

To deny someone access to your applications, follow these steps:

1. Click Add User. (This might seem counterintuitive, since you're excluding a user, but what you're really doing is adding this user to your Deny List.)

   The Select a User box opens.

2. Click the drop-down arrow on the "Make a selection" menu. Select "Search for a specific user".

   The Search for a User box appears.

3. In the text box, type in the name, email address, or screen name of the user you want to deny. Click OK.

   The user's name appears in the Search Results area of the Select a User box.

4. If the name's not already highlighted, select the name you want. Click the Add button.

   The name of the user you're denying jumps to the right-hand list of names.

5. Repeat if you want to deny more than one user. When all the users you want to deny are in the right-hand list, click Done.

   The name of the user you've denied appears in the Deny List on the Deny tab of your Manage Billing Account page.

6. Click Save Changes.

   You've locked out that user. Users on the Deny List have zero access to the applications in the account, even if someone has given them permissions to access a particular application.

But what if Harold H. Brown has retired to Maui, but Harold G. Brown is still on your team—and you denied access to the wrong Hal? If you make a mistake and deny a user who should have access, it's easy to fix. On your Manage Billing Account page, click the Deny tab and find the user whose access you want to restore. Turn on the checkbox in the "remove" column (to the left of the user's name), and then click Save Changes. Voilà—Harold G. Brown is back in business. (Don't forget to go back and deny Harold H. Brown, just in case he gets tired of sipping daiquiris on the beach and wants to peek at some data that's no longer his business...)

Users with Access tab

This tab shows you a list of all users who have access to applications within the account, as shown in Figure 1-12. From this tab, you can take the following actions:

- **Send an email.** Click any user's name to open a box that lets you send that person an email. Or you can copy and paste the email address into your own email program.

NOTE

QuickBase hides the email addresses of users who've chosen a screen name, marking their email addresses *private*. If you want to contact someone with a private email address, click his name and send the email through QuickBase.

- **View all applications that a user has access to.** Click the "apps" link to get this information.
- **Check a user's status.** If you've invited someone to join an application and they haven't responded, you can follow up with that person; just click his name to fire off an email.
- **Remove a user.** When you click the "remove" link, QuickBase gives you the option to deny the user access to the QuickBase applications in your account or simply to remove that user from a group you've assigned her to (or both). For example, if Tina Kulak jumps from Sales to Marketing, you still want her to have access to your QuickBase applications—just the appropriate ones for her new role. So you'd take Tina out of the Sales group and add her to the Marketing group. (See "Creating a Group and Adding Members" on page 373 to learn how to add a user to a group.)

TIP

You can also deactivate a user by clicking the "remove" link—if you "own" the user's email address; see "Deny? Deactivate? What's the Diff?" on page 33.

- **Search for a user.** Use the left-hand Search box to find a particular user in a long list. Just type in the name you're looking for and click Search. To return to the full list, click List All.
- **Reactivate a user.** If you've deactivated someone's QuickBase account (see "Deny? Deactivate? What's the Diff?" on page 33) and want to restore that person's access to the site, click the Reactivate Users link.

UP TO SPEED

Deny? Deactivate? What's the Diff?

When you want to keep a user away from your applications, you can either *deny* that person or *deactivate* her. To some extent, the option you choose depends on the level of control you have over that individual. In QuickBase terms, it depends on whether or not you "own" the user's email address.

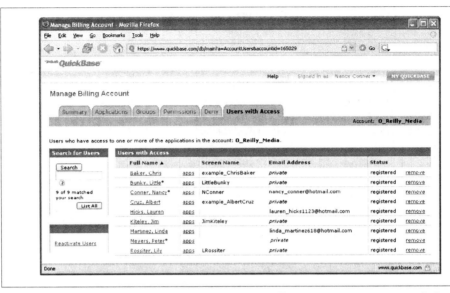

Figure 1-12. The Users with Access tab on the Manage Billing Account page gives you the lowdown on QuickBase users who have access to your account. Click a name in the Full Name column to send that user an email through QuickBase. Click "apps" to see a list of the applications a user currently has access to. The Status column tells you whether or not a user has registered with QuickBase. Click "remove" to deny a user access to applications in this account or to remove the user from any groups he belongs to.

Here's an example of when you own a user's email address. If everyone in your company registers using their work email address, such as *lizjones@yourcompany.com* or *fred-jefferson@yourcompany.com*, QuickBase recognizes the billing account administrator as the person who "owns" all the addresses that end in *@yourcompany.com*. Their access to QuickBase is through your company, and you have the right to keep anyone whose email address you own out of your company's QuickBase account. So if Liz Jones takes a job with a rival company, you can deactivate *lizjones@yourcompany.com*. That means the person associated with that email address no longer has any access to QuickBase at all—she can no longer sign in. So if Liz wants access to Quick-Base, she'll have to get it through her new company, using a new email address.

On the other hand, maybe you invited a freelance consultant to lend a hand in your requirements-gathering process. This consultant's email address *doesn't* end with *@yourcompany.com*—maybe it's *whizkid@IThotshots.com*. When the project's over, you don't have the right to refuse whizkid all access to QuickBase—the consultant might need access to another client's applications or might have his own QuickBase account for that matter. So of course you don't have any right to kick him out of QuickBase entirely—you only have the right to keep him away from applications in *your* company's account. In this case, at the end of the project you'd deny *whizkid* access to *your* QuickBase applications. He can still sign in to his own account or to other QuickBase accounts to which he has access, he just won't be able to view or work with your company's applications.

Deactivation doesn't have to be forever. If Liz Smith sees the light and abandons your competitor to come back to work for you, you can reactivate her with a couple of clicks. On the left-hand side of the Users with Access tab on your Manage Billing Account page, click the Reactivate Users link. The page that opens shows a list of deactivated users. Find the user you want to reactivate and click the reactivate button to the right of that name. (If your company has more than 20 users, you'll see a search box instead of a list. Type in the user's name and click Find.)

Alert! Alert!

The left-hand side of your My QuickBase page displays an alerts link, shown in Figure 1-13. An *alert* is a message about your QuickBase account that typically deals with one of the follwing issues:

- Another QuickBase user has invited you to join an application.
- Another QuickBase user wants you to take over management or ownership (or both) of an application; see Note on page 30 for an explanation of how these two terms differ.
- A table in an application you manage has reached 90% of its capacity.
- QuickBase is letting you know that your account is getting close to its service plan limit. If you're a billing account administrator, check out "Billing Account Administration" on page 25. QuickBase alerts you when your account is about to reach its limits for users, application size, or file attachments so you can deal with the situation—by upgrading the account to handle more users or data, for example —before you hit those limits and people's work gets interrupted.

NOTE

Busy people can easily overlook a new alert on their My QuickBase page. To make sure that you don't miss an important alert, QuickBase also emails you whenever you receive a new alert that requires your action, like a request to take over an application's ownership. The email includes a link you can click to go straight to the alert.

To read an alert, click the left-hand "unread alerts" link. This opens your My Alerts page, shown in Figure 1-14. Alerts appear in a table, with the most recent at the top. Any alerts you haven't yet read appear in boldface; any that you've read but haven't deleted are in a normal (non-bold) font. Find the alert you want to read and click its title in the Summary column. If an alert requires some action from you (someone wants you to take over management of an application, say), follow the instructions in the alert. For example, to accept an application transfer, click Continue→Accept. When you're finished reading an alert, click Done. (Or, if you're *really* done with that alert once and for all, click Delete.)

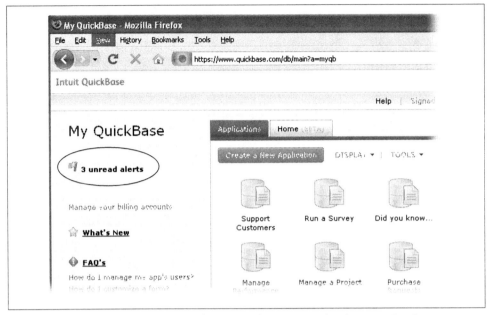

Figure 1-13. Alerts keep you informed of important happenings related to your QuickBase account. Look on the left side of your My QuickBase page to see whether you have any unread alerts (circled). To see your alerts, click the circled link.

NOTE

When an alert requires action from you, QuickBase lets you know. Check the status column: If an alert's status is "notify," that alert is just FYI—you don't have to do anything about it. If the status is "pending," QuickBase is waiting for you to do something about that alert (like accept an application transfer request). After you've acted on a pending alert, QuickBase changes the alert's status to "handled."

You probably don't want dozens of alerts hanging around after you've read them. You can delete an alert as soon as you've read it, or delete alerts from the My Alerts page. To delete one from My Alerts, turn on the checkbox to the left of the alert's title (same goes for any others you want to delete), and then click the Delete button at the top or the bottom of the table.

Getting Started with Applications

Just as your My QuickBase page is your control center for everything you do in Quick-Base, each application has its own home page: the *Dashboard* (Figure 1-15). The Dash-board is your starting point for working with any application. Usually, it's the page you see when you open an application. (If you're invited to join an application ["Accepting

---

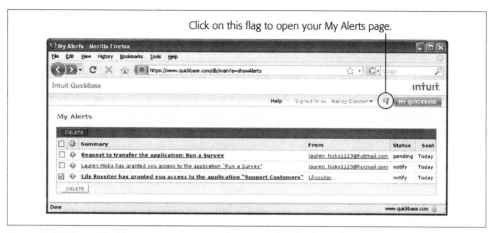

Figure 1-14. Your My Alerts page shows you the name of each alert, who sent it to you, its status, and when it was sent. To read the full text of any alert, click its title. You can get to this page from any other QuickBase page by clicking the circled flag.

an Invitation" on page 6], the link in the email welcoming you takes you directly to the application's Dashboard.)

Getting to the Dashboard of any application is a snap. From My QuickBase, look in the Applications box for the application you want, then click its name (in Details display) or its picture (in Icons display). Or, if you're knee-deep in an application's records and want to get back to the Dashboard, click the application's name in the upper-left corner of any page in the application. (Next to the application's name is a little picture of a house, reminding you to click here to return to this application's home page—its Dashboard.)

Administrators can create and assign different Dashboards for different roles (for an explanation of roles, see "Managing Roles" on page 351). So if you're looking at a Sales Leads application, for example, you'll have a different Dashboard depending on whether you're a Viewer, a Sales Rep, or a Manager. Figure 1-16 and Figure 1-17 illustrate the difference between the Sales Leads Dashboards for a manager and a sales rep.

Administrators can do all sorts of nifty things from their Dashboard (see "The Administrator's Dashboard" on page 271 for details). If you're a QuickBase user who's joining someone else's application, your options are more limited (but almost as nifty). You can:

- Open an existing *report* (a report is how QuickBase displays your data).
- View a particular *record* (a piece of information your application holds, like a purchase request or a work order).
- Add a record to the application.
- Modify an existing record within the application.

Info box

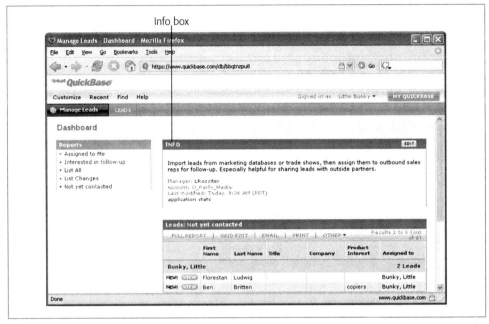

Figure 1-15. An application's Dashboard is both your starting point and your control center for working with an application. The Info box tells you the purpose of the application and who manages it. Below that is a report displaying some of the application's data. On the left, the Reports menu lets you choose among existing reports, giving you different ways to look at the data this application holds.

- Find records you've worked on recently.
- Create a new report.
- Modify a report you've created—as long as you have Save Shared Reports permission.
- Create notifications to alert you about additions or modifications to the application's data.

The sections that follow dish up all the juicy details.

Open an Existing Report

Reports are an amazingly helpful QuickBase tool: They let you display your application's data in different ways to make it easier to find what you're looking for.

For example, in the Manage Leads application shown in Figure 1-15, a sales rep might want to see only those leads that have expressed interest in a follow-up call—a report already exists to put that information right at his fingertips. The sales rep would select the "Interested in follow-up" from the left-hand Reports menu, then pick up the phone and start calling.

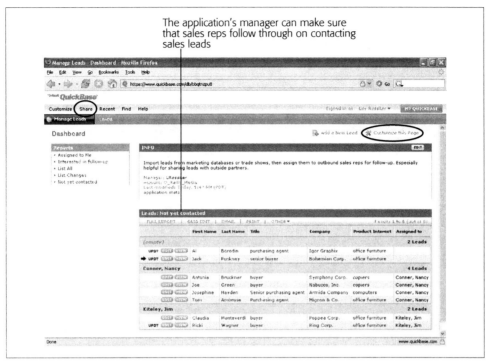

The application's manager can make sure that sales reps follow through on contacting sales leads

Figure 1-16. The Dashboard for the manager of the Manage Leads application shows all leads that haven't been contacted yet, organized by sales rep. Leads that need to be assigned to a rep appear first, under "(empty)". Application managers can customize their Dashboard by clicking "Customize this Page" (circled). Application managers can also manage the application's users by clicking Share (also circled).

As another example, in a Work Orders application, a property manager might want to know how many repairs the tenants are paying for versus how many the management company is paying for. To find out, she'd choose the "% of Billable vs Nonbillable" report to see this info in an easy-to-read chart. In contrast, a maintenance supervisor might want to see all the work orders for the current month or a list of all work orders ranked by priority. And a maintenance *worker* would want to check out the My Assigned Work Orders report. The different reports let people who need the data see it in the way that makes most sense to them.

Chapter 2 explains everything you ever wanted to know about reports (including how to create your own). The Dashboard page's left-hand Reports menu lists a smorgasbord of pre-existing reports to choose from. Click any title to display the report you want.

Sales reps have a different report
on the Dashboard than the
application's manager has

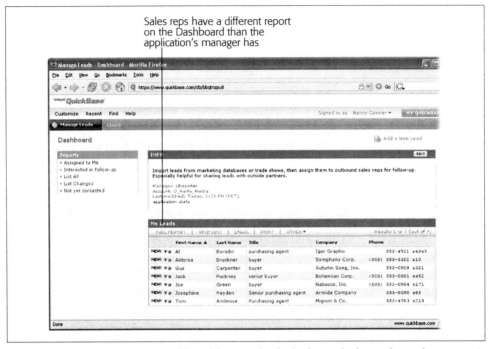

Figure 1-17. At first glance, the Dashboard for an individual sales rep looks similar to the manager's Dashboard, but there are some important differences. For one thing, there's no "Customize this Page" button or Share menu. Also, the only sales leads listed on the Dashboard are those assigned to the sales rep who's viewing the Dashboard. So the first table this sales rep sees is the one that's most important to her—her own leads.

View a Record

No matter how much data you pack into your QuickBase application, it won't do you any good if you can't look at it. Imagine attempting to fix a software bug when you don't know what the problem is, or trying to figure out this month's payroll when you can't see anybody's timecard. Kind of like playing darts while blindfolded.

When you want to look at a particular record, click the record's Display button (it's either a button that says VIEW or a small blue dot, depending on how you've set your User Preferences—see "Managing Your Account Information" on page 19). The record opens so you can see its details.

Add or Modify a Record

It's easy to add a new record to an application. For example, say you work in a property management office and a tenant calls to report a broken second-story window that needs fixing, thanks to Junior's amazing pop fly. You go to the Dashboard page of the Work Orders application, look in the upper-right corner for the "Add a New Work

Order" link, and click it. (If you're working in a multi-table application, you need to find the table you want to add the record to. Table names appear in the blue bar at the top of the page: click the table name, and then click "Add a New Record".) The Add Work Order page opens, letting you create, prioritize, and assign the work order (thanks to the easy-as-pie maneuvers you'll learn in Chapter 4, you can have QuickBase automatically email your instructions to your expert window-fixing specialist). When you've finished entering the information, click Save and you're done. Help is on the way to your tenant—until the next time the kids play baseball.

Whatever kind of records you're working with in an application, you can easily add a new one. If your application consists of just one table holding just one type of record, look for the upper-right "Add a New Record" link. The exact name of this link depends on the kind of records your table holds. For example, in a Document Library application, the link will say "Add a New Document", and in a Purchase Order application, the link will say, "Add a New Purchase Order". If an application contains more than one kind of record—such as work orders and rental units—you need to choose the right table before you can add a new record. So if your real estate management company has bought a new apartment complex and you need to create a new record for each unit, you'll look in the blue bar at the top of the page for the table name (in this case Properties/Units). Click the table name, and then select "Add a New Record"—again, the name of the record depends on the type of record you're adding.

Modify a record

Sometimes you need to change the information in an existing record. For example, say you've scheduled the work order to fix a tenant's broken window pane, and then the same tenant calls to report that an unfortunate croquet accident has demolished the screen door. You want to update the work order to include both repairs.

The first thing to do is find the record. A quick way to do this is to open a report that you know holds the record. So start by checking out the Dashboard page's left-hand Reports menu. Looking back at Figure 1-15, you might choose Current Month's Scheduled Work Orders or Open Work Orders by Priority.

Find the record you want (see the next section), and then click Edit. (This might be a button with the word "Edit" or the letter E, depending on how you've set your User Preferences.) The Edit Work Order page opens. Make your changes, and then click Save. Then hope the tenant sends the kids to a movie before they decide to play murder ball.

When you edit an individual record, QuickBase gives you several options of how to proceed after you've made your changes. These options appear as buttons at the bottom of the Edit page:

- Click Save to save your changes and return to the last page you viewed.

- Click Save & Next to save your changes to this record and jump ahead to the next record.
- Click Skip to go to the next record without making changes to this one.
- Click Delete to erase this record from the application.

Find an Existing Record

When an application grows to hold hundreds and hundreds of records, you can't easily find the record (or group of records) you're looking for just by eyeballing the list. That's what Find is for.

To search for records in an application, click Find in the application's menu bar. The Find box opens, with a text box where you can type in what you're looking for: a product name, an address, a date. Type in your search criterion and click Find. Quick-Base takes you to the Search Results page, which lists all matching records.

TIP

To quickly find a record you've worked on recently, click Find, and then scan the list of records under Recent, at the bottom of the Find box. QuickBase lists the last eight records you've worked on. Click any record to open it.

What if typing a search term into the Find box still doesn't dig up the record you're looking for? Try Advanced Find. From the menu bar, click Find→Advanced Find. QuickBase opens the Advanced Find page, where you can tell QuickBase what to search for in specific fields. For example, if you can't recall the name of the sales lead who called before lunch to cancel her appointment, but you just *know* her last name begins with a *W*, it's not going to help you to search for every record that contains the letter *w*. But with Advanced Find, you can tell QuickBase to search the Last Name field and return all records that start with a *W*. You can search more than one field at a time, too, to narrow your results and home in on just the record you're looking for.

Find a Record You've Worked on Recently

If you've just added or edited a record and you need to find it, the Dashboard page makes it easy. Say you've updated the price list for your office supply company, and then 10 minutes later you realize that you made a mistake: You mixed up the price of a new super-fast, multi-featured photocopier with the price of a case of toner. Before your in-the-field sales reps start giving photocopiers away, you want to fix the error—fast.

If you're looking for one of the last few records you've worked with, click Recent in the menu bar and see which records it lists. But maybe you've just modified several dozen records—and Recent can't show them all. You can still find the record quickly. On the

Dashboard page of the application that holds your price list, look in the left-hand reports menu for List Changes. Click it, and the page that opens displays new and recently updated records. From there, click the Edit button to change a record or the Display button to view it.

Create or Modify a Report

You need permission to create and modify reports. If you don't have permission, you'll know—the Customize button on the Dashboard page's menu bar will *not* have "Create a new" as an option. To get permission to create or change shared reports, email the application's manager. (To find an application's manager, look in the Dashboard page's Info box; click the manager's name to send an email.)

Create a new report

You can create a new report from an application's Dashboard page (or from any other page in the application, for that matter). Just follow these steps:

1. On the menu bar, click Customize→Create a new→Report. (If you're in a multi-table application, choose the table for which you're creating the report.)

   This opens the Report Builder.

2. Select the kind of report you want to create: Table, Grid Edit, Summary, Calendar, Chart, Timeline. (Chapter 2 tells you more about each kind of report, including what they look like and how they can present your data.)

   A box appears that lets you choose the data you want to display and how you want to display it.

3. Make your selections, and then click Display.

   QuickBase shows you how the new report will look.

4. If you're not happy with the displayed report, click the upper-right "Customize this Report" link to return to the Report Builder.

   Back in the Report Builder, you can make changes and display the new report again.

5. When you're happy with the new report, look at the top of the screen for New Report: Save. Click the Save link.

   A box appears, asking you to name the new report and select whether you want it to be a Personal Report or a Shared Report. *Personal Reports* are for your own viewing pleasure; no other QuickBase users can see them. (If you don't have permission to save shared reports, Personal Report is your only option.) *Shared Reports* are available to everyone who has access to the application. If you select Shared Report, the box expands so you can specify which roles have access to your new report and, if you want, write a description to explain what's in it.

6. When you've filled out the Save Report As box to your satisfaction, click OK.

   Your new report is ready to go!

Modify a report you've created

To change a report that you've created and saved, first open the report. In the blue bar at the top of the page, click the type of record the report holds (such as Leads, Units, or Tasks). The menu that appears is divided into Personal Reports (if any) and Shared Reports. Click the name of the report you want to change. When the report opens, click the upper-right "Customize this Report" link. The Report Builder opens. Make the changes you want, just as you would in step 3 of the previous section, and follow the steps from there.

Stay on Top of Things with Email Notifications

When a record changes, QuickBase flags it with an update icon. But those flags can multiply fast, and you probably care more about some changes than others. If you want to know when a record changes in a specific way—a record is deleted, for example, or someone writes a new response to a survey you designed—you can have QuickBase send you an email notification of the change.

1. From any page in the application, click Customize→Create a new→Email Notification. (If you're in a multi-table application, QuickBase asks you which table you want. See "Single-Table or Multi-Table?" on page 231 for more on multi-table applications.)

   The Emails: New Notification page shown in Figure 1-18 opens.

2. Type in your information.

   In the Notification Name box, give the notification a name, like *New Task Added* (this makes it a lot easier to manage multiple notifications). Make sure that Notify Whom is set to Me (see "Sending Notification Emails to Others" on page 165 to learn about sending email notifications to others). Select when you want to be notified: you can receive a notification when a record is added, modified, or deleted, or any combination of the three. Type in a Subject for the email, or leave it blank for QuickBase to use its usual subject line, which depends on the application and the kind of change you want to know about—if you've set up a notification for whenever someone adds a new task to your project management application, for example, the subject line says something like *Manage a Project: Tasks — Task #86 Added.*

   Use QuickBase's default message (a basic notification regarding the type of change) or select Custom to write your own ("Signing Up for Emails for Yourself" on page 162 tells you more about creating custom messages). Next, decide

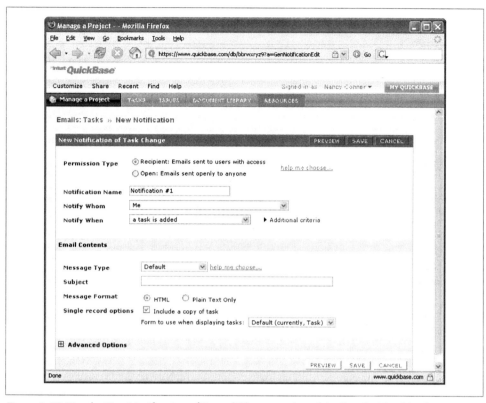

Figure 1-18. Use the New Notification of Record Change section of the Emails: New Notification page to specify the kind of change you want to know about. In this example, which deals with tasks in a Project Management application, QuickBase emails you every time a task gets changed in the Tasks table of the Manage a Project application. In the Email Contents section, you can spell out the subject line for such notification emails and, if you want, create a custom message.

whether you want your message in HTML (which can display graphics) or plain text. Finally, turn on the "Include a copy of record" checkbox if you want Quick-Base to include the new or changed record in the email. (In Figure 1-17, this checkbox says "Include a copy of task" because that's the kind of record you're dealing with in the Tasks table.) When you're done, click Preview (to check out the email notification) or Save (to start the notifications rolling in).

POWER USERS CLINIC

Getting the Most Out of Your Email Notifications

If you don't want a zillion emails a day zooming your way, overwhelming you with updates that you don't really need to know about, you can fine-tune your email notifications. You can do this when you create a brand-new notification, or you can do it for a notification that already exists.

If the notification already exists, click Customize→Tables to get to the Tables page. (In a multi-table application, select the table you want from the list on the left side of the screen.) Click the Emails tab to display notifications you've already created. Find the notification you want to fine-tune and click its name (this is why naming your notifications is a good thing). The Emails: Notification page opens, which looks just like the page you used to create the notification in the first place, except all the info for this notification is already filled in.

On the Emails: Notification page, there are two sections of interest: "Additional criteria" next to the "Notify when" drop-down list, shown in Figure 1-19, and the Advanced Options section, shown in Figure 1-20. (If you can't see these sections, click the arrow next to "Additional criteria" and the plus sign next to Advanced Options.)

Here's how to fine-tune QuickBase's criteria for shooting you a notification email under "Additional criteria":

* **Select a specific field you're interested in.** If you want notification only when a lead's phone number changes, for example, or when someone puts a new comment in the Comments field, you can restrict your notifications to changes in those fields. When you turn on the "When specific fields change" radio button, QuickBase shows you which fields are available. Just pick the ones you want.

* **Specify additional criteria.** If you want, you can select a field and choose other criteria from the drop-down lists. If you specify more criteria, QuickBase will send you a notification only when those criteria are met. For example, you can select "Modified by," "is not," and your own name. That way, QuickBase won't sling you a bunch of emails about changes you already know about because *you* made them. Or, if you're a sales rep who's on the road, you can elect to get notifications pertaining to a certain Zip code within a certain date range. Click the "more lines" button when you want to add a bunch of conditions to sending a notification.

Farther down the Email Notification page is the Advanced Options section. Here's what Advanced Options lets you do:

* **Select the kind of operation that triggers an email.** You can choose whether you want to receive an email when a single record changes (someone adds or edits a record), when multiple records change (someone imports a bunch of new records all at once), or in either case.

* **Choose who's sending the email.** Your choices here are *notify@quickbase.com* or the application manager's registered email address. If you don't want to confuse automatic notifications with other correspondence from the application manager, choose *notify@quickbase.com*.

If the application has custom forms ("Customizing Forms" on page 439), there's another advanced option called Data Form. This simply lets you choose which custom form you want to use for your email notifications.

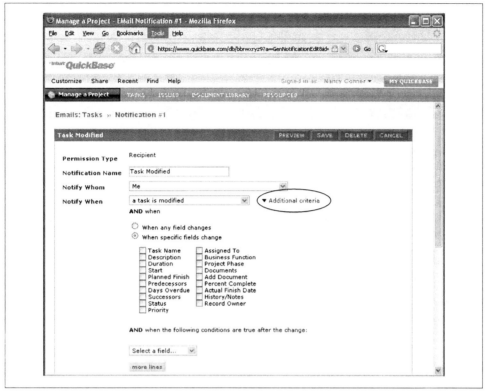

Figure 1-19. Click the triangle next to "Additional criteria" (circled) to display these options. The specific fields (sections within a record) come from the application you're working with—this example is for the Tasks table of a Project Management application. Another application (Manage Sales Leads, for example) would show a different set of fields specific to that application. Choosing the fields and conditions that trigger a notification email gives you lots of control over what shows up in your inbox.

Getting Help

QuickBase is so easy to use, you'll jump in and be working with applications in no time: adding, editing, and deleting records, designing custom reports, and a whole lot more. You've got this book to guide you, and Intuit also offers tons of helpful resources. When you need some assistance with QuickBase, go to the gray bar at the top of any QuickBase page and click Help→Help & Support to open the QuickBase Support page, shown in Figure 1-21. From the Support page, you can connect to any of the following resources:

- **Online Help.** Click this link to open a searchable database of Help files on every conceivable topic. Use the upper-left Search box to find a specific topic or click Index to browse or search an alphabetized list of all things QuickBase.

- **Training and Tutorials.** Intuit offers a number of training resources for new QuickBase customers. Click Live Online Training to sign up for a one-day live tutorial (starting at $399 per participant) with Intuit partner Real World Training.

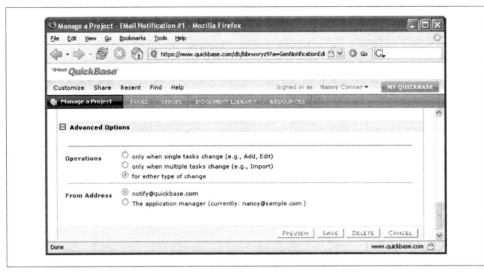

Figure 1-20. If you don't want to know about every single little record change, turn on "only when multiple tasks change"; QuickBase will email you about changes that affect a bunch of records, like an import. Usually, QuickBase names itself as the sender of notification emails; if you tend to pay better attention to email that comes from a person (as opposed to a database), select the application manager as the sender.

Or click Self-paced Training to see a list of free training videos you can watch right away.

TIP

QuickBase staff conducts free, live seminars over the Internet (called *webinars*) to get you up to speed with your new QuickBase account or cover popular topics such as customizing QuickBase, process and workflow, and using QuickBase for projects. Topics change frequently, so to see what's on offer and sign up for a webinar, go to *http://quickbase.intuit.com/webinars*. To see a video recording of a past webinar: From the QuickBase Support page, look in the Video Tutorials section and click the "recorded Webinars" link.

• **QuickBase KnowledgeBase.** If you're looking for troubleshooting tips or work-arounds to thorny problems, take a look at the KnowledgeBase. It's written by Intuit staff and aimed at intermediate-to-advanced QuickBase users.

• **QuickBase Community.** When you need help with a problem, there's no better mentor than someone who's already been there and done that. Click this link to open the QuickBase Community forums page. You can search past discussions or start your own by asking a question. Type your question into the box above the list of discussion topics and then click the big, blue Ask button. After you click but before posting your question, the site shows you a list of related topics; if your question has already been asked and answered, you can read that conversation

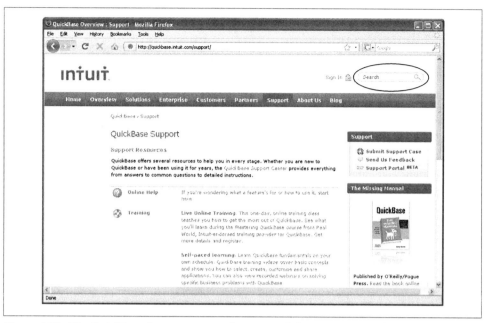

Figure 1-21. The QuickBase Support page gathers many help resources together in one place. To search all QuickBase help resources, type a word or phrase into the upper-right Search box (circled) and then click the magnifying glass or press Enter.

(just click its title). If you don't see your specific question, go ahead and post it to the forum by clicking Ask My Question.

- **Submit Support Case.** If you need help from the folks at Intuit, click this right-hand link to open a form that lets you email them your question. On the first page of the form, type in your QuickBase-registered email address and, from the Contact Type drop-down list, choose Submit Support Case, and then click Next. The next page of the form has two required fields (Subject and Message Details) and two optional fields (Phone Number and File Attachment). When you've described your issue, click the Submit Support Request button, and someone will get back to you by email or, if you've given a phone number, by phone.

TIP

You can also submit a support case from your My QuickBase page: In the left-hand Support section, click the "Submit a help request" link.

QuickBase Calling: Using QuickBase on Your iPhone

You can access QuickBase from anywhere using your iPhone. This is a great way to view your data or keep it up to date when you're not near a computer. Just fire up your iPhone's Web browser and sign into QuickBase. Once you've done that, you can check reports and add, edit, or delete records. In fact, you can work with an application's data just the same as if you were in the office sitting at your desk.

When you're working with QuickBase using your iPhone, it's best to focus on working with the info an application contains. More complex tasks, such as customizing an application's structure, are best left until you can work from a computer. Here are a few other things to keep in mind when you're working with QuickBase from your iPhone:

- QuickBase Help uses a pop-up window to display Help pages. If your pop-up blocker is turned off, Help pages won't display.
- You can't use the Home tab on your My QuickBase page. Currently, your iPhone's Safari browser doesn't support it.
- You can't upload attachments. You can, however, download files in any format that Apple supports, such as PDFs, Word documents, Excel spreadsheets, and so on.
- Dragging and dropping doesn't work. If you need to move columns in a table, use Report Builder.
- You can't manage tokens in an application.
- If you have rich text pages as part of an application's Dashboard, entering the Dashboard editor will crash your phone's Safari browser.
- If you're using the User Picker to choose recipients of an emailed record or report, work in small batches. If User Picker is open and Safari refreshes the page, you'll lose the recipients you've chosen.

Different Ways of Displaying Your Data

Like any self-respecting program, QuickBase is considerate enough to let you look at your data in whatever way makes most sense to you. From Excel-style tables to calendars, charts, and timelines, QuickBase's wide range of built-in *reports* lets you sort, organize, and display your content almost any way you like. If you can imagine it, QuickBase probably has a report to make your vision appear onscreen.

And the best part is how flexible these reports are. Don't like a crowded table with too many columns? QuickBase lets you choose the columns you want to display. Going for a high-impact graphic to illustrate sales trends at a glance? No problem. Or perhaps you want to find out which project tasks are on track—and which have fallen behind; just whip yourself up a custom report and, with the click of a link, you (and your co-workers) can see your handiwork.

Creating a custom report ("Creating a Report from Scratch" on page 61) does take a little bit of work. So before you get your hands dirty trying to design your own, the first part of this chapter takes you on a quick tour of QuickBase's standard report formats: the table, the calendar, the chart, and the timeline.

Plus, every built-in application comes loaded with ready-to-use reports based on the standard formats. For example, the Track Tasks application has a My Tasks report, which presents all your assignments in an easy-to-read table. Once you learn your way around one table, you'll find it a snap to view and manipulate Table reports in your applications. Same goes for all the other report formats.

QuickBase's Report Formats

When you open an application, its Dashboard shows you a report or two. For example, if you're a sales rep and you open the Manage Leads application, the Dashboard shows a handy table listing your assigned leads. If you're a project manager, the Track Tasks Dashboard shows a table of overdue tasks and a pie chart of open tasks, sliced up by status. Changing between reports is simple. From the Dashboard page, click the report you want in the left-hand Reports menu, which lists all the existing reports for that

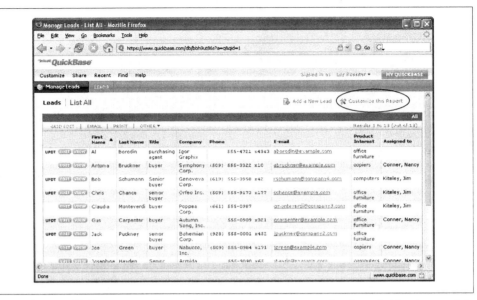

Figure 2-1. In a Table report, each record appears in its own row; each column holds whatever info you're tracking: first name, last name, title, email, and so on. To narrow down the records and fields you're looking at, click the "Customize this Report" link (circled), which opens the Report Builder (see "Create a new report" on page 43).

application. In a multi-table application, of course, you'll have several tables to choose from. From anywhere in the application, simply click the name of the table you want in the Table bar—the blue bar at the top of the page just below in the menu bar. A menu appears listing all the reports for this table; just select the report you want. The following sections explain each report format.

Table Reports

In QuickBase, the most common way to display data is in a table, which shows your data in rows and columns (Figure 2-1). Each row represents a record, and each column represents a field within that record. If you've ever used an Excel spreadsheet, a Table report will look like an old friend.

Grid Edit Reports

A Grid Edit report, such as the one shown in Figure 2-2, looks a lot like a Table report. (In fact, you can magically convert most QuickBase tables to Grid Edit reports by clicking the table's upper-left Grid Edit link.) What you can do in Grid Edit that you can't do with a table, though, is edit individual cells or ranges of them, just as you would in a spreadsheet. That can be a *major* timesaver if you're editing lots of data; rather

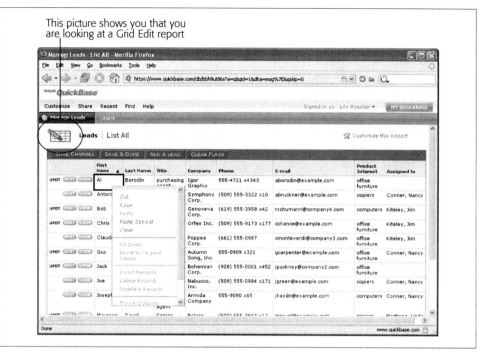

Figure 2-2. Grid Edit reports let you edit fields directly in the table; you don't have to click the Edit button and slog through one record at a time. Click any cell to select it; QuickBase responds by marking it with a thick black line. (You can also select a range of cells: click a cell, and then hold down the mouse button while you drag the cursor to select more cells.) Once you've made your selection, right-click for a menu of changes. When finished, click Save Changes (at the top of the table) to save your edits and remain on this page; click Save & Done to exit the report.

than having to open each record separately, you can click-and-peck your way through your grid-editable table. Your wrists will thank you.

When you're looking at a Grid Edit report, double-click a cell to make a quick change to just that cell. If the cell you've double-clicked is a multiple-choice field (such as Priority), a drop-down menu appears, listing choices like High, Medium, and Low.

The caption for Figure 2-2 explains how to select a range of cells—useful when you want to make a bunch of changes en masse. Once you've made your selection, right-click for a pop-up menu that offers these options (which options you can use depends on what you've selected):

- **Cut.** The old reliable. Works the same as the cut command in Word, Excel, and pretty much every other program.
- **Copy.** Make a duplicate of whatever's in the cell.
- **Paste.** Works hand in hand with Cut and Copy: Choose Paste to insert what you've copied or cut into a new cell.

- **Paste Special.** Opens a pop-up box that lets you paste in clipboard data from another program.
- **Clear.** Erases the contents of the cell.
- **Fill Down.** When you select this option (which works only for a range of cells), QuickBase copies the uppermost value in each column you've selected and pastes it into the cells below. It's a great way to add the same entry to a whole bunch of stacked cells.
- **Reset to Original Values.** This option takes the "oops" out of editing. QuickBase resets the cells you've selected to the values they had when you opened the Grid Edit report. (This *doesn't* work, though, for changes that you've saved.)
- **Insert Records.** When you've selected one or more rows, QuickBase inserts a blank row above the range you've selected.
- **Delete Records.** This doesn't just take rows out of your table—it marks records for utter and complete destruction. (So if you want to save a record but clear some of its fields, *don't* use this option; use Clear instead.) When you choose Delete Records, QuickBase draws a line through the records you've marked for deletion; when you save your changes, those records are gone for good.
- **Undelete Records.** If you've marked records for deletion and have a change of heart, this option gets rid of that strike-through line.
- **Undo.** Whatever you've just done, this option undoes it. (It doesn't matter if you've selected a bunch of different cells when you click it; Undo reverses whatever you just did.)

TIP

When two tables are related, you can embed a Grid Edit report in the master table's forms, showing detail records related to a particular record in the master table—and letting you edit those detail records without leaving the master form. For example, say you're looking at a record from the Customer table. An embedded report shows all the records from the Orders table that belong to that customer. By displaying the orders in Grid Edit mode, you can add new orders, update their status, or enter notes, and then save all those changes with just one click.

Summary and Crosstab Reports

Summary and Crosstab reports display data in a table format, but they're better than plain-vanilla tables when you want a bird's-eye view of your data. For example, a Summary report like the one shown in Figure 2-3 combines groups of similar records and presents you with key totals. So your table doesn't show every sale in each region or each team member's task—it shows *total* sales and *total* tasks, emphasizing the bottom line. Crosstab reports offer slightly more information-rich tables by listing records in both rows and columns. The concept is easier to understand if you look at an example,

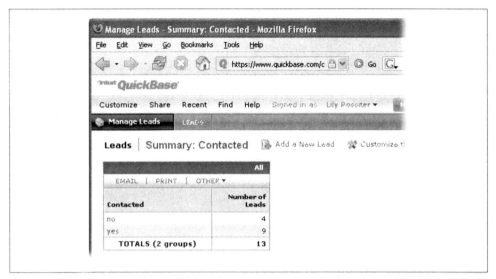

Figure 2-3. This Summary report displays the total numbers of leads that have been contacted (the "yes" row) and those that haven't (the "no" row). For the complete records in Table format, click the word "no" or "yes."

like the one shown in Figure 2-4. Crosstab reports are a good way to show results that answer two or more questions. For example, if your novelty company wants to know which product—red rubber clown noses, squirting lapel flowers, or joy buzzers—sells best in certain cities, a Crosstab report shows at a glance that clown noses are big in Des Moines, while Wichita prefers joy buzzers.

Calendar Reports

A Calendar report (Figure 2-5) does just what its name suggests: displays data on a calendar. In Calendar reports, you can look at the scheduled start dates or end dates of various tasks, or see when records were created or modified. So, for example, you can keep an eye on deadlines as they approach.

TIP

If you've created a report that you want to check at regular intervals—a weekly task list, for example, or a monthly HR update—you can set up subscriptions to that report. When you subscribe to a report, you receive a fresh, updated report by email at an interval you choose: daily, weekly, or monthly. And if you have administrator-level access to the application, you can subscribe other application users to the report, too.

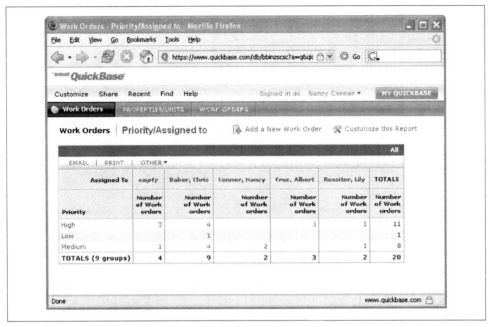

Figure 2-4. Crosstab reports add a new dimension to your data. This example shows outstanding work orders, and it shows them in two dimensions: the priority of each work order and who's assigned to the job. At a glance, you can see how many work orders have a priority of high, medium, or low, and how many work orders each employee has. For example, you might not want to assign Chris Baker any more work orders until he's taken care of the four high-priority jobs he's already got on his plate.

Chart Reports

They say a picture is worth a thousand words, but a good chart is probably worth a few more, thanks to its ability to show trends and relationships at a glance. Even though tables are a good way to present information, rows and rows of data lack the visual oomph of a chart. QuickBase offers several kinds of Chart reports:

- **Bar chart.** In this kind of chart, different bars of equal width vary in height to show different amounts of data. For example, the bar chart in Figure 2-6 shows the number of purchase orders per requester. Bar charts are easy to read and work great for making comparisons. Ask yourself what you want your chart to illustrate—if your answer includes a word like "rank" or "compare," you've got a good candidate for a bar chart.

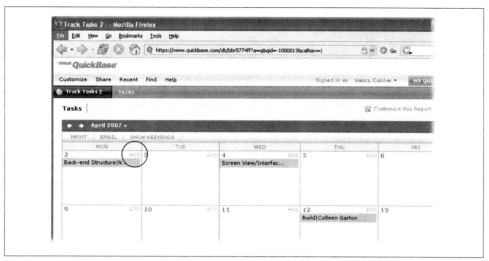

Figure 2-5. This report shows task start dates in a calendar format. Use the right- and left-pointing arrows next to the month to move the report a month forward or a month back. Click the downward-pointing arrow after this month's name to zip right over to any month and year you choose. To view a task's details, click its name. To add a new task, look in the upper-right corner of any date box and click ADD (circled for Monday, April 2).

NOTE

QuickBase offers four different types of bar charts: straight-up bar charts like the one shown in Figure 2-6; horizontal bar charts, which flip the bars sideways so they reach from left to right; stacked bar charts, which add another dimension to the picture by breaking each bar into different colors (each color represents part of a whole, like different sales offices within a region); and horizontal stacked bar charts, which turn the stacked bar chart on its ear. For tips on building bar charts, jump ahead to "Bar charts" on page 87.

- **Pie chart.** Pie charts, like bar charts, are also easy to read, serving up your data in wedge-shaped slices (Figure 2-7). These charts, which show the relationship of different parts to the whole, are great for showing proportions or percentages, like sales figures per region.

- **Line chart.** This type of chart displays your data as a series of points connected by a line (Figure 2-8). If you want to show growth or decline, use a line chart.

TIP

Line charts are ideal for showing trends by plotting data over time, such as sales per month.

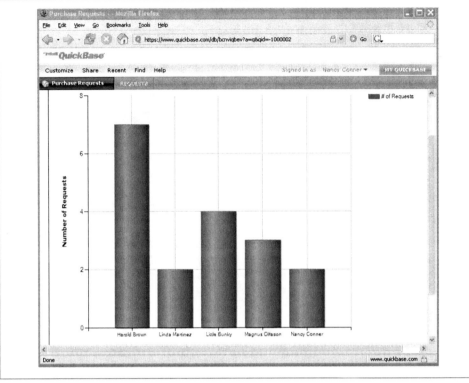

Figure 2-6. This basic bar chart shows the number of purchase orders according to requester. As you can see, Harold Brown has filed a lot more purchase requests than any of his colleagues. A bar chart really makes these differences jump out at the viewer.

- **Area chart.** An area chart is a line chart with a fancy hairdo. This kind of chart emphasizes changes in values by coloring in the segment of the chart that's *below* the line connecting data points. Figure 2-9 shows an example.

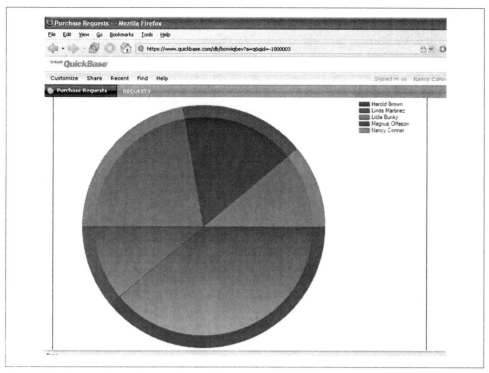

Figure 2-7. This pie chart slices up the number of purchase orders per requester, showing that all by himself, Harold Brown accounts for almost half of all purchase orders. The underlying data is the same as Figure 2-6's bar chart, but a pie chart helps you see things differently.

number of work orders per week, but you want to know *which* repairs tenants requested most often. Is there an easy way to look at the records that created the chart?

There sure is. QuickBase charts use Flash technology to make them interactive. In other words, that's not just a pretty picture you're looking at. In a pie chart, click any wedge to see the records associated with that wedge. Bar charts work the same way—hover your cursor over a bar to see the actual value associated with that bar; click the bar to see the records behind it. Same thing with the points plotted on a line or area chart— click a point to get a look at its records. And to see *all* the records behind a chart, click the chart's title.

Timeline Reports

When you're working against a deadline, a Timeline report gives you a good look at what your team has to do and how long they've got to do it. A timeline displays records, such as tasks, each with its own start date and end date. Timelines are great for spotting potential bottlenecks, as shown in Figure 2-10.

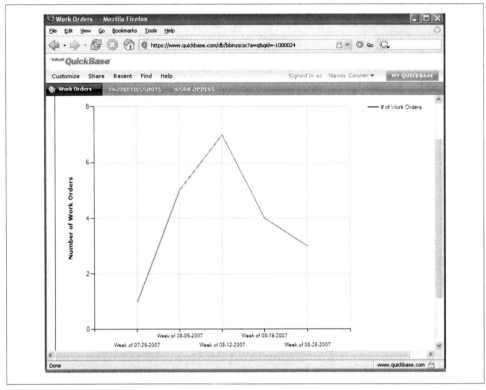

Figure 2-8. Line charts plot data points and then connect those points with a line, showing peaks and valleys. This style of chart is particularly good for illustrating trends over time. This simple line chart shows that work orders peaked sharply during the week of August 12, and then declined.

Creating, Editing, and Printing Reports

Reports are so flexible you can do just about anything you want with them. You can create a report that displays data in a whole new way, or you can tweak an existing report so that it shows exactly what you want to see. When you've got a report looking just right, you can save it, print it, or copy it. (You can also copy a report to use it as a starting point for creating a new report.) Or, if there's a report you don't need anymore, you can delete it. This section explains all.

NOTE

When you've got a great report, tell the world! Chapter 4 teaches you all you need to know about sharing your QuickBase reports, from emailing a report to spiffing up your Word documents with imported QuickBase charts.

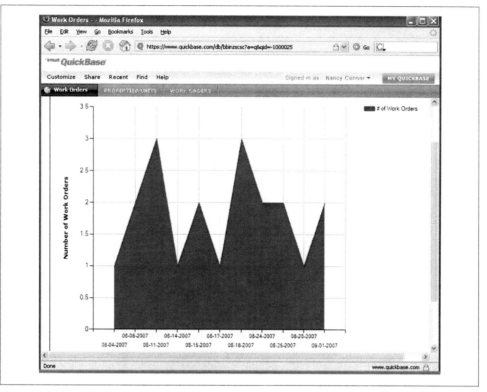

Figure 2-9. An area chart makes a bold statement, emphasizing peaks and valleys by filling in the area below the line with color.

Creating a Report from Scratch

If you use any of QuickBase's prebuilt applications (Chapter 6 explains all about those), each one already has a number of reports built right in. For example, the Track Tasks application comes with more than a dozen reports including My Tasks, Calendar of Tasks This Month, Open Tasks by Assigned to, Tasks Due in Next 30 Days, and so on.

That's a lot of different ways to look at your data! (And that's just for one application.) Chances are you'll find prebuilt applications have all the reports you need. But maybe not. Or maybe you'll create your own application (Chapter 7 tells you how), in which case you'll definitely need to know how to cook up your own reports. Either way, follow these steps to create a new report:

1. Open any application and then, in the menu bar, click Customize→Create a new→Report. If you're in a multi-table application ("Single-Table or Multi-Table?" on page 231), choose the table you want to create the new report for. Or, if you're the type who likes to minimize clicks so you won't wear out your mouse,

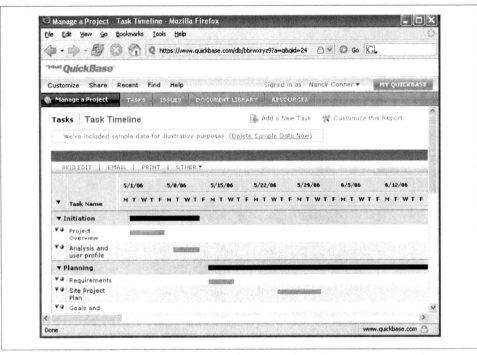

Figure 2-10. This timeline shows this project's tasks' start and end dates over a six-month period. At a glance, you can see which project phases overlap and when you're going to need to order extra Mountain Dew for the programmers.

you can take this shortcut: Click the table name in the Table bar (the blue bar at the top of your screen), and then select "Create a New Report".

The Report Builder window, shown in Figure 2-11, opens. Think of Report Builder as your launchpad for creating or modifying a report.

2. Choose a report type (Table, Grid Edit, Summary, Calendar, Chart, or Timeline).

Depending on which report you select, Report Builder changes to offer you options specific to that kind of report. Figure 2-11 shows Report Builder for Table reports. Other reports have different sets of options—keep reading to learn more about options specific to Table and Grid Edit reports ("Table Reports" on page 70), Summary reports and Crosstab reports ("Summary and Crosstab Reports" on page 78), Calendar reports ("Calendar Reports" on page 84), Chart reports ("Chart Reports" on page 87), and Timeline reports ("Timeline Reports" on page 96).

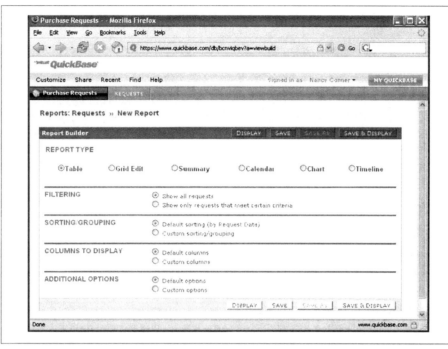

Figure 2-11. Build your new report with the Report Builder. First, choose the kind of report you want in the Report Type section; once you make your choice, QuickBase presents you with options specific to that report. (For example, if you select Chart, you have to pick whether you want to create a bar, line, area, or pie chart.) You can also customize your display: whether to display all records or just those that match certain criteria; how to sort, group, and display the data; and so on.

NOTE

Sometimes—not always—Report Builder lists one other report type as an option: Grid Edit. This report lets you edit records as though you were working with a spreadsheet. (To read more about Grid Edit reports, jump back to "Grid Edit Reports" on page 52.) When you're creating a brand-new report, Grid Edit's options in Report Builder are the same as for a Table report.

---

3. Select the options for your new report (for all the juicy details about those options, see the section on creating specific report types), and then click Display. Although these options vary according to report type, the following options are common to all reports:

Filtering. You can display all records or only those that meet certain criteria, which you define. For example, you might choose to display tasks assigned to a certain person or purchase orders that still need approval. If you like, you can filter by more than one criterion—just click the "more lines" button to add another field to your filter.

Additional options. You can define a custom formula column ("Using Formulas to Design Reports" on page 435) for your report. Custom formula columns are an advanced feature that you probably won't use for most reports. That said, if you want to create a custom column for just this report and you don't have administrative privileges ("Managing Your Billing Account" on page 23), turn on the "Define a custom formula column for this report" checkbox and type your custom formula into the text box that appears. (If you've got administrative privileges, then you'd most likely add a new field to the form ["Customizing Forms" on page 439] to create a custom column.)

Once you've made your selections, QuickBase displays your new report.

4. If you want to make changes, click the upper-right "Customize this Report" link to go back to Report Builder and tinker with the report some more. If you're happy with the report, look above the report you've created for the Save link and click it.

The main screen grays out, and the Save Report As box opens, shown in Figure 2-12.

5. Give your new report a descriptive name (so you can find it again later) and choose whether you want the report to be for your eyes only (Personal Report) or for everyone to see (Shared Report).

NOTE

Unless you have permission to save shared reports, your only option is to save your new report as a personal one. If you don't have permission and you think the world should see your cool new report, talk to the application's manager. (The manager of each application is listed on your My QuickBase page when you view your applications in Details display.)

If you choose Shared Report, the box expands to give you some more choices; Figure 2-13 explains your options. Whether you've chosen to keep your report personal or share it with other application users, click OK to save the report.

TIP

If you've got several reports from different applications that you find yourself checking frequently, put those reports in a central location: the Reports tab of your My QuickBase page. Chapter 1 ("Keeping Tabs on Your Data: Using the Home Tab" on page 15) explains how to add reports to your My QuickBase page.

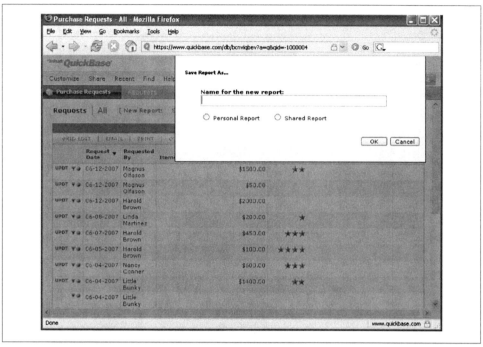

Figure 2-12. Immortalize your newly created report using the Save Report As box. Give your new report a name and decide whether you want to save the report for your personal use or to share it with other QuickBase users who have access to this application. If you choose Personal Report, click OK and you're done. If you choose Shared Report, the box expands and you have some more decisions to make, as Figure 2-13 shows.

TIP

When you display a new report to see how it looks, you might want to go back and make some changes. To get back to Report Builder, click the report's "Customize this Report" link. *Don't* click your browser's Back button—that returns you to Report Builder, but all the work you just did has disappeared, leaving you back at Square One. (If you hit Back by mistake, don't despair—or start all over again. Click your Web browser's Forward button, and then click that Customize link.)

Edit, Copy, or Delete a Report

Sometimes an existing report is close to what you want, but not quite there—maybe a table has too many columns or you want to label the wedges on a pie chart with actual values rather than percentages. It can be easier to modify a report than create a whole new one from scratch (although that's pretty darn easy, too). Or, if you don't want to make changes to an existing report, you can always copy the original report and use the replica as the basis for a new report, saving yourself a step or two. Finally, if a report has outlived its usefulness, you can get rid of it.

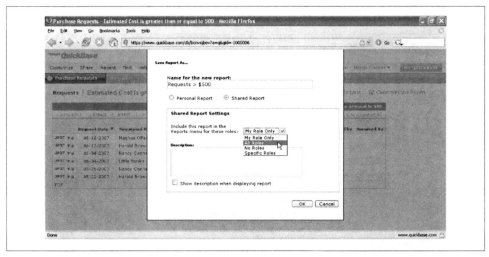

Figure 2-13. It's nice to share. If you decide to share a report you've created, first specify the roles of the people who can see it. Then, if you want, enter a description of the report. (If you make the name descriptive enough, you may not need to enter anything in the Description box.) If you write a description and want to display it along with the report, turn on the checkbox at the bottom of the box.

Whether you want to edit, copy, or delete a report, you start off the same way:

1. Open the application that holds the report you want.

   You can always find this in the Applications section of your My QuickBase page.

2. In the menu bar at the top of any page in the application, click Customize→Tables.

   QuickBase whisks you off to the Tables page, shown in Figure 2-14. If you're in a multi-table application, select the table you want from the left-hand list.

3. Click the Reports tab.

   QuickBase displays all the reports that exist for the table you've chosen.

How you proceed from there depends on what you want to do.

Editing a report

If you're already looking at a report and you want to tweak it, click the report's "Customize this Report" link, then tweak away. If you're elsewhere in the application, find your way to the Reports tab of the Tables page as described in the previous section. Then follow these steps:

1. Find the report you want to edit, and click its name.

   Report Builder opens.

2. Make whatever changes you want to the report. When you're finished, click Display to see how the new report looks, Save to overwrite the report you started with,

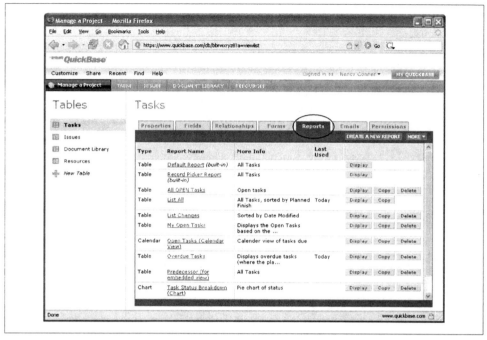

Figure 2-14. In all your QuickBase applications, the Tables page offers a central location for working with tables. When you want to tweak a report, this is the place to go. On the Tables page (Customize→Tables), click the Reports tab to see a list of all the reports related to the current table. From here, you can open, copy, or delete a report. To go straight to Report Builder and edit a report, click the report's name.

Save As to save this report with a new name, or Save & Display to overwrite the report you started with and display the new version. (If you click Display, don't forget to click the Save or Save As link on the display page to save it.)

QuickBase saves the edited report.

TIP

If you've edited a report and you don't like the way it looks when you display it, click the Revert link at the top of the page. That discards your changes and puts the report back to the way it was.

Copying a report

Go to the Reports page as described in the previous section, and then follow these steps:

1. On the Reports tab of the Tables page, find the report you want to copy, and look to the right of its name for the Copy button. Click Copy.

QuickBase creates a new report that's an exact copy of the one you selected. To distinguish the copy from the original, QuickBase adds the word *copy* to the end of the report's name. The new report appears in the Reports list with a thick black arrow pointing to it.

2. To make changes to the new report, click its name.

   Report Builder opens. Here, you can rename the report and edit it in any way you like.

3. When you're finished, click Display to see how the new report looks, Save to save it with its current name (which includes the word *copy*), Save As to save the report with a new name, or Save & Display to save the report with its current name and see what it looks like. (If you click Display, don't forget to click the Save or Save As link on the display page to save it.)

   QuickBase saves your new report.

TIP

When you want to create a new report that's similar to an existing report, copy the existing report and then edit and rename the copy.

Deleting a report

Go to the Reports page and then follow these steps:

1. Find the report you want to delete. To its right is a Delete button; click it.

   QuickBase asks you to confirm that you want to get rid of this report.

2. Click OK.

   QuickBase deletes the report and updates the Reports list to show it's gone.

Print a Report

If you want to include a report in a written document (or it just looks so darn good that you want to tack it up on your wall), all it takes is a couple of clicks.

NOTE

If you simply want to print whatever's on your screen, you can do so in a flash from the Customize menu. Click Customize→"Print this page". QuickBase opens two new windows: one displaying the page as it'll be printed and the other to let you select the number of copies and send the document to your printer. If your report stretches beyond what you can see on your screen, QuickBase cuts off the part you can't see. If that's the case, follow the steps below to print your report in all its glory.

Here's how to print a report that's displayed as a table (including Summary and Cross-tab reports):

1. Display the report you want to print. Find the Print button at the top of the table (it's in the gray bar just above the data) and click it.

   A box appears, asking whether you want to print the report as it appears on your screen or as individual records (one record per page).

2. Make your selection and click OK.

   QuickBase opens a new browser window with your table in it. A Print dialog box also opens.

3. If you want, adjust the properties of your print job (paper orientation, number of copies, and so on). When everything's all set, click OK.

   You've got a printed version of your report.

TIP

If you want to see how your report will look on paper before you print it, click Cancel in the Print dialog box. In the browser window that displays your about-to-be-printed report, select File→Print Preview. From there, click the Page Setup button to make adjustments. Click the Print button to bring back the Print box and then go ahead and print your report.

Printing a Chart report is similar. Because charts are Flash files (which let you interact with them), when you click the Print link above a chart, QuickBase converts the chart to an image file, which you can then print.

Use the same procedure for printing calendars and timelines. After you click the report's Print button, QuickBase opens the report in a new browser window and reminds you that these reports look best in Landscape orientation (rather than Portrait). Select File→Print, and proceed with step 3 in the previous list.

TIP

Calendars and timelines print best if you set the margins to half an inch.

Tips for Creating Specific Report Types

When you're creating a report, the options QuickBase gives you depend on the kind of report you're working on. When you select a report type (Table, Calendar, or whatever), Report Builder magically transforms itself to ask you for the precise information it needs to create that kind of report. The following sections step you through each set of options.

Table Reports

For tables, Report Builder asks you to define the criteria you want for the report you're creating. For example, you might want your new Work Orders table to display only high-priority work orders or your Purchase Requests table to list all requests over $5,000. You might want sales leads grouped by region or by product interest. And you might want to show only a few columns, rather than cluttering up the table with lots of extraneous information. However you want to organize your table, whatever info you want it to show, you can customize a report to get your table *exactly* the way you want it.

When you're creating a Table report, QuickBase presents you with the following sections:

- **Filtering.** This section is where you tell QuickBase which records to display in your new report. There are, of course, many reasons to filter records: You might want to display unassigned tasks, leads, or work orders; documents modified in the past week; high-cost purchase requests; and so on.

  Displaying only those records that match criteria you choose is one of the most common reasons to create a new report. And doing so is easy, as you can see in Figure 2-15. In Report Builder, click the "Show only records that meet certain criteria" radio button, and then select the field you want to filter and tell QuickBase how to filter it. (Filtering criteria, of course, depend on the field you select. If you want to see records modified in the past week, for example, you'd select "Date Modified" and then set the criteria to show only those records changed within the past week. If you wanted to see tasks assigned to a certain person, you'd select "Assigned To," then "is," and then the name of the person you're interested in.) You can filter on several criteria by clicking "more lines" and choosing other fields until you're done. Just don't filter out too much or your new report will have nothing to show for itself!

  TIP

  Use OR to find records that match either of two possibilities: tasks assigned to Shari Ozawa OR to Jim McClendon, for example. Just make sure that you type *OR* in capital letters. (If you don't, QuickBase sees *or* as a word in the search rather than an instruction on how to search.)

- **Sorting/Grouping.** In this section, shown in Figure 2-16, you can tell QuickBase how to organize the data it displays in your new report. You can choose from the standard organization QuickBase uses for this table (look at "Default sorting" to see what that is—it might be by first name, date created, priority, or whatever), or you can sort according to your own criteria. You can sort in ascending order (low to high) or descending order (high to low). You also have the option of grouping the results. So if you're sorting purchase requests by request date, for example, you

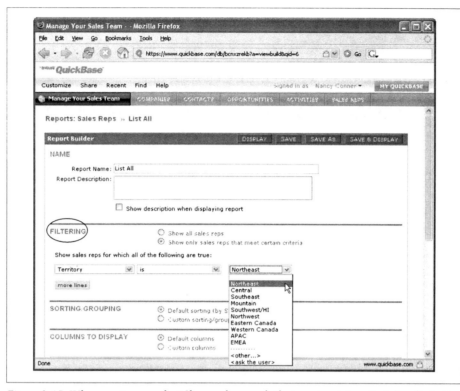

Figure 2-15. When you turn on the "Show only records that meet certain criteria" radio button (here, it says "sales reps" instead of "records" because that's the kind of record you're dealing with in this table), the Filtering section (circled) expands so you can choose the criteria you want QuickBase to match. In this example, the new Table report will look for and display only those sales reps who have Northeast in the Territory field—so your table won't show accounts in the Southeast or Central region, for instance. Click the "more lines" button if you want to add more filtering criteria; you could display, for example, all sales reps in the Northeast territory who've won deals in this year or this period.

can group the results by the day, week, month, quarter, year, and so on. Or if you're sorting purchase requests by who approved them, you can group the results by the approver's name, so that all the purchase requests approved by Andrew Aho appear in one group, all the purchase requests approved by Beverly Berlioz appear in another, and so on, with each group showing the total cost of the requests approved by that person.

- **Columns to Display.** This handy section lets you choose and order the columns you want your table to display. Remember: In the previous two sections of the Report Builder window you were picking which records (think: rows) to select (Filtering) and how to sort and group them (Sorting/Group); this section lets you decide which *columns* show up in your report. The default columns in a report depend on the application you're in. (If you want to see what the default columns

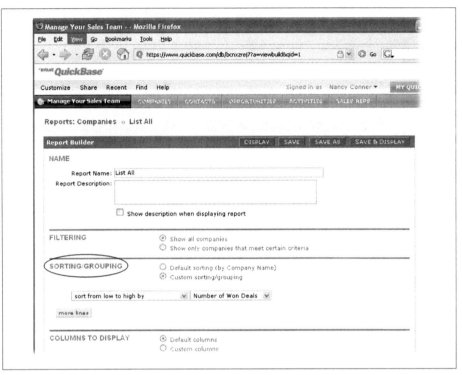

Figure 2-16. In Report Builder's Sorting/Grouping section (circled), you can either select the default sorting criterion (in this case, the default sort for accounts is by Company Name) or choose a different field to sort on. In the example, the Table report will sort accounts in ascending order according to how much business each account brought in last year. As in the Filtering section, you can sort by more than one field; just click the "more lines" button to add another sorting criterion.

are, click the "Custom columns" radio button and, when the section expands, click "Set to default columns." The default columns appear in the Your Columns box. To clear Your Columns, click "Remove all columns.") When you turn on the "Custom columns" radio button, QuickBase presents the options explained in Figure 2-17.

- **Additional Options.** This section, shown in Figure 2-18, gives you still more options for creating a table:

Format. Most of the time, your choice here will probably be Normal, which is best for displaying your report in a Web browser. But you do have a few other options: Plain Text displays your report as unformatted text. It ain't pretty, but the info's there. Comma- or tab-separated values let you export the data ("Exporting Data" on page 137) to a spreadsheet program. To display your data in an XSL style sheet, choose either "XML (flat)" or "XML (structured)."

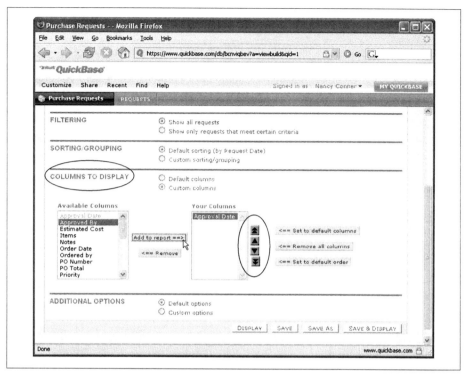

Figure 2-17. In Report Builder's "Columns to Display" section (circled), pick which columns you want to appear in your report and what order you want them in. In the Available Columns box, highlight a column name and then click the "Add to Report" button to move that column to the Your Columns box. You can change the order of columns in your new table by using the arrow buttons (circled); single arrows move the selected column up or down in the list by one slot, and double arrows move it up or down by three slots. "Set to default columns" restores QuickBase's original selection of columns; "Set to default order" puts them back in their original order.

Show Main Table. When you select sorting and grouping options as described earlier, you can display both the main table and a *summary table*, which shows just the sorted and grouped info (see the next list item). If you want your report to show only the summary table, turn off this checkbox (it's turned on by default). If you show both the main table and the summary table, the main table appears first; scroll down to see the summary table.

Show Summary Table. This option comes into play only if you've sorted and grouped your data. The summary table's a snapshot of numeric fields that display totals, averages, or both. For example, if you're creating a report of purchase requests sorted and grouped by requester, your summary table will present columns showing the number of requests by each requester and the total estimated cost of each requester's requests. Figure 2-19 shows what that looks like.

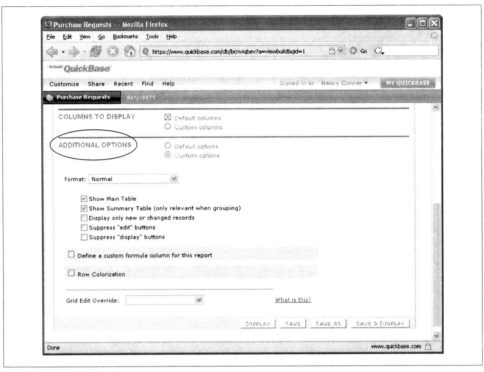

Figure 2-18. The Additional Options section (circled) offers a grab bag of ways to customize your Table report. When you turn on the "Custom options" radio button, it displays the default options: Normal format (the way you're used to seeing QuickBase tables); showing both Main and Summary tables for grouping; putting Edit and Display buttons on the screen; displaying a gray background for rows; allowing grid edit; and so on. You can change as many of those options as you like.

Display only new or changed records. This is a quick way to show only those records that someone has added or modified since you last looked at this report.

Suppress "edit" or "display" buttons. If you want a clean-looking table for a report, you can hide the Edit and Display buttons.

Define a custom formula column for this report. This lets you create a field that you'll use just for this report. For more on custom formulas, see "Using Formulas to Design Reports" on page 435.

Row Colorization. QuickBase's white and gray rows are perfectly fine, but sometimes you need a little color in your life. To call attention to certain records, such as high-priority or overdue tasks, apply a custom color to their rows. When you turn on the Row Colorization checkbox, a text field appears, asking you to type in a row colorization formula. All that means is that you have to let QuickBase know which rows you want colored and what color you want them to be. You do this by using an *if ()* formula —a moderately user-unfriendly system that's not too hard once you get the hang of it.

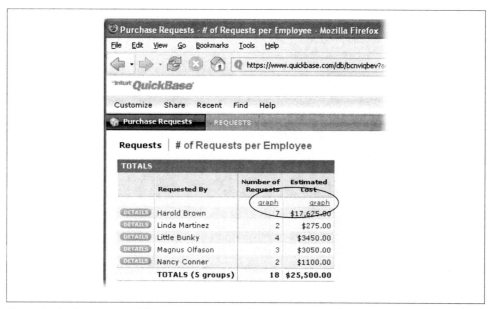

Figure 2-19. A summary table summarizes an application's numeric fields when these display totals, averages, or both. In this example, the summary table shows totals for the Number of Requests and Estimated Cost fields. One cool feature of summary tables is that you can see a graph of any field with just one click—click the "graph" link (circled) above the data in any column to see a bar graph of that column's figures.

Full details on writing custom formulas are in "Writing Formulas" on page 417, but here's a quick and dirty example: Imagine that you want to highlight high-priority work orders an urgent shade of fire-engine red. Type this into the Row Colorization text box: *if ([Priority] = "High", "red", "")*. Or, to highlight overdue tasks with a guilt-inducing yellow, type this: *if ([Due Date] < Today(), "yellow", "")*. You can get fancier with row colorization, using different colors to highlight different things—see the box in "Color My World" on page 76 for full details. Also, if you're new to playing with colors, click the Help link above the box where you type in your formula: It opens a new window displaying QuickBase's handy Help page on using this feature.

Grid Edit Override. Grid Edit, explained in "Grid Edit Reports" on page 52, is a report that lets you edit a group of records in the same way you'd edit a spreadsheet—copying and pasting from one cell to another, filling down, adding or deleting multiple records all at once, and so on. Tables usually have a Grid Edit link at the upper left (you can see an example back in Figure 2-1). When a user clicks Grid Edit, QuickBase normally shows the same columns that appear in the original table from which the user got to the Grid Edit page. Sometimes, though, you might not want Grid Edit to show the exact same fields as in the original table. That's where Grid Edit Override comes in. If you don't want users to be able to grid edit this report at all, select <Disable> from the drop-down menu here. At the other extreme, select <All Fields (built-in)> if you want *every* field the table contains to show up as a column in Grid Edit. Or, if you've created any custom forms for this table, you can select the one you want here.

You can use hexadecimal color values ("Customizing an Application's Appearance" on page 215) instead of numbers to give yourself more control over the shades —when you're working with hexadecimal values, there are way more colors than in a boring old rainbow.

("Customizing an Application's Appearance" on page 215)

NOTE

One thing you *can't* do to custom color your reports is highlight a column using color. These formulas only work for rows.

POWER USERS' CLINIC

Customizable Reports

You can create a report that asks users to select which items to display from a list of criteria you define. For example, you can create a report that asks users to choose a region when they want to look at sales leads. This is an amazingly powerful tool that's sure to dazzle your boss, your co-workers, and your fellow QuickBase aficionados.

The easiest way to learn about this feature is to just go ahead and use it. The following steps show how to have QuickBase prompt users to select the records it searches for and displays:

1. Open the application you want and, from the menu bar, select Customize→Tables. This gets you to the Tables page. (If you're in a multi-table application, choose the table you want.) Click the Reports tab to see the list of reports for that application. If you want to edit an existing report, click its name. If you want to create a brand-new report, click the upper-right Create a New Report button.

   The Report Builder page opens. (Jump back to Figure 2-11 for a look at this page.)

2. In Report Builder's Filtering section, turn on "Show only records that meet certain criteria."

   The Filtering section expands to let you choose the criteria you want QuickBase to match.

3. In the "Select a field" drop-down list, choose the field you're interested in.

   Depending on the field you select, other options appear to the right.

4. In the second column, choose the *operator* you want to use to filter the data. (An operator is a keyword or key phrase that lets you work on data; for example, an operator sets true/false conditions—either retrieving or excluding all records that contain a certain word.)

   QuickBase displays a third column, depending on the operator you choose.

5. If the third column contains a drop-down list, select <ask the user>. If it contains a text box, type _ask1_ or <ask the user> into the box. Click Display to see how the report prompts the user for a selection criterion.

   QuickBase displays the prompt box that a user looking at that report will see.

6. Test out the prompt: Select a criterion and click OK.

   QuickBase shows the report according to the criterion you chose.

7. If you need to make changes, click the report's "Customize this Report" link to reopen Report Builder. If everything looks OK, click the Save or Save As link. (If you've created a whole new report, Save is your only option. If you've edited an existing report, click Save to overwrite the old report or Save As to save this report with a new name.)

QuickBase saves your report. Now, whenever anyone chooses this report, QuickBase prompts them to enter their selection criterion.

If you want to prompt users to select criteria for two or more fields, you can. In Report Builder's Filtering section, click the More Lines button to increase the number of fields.

Summary and Crosstab Reports

You create both Summary and Crosstab reports using the Summary Report Builder. That makes sense, given that they're both souped-up variations on the same theme: tables that help you pluck key info from large amounts of data. (For a refresher on the difference between these reports, jump back to "Summary and Crosstab Reports" on page 54.) To get started, select Summary as the Report Type in Report Builder. As you build your report, you'll decide whether you want to create a Summary (Figure 2-20) or a Crosstab (Figure 2-21) report. You make this decision in the Crosstabs (Column Groupings) section. The rest of this section explains your options.

- **Data To Summarize.** In this section, you select the fields whose data will make up your report. The values you select here label column headings (in a Summary report) or column subheadings (in a Crosstab report). Use the left-hand drop-down menu to select the fields you want your table to display. For example, Figure 2-21 shows an application for managing sales leads, and the column heading (chosen in this section) is "# of Leads." You'll find only numeric fields listed in this drop-down. That's because only numbers can be summarized, which means added up, averaged, or used for some other kind of calculation—after all, summarizing is the whole point of a Summary report. Depending on what you choose from the leftmost drop-down, a new drop-down may appear, called Summarize By. Summarize By gives you these choices for creating your summary:

  —**Totals.** This option adds up your data's values within each group.

  —**Averages.** This shows the value that marks the middle of your data set. Your high-school math teacher would call this the arithmetic mean. Remember? If you bought three DVDs—spending $8.99, $12.98, and $26.99—your average cost was $16.32 (add the prices and divide by the number of discs you bought). That's the kind of value this choice shows.

  —**Maximums.** This option shows the highest value within the group of records.

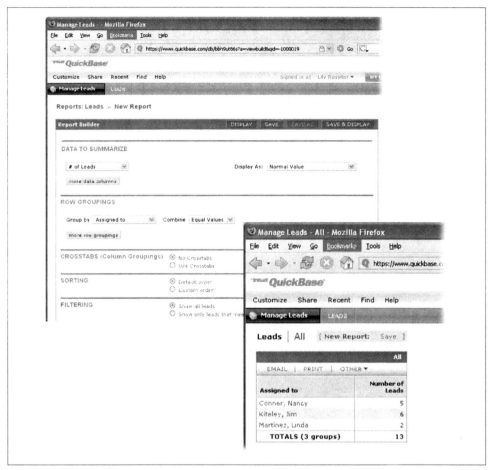

Figure 2-20. Top: When you create a Summary report, first choose the data you want to summarize (this will provide your column headings) and then choose the information that will appear in each row. Next, tell QuickBase how to arrange that information by setting the options in the Sorting and Filtering areas. Notice that, to display a Summary report, the No Crosstabs radio button is turned on. Bottom: The result: A Summary table showing the number of leads assigned to different sales reps. The table lists the number of leads per rep and the total of all leads at the bottom.

— **Minimums.** The flip side of the previous option, this one shows the lowest value within the group.

— **Std. Deviation.** Here's another one for your old math teacher. The standard deviation shows the spread of a set of values around the set's average. When you look at an average, it doesn't tell you anything about the spread of values: for example, if you bought a dozen DVDs and the average price was $16.32, did most of the DVDs cost around sixteen bucks or did you buy a lot of cheap DVDs and one really expensive, super-deluxe edition? Calculating the standard devi-

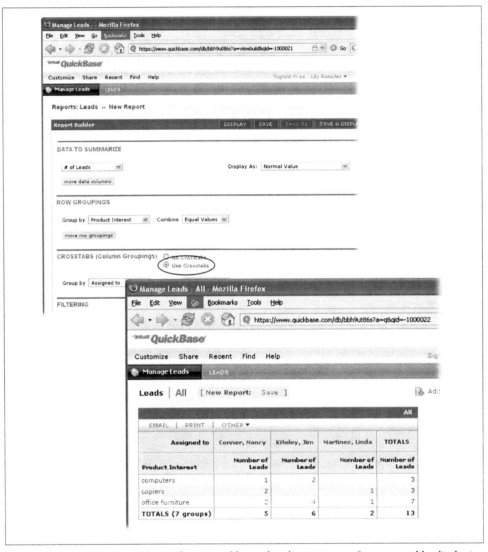

Figure 2-21. Top: Creating a Crosstab report adds another dimension to a Summary table, displaying records in both columns and rows (see "Summary and Crosstab Reports" on page 54 for full details on how these amazingly helpful reports work). In this example, the Use Crosstabs radio button (circled) is turned on, making the section expand so that you can choose a column grouping—in this case, names in the Assigned To field form the columns. In each column, under the name of each sales rep is the subheading "Number of Leads" (selected in the Data To Summarize section). Rows group data by the field you select (Product Interest, in this case). Bottom: The result: The Crosstab report adds another dimension to a Summary table. Not only do you see the number of leads per sales rep (and in total), you also see how product interest breaks down, both by type of product and by sales rep.

ation (or better yet, having QuickBase do the math for you) gives you an idea of how the values relate to the average.

The right-hand drop-down, Display As, is optional. Its menu shows the different ways your report can display the contents of the field you've chosen to summarize. Here are your options:

— **Normal Value.** This is the usual display choice. It means QuickBase doesn't do any fancy footwork with your numbers.

— **Percent of column total.** When you choose this option, QuickBase displays each value as a percentage of the entire column (so the numbers display add up to 100%).

— **Percent of crosstab total (Crosstab reports only).** The previous option shows values as a percentage of the total in each column; this options shows the percentage of each *row* that a value represents. Figure 2-22 shows you what this looks like.

— **Running total down column.** When you display normal values, QuickBase adds up the numbers and gives a total at the bottom of a columns. This display option shows running totals as you read your report from top to bottom, showing how the numbers increase as new values are added.

— **Running total across crosstab (Crosstab reports only).** Just as the previous option shows a running total from top to bottom, this option keeps a running total as you read your table from left to right.

One lonely little column probably isn't enough data, but it's easy to create others to join the party. Click the "more data columns" button to add another column, and make your choices. If, on the other hand, you went a little crazy with your columns and your Summary report is too wide for your computer screen, click the "fewer columns" button. This removes columns from the report you're creating, starting at the bottom and working upward.

• **Row Groupings.** Each row of a Summary report represents a group of records, and this is where you specify how you want those records grouped. Here, you pick the field you want to use to group records—that's what the "Group by" drop-down is for—and organize those groups using the Combine drop-down. First, choose the field you want for your rows. In Figure 2-20, for example, each row is the name of a sales rep that appears in the "Assigned to" field. So, for instance, all the records that have the name Jim Kiteley in the "Assigned to" field (there are six total) are grouped into that one row. Once you've chosen the field to group by, use the Combine drop-down to tell QuickBase how you want your groupings organized. This depends on the type of field you've chosen in the "Group by" drop-down. To organize text fields (names, tasks, priority, and so on) alphabetically, select Equal Values, which tells QuickBase to combine all identical terms into one row. (Other combination choices might be First Word or First Letter.) You can combine date fields by day, week, month, quarter, year, decade, or equal values. You can combine

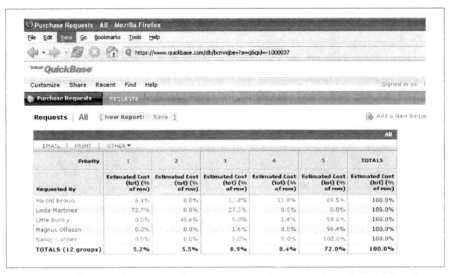

Figure 2-22. When you display your data as a percent of the crosstab total, QuickBase figures the percentages for each row, adding them up to 100% in the rightmost column. This example, from an application to manage purchase requests, shows what percentage of each employee's purchase orders fall into each priority level. Not surprisingly, almost everyone thinks most of their requests deserve top priority.

numeric fields (like estimated cost) by equal values or in number ranges, like hundreds or thousands—so you might show, for example, the number of purchase requests that cost less than a hundred dollars, that cost between $100 and $200, between $200 and $300, and so on.

- **Crosstabs (Column Groupings).** If you're creating a Summary report, jump right over this section (just make sure the No Crosstabs radio button is turned on). But if you want another dimension to play with, you can create it here. In Report Builder's previous sections, you've already selected the data your report will summarize and the information that will be grouped into its rows. When you turn on the Use Crosstabs radio button, you can group your report's columns by a specific field. A Crosstab report cross-tabulates; all that means is that a field (that you choose) groups other fields together. To see what this looks like, take a look at Figure 2-23. After you've turned on the Use Crosstabs radio button, use the "Group by" drop-down to select the field you want over the fields that will be grouped together in subheadings. (The grouped fields are the ones you selected back in the Data To Summarize section.)

- **Sorting (Summary reports only).** Sorting for Summary tables works similarly to how it works for regular tables ("Table Reports" on page 70)—use this section to let QuickBase know how you want your data organized. For a Summary report, you can set your own custom sort order. For example, you might want to list purchase requests from lowest to highest (or vice versa). Your options for sorting

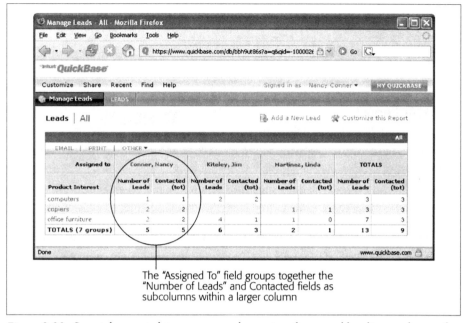

The "Assigned To" field groups together the "Number of Leads" and Contacted fields as subcolumns within a larger column

Figure 2-23. Crosstab reports let you group columns together as subheadings under another column, letting you fit a lot of data into one easy-to-read report. In this example from a Sales Leads application, the "Assigned to" field groups together the Number of Leads and Contacted fields, letting you see at a glance whether your sales reps are following up on their leads. Rows break down the data by product interest. As you can see, if Jim Kiteley wants to sell any office furniture, he'd better hurry up and make some calls—he's behind on contacting leads with that product interest.

come from the fields you chose in the "Group summary by" and "Columns to display" sections.

NOTE

There's no Sorting section for Crosstab reports. When you turned on the Use Crosstabs radio button, the Sorting section magically disappears.

- **Filtering.** The Filtering section for Summary and Crosstab reports works the same as it does in Table reports, described in "Table Reports" on page 70.

- **Additional options.** There's only one additional option here: to create a custom column for this report only. See "Writing Formulas" on page 417 for more on creating custom formulas.

Calendar Reports

Remember those old movies that showed time passing by flipping pages on a calendar?
Don't let your days get away from you that quickly. Use Calendar reports to keep track,
day by day, of how a project's tasks are progressing.

As you can see in Figure 2-24, Report Builder has some sections unique to Calendar
reports. In the Calendar section, adjust the following settings:

- **Create a Calendar report based on the field.** Do you want the calendar to display
  records (tasks, for example) according to their start date, end date, or the date
  someone created or modified records? Make your selection by picking from the
  drop-down menu.

  Show durations on this calendar/End Field. You don't have to limit your Calendar report to showing just start dates or just end dates. Showing durations on
  your calendar means that QuickBase displays how much time has been allotted to
  a record, such as a task. This option lets you show both the start date and end date
  of a task, for example, connected by a colored bar. It's a fantastic way to track tasks
  and projects that span days or even weeks. To show durations, select Start Date as
  the basis for creating your calendar (see the previous item in this list). Then in this
  section's End Field drop-down menu, select the field that represents the end of the
  task or project whose duration you're showing (you might select the End Date field,
  for example, or a Formula Date field that calculates the end date of a project based
  on the number of days expected to complete a task). The result will look like
  Figure 2-25.

- **For each day display.** Choose the field you want QuickBase to display on the
  calendar, such as the name of a task, an activity, or the person it's assigned to.

- **And.** If you want to display information from a second field, like priority or someone's name, here's where you do it. (In Calendar report, users can click the text
  that appears for any date to see the whole record, so displaying a second field may
  not be necessary.)

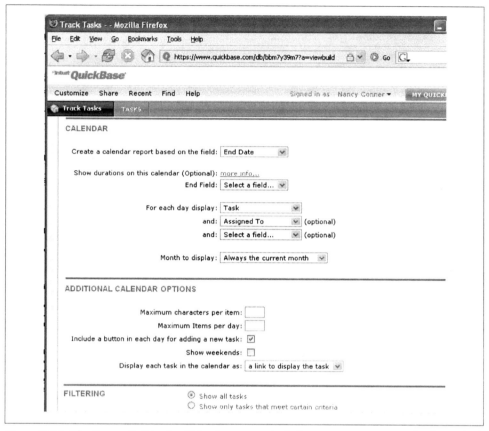

Figure 2-24. The Report Builder for Calendar reports includes settings unique to calendars: which dates to display, which month you want to appear first when someone looks at the report, the maximum number of records to display for one day (and how long a record name can be), and so on. It's helpful to include an Add button on each date of your calendar to make it easy for viewers to add a new record. Similarly, displaying each record as a link lets viewers see the details of any record right from the calendar. If your team's on call 24/7, you can display weekends, but if you're strictly a Monday-through-Friday operation, you can leave off Saturdays and Sundays. Finally, showing durations on your calendar is like adding a timeline to it; this option stretches a bar between a task's beginning and end dates.

- **Month to display.** Your choices here are the current month, next month, last month, or a specific month that you choose (for example, you might want to display the month that marks the target date for the end of the project). Whichever you pick becomes the default month for this report. (Of course, anybody looking at your calendar can move on from there to look at another month.)

In the Additional Calendar Options section, you've got these choices:

- **Maximum characters per item.** QuickBase is set to display up to 23 characters (including spaces) for each item. You can shorten or lengthen this number as you

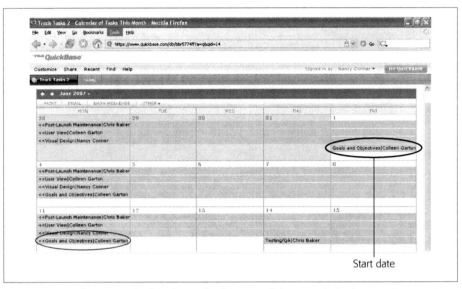

Figure 2-25. A duration calendar shows the duration of the records (tasks, activities, projects, and so on) that it displays. In this example, Colleen Garton's assignment is to begin the Goals & Objectives task on June 1 and finish it 10 days later, on June 11.

like. Keep in mind, though, that too many characters will clutter up the calendar, making it look crowded and hard to read. Too few, on the other hand, can leave viewers guessing about what, exactly, the calendar is displaying.

- **Maximum items per day.** You can limit the number of items that QuickBase shows for a given calendar date. If there are more items for that date than QuickBase can display, it shows a "more" link, which takes viewers to a table that lists all the items associated with that date.

- **Include a button in each day for adding a new task.** Turn on this checkbox and QuickBase does just what it says: puts an Add link in the upper-right corner of each date of the calendar. When a user clicks the link, QuickBase jumps to the Add Record page (Figure 3-1), with the date already filled in to match the date of the Add link the user just clicked.

- **Show weekends.** If you're on a strictly Monday-through-Friday schedule, there's no need to display empty Saturdays and Sundays. Turn off this checkbox, and your calendar shows Mondays through Fridays only.

- **Display each record in the calendar as.** Your choices here are "text only," "a link to edit the record," and "a link to display the record." If you link to the record, someone looking at your calendar can click any task and see the full record associated with that task. If you select "a link to edit the record," users who have permission (Note on page 7) can click the link, open the record, and modify it as needed.

Chart Reports

You might want to capture a lot of information in each record—notes from sales calls; the names of contacts' spouses, kids, and pets; exactly which faucet keeps leaking in Apartment 2B—but that doesn't mean you want to display it all when you create a report. Charts take out the unnecessary details, giving viewers an easy-to-grasp snapshot of what they need to know: how December sales compared with last year, who's submitting the priciest purchase requests, and which sales rep wins the trip to Hawaii for selling the most jet-powered pogo sticks. QuickBase offers so many different kinds of charts—seven in all—you'll be tempted to spend all day playing with them.

To create a chart, open the application you want and make your way to Report Builder (Customize→Create a new→Report or take a shortcut by heading to the Table bar, clicking the name of the table you want, and then selecting "Create a New Report"). Select Chart, and Report Builder displays the Chart type section, with a drop-down menu offering all your choices: pie, bar, horizontal bar, stacked bar, horizontal stacked bar, line, and area. Choose the type of chart you want to create. The sections that follow describe each kind.

Pie charts

Creating a pie chart's a piece of cake. You might create a pie chart to show how resources are allocated on a project or to illustrate how different regions contributed to the year's total sales. Figure 2-26 shows how Report Builder looks when you're creating a pie chart.

Imagine you want to create a pie chart showing how many resources are allocated to each group on a project, listing the groups by business function. There are two elements you need to define: what each wedge represents (in this case, each wedge shows the number of resources) and how to determine the size of each wedge (the more resources a group has, the bigger the wedge). Figure 2-27 shows the result. Or here's another example: if you wanted to show sales per region, each wedge would represent a region, and the size of each wedge would represent the amount of sales for that region.

Pie charts are easy to take in at a glance, but to make them crystal clear, but sure to label each wedge. To do so, go to the Data Labels section. Turn on the "Data labels always visible" checkbox and choose the kind of label you want your chart to display. You can label each wedge with a name (to show what it represents). To get even more specific, you can also label each wedge with the number it represents (value) or its percentage of the whole (percent).

Bar charts

QuickBase offers four flavors of bar chart: vertical, horizontal, stacked, and horizontal stacked. Vertical (Figure 2-28) and horizontal bar charts are great for making comparisons; for example, you might want to rank different products in terms of sales or show

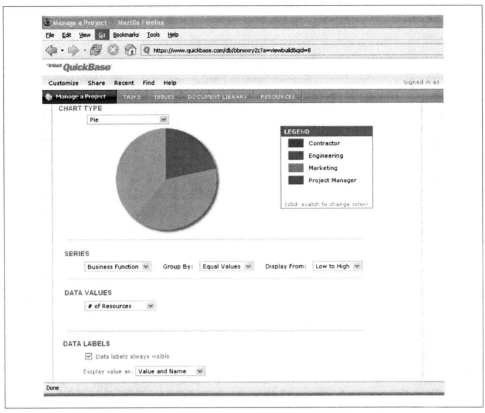

Figure 2-26. In a pie chart, the Series section determines what data is used to form the wedges. The chart being built here will show how resources are allocated to each group involved in the project. After you know what the wedges represent, specify the data values, which determine the size of each wedge. In this example, the number of resources determines wedge size, so if Marketing has twice as many resources as Engineering, the Marketing wedge will be twice as big as the Engineering wedge. To change the color of any wedge, click the color swatch in the Legend box and select a new color from the palette that appears.

which departments are putting in the most hiring requests. When you want to add another dimension to the data, use a stacked bar chart (Figure 2-29). This kind of chart combines a bar chart's knack for showing comparisons with a pie chart's ability to break a whole into its parts. For example, using a stacked bar chart lets you show not only how many hiring requisitions each department's submitting but also can break down the types of positions requested. You can display the bars of a stacked bar chart either vertically or horizontally.

To create a bar chart report, you have to define the x axis (which runs along the bottom of your chart) and the y axis (which runs up the left-hand side of the chart). For example, to create the bar chart in Figure 2-28, which shows how many tasks are in each status category, you'd define the x axis as Status (the fields you're comparing) and the y axis

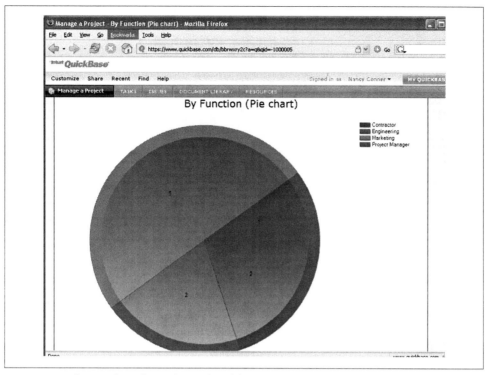

Figure 2-27. This pie chart shows the results of the Report Builder settings in Figure 2-26. To make your pie chart easy to read, be sure to use strongly contrasting colors for the wedges. Labeling each wedge makes it clear to the viewer what each wedge represents and the precise size of each wedge in relation to the whole.

as # of Tasks (which determines the height or length of each bar). Figure 2-30 shows where to fill in these criteria.

Click the Display button (it's at both the top and the bottom of the Report Builder window), and you've got a simple bar chart, with tasks broken down by status. (If that's all you want, don't forget to save; click the Save or Save As link at the top of the page.)

What if you want to show more detail? That's what the stacked bar chart does (see Figure 2-29), showing how many tasks in each status category belong to different departments within the company. When you break down the data in this way, you're creating a *series* within your chart. In the Series section of Report Builder, select the field you want to add to the chart, as well as how you want to group your data. The stacked bar chart in Figure 2-29 has Business Function selected in the Series section, grouped by Equal Values, and displayed from Low to High.

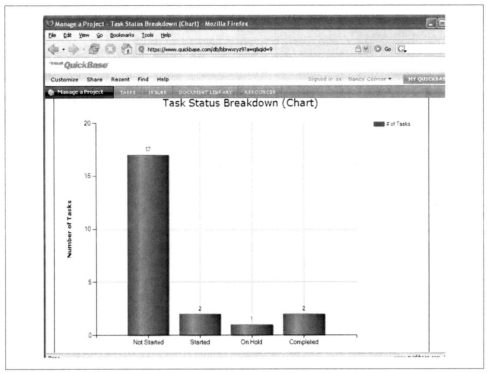

Figure 2-28. A basic bar chart helps you make a simple comparison of different items. This example compares a project's tasks according to their status: not started, started, on hold, or completed.

TIP

If you make a selection in the Series section when you're creating a vertical or horizontal bar graph, QuickBase creates a number of smaller bars in different colors to represent the field you chose. Figure 2-31 shows an example.

Your final decision in creating a bar chart is whether to display data labels. If you want to label each bar with the number it represents (the y-axis value), turn on the "Data labels always visible" checkbox. When you turn it on, a drop-down menu appears so you can specify the value you want to use for your data labels:

- **Value.** The actual number, such as how many tasks make up each bar.
- **Percent of Series.** Useful in a stacked bar chart because it shows you the percentage of each band in each bar—how many tasks Engineering hasn't started yet, for example. In a regular bar chart, selecting this option shows you how much each bar contributes to the whole.

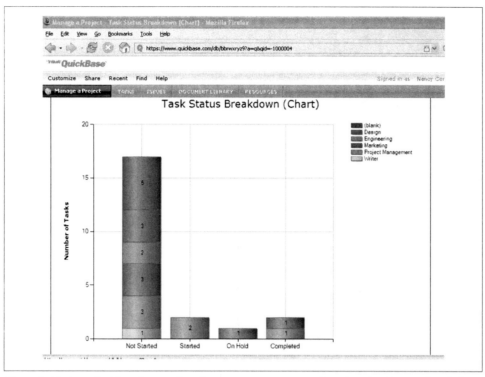

Figure 2-29. A stacked bar chart makes the same comparison as a bar chart but lets you break down each bar, showing what parts make up the whole. This example still has the same number of not started, started, on hold, and completed tasks as the chart shown in Figure 2-28, but each bar consists of colored bands that shows who's responsible for the tasks in each status category: Design, Engineering, Marketing, Project Management, Writer, or unassigned (blank) .

UP TO SPEED

Logarithmic Charts

Whatever kind of bar chart you're whipping up, you have the option of turning on an unassuming-looking little checkbox in the "Data (y-axis) Values" section: Logarithmic Scale. Even though that sounds like something a lumberjack might use, it's helpful if you have a situation where one of your bars is literally going off the chart.

Say you work for a candy company, and the superstarlet of the moment is caught on camera unwrapping a stick of your glow-in-the-dark bubble gum. All of a sudden, everyone everywhere is buying Bubble-Glo gum. It's outselling all your other confections by a mile. When you create a bar chart to show monthly sales figures, Bubble-Glo dwarfs all the other products—so much so that you can barely make out those stumpy little bars way down at the bottom of the chart next to the giant redwood that represents Bubble-Glo.

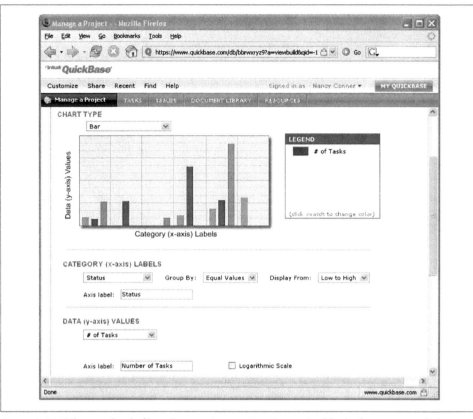

Figure 2-30. Whatever kind of bar chart you're creating, Report Builder looks pretty much the same. (The only difference is the illustration of the chart type—the other sections are identical.) When you define the x axis and the y axis (the example in the Chart Type section reminds you which is which), you can either use the field names you choose as labels (that's the default) or type your own into the text box. These settings create the bar chart shown in Figure 2-28.

To make your chart easier to read, turn on the Logarithmic Scale checkbox. What it does is change the background scale in some places to compensate for big differences between bars. Without logarithmic scale, the values on the y axis (going up the left-hand side of the chart) march along in steady increments: 100 cases of candy, perhaps, then 200, then 300, and so on. Logarithmic scale squeezes some of those lines together where a big jump causes it to condense values. So when you go from 1,550 cases of your next-best seller to 10,000 cases of Bubble-Glo, your chart shows the amazing difference in sales *and* lets viewers make out the less frenzied numbers for your other products.

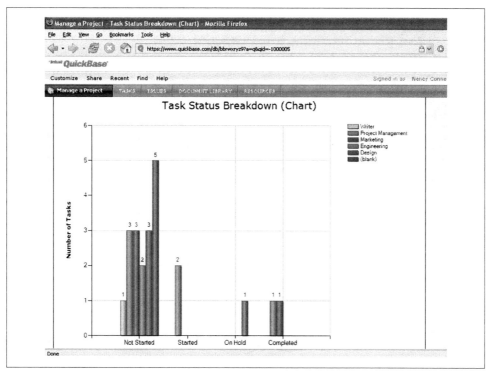

Figure 2-31. When you create a series for a bar chart, QuickBase creates a number of small bars in different colors to show how each section breaks down. This chart came from the same settings as the stacked bar chart shown in Figure 2-29.

Line charts

Even though the results look different, you create a line chart in Report Builder exactly the same way you create a bar chart: select a criterion to define the y axis (in this case, the y axis represents plot height) and another to define the x axis. Line charts are most useful for showing trends over time, so you'll probably select some time element—like weeks, months, or quarters—for the x axis. For example, you can chart sales trends from month to month over the course of a year or track how long it takes to complete tasks or resolve issues on a project.

As with bar charts, you can create a series, which adds more lines to your graph. For example, if you're charting the number of work orders scheduled each week, you can choose "Assigned to" in the Series section to create a separate line for each worker, as shown in Figure 2-32. You can also label data elements (here, data elements are the points that your line graph charts) by turning on the "Data labels always visible" checkbox.

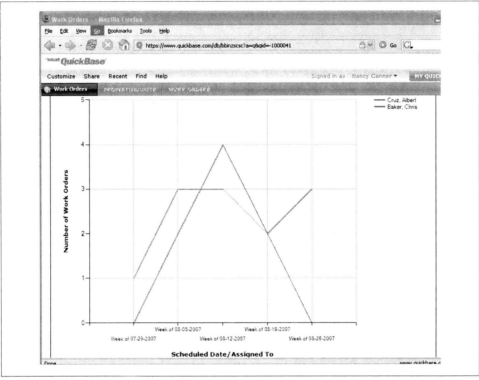

Figure 2-32. When you create a series for a line chart, you create a line for the contents of each field you choose for the series. Here, the Series field is "Assigned to," so each line represents the work orders assigned to one worker. Be careful not to clutter up your chart with too many lines—this can make the chart crowded and confusing.

Area charts

For this style of chart, which fills in the area beneath the line that plots points, Report Builder offers the same settings and criteria as for a line chart. Figure 2-33 shows an area chart that uses the same criteria as the line chart in Figure 2-32.

UP TO SPEED

Tips for Creating Great Charts

You can do so much with QuickBase charts, it's easy to get carried away. But before you go hog wild with your chart reports, changing colors here and adding another line there, keep in mind that a chart's only as good as the information it conveys. If you try to do too much with a chart or if you design it in a way that's difficult to read, all your hard work—not to mention the point you're trying to make—will go right over viewers' heads.

Here are some basic principles of good charts:

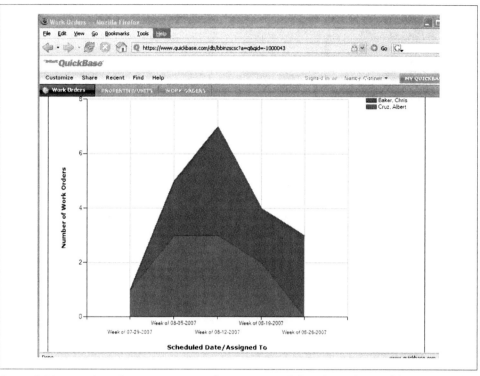

Figure 2-33. Area charts have a strong visual impact. As with line charts, be careful not to crowd in too many elements—if you were comparing the work orders of more than three or four workers, this chart would become very difficult to interpret.

- Keep it simple. Each chart should hold one message, like "Sales are up." If you're trying to convey two messages—"Sales are up overall, except our automatic potato peeler isn't doing as well as we expected based on last year's sales projections"— you need two charts.

- In the same vein, leave out all unnecessary details. Anything that doesn't contribute to your chart's single, basic message doesn't belong in the chart. Your chart should be a tightly focused snapshot of some aspect of the data. If you don't need a fourth line in your line chart, leave it out. (And more than four lines puts your chart in danger of looking like a game of Pick-up Sticks.)

- A little color is good. Color makes contrasting elements stand out. But use color sparingly—too much can make viewers go cross-eyed. In general, four colors is a good maximum.

- Label a chart's elements. In a bar, line, or area chart, label the x and y axes; in a pie chart, label the wedges. Include a legend to show what's what. Don't make viewers guess.

- And while you're labeling, be sure to use both upper- and lower-case letters. US-ING ALL CAPS LOOKS LIKE SHOUTING AND CAN BE TOUGH TO READ.

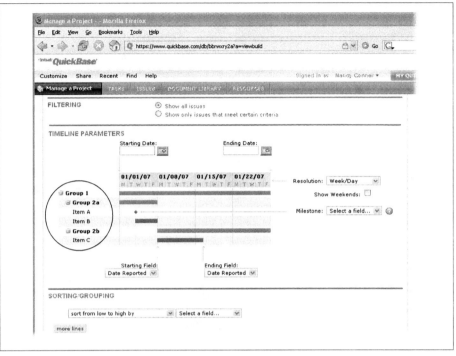

Figure 2-34. QuickBase Timeline reports give an overview of your project as it unfolds through time. Report Builder's options let you specify how much time you want your timeline to cover and whether to show project milestones. Add another level of detail by creating subgroups (circled) that break down tasks or issues by another level.

Experiment with different chart reports. Try presenting the same information in a vertical and a horizontal bar chart, for example, and then ask people which one has more impact or is easier to read. Or test out multiple pie charts versus a stacked bar chart, or a line chart versus an area chart, in the same way. When you pay attention to the chart's message and the viewer's ease in getting that message, you'll wow 'em with your charts every time.

Timeline Reports

There's no better way to drive home the point that time is indeed money than by showing a timeline, with its visual representation of interrelated tasks. Help keep your team on target by following these steps to create a Timeline report:

1. In the application you want to create a timeline for, open Report Builder ("Create a new report" on page 43) and select Timeline.

   Report Builder displays a Timeline section, as shown in Figure 2-34.

2. You've got several decisions to make in the Timeline section:

Starting Date/Ending Date. These dates indicate when your whole timeline begins and ends. You don't have to select any dates here. If you leave these boxes blank, QuickBase looks at the start of the earliest item and the end of the latest item (based on the records you specify) and figures out the start and end dates for itself. (If you're working on a long-term project, though, it's a good idea to specify the chunk of time you want the report to show.)

NOTE

If you choose specific start and ending dates here, QuickBase may expand them automatically. Whether or not QuickBase messes with your dates depends upon the resolution you set in the Resolution drop-down.

Resolution. The resolution of your timeline is how you want the time segments broken down. From the Resolution drop-down menu, choose the unit of time you want your timeline to display: week/day, month/week, quarter/month, year/month, or year/quarter. (If you choose week/day, you have the option to display weekends.)

Milestone. Nobody likes to blunder along in a seemingly endless project without any lights to mark the end of the tunnel. That's why, in timelines, milestones are such a powerful feature. Milestones show a project's landmarks. If you want to add milestones to your Timeline report, you need to do a little setup first. Take a moment to create a checkbox field for the table—you can give it an imaginative name like, hmmm, *Milestone*. (Click Customize→Create a new→Field, then add your checkbox field. Jump over to Chapter 6 for the lowdown on adding a field to a table.) After you've created your checkbox, it appears in the Milestone drop-down. Select the checkbox field you created from the drop-down menu. Now, when you create your Timeline report, any record that has the checkbox turned on displays a diamond symbol to indicate a milestone. It may not be as much fun as a celebratory pizza party, but it shows your team they're making progress.

Starting Field/Ending Field. The selections you make in these drop-down menus tell QuickBase where to begin and end each task, issue, or whatever you're putting on the timeline. If you're tracking tasks, for example, you'd select Start Date and End Dates. If you're keeping an eye on how long it takes to resolve issues that arise during a project, you'd pick Date Reported and Date Resolved. (Your choices reflect the date fields in your table.)

Sorting/Grouping. After you've set your timeline's parameters, you can tell QuickBase how to group and sort the data your timeline holds. You might sort tasks by project phase, for example. You can add more info to your timeline by creating subgroups in this section. Click the "more lines" button, then add the field you want for the subgroup. So, for your timeline that groups tasks by project phase, you might subgroup records by who's assigned each task. To see what groups and subgroups look like, glance back at Figure 2-34.

Columns to Display. Tell QuickBase which columns you want your timeline to show. For timelines, this section works the same way it does for tables.

When you're finished making your selections, click Display to see what your timeline looks like.

3. If you want to make changes to the timeline, click the timeline's "Customize this Report" link to go back to Report Builder. If you're happy with it as is, click Save or Save As.

Automatic Milestones

Imagine you're creating a timeline to track tasks for a big project. You've created a number of tasks that have no duration, such as Sign-off Due, and you want such tasks to show up on your timeline as milestones. But you don't want to go back and click through a bunch of records to hunt down all the no-duration tasks and turn on the Milestone checkbox.

This trick was invented just for you: You can create a Milestone checkbox that is automatically turned on for any task that has no duration. When you add the checkbox field (Customize→Create a new→Field), *don't* select Checkbox as the field type. Instead, select Formula—Checkbox to create a souped-up version of that boring old "click me on, click me off" checkbox. When QuickBase has created the field, it lands you on the Tables page, with the Fields tab selected. Find the checkbox field you just created and click its name. The Field Properties page opens. In the Formula box, type this: *If([Duration]=0,true,false)*. Now, any tasks without a duration will automatically turn on this checkbox all by themselves—giving you a few extra minutes to enjoy your coffee break.

Back in Report Builder, select your new checkbox from the Milestone drop down. Now your Timeline report will show the milestones you created. One caveat: Milestones are based on the end date of an event. So any tasks that have a blank Ending Date field won't show up on your timeline, even if the Milestone checkbox is turned on.

CHAPTER 3

Working with Data and Documents

QuickBase is a super-powerful database, but until there's stuff inside its mighty self, it's really just an empty program. Fortunately, QuickBase makes it easy to gather your data and documents in one location, so everyone on your team can start working quickly—no fuss, no muss, no chasing missing documents from cubicle to cubicle.

This chapter shows you how to get information into QuickBase, from individual records to complex documents, and how to work with the information once it's there. Whether you need to import an entire spreadsheet, change a single phone number in a contact list, or track revisions to an evolving specification, QuickBase makes it easy.

Ever spend hours revising a report, only to find out someone else overwrote your changes? With QuickBase, that's a thing of the past—you can reserve a report while you're working on it, preventing others from modifying it until you're done. Here's a quick rundown of the other big topics you'll learn about in the following pages:

- Adding a new record to an existing application
- Importing data
- Uploading documents
- Finding information within an application
- Editing existing records or documents
- Deleting records or documents
- Getting your data out of QuickBase
- Restoring a previous version of a document

Getting Data and Documents into QuickBase

Whether you're updating an existing application by adding a single new record or sucking in heaps of contact info, product listings, or whatever, QuickBase gives you plenty of ways to import your data and documents.

Adding a New Record

When you want to add a new record to an application, just follow these steps:

1. Open the application you want to add the record to. If you're in a single-table application, look in the upper-right corner of any page for the Add a New Record button and click it. Or click the name of the table you want in the blue Table bar near the top of your screen, and then click "Add a New Record".

   The Add Record page, shown in Figure 3-1, opens.

2. Type in the info you want to add.

   Some fields are optional; those marked with an asterisk (*) you have to fill in.

3. If you have more records to add after this one, click Save & Add Another.

   QuickBase saves the info you've entered and presents you with a fresh new Add Record page.

4. When you're all done adding records, click Save.

   QuickBase saves your work and shows you the last record you added. You can inspect the record and edit, email, or print it (just click the Edit, Email, or Print buttons, which appear at the top and bottom of each record).

Copying a Record

If you're adding lots of new records that have similar content—like maybe you're entering work orders for a 600-unit apartment complex and you don't feel like typing *Luxury Towers, Miami, FL* over and over again—you can copy an existing record, make pertinent changes, and save the new record as many times as you need to. Here's how:

1. Open a report ("Open an Existing Report" on page 38) that holds the record you want to copy and click that record's Display button. (This is a button that says VIEW or V, depending on how you've set your user preferences; see "Edit user preferences" on page 20.)

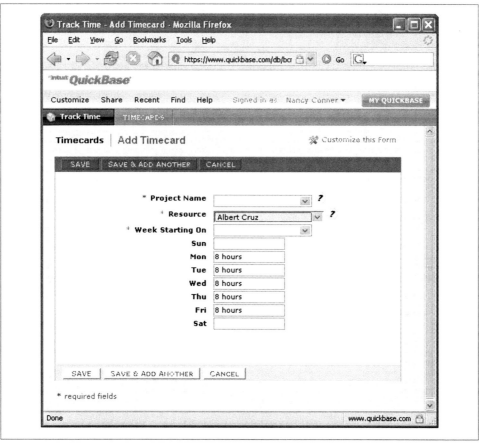

Figure 3-1. This particular Add Record page is what you see when you're adding a new timecard to a time-tracking application. (Other kinds of records, such as issues or resources, have different Add Record pages.) Got a question about what a field requires? Look for a question mark to the right of the field; click it to get a pop-up window with helpful tips about the kind of info you need to enter.

A page opens, showing you the details for that record.

TIP

If you're looking for a record you just added or modified, use the List Changes report to find it easily.

---

2. Look at the bottom right of the record for the Add Similar button; click it.

   The Add Record page opens, with the fields already filled in.

3. Make whatever changes you want, and then click Save.

   QuickBase displays the new record. If you didn't change a thing in the new record —in other words, if it's identical to the record you copied—you can tell them apart by their Record IDs. The new copy will have a higher Record ID number than the original. (See the box in "The Key to Importing Data" on page 102 for more about what Record IDs do.)

4. If you want to make a copy of this new record, click Add Similar again.

   The prefilled Add Record page opens again.

TIP

When you're adding similar records, always click Save→Add Similar. This brings up the prefilled Add Record form. If you click Save & Add Another, you get a blank Add Record form, which means a lot more typing.

Importing Data into QuickBase

An easy way to get lots of data into QuickBase in one fell swoop is to *import* it. Quick-Base is on pretty good speaking terms with all major spreadsheet and database programs, and can handle almost any type of word processing document you send its way. So if you've been tracking job applicants, sales leads, or billable hours using a program like Excel, for example, you can easily move that data into QuickBase.

NOTE

This section tells you how to import data into an *existing* application. To import data when you're creating a *new* application, see "Creating an Application by Importing Data" on page 245.

UP TO SPEED

The Key to Importing Data

When you import data into an existing application, QuickBase does one of two things:

- Creates new records
- Updates existing records

In other words, brand-new data creates brand-new records, and new data about records already in QuickBase updates those records.

How can QuickBase tell the difference? The key is something called, appropriately enough, the key. To be precise, QuickBase uses a *key field,* which is a field that must contain a unique value for each record. All QuickBase tables have a key field—usually it's the Record ID number. In most cases, QuickBase creates a Record ID field in a table and, whenever you create a new record, automatically assigns a unique Record ID number. But you can set the key field to be *any* field that makes sense in your application. The only essential is that the field you choose has to be one that allows a unique value for each individual record.

For example, let's say you're working with a payroll application in QuickBase. You don't care about the Record ID number QuickBase assigns each employee; you want the key field to be the Employee ID number that your company assigns each of its workers. You know, of course, that this is a unique number for each record: even if two Sara Smiths work for your company, each Sara has her own Employee ID number. So this number makes a good—and meaningful—key field. In this scenario, when you import payroll data, QuickBase uses the Employee ID field to figure out where the incoming data should go. Workers who are already in your QuickBase application get their payroll records updated; new employees get fresh records created for them by QuickBase.

You can base your key field on a number or on text—the important thing is that it have a unique value for each record.

Here's how to set a key field:

1. Open the application for which you want to set the key field and then, from the menu bar, click Customize→Tables.

   The Tables page appears. If it's not already selected, click the Fields tab. (In a multi-table application, the application's different tables appear in a list on the left-hand side of the page. If necessary, click the name of the particular table you want.) The Fields tab of the Tables page lists the different fields in a particular table. In the Field Label column is the name of each field; next to one of these names is a picture of a key. Bingo—that's the current key field.

2. Click the upper-right "Set the Key Field" button.

   A box called "Change the Key Field" appears. In the box is a drop-down menu, showing the current key field.

3. Click the drop-down arrow to see a list of other fields in the table. Choose the field that you want to be the key field, and then click OK. Only a field that contains unique values can be a key field—in other words, you probably can't pick "Assigned to" as a key field because employees' names get repeated over and over in that field in different records. If you try to set a field that doesn't hold unique values as a key field, QuickBase displays a box explaining that it's not a good choice, and asks you to try again.

You've reset the key field for your table. Note that changing the key field in one table of a multi-table application may affect other tables in that application. If that's going to happen, QuickBase warns you. To find out more about linked tables, take a look at Chapter 10.

TIP

A quick, easy way to get data into your application is to set up a form on your Web site that lets visitors add data to your QuickBase application—whether or not they have a QuickBase account. Find out how in "Collecting Data via Web Page Forms" on page 459.

Import using copy and paste

QuickBase gives you several different ways to import your data. One of the simplest methods is to just copy and paste, like so:

1. **Open the document you want to copy from. Highlight the content you want to import, and then select Edit→Copy.**

   For example, you can copy a table from a Word document, or you can copy a group of rows or columns from a spreadsheet program.

2. **In QuickBase, open the application you want to copy the data *into* and then choose Customize→Import/Export.**

   The QuickBase Import/Export page opens.

3. **Turn on the "Import into a table from the clipboard" radio button.**

   The box you're working in expands, giving you a place to paste the data. (If you're working in a multi-table application, the expanded box also has a section that asks you to pick the table you want to import to.)

4. **Choose the table you're importing to (if you're in a multi-table application). Click inside the Paste Data text box, and then paste in your data (Edit→Paste or Ctrl+V on a PC; ⌘-V on a Mac). Click the Import Data button.**

   The Import page appears, as shown in Figure 3-2. This page, which displays a temporary table showing the data you've pasted in, asks you to verify that Quick-Base has copied the data into the appropriate fields; you'll learn how to fix any errors in the next step.

TIP

If you think the Import page's table would be easier to read flipped on its side (so that the radio buttons appear as a column down the left-hand side of the table), look below the table for a link labeled "Click here to flip this chart's orientation." Click the link to see this table in a whole new way.

---

5. **Check to make sure that field labels (which become column headers in your QuickBase table) are correct and that your data is correctly positioned. Use this checklist:**

   Does the row called "Field Labels Row 1" contain field names from your destination table (in other words, does it show the headings for table columns)? If yes, you're in good shape. But if this row holds individual data values (like phone numbers or people's names), turn off the "First Row is List of Field Names" checkbox to move those data values down into the body of the table.

   Does the data under each field name belong in the field that appears at the top of the column? If the content of a column doesn't match its label (for example, if the Last Name column contains Zip codes), click the drop-down list at the top of that

---

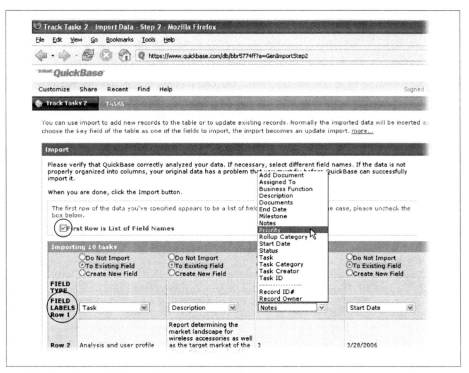

Figure 3-2. Before QuickBase takes the plunge and imports new data into an existing table, you've got to check and make sure that everything looks the way it should. Field labels (circled) become column headings in your QuickBase table. Look at each column to make sure its field label matches the data beneath it. For instance, the third column in this example—showing a number—has Notes as its field label; click the drop-down menu to change that label to the correct one: Priority. Radio buttons at the top of each column let you create a new field, if necessary, or tell QuickBase not to import the values in that column.

column to choose the correct field label. When all the field labels match the content that appears below them, you're good to go.

6. When the data looks right, click Import. (If there's a problem, jump ahead to the box in "Import Duties" on page 106 to help QuickBase get your data straight.)

QuickBase imports your data and shows you a confirmation page.

If the act of importing will cause QuickBase to set up some new fields (that is, columns) in an existing table, you get a warning that asks you to confirm that you really want to set up these new fields. If you want to add new fields, click OK. If you want the table's fields to stay the way they are, click Cancel. When you cancel, you don't import any data. Instead, QuickBase goes back to the Import page. There, you can choose not to import the data from the columns in question (turn on the Do Not Import radio button for any columns you want to leave behind), or you can import the data in those columns into existing fields (turn on the To Existing Field radio button and choose the field name you want from the drop-down menu beneath it). When you've got the settings you want, click Import.

FREQUENTLY ASKED QUESTION

Import Duties

I'm trying to import data into QuickBase, but when I look at the data on the Import page, it's all messed up. How can I make sure QuickBase imports my data correctly?

QuickBase is smart, but it's not a mind-reader. Sometimes when you're importing data, you have to tweak things a bit to make sure that the data ends up in QuickBase looking the way you want it to. Here are four common data-importing problems you might encounter:

- **The first row of the table shows data values, not field names.** If the "Field Labels Row 1" row shows data values that should be in the *body* of your table, turn off the "First Row is List of Field Names" checkbox.

- **The values in a column appear in the wrong field.** At the top of each column is a drop-down list. Click the list and find the name of the field you want.

- **QuickBase doesn't list the name of the field you want the values to appear in.** Turn on the Create New Field radio button for that column. If your table had a column header in the original document (that is, the one you copied it *from*), it appears in a text box that pops up. You can edit that field name or type in a brand-new one. Make sure that the field type (text, numeric, date, and so on) is correct.

- **A column of values that you don't want to import has shown up in QuickBase.** At the top of that column, turn on the Do Not Import radio button, and QuickBase will exclude those values from the import.

Import from a file

Copying and pasting works great for the small stuff, but when you've got a whole file you want to get into QuickBase, you can import the whole shebang all at once. When you import from a file, your files need to be in one of two special formats—TSV (short for *tab-separated values*) or CSV (*comma-separated values*)—for the import dance to work. These formats, which are available as save-as options in most spreadsheet and database programs, use tabs or commas to mark off distinct blocks of data. For example, say you have a spreadsheet that lists customer information, like this:

Acct #	Last Name	First Name	Street	City	State	ZIP Code	Phone #
1234	Ortiz	Jorge	7 Magnolia Lane	Camp Hill	PA	17011	717-555-8463
1235	Hauser	Trudy	12 Dryden Rd.	Jacksonville	NY	14854	607-555-4721

Saving the spreadsheet in CSV format automatically takes the customer information out of cells and inserts a comma between each data element, like this:

```
1234, Ortiz, Jorge, 7 Magnolia Lane, Camp Hill, PA, 17011, 717-555-8463↵
1235, Hauser, Trudy, 12 Dryden Rd., Jacksonville, NY, 14854, 607-555-4721
```

QuickBase can then read the CSV file and funnel its data into a QuickBase table. After you save the file, make sure it has either a .TSV or a .CSV extension—that's how you know it's ready for importing.

TIP

QuickBase does best importing lean spreadsheets that don't contain any extra info. For example, get rid of any rows that have explanations or comments (you can always paste them back in later). What you do want, of course, are your column headings (field names) and the actual data.

When you're ready to import a file into QuickBase, just follow these steps:

1. Open the QuickBase application you want to import your data into and select Customize→Import/Export.

   The Import/Export page appears.

2. Turn on the "Import into a table from a file" radio button.

   The box you're working in expands so you can choose a file to import. (If you're working in a multi-table application, the expanded box also has a section that asks you to pick the table you want to import *to*; select your choice from the Pick Table drop-down list.)

3. Click the Browse button so you can choose the file to import.

   A File Upload box opens, allowing you to find and select your .TSV or .CSV file.

4. Select the file you want to import, and then click Open.

   The file appears in QuickBase's Choose File box.

5. Click Import From File.

   The Import page appears, with QuickBase's analysis of the data in your file.

6. Verify that everything looks the way you want it to—that the field names are correct and data values show up where they belong. If it's all good, click Import. (If things

look a little screwy, take a look at the box in "Import Duties" on page 106 for some quick fixes.)

QuickBase imports your data and opens a confirmation page.

Tips and Tricks for Importing Data

Whether you're creating a new application or working with an existing one, QuickBase makes it a snap to import data from an Excel spreadsheet. In some situations, though, importing data can be a wee bit tricky. Sometimes, a spreadsheet that looks perfectly fine to you will make QuickBase go "Huh?" And importing data into an existing application—especially a multi-table application with related tables—requires a few tweaks to get the right data into the right table.

To make imports go as smoothly as possible, you first need to make sure Excel and QuickBase are ready to talk. This section clues you in on how to get your spreadsheet squeaky clean (so QuickBase understands its data) and offers tips for getting your data into an existing multi-table application without messing up the relationships between your tables.

NOTE

If you're importing records that have a User field, you can import only up to 1,000 records. (Chapter 7 tells you all about field types, including User fields.) This limit applies only to records that contain a User field. To get around this limitation, break your humongous import into several smaller chunks, making sure each chunk has fewer than 1,000 records.

Cleaning up Your Spreadsheet

Excel is easy to get along with. It lets you enter your data in any way that makes sense to you. So you might have a title that stretches across a few cells at the top of a worksheet, or maybe you have a separate worksheet for each record. Basically, you can type in whatever you want in any cell, and Excel's fine with it. QuickBase, on the other hand, is a little pickier. So you may have created a spreadsheet works in Excel but confuses QuickBase.

Like any database, QuickBase craves data that's structured in a consistent manner. You'll save yourself massive amounts of time and frustration if you make sure—*before* you import—that QuickBase can understand your spreadsheet as easily as you can.

QuickBase likes its data organized just so: one complete record per row, and columns that hold the same kind of information all the way from top to bottom. Before you import data from a spreadsheet, make sure each column has a header describing what's in the column; *you* might know that Column B holds the names of sales reps and Column E lists customer contact names, but there's no way for QuickBase to know

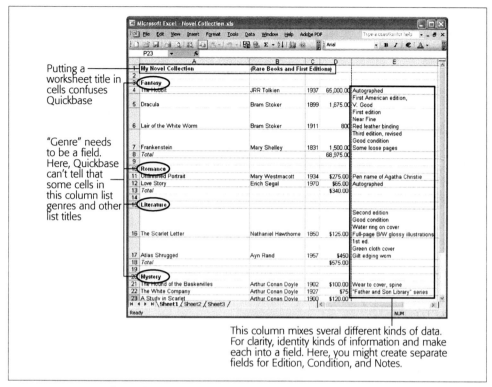

Putting a worksheet title in cells confuses Quickbase

"Genre" needs to be a field. Here, Quickbase can't tell that some cells in this column list genres and other list titles

This column mixes sveral different kinds of data. For clarity, identity kinds of information and make each into a field. Here, you might create separate fields for Edition, Condition, and Notes.

Figure 3-3. As an intelligent human being, you probably have no trouble interpreting this spreadsheet, which catalogs a rare book collection. As an intelligent database program, however, QuickBase needs a little help. For starters, get rid of the worksheet's title at the top of the screen. Next, give each column a header—even though it's clear to you that the columns list title, author, publication date, value, and notes, QuickBase won't know what to call these fields unless you tell it. There's no need to import the Totals rows into QuickBase, because QuickBase will add up values for you. And take a look at Column E, which has notes on each book. The info it holds is a bit of a mixed bag. You can break out several kinds of data from this column, such as Edition, Condition, and Notes. Column A also mixes up kinds of data: genre and title. Each type of information should become its own field in QuickBase; before you import, create the appropriate columns in Excel to break down this data.

what a column holds if you don't tell it. Figure 3-3 shows a spreadsheet that's hard for QuickBase to understand.

Before you import data from Excel into QuickBase, take a few minutes to look over your spreadsheet. Try to see it from QuickBase's point of view. Go through the spreadsheet row by row and ask yourself:

- **Does each row represent a single record?** The spreadsheet in Figure 3-3 fails already. Some rows, such as rows 4-7, represent single records; but others, such as the different genre types, actually represent fields (types of data), not records.

- **Does each record (row) contain all the information it needs to be complete?** If you rearranged the rows, would the spreadsheet still make sense? If you reordered the rows in Figure 3-3, for example, the information about genre would no longer be meaningful, so the genre should instead be included as part of each row.

Then, go through column by column with these questions in mind:

- **Does each column have a label at the top to identify its contents?** Labeling your spreadsheet columns tells QuickBase what to call each field. So make sure each column is clearly labeled and that you haven't included any title information like the "My Novel Collection" field in Figure 3-3.

- **Does each column contain one (and only one) kind of data?** Unlike rows, each column should *not* contain an entire record. Columns specialize in just one kind of information.

When you can answer yes to all these questions, your spreadsheet is set up in a way that QuickBase will understand. Figure 3-4 shows a cleaned-up version of the spreadsheet from Figure 3-3, and Figure 3-5 shows how smoothly the cleaned-up spreadsheet imports into QuickBase.

NOTE

It's okay to have some empty cells in your worksheet. After all, you may have a record that's only partially complete. For example, the spreadsheet documenting your rare book collection may have notes on the condition of some books but not of others. As long as you've got a Notes field—a clearly labeled column that holds notes on individual records—QuickBase will create the field. If a particular record has data in the Notes column, QuickBase imports that data. But if the Notes column is empty for another record, QuickBase leaves the field blank for that record.

The following list describes a few potential pitfalls to check for before you import from a spreadsheet into QuickBase. After you've organized your data and fixed these other spreadsheet-to-QuickBase issues, you're good to go for a fast, easy import.

NOTE

If you're creating a new application with the data you import, you'll find step-by-step directions in "Creating an Application by Importing Data" on page 245. To import data into an existing application, take a look at "Importing Data into Quick-Base" on page 102. And keep reading for pointers on importing into a multi-table application.

- **Delete totals.** If your spreadsheet is set up to show totals in a column or a cell, delete the column or row that holds the totals. If, for example, you have a column called Totals whose contents appear automatically thanks to an Excel formula, QuickBase will interpret that column as data that you typed in yourself. In other

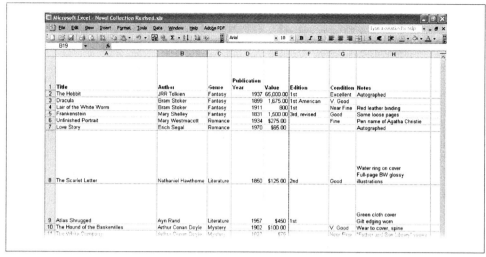

Figure 3-4. Now this spreadsheet is ready for a smooth import into QuickBase. The column headers will become QuickBase field names, making both tables and forms easier to read and use. Edition, Condition, and Notes have become their own fields instead of being jumbled together in one column, and a Genre field has been added to each record.

words, QuickBase thinks of your Totals column just like any other column of data in the spreadsheet and ignores the formula that generates the data. This can be confusing when the column shows up in QuickBase—instead of a dynamic total that changes when you enter new data, the column holds static numbers (old totals) that no longer apply. QuickBase adds up numbers automatically, so it'll create new totals for you in the application.

- **Delete formula cells.** QuickBase's lack of understanding of Excel formulas isn't limited to ones that calculate totals: Excel formulas don't work in QuickBase, period. So if you include formulas in your Excel spreadsheet, you're just cluttering it up with unnecessary information that you'll have to remove later. If you have cells that contain Excel formulas, get rid of them before you import—or at least delete the formulas.

  So how do you get QuickBase to do the calculations you did in Excel? Jump over to Chapter 11, which tells you all about writing formulas in QuickBase.

- **Clean up individual cells.** In spreadsheets, you often see cells that hold lists like milestone dates or names of multiple clients at a single organization. Such lists don't translate well into QuickBase. You can import them into a multi-line text field, but that's not going to help you keep your data organized or make your records easy to find.

  If your spreadsheet has cells that contain lists rather than single pieces of information, take a close look at those cells. You'll probably find that each item in the list would work better as an individual record or field. If that's the case, you'll have to roll up your sleeves and make some changes to your spreadsheet before you import

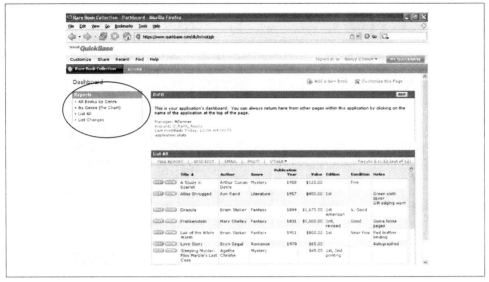

Figure 3-5. By starting with a nice, clean spreadsheet, you get a quick, easy import—and a table that makes sense. Notice that QuickBase is already thinking ahead by creating a couple of reports you might want to see: List All (shown on the Dashboard) as well as a table of all books sorted by genre and a pie chart filtered according to genre. (See the upper-left Reports menu, circled.)

it, putting those individual items into rows or cells of their own. The extra work will be worth it, though, once you've smoothly imported all that data into Quick-Base.

Importing into a Multi-Table Application

As you probably know, Excel spreadsheets can grow huge, as people cram all kinds of information into one ginormous spreadsheet. A major advantage of using QuickBase to organize your data is that QuickBase lets you break all that information into a series of tables—with each table holding a specific kind of information—and then link those tables in various ways. For example, imagine you sell textbooks to college instructors. At each university, you're likely to have a number of different contacts in various departments. For each potential customer, you have to type in the name of the university, the person's department, and the university's address—over and over. And when the English Department changes its name to the Center for the Study of Literatures and Cultures or moves from 816 North Hall on South Campus to 302 East Hall on West Campus, you've got a lot of records to change.

In QuickBase, you can create a table for each kind of information you want to track. In the textbook-sales example, you might have one table called Schools for the colleges and universities in your territory, and another called Contacts for the names of instructors you call on. By linking those tables in a relationship, you can easily update information across the board. So when Anytown College gets a hefty donation and changes its name to Big Bucks Philanthropist University, you only need to change the name once, in the Schools table. Thanks to relationships, QuickBase automatically changes the school's name in any tables linked to the Schools table, like the Contacts table, where the records for each instructor at that school will reflect the new name.

TIP

If you're using your spreadsheet to create a new application (see Chapter 7), you can import the spreadsheet in one fell swoop, creating a monster table. Then you can divide and conquer by splitting the big table into smaller ones. To see how to turn a field (or fields) into a whole new table, see "Turn a Field into a Table" on page 319.

Organizing your data. Start by taking a look at your spreadsheet. It holds a lot of info that should be grouped into different tables when you move it over to QuickBase. Which columns go together? Which seem like they belong to a different grouping? Next, look at the QuickBase application that will hold your data. Decide which columns of the spreadsheet belong in which table. Taking a few minutes to do this is half the battle of moving data from your spreadsheet into an existing multi-table application.

For the textbook-sales example, Figure 3-6 shows a list of contacts and institutions. Imagine you want to get this info into an existing multi-table QuickBase application, one with related tables called Schools and Contacts. Looking at the spreadsheet, it's easy to see which data belongs to which table: You want to import the School and Location columns into the Schools table and the First Name, Last Name, and Job Title columns into the Contacts table.

Because you can import into just one table at a time, you'll do two imports. Now the question becomes, "Which import should I do first?" The next section has the answer.

NOTE

Before you start importing, make sure your spreadsheet is set up in a way that Quick-Base can understand. For tips on making your spreadsheet QuickBase-friendly, flip back to "Cleaning up Your Spreadsheet" on page 108.

Importing data into a master table. Relationships between QuickBase tables are one-to-many relationships: one manager has many employees, one library holds many books, one customer has many orders. The table on the "one" side of that relationship is called the *master table;* the table on the "many" side is called the *details table*. In the textbook-sales example, one college has many instructors, so the master table is Schools and the details table is Contacts. (Chapter 10 tells you everything you ever needed to know about table relationships.)

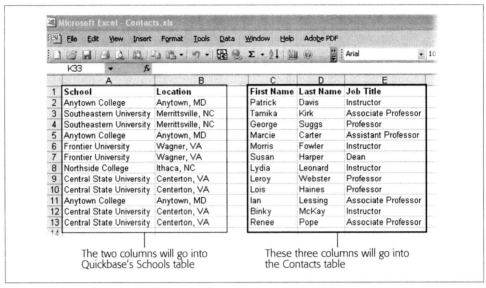

Figure 3-6. One spreadsheet can contain information that belongs in separate, but related, QuickBase tables. Here, it makes sense to include institution names and locations in the Schools table, and potential customers' first names, last names, and job titles in the Contacts table.

Why do you need to know this? Because to make your import work, you need to import data to the master table first—and you can't do that if you don't have a clue which table is which.

TIP

Still not sure which table is the master table and which is the details table? QuickBase can tell you if you're in doubt: Open the application that holds the related tables. From the menu bar, choose Customize→Tables, select one of the tables you want to import *to* from the left-hand list, and then click the Relationships tab. (You can also get to the same place via this route: Customize→Application→Tables→relationships.) The Relationships tab of the Tables page lists all of a table's relationships. The master table is on the left, and the details table is on the right.

Once you've identified which data is going to the master table, make sure that the values you're about to import are unique. This will spare you the headache of duplicate records in QuickBase. In the Schools table, for example, you want just one record per institution —you don't want a dozen different records that all hold identical info for Frontier University.

If you're using Excel, filtering for unique values is easy. Select the column or columns you're going to import, and then go to the menu bar and choose Data→Filter→Advanced Filter. In the dialog box that opens, turn on the "Unique records only" checkbox, and then click OK. The columns you selected now show just one record for each value—no duplicates.

NOTE

When you filter for unique values in Excel, it looks like some of your records have disappeared. Don't panic—they're still there. To see all the records in your spreadsheet, select Data→Filter→Show All. Whew! Everything's back to normal.

Cast an eye over the records that are left in the column or columns you want to import. Are there any typos or other inconsistencies? Duplicate records have a funny way of sneaking into a spreadsheet. For example, maybe you typed "Central State University" in some places and "Central SU" in others. If you need to clean up values further, do so, and then filter for unique values again.

Once you're sure that you've rid the spreadsheet of pesky duplicate records, copy the columns you want to import into the master table. (Highlight the columns by clicking on their headers (labeled A, B, C, and so on); Shift+click to select contiguous columns, and Ctrl+click to select non-contiguous columns. Then select Edit→Copy from Excel's menu bar or press Ctrl+C.) Then import the data by pasting it into the master table in QuickBase. For a refresher on how to import into a QuickBase table, skip back to "Importing Data into QuickBase" on page 102.

Keeping master records and details records together

In your spreadsheet, it's easy to see which details (contact names and job titles) belong with which master records (college or university). But when you split up the spreadsheet into different QuickBase tables, how do you make sure that information stays related?

You've got two choices: You can change the key field of the QuickBase table, or you can export records from the master table back into Excel and match them up there. Which route you take depends in part on whether you're creating a brand-new master table in QuickBase or you're importing new records into an existing table that already has some records in it. Changing the key field of a table that already holds records can be iffy; doing so might mess up existing relationships with other tables. So if you're exporting to a table that's already got some information in it, skip ahead to Method 2.

- **Method 1: Changing the master table's key field.** As Chapter 3 explains, a key field is a field in a table that must contain a unique value for each record, such as a product number or an employee ID. In QuickBase, the key field is usually a record ID number, but it can be any value, as long as that value is unique for each record in the table.

   When you import into a multi-table application, one way to make sure related information stays connected in the master table and the details table is to turn one of the columns you just imported into the master table into a key field. In the example, a good key field would be School—the field that holds the college or university name. Each college or university has a single name, so that name can be the unique value for each institution listed in the master table. The advantage of this method is that the values in the key field will be familiar—they're the values that were listed on your spreadsheet, rather than a hard-to-remember record ID number assigned by QuickBase.

NOTE

"The Key to Importing Data" on page 102 gives step-by-step instructions for setting a key field.

Changing the key field works best if your import creates a brand-new multi-table application. If you're importing into an existing multi-table application, with related, data-filled tables, use Method 2. It's a little more complicated, but the extra steps are worth it to make sure that importing new data doesn't break any existing relationships.

- **Method 2: Exporting back to Excel and using VLOOKUP.** You can also match up master and details records by exporting information from QuickBase back into Excel, and then using VLOOKUP—a tool in Excel 2003—to match master and details records. In an existing application, you may not want to change a master table's key field, so this method works best when you want to keep your existing QuickBase tables and their relationships exactly as they are.

  Even though it looks kind of like a typo, VLOOKUP stands for "vertical lookup." VLOOKUP tells Excel to search for a value in one place and insert that value in another place. In other words, VLOOKUP scans the values in a single column of the spreadsheet, from top to bottom. Then, when it finds a match, it gets other information from the row that contains the matching cell. Use VLOOKUP when the value you're matching lives in a column to the left of the information you want to retrieve. For example, in your textbook-sales workbook, you might have one worksheet called Contacts and another called Schools. Say that the Contacts sheet uses a school code—a numeric ID—for each contact; the Schools worksheet contains the school name and address for each school code. When you're working in Excel and you type a school code into the Contacts spreadsheet, VLOOKUP can tell Excel to find that code in the Schools spreadsheet and insert the relevant school name into the Contacts spreadsheet. Cool, huh?

  But what good does that do your QuickBase application? Well, when you're importing records from Excel into an existing multi-table QuickBase application, VLOOKUP lets you match up details records in Excel with their QuickBase master key fields, getting your info into QuickBase while preserving existing relationships between tables. Even cooler.

Using VLOOKUP in Excel

Using the VLOOKUP function takes a bit of Excel expertise, but once you've mastered it, it's super helpful for quickly finding and matching up information in a large spreadsheet crammed with data. As a simple example to show how VLOOKUP works, recall the textbook-sales example. In your Excel workbook, you've got two worksheets: Contacts holds information about faculty members; Schools holds the names and addresses of the colleges and universities in your territory. The Contacts worksheet has a column called School Code; you want Excel to use that code to find the name of a university on the Schools workset and insert it in the Contacts worksheet. And that's where VLOOKUP comes in.

VLOOKUP is a search-and-copy function that scans a spreadsheet's columns, reading down a column until it finds a match. When it's found the match, it returns information from the row that holds the matched value. To use VLOOKUP, you need to supply three arguments (there's a fourth argument that's optional). These arguments tell VLOOKUP what to search for. In spreadsheet-ese, the arguments look like this:

VLOOKUP(lookup_value,table_array,col_index_num,range_lookup)

In plain English, here's what each argument means:

- **lookup_value.** This argument is your starting point; it tells Excel the value that you want to find. In this argument, you give Excel the coordinates of the cell (such as *B1* to indicate the cell at the intersection of column B and row 1) that holds the contents you want to VLOOKUP to search for. For example, take a look at Figure 3-7. If you want to find the name of the school Patrick Davis works for, the cell that holds his school code is D2. So for the first part of your function, that's exactly what you'd type: *D2*.

- **table_array.**This argument lets Excel know which cells you want to search through, in a grid that consists of two or more columns and several rows. For example, to search the cells in a grid that has cell A2 in the top-left corner and cell B6 in the bottom-right corner, type this: *$A$2:$B$6*. Notice that, for this argument, each part of the cell coordinates is preceded by a dollar sign (cell A2 becomes *$A$2* and cell B6 becomes *$B$6*) and the top-left and bottom-right coordinates are separated by a colon. If you want Excel to search a different worksheet in the workbook than the one you're on now, preface this argument with that worksheet's name, followed by an exclamation point. So *Sheet2!$A$2:$B$6* searches the grid of cells between A2 and B6, but on Sheet 2 instead of the current worksheet.

What if you've named your worksheet, rather than going by the numbers? For example, in the textbook sales workbook, there's a spreadsheet named Contacts and another named Schools. In that example, you need to give Excel a little help to find the right worksheet, like this: *[Sheet2]Schools!$A$2:$B$6*. Type the sheet number in square brackets, followed by the sheet's name and the exclamation point. (To find the worksheet number, count the tabs at the bottom of your screen,

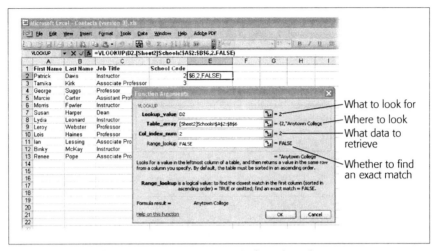

Figure 3-7. Excel helps you write your VLOOKUP formula with its Function Arguments wizard. Type each part of the formula (each argument) into the appropriate text box—if you make a mistake, QuickBase gives you an error message to the right of the argument that has the problem. This example tells Excel to find the value in cell D2, then go to the Schools worksheet and search for that value in the range of cells between A2 and B6; when Excel finds an exact match, it reads along the row that contains the match and retrieves the information from Column 2. In the blink of an eye, Excel inserts that information in the cell where you inserted the function (here, that's cell E2).

starting from the left: the leftmost tab is Sheet1, the next is Sheet2, then comes Sheet3, and so on.)

- **col_index_num.** Excel goes down a column to look for the data you told it to find. When Excel finds a match, it moves to the right, searching for the contents of a particular cell. This argument specifies which cell to find by naming the column that holds the information you want to retrieve. If, for example, the Schools sheet holds school names in the second column, you'd type 2 here.

- **range_lookup.** This argument is optional, so you can leave it out if you want. Range_lookup tells Excel whether it can return partial matches or only exact matches. Its value can be either true or false. If you set it to TRUE (or leave it out), Excel returns partial matches. If you set it to FALSE, Excel finds only exact matches. If there is no exact match, Excel gives you an error value of #N/A, which means "value not available".

To write a VLOOKUP formula, click inside the cell where you want the looked-up data inserted, and then look just above the spreadsheet's top row and click *fx* (that's the Insert Function button). Excel has a handy wizard, shown in Figure 3-7, that walks you through setting up VLOOKUP arguments, making formula writing a little easier by breaking the formula into its arguments. As you type in each text box, Excel types the same thing into the Function bar and the cell where you're inserting the function. If you make a mistake when you're typing, Excel lets you know so you can try again.

When your formula looks good, click OK—and watch VLOOKUP work its magic. It finds the data you want from the Schools sheet and inserts it in the Contacts sheet.

Once you know what you want to search for and what you want to retrieve, you can fill in the arguments VLOOKUP needs to do its job. Figure 3-7 uses VLOOKUP to find the name of the school Patrick Davis works for and insert that name in column E. Here's the formula for doing that:

=VLOOKUP(D2,[Sheet2]Schools!$A$2:$B$6,2,FALSE).

- **What to look for:** The contents of cell D2. In the example, that's the School Code in Patrick Davis's record.
- **Where to look:** On the worksheet named Schools, in the grid that has cell A2 in the upper left and B6 in the lower right.
- **What to grab when it finds a match:** Whatever's in the cell in the second column of that record. In the example, that's the school name, Anytown College.
- **Whether to find a partial or an exact match:** Exact matches only.

Start by exporting records from your application's master table back into Excel. You don't need to export all the data from QuickBase to Excel, just two fields: a field you can use to match the values you've got in Excel (such as Company Name, Client, or Property), and the key field that QuickBase has assigned to each record (probably Record ID). Put these values on another sheet in the workbook that holds the data you'll import into the QuickBase details table. (To create a new worksheet in your Excel workbook, select Insert→Worksheet. To move from one worksheet to another within the same workbook, click the tabs at the bottom of the screen.)

In the textbook-sales example, Schools is the master table. From the Schools table, you'd want to export the School Name field and the Record ID field (which is the key field for this table). Make sure that your lookup value (School Name) is in the left-hand column and the values you want Excel to return (Record ID) are in the right-hand column.

TIP

To export just two fields, rather than all the fields in your QuickBase table, create a report that shows only the fields you want to export. (In Report Builder's "Columns to Display" section, move the two fields you want from Available Columns to Your Columns, and then click Display.) At the top of your new report's table, click Other→Export this Report to a Spreadsheet. Select the spreadsheet program you want to export to (Excel is the default), and then click OK. Your computer fires up Excel and opens a spreadsheet with the fields you exported.

After you've exported the fields into Excel, make sure that the School column is sorted alphabetically from A to Z. (If you've exported a field that contains numbers instead of names, sort it numerically in ascending order.) When you've done that, make a column in your Excel spreadsheet where VLOOKUP will match the master records you exported from QuickBase with records you'll soon import into your QuickBase details table. In the example, you'd call this column something like School Code.

When you click the Insert Function button (it looks like this: *fx*) at the top of a worksheet to create a formula, Excel launches a wizard that breaks down the arguments you need to supply to VLOOKUP (see the box above for an explanation of these arguments and how to use the wizard). Type in the appropriate arguments, and then click OK. Excel fills in the Record ID—or whatever the master table's key field holds—for that record.

NOTE

Typing in VLOOKUP arguments one at a time for each cell in your spreadsheet would be *very* slow going. To speed things up, you can copy the function to other cells in the same column. Start by clicking in the cell that holds a valid VLOOKUP function. (In Figure 3-7, that would be D2.) A black outline appears around the cell, with a handle in the lower-right corner. Grab that handle and drag it down the column to cover the range you want. When you release the mouse button, Excel applies that function to all the cells you selected—in a flash, each cell contains the data you told VLOOKUP to find.

When you've got a column that holds the content of the key field for each record that will go into the details table, you're ready to import the details table's data into Quick-Base. Figure 3-8 gives you an idea of how this looks.

Importing data to the details table

Whether you've kept master and details records linked by changing the master table's key field or by using VLOOKUP to associate details records with master record IDs, your next step is to import the data you want to go into your QuickBase details table. Doing so takes just a few seconds. In Excel, make sure that all the data that will go into the details table is visible. (Data→Filter→Show All does the trick.) Then, highlight the columns you want to import. Copy them (select Edit→Copy, or press Ctrl+C), and then do a quick-and-easy import by pasting those columns into the QuickBase details table. Make sure that the field that holds the master table key field info is the details table's reference field.

Voilà! You've imported related data into two linked QuickBase tables while maintaining the relationship between those tables, as Figure 3-9 shows. If you have data in your spreadsheet that needs to go into other linked tables, just repeat the process described in this section.

This formula…

```
Microsoft Excel - Contacts (version 3).xls
File   Edit   View   Insert   Format   Tools   Data   Window   Help   Adobe PDF
```

```
                                                        Arial
E2              fx   =VLOOKUP(D2,[Sheet2]Schools!$A$2:$B$6,2,FALSE)
     A          B          C                    D                E                 F
1  First Name  Last Name  Job Title             School Code
2  Patrick     Davis      Instructor                         2   Anytown College
3  Tamika      Kirk       Associate Professor               3
4  George      Suggs      Professor                         3
5  Marcie      Carter     Assistant Professor               2
6  Morris      Fowler     Instructor                        4
7  Susan       Harper     Dean                              4
8  Lydia       Leonard    Instructor                        5
9  Leroy       Webster    Professor                         6
10 Lois        Haines     Professor                         6
11 Ian         Lessing    Associate Professor               2
12 Binky       McKay      Instructor                        6
13 Renee       Pope       Associate Professor               6
14
15
```

… finds the information you
want and inserts it here

Figure 3-8. The VLOOKUP formula in Excel's formula bar (circled) searches through the info you imported from the QuickBase master table and, when it finds a match, puts the Record ID in the appropriate cell in column F (School ID). In this figure, Excel searched cells A2-B6 of worksheet 2 and filled in the School ID value 2, which corresponds to Anytown College. Once you've written a successful VLOOKUP formula in one cell, you can copy it to other cells in the same column, supplying data in a snap. When you've got the record IDs from the master table, you can import data from this spreadsheet into your QuickBase details table, maintaining the table relationships that already exist in QuickBase.

Adding Documents

If you've ever been in a meeting where everyone had a different version of the "same" report, or if you've ever hit the road to find that you forgot to download the latest product information to your laptop (resulting in a frenzied email exchange with the home office), you'll love the way QuickBase provides a centralized, accessible repository for up-to-the-minute versions of all your important documents: sales brochures, contracts, reports, specifications—whatever you need to keep things running smoothly. In fact, you can upload any kind of file—not just documents—to QuickBase and share them with other QuickBase users. (Just keep in mind your billing account's limitations for attached files; see Table 1-1.)

Getting a document into QuickBase is a snap. Open the application you want to add the document to. From the blue Table bar, click the name of the table you want (such as Document Library), and then select "Add a New Document". (Or, if you see an "Add a New Document" link in the upper right, just click that.) The Add Document page, shown in Figure 3-10, appears. This page is a form that lets you add a new record—in this case a document—to your QuickBase application.

Quickbase looks up and displays this information from the master table. Click a link for more information about a particular record.

Figure 3-9. After you've imported your Excel data into the details table, that table can look up and display information from the master table. Here, by importing data from the master table's key field, you can have the details table show which contacts belong to which school.

Click the Browse button to summon the File Upload box. When you find the document you want, click Open. The document's filename appears in the Attachment text field. Click Save when you're finished (or Save & Add Another if you've got more documents to add).

When you're done adding documents, QuickBase shows you the details of the last document you added, as shown in Figure 3-11. Later, if you want to find this record again (which lists the details of the document), you can use Find or open a report that contains the record (such as Alphabetical, Documents by Author, or List All). Find the record you want and click the Display button to view it—a page just like the one in Figure 3-11 opens.

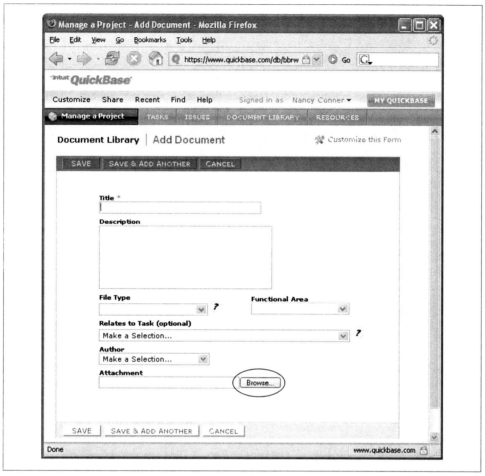

Figure 3-10. Adding any kind of document to a QuickBase application is easy: just enter a title, fill out any of the other fields (they're all optional), and then click the Browse button (circled).

Finding, Changing, and Exporting Data

Once you've got some data in QuickBase, you'll want to work with it: find records to update or edit, delete deadwood you no longer need, export it into a spreadsheet, and so on.

Finding Information

As your QuickBase applications—and the data they hold—grow, it might seem like you're going needle-hunting in a haystack when you want to find a particular record

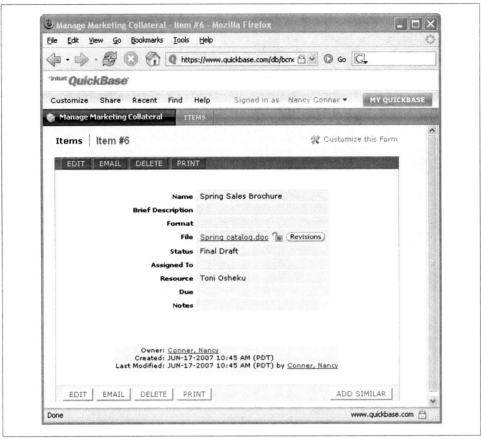

Figure 3-11. After you've added a document to an application, QuickBase shows you its details. The Name field is the name you entered on the Add Document page; the File field shows the document's actual filename. Click the Revisions button to see a record of all the changes that have been made, if any. The open padlock indicates that no one has reserved this document (see "Reserving a Document" on page 141).

or application. Not so. QuickBase lets you do lightning-fast, precise searches to pull up what you're looking for, no pitchfork required.

Search for an application

When you're a busy person working on tons of projects, your QuickBase Applications list can get pretty long, making it hard to find the application you want when you want it. You don't have to scroll endlessly through your application list to find the application you need. Start on your My QuickBase page; in the Applications box, click Tools→"Search for an application". In the "Search for an Application" box that pops up, type all or part of the application's name into the text box, and then click Search.

If you can't remember the application's name, you can still find it. Instead of trying to guess the name in the "Search for an Application" box, just leave the text box blank and click Search. QuickBase zips you over to the "Search for an Application" page, where you have these options:

- Search for text in an application's name or description (in case you suddenly remember that elusive name).
- List all applications you have access to.
- List all the applications you manage.
- List all applications that a group has access to (you have to type in the group's name).

Make your selection, and then click the Search button. QuickBase shows a list of the applications you asked it to find. To go to an application's Dashboard, click its name.

If you have 20 or more applications in your My QuickBase list, all that work has earned you a reward: a special Search box to make finding your applications easier. Once your Applications list hits 20, a "Search for an Application" box appears on the right side of your My QuickBase page, just below the Alerts box. Simply type in an application name and click Search, to save yourself a step in searching.

Search for information inside an application

You don't have to go through record after record to find information that's buried deep inside an application—QuickBase does super-fast searches for you. To search inside an application, whether it's single- or multi-table, start with the menu bar. Click Find, and the Find box appears, asking for your search criteria. Type in the word or words you're searching for. (If you're in a multi-table application, the Find box also has a drop-down list where you can choose the table you want to search, or just search all the tables in that application.) When your search is set to go, click Find. QuickBase looks through all the records and file attachments within that application, and then shows a list of matching results.

No luck? See the next section on Advanced Find. Sometimes, superhero Advanced Find is better at ferreting out text inside an attached document than its mere-mortal sibling Find.

TIP

When you type two words into the Find box, QuickBase looks for records that contain both words. So if you type in *Leroy Phillips*, QuickBase will find all records in that application that contain the name *Leroy* and the name *Phillips*. If you want the exact name Leroy Phillips, throw some quotation marks around the name, as you would when searching in Google. (Be aware, though, that using quotes to find an exact phrase works only in this Find box—it won't help you out in Advanced Find.) You can broaden your results by telling QuickBase to look for *any* of the words in your Find box: Type *Leroy OR Phillips* (the word *OR* must be all caps), and Quick-Base returns all the records that have either of these names: not only Leroy Phillips but also Mary Phillips, Charles Leroy, and so on. Type *Leroy OR Phillips OR Smith*, and QuickBase shows you all the records that contain at least one of those names.

Fine-tune your searches with Advanced Find

Often, you need to search for records in ways that go beyond typing in a search term. Say you want to find sales made within a certain date range or tasks assigned to a particular member of your team. The Advanced Find option lets you filter records according to criteria that you choose.

When you click the Find menu at the top of the screen, the box that opens has a link in the lower left called Advanced Find. Click it to go to the Advanced Find page, shown in Figure 3-12.

Here's how to use the Advanced Find page:

1. If you're searching a multi-table application, go to the upper-right Table drop-down menu and select the table you want to search.

NOTE

This menu doesn't appear in single-table applications.

---

2. On the left side of the page, click the box that says <Some field>.

   A menu of field names, tailored to the application and table you're searching, appears.

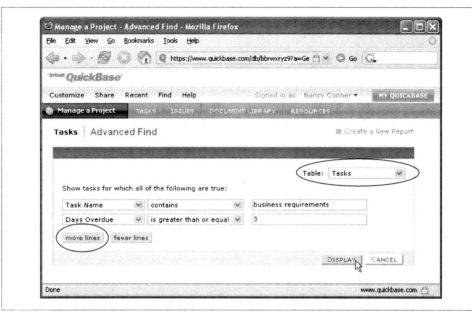

Figure 3-12. Use the Advanced Find page to hone your searches. Each drop-down menu lists different fields in that particular application; select a field that interests you, and then tell QuickBase what to look for in that field. This example is searching for tasks whose name contains the phrase "business requirements" and are at least three days overdue. If you want to include more search parameters, click the "more lines" button (circled) to add more drop-down menus. If you're searching a multi-table application, the upper-right Table menu (also circled) lets you specify which table you want QuickBase to search.

TIP

If you want to search all the fields in an application, leave this box set to <Some field>. If you want to search inside documents attached to this application, select <Some attached file>.

---

3. Choose the field you want to search, and then set your search parameters.

   The middle box has a list of criteria you can use to filter the data. For example, if you're searching for text, you can choose from criteria such as *contains, does not contain, is, starts with,* and so on. If you're searching for numbers, the middle box contains choices like *is less than, is greater than or equal,* and so on. Use the third column to specify *what* you're looking for: a name, a word, a phrase, a date, a value —whatever.

NOTE

You *can't* use double quotes ("New York", for example) to search for an exact phrase in Advanced Find.

---

4. QuickBase makes it easy for you to specify exactly what you're looking for by providing drop-down menus tailored to the kind of information you specify. For example, if you select Date Created from the left-hand menu, then the other menus change, presenting only what's useful for a date search.

TIP

As with the Find box, when you're looking for records that contain *any* of several words, separate your search terms with *OR* in capital letters. If you want to find sales contacts in Topeka, Indianapolis, and Wichita, for example, type *Topeka OR Indianapolis OR Wichita*.

---

5. When you've set all your search parameters, click Display.

QuickBase shows you the results of your search.

TIP

To refine your search results, click the Search Results table's Customize link (it's in the bar across the top of the table). The menu that appears lets you sort the results further (select "Sorting & grouping"), rearrange the columns (Select "Default column list"), or choose a different report to display them (Select "Edit this report in the Report Builder"). For more on using Report Builder to refine a report, see "Editing a report" on page 66.

Save search results

When you've spent time sifting through masses of records to find a particular group, you don't want to have to repeat your search every time you need those records. So it's a good thing you don't have to. Say hello to the Save link (yep, the same one you learned about back in Chapter 2).

When you save your search results, they're not frozen in time at the moment you did the search. Say that first thing in the morning you searched for all clients in the 90210 Zip code and saved the results, and then took a coffee break. While you were enjoying your double nonfat mocha latte, your coworker updated some records within that Zip code. When you get back to your desk, you open your saved search—like magic, the records you saved reflect the updates that happened during your break. When you save a search, the records in it are always up to date.

NOTE

If you search "All tables" in a multi-table application, there's no Save link on the results page. That's because when it searches multiple tables, QuickBase displays multiple reports, all at the same time. In order to save the results in a multi-table application, you need to search its tables one at a time.

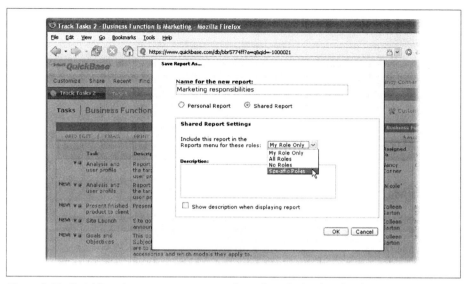

Figure 3-13. QuickBase lets you save your search results, which is handy when you need to focus on a particular subset of records within an application—like all employees who opted for dental insurance or all clients who've expressed interest in a particular product line. Give your new report a name and, if you want, a description. You can restrict a saved report to your own role, so that only you and anyone else who shares your role can see it. If you want to make the search results available to more people, choose Specific Roles. QuickBase shows you the roles with whom you can share the report; check the appropriate boxes.

It takes only a couple of seconds to save your search results:

1. Above the Search Results table, look for New Report: Save; click the Save link.

    The Save Report As box, shown in Figure 3-13, appears.

2. Type in a name for your new report. Then choose whether you want to save your search results as a Personal Report (for your eyes only) or a Shared Report (available to all application users). If you don't have permission to save reports, Personal Report will be your only option.

    When you name the report, make the name something descriptive that'll jog your memory later on; *Employees on Dental Plan* is a lot clearer than *New Report*. If you're saving this report as a Shared Report, the box expands to ask for some more info. You can choose which roles can see the report and, if you want, write an optional description. If you write a description and want to see it when you look at this report, turn on the "Show description when displaying report" checkbox.

3. When everything in the Save Report As box looks good, click OK.

    QuickBase saves your search results; to summon the results at any time, click Reports in the application's menu bar and select your report from the list.

Searching for Data and Replacing It

Just like the popular tool in Microsoft Word and Excel, QuickBase comes with its own Search and Replace feature that can save you boatloads of time when you need to make changes throughout an application.

NOTE

You may not have permission to change all the records in a specific report. If you don't, QuickBase changes only those records you have permission to change.

Use Search and Replace for a User field

Sometimes you need to reassign tasks from one employee to another. An employee may leave the company, move to another project, or have a family emergency. But someone still has to take care of business, and you want to transfer tasks between workers without clicking through dozens of individual records.

When you make this kind of alteration, you need to change what's known as a *User field*, which is QuickBase's holding tank for user information in an application. For example, you might need to change a User field such as "Assigned to" from one person to another. (For more on field types, including User fields, see "Assigning field types" on page 235.)

Here's how to do a fast search and replace when you're changing a User field:

1. Open (or create) a report that holds all the records you want to change (see Chapter 2 for the skinny on creating reports). Above the records is an Other link with a downward-pointing arrow, shown in Figure 3-14; click the arrow. From the menu that appears, select "Search & Replace (in this report only)".

   The Search and Replace box opens.

2. Click the "In the field" drop-down list (see Figure 3-15) and select the User field that you want to change.

   When you select a User field, the Change and To fields display buttons labeled Select User. These buttons let you select actual QuickBase users, rather than typing in the name and other info that QuickBase already has stored.

3. In the Change field, click the Select User button.

   The "Select a User" window opens, giving you a bunch of options: select a user from this application or from a group, search for a particular user ("Basic Sharing" on page 280), or create a new user ("Basic Sharing" on page 280).

4. Select the user you want to replace.

   For example, say Lida Martinez has called in sick, and you want to reassign her tickets to Tim Germaine. In that case, you'd select Linda Martinez. If you're looking

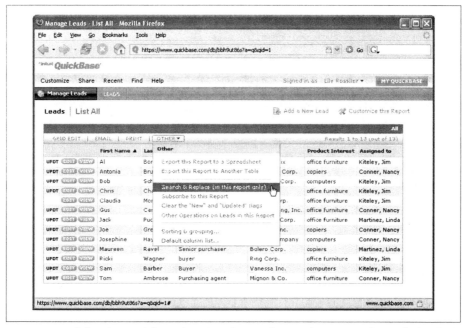

Figure 3-14. Click Other, and then select "Search & Replace (in this report only)" to find multiple records and replace specific information inside those records.

for a user already associated with this application, choose a name from the "Users in this application" list. Click Done.

Back in the Search and Replace box, the name of the user you've chosen appears in the Change field.

5. In the To field, click the Select User button.

Now you're selecting the user who'll *replace* the user whose name appears in the Change field. Again, the "Select a User" window opens, with the same options as in step 3.

6. Select the user who's replacing the user in the Change field, and then click Done.

In the example, Tim Germaine is taking on the assignments of the ailing Linda Martinez, so you'd choose Tim Germaine. Now the Search and Replace box resembles the example shown in Figure 3-15, with the names of the users you're changing filled in.

7. Click OK.

QuickBase opens a confirmation box, letting you know how many records it's about to change.

8. If the changes look OK, click Replace.

To see the applied changes, refresh the report in which you made them by clicking your Web browser's Refresh or Reload button.

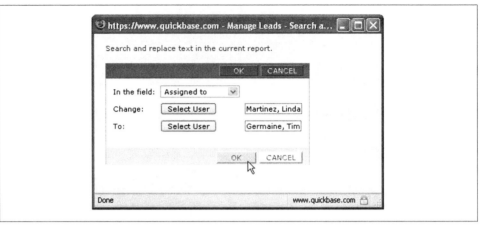

Figure 3-15. The Search and Replace box can be a huge timesaver. Select the person you want to replace by clicking the Select User button next to the Change label. Then identify the new guy or gal by clicking the same button next to the To label.

Use Search and Replace for a checkbox field

Imagine you're a sales rep who's just hit the road to woo new clients. After a long day of meeting and greeting, you want to update the Sales Leads application to reflect the fruits of your labor. No need to wear out your mouse-clicking finger turning on the Contacted checkbox over and over again. When you need to change a bunch of checkboxes (either turning them on or off en masse), use Search and Replace:

1. Open or create a report ("Creating a Report from Scratch" on page 61) that has all the records you want to change. Click Other, and then select "Search & Replace (in this report only)".

   The Search and Replace window opens.

2. Click the "In the field" drop-down list and select the checkbox field you want to change.

   In this example, you'd select Contacted.

3. Make your change.

   To turn on a checkbox that's currently empty, type *no* in the Change text box and type *yes* in the To text box. To clear a box that's currently turned on, type *yes* in the Change text box and type *no* in the To text box.

   Think of it like this: What you type into the To field is the result you want. So if you want to turn on the checkbox, make sure the To field says *yes*. If you want to clear the box, make sure the To field says *no*.

4. Click OK.

   QuickBase displays a confirmation window, letting you know how many records your change will affect.

Figure 3-16. When searching for and replacing data, make sure the old data (what you want to find and change) is in the Change field and the new data (what you want to change it to) is in the To field. You can limit your search to whole fields (for example, if you want to change one particular person's email address, such as ahicks@abccompany.com) or tell QuickBase to match the upper- and lower-case letters exactly as you've typed them.

5. Click Replace to confirm the change.

   QuickBase flips around the checkboxes you chose.

Search and Replace for other kinds of data

When you want to find and replace data that's *not* in a user field or a checkbox field, these are the steps to take:

1. Open or create a report ("Creating a Report from Scratch" on page 61) that holds all the records you want to change. Click Other, then select "Search & Replace (in this report only)".

   The Search and Replace box appears.

2. Click the "In the field" drop-down list and select the field in which you want to make a change. Type the word you want to search for into the Change field. Type the word you want to replace it with in the To field.

   For example, say your business partner ABC Company has changed its name to XYZ Company, and all the employees' email addresses are about to change from *employeename@abccompany.com* to *employeename@xyzcompany.com*. You'd type the old email address, *@abccompany.com*, into the Change field and the new email address, *@xyzcompany.com*, into the To field. Figure 3-16 shows you how this would look.

3. If you want your search to match the whole field you've typed or the case of your letters, turn on the relevant checkbox. When everything looks good, click OK.

A confirmation box appears, telling you how many records you're about to change.

4. Click Replace.

QuickBase changes your records. Refresh the report you started from (click your browser's Refresh or Reload button) to see the results.

TIP

If you have administrative privileges, you can also search and replace within an application's schema (as opposed to its data). If the data represents the guts of an application, the schema is its skeleton—the structure that holds the data. An application's schema includes field, report, and form labels; field properties; form properties; and so on. Say you want to relabel all the "work orders" in an application as "tickets." Select Customize→Application→Misc.→"Search & Replace in Schema." Type in your search term (in this case, *work order*); if QuickBase finds fields, reports, or other elements of the schema that contain the term, it shows them to you and presents a Replace box. Type in the replacement term (*ticket*, in this example) and click "Replace in Selected Items". Click OK to confirm, and QuickBase makes the change.

Modifying an Existing Record

Change happens. People come and go, addresses and phone numbers change, the new boss wants to have status meetings on Tuesdays. QuickBase makes it easy for you to make changes to existing records. Just follow these steps:

1. Find the record you want to change.

   To do so, go to the application's Dashboard and look in the left-hand Reports menu for a report that holds the record, like List All or Assigned to Me. Or, from the menu bar, click Find, enter a keyword into the box that appears, and then click the Find button.

TIP

Often, the fastest way to find new and updated records is to select the List Changes report. This report shows all records that have changed since the last time you viewed the application.

---

2. A list of records appears. To the left of each record, you see an Edit button—a button labeled either EDIT or just E, depending on how you set your User Preferences.

NOTE

If there's no Edit button, you don't have permission to change records in that application. If you think you should have this ability, contact the application's manager. (Look on the application's Dashboard page or in the Applications Details display on your My QuickBase page to find out who the permissions czar is.)

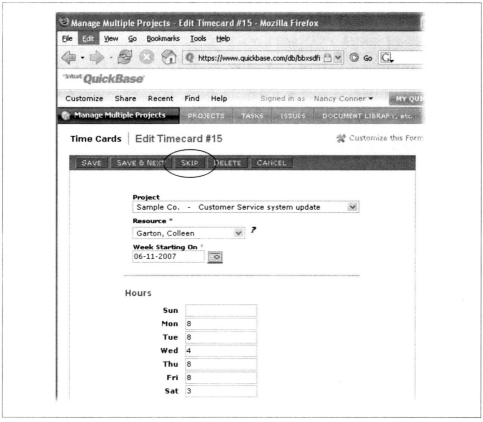

Figure 3-17. The Edit Record page looks a lot like the Add Record page, except the fields hold previously entered information. To edit a text field, just click the box and start typing away. When you're editing a bunch of records at once, click Save & Next when you're finished with one to move ahead to the next record. You may not need to edit every record in an application; click Skip (circled) to move on when you don't want to change the current record. When you're completely done making your changes, click Save.

3. Click the Edit button of the record you want to change.

   The Edit Record page opens (Figure 3-17) showing editable versions of all the record's entries.

4. Make the changes you want; if there are other records you want to edit, click Save & Next.

   QuickBase saves your changes and opens the next record. (If you don't need to make any changes to that record, click Skip to jump to the next one.)

5. When you're finished, click Save.

   QuickBase saves your changes and returns you to the last report you were in.

Deleting Records

If you don't want old records lying around cluttering up your application, you can clean house by deleting them. Make sure, though, that you really want to get rid of any records you delete—in QuickBase, deletion is *forever*.

You can delete a single record in just a few steps:

1. Open a report that contains the record you want to delete.

   You might, for example, start from the application's Dashboard page and select the List All report. Or use the Find drop-down menu ("Search for information inside an application" on page 125).

2. To the left of the record is an Edit button (a button that says EDIT or the letter E, depending on how you've set your User Preferences). Click it.

   The Edit Record page opens.

3. At the top and bottom of the record is a row of buttons. Click the Delete button.

   Because a deleted record is really, really gone, QuickBase asks if you're sure you want to delete this one.

4. Click OK.

   QuickBase deletes the record.

Delete a bunch of records from an application

When you've got a whole list of records to delete, it's tedious and time consuming to get rid of them one by one. So QuickBase lets you virtually shred a bunch of records with just a couple of mouse clicks:

1. Create a report ("Creating a Report from Scratch" on page 61) that contains all the records you want to delete—and only those records.

   For example, you might create a report that shows only closed tickets or records created before a certain date.

2. From that report's page, click Other→"Other Operations on Records in this Report".

   A new window pops open, showing the operations you can perform: Change Owner, Delete, and Show Expanded URL.

3. Click Delete.

   Once again, QuickBase wants to make sure you clicked what you meant (and meant what you clicked). Another window opens, telling you how many records you're about to delete and asking if you really want to delete them all. If you meant to get rid of 12 records and QuickBase tells you you're about to delete 200, now would be a good time to click the Cancel button.

4. Click the Delete Records? button.

QuickBase confirms that the records are gone. Click "Close this Window" to close the confirmation window. The last report you were in still shows the records you just deleted. To make sure they're gone, refresh the page (click your browser's Refresh or Reload button).

Delete all the records in an application

One way to delete *all* the records in an application is to go to the application's Dashboard page, open the List All report, and then follow the steps to delete a bunch of records. But there's another option that's just as easy:

1. Open the application whose records you want to clear out. Then select Customize→Application.

   QuickBase takes you to a page that lets you change various setting for your application. Click the Misc. tab to get to the page shown in Figure 3-18. From here, you can do a number of different things (which is why they call it the Miscellaneous tab), depending on your permissions. If you don't see a link that says Delete Data, it means you don't have permission to delete all the records from this application; talk to the application's manager to get the green light. (To find out who that is, click the Show Application Statistics link.)

2. Click the Delete Data link.

   You can only delete data from one table at a time. So if you're in a multi-table application, tell QuickBase which table you want. A confirmation window opens, asking whether you *really* want to delete all those records.

3. If you're sure you want to go ahead, click "Yes, delete all Records."

   A Confirmation page opens letting you know the records are history. Since you've deleted just the records and not the application, QuickBase takes you back to the application's Dashboard.

Exporting Data

Just as it's easy to get your data *into* QuickBase, it's a cinch to get it out. When you export data from QuickBase to a spreadsheet program (like Excel) or database program (like Access), you have three data formats to choose from:

- **Tab-separated values (TSV) format** saves your record in text format, one record per line, separating one field from the next with a tab. TSV is a good format to use if you're exporting to a spreadsheet program.

- **Comma-separated values (CSV) format** also saves your record in text format, with one record per line, but uses commas, instead of tabs, to separate fields. Many database and spreadsheet programs understand CSV format, so if you're not sure which format to use, this is a good one to try.

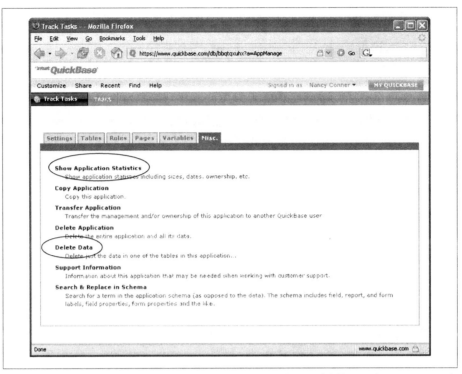

Figure 3-18. The Miscellaneous tab gives you a quick rundown of different things you can do with an application. To delete all the records from this application, click Delete Data (circled). If the Delete Data link doesn't appear here, find the application's manager by clicking Show Application Statistics (also circled) and contacting the that person to change your permissions.

- **Extensible markup language (XML).** XML is a highly customizable, increasingly popular format used to organize data so that different computers, operating systems, and programs can quickly exchange records. XML lets you share your data on the World Wide Web, on intranets, in databases, and so on.

Here's how to export data out of QuickBase:

1. Open the application you want to export from. Then click Customize→Import/Export.

   The Import/Export Page opens.

2. Turn on the "Export a table to a file" radio button.

   The Import/Export box expands, as shown in Figure 3-19.

3. If you're exporting from a multi-table application, select the table you're exporting *from* in the "Choose a table" drop-down menu. Then pick the format for the exported data (see above). Click "Export to File."

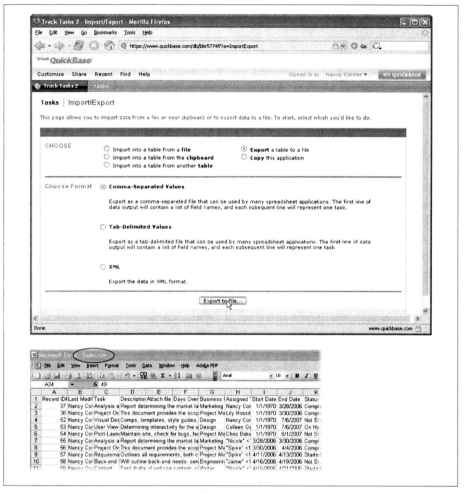

Figure 3-19. When you ask QuickBase to format your records as comma- or tab-separated values (top), QuickBase actually creates a file (bottom) that you can export into Excel (or any other program that recognizes those formats). QuickBase comes up with a name for your file (here, Tasks.csv, circled) that combines the name of the table you exported from with the format you used. Now you can work with the file just as you would any other spreadsheet. When you're done, save it as a .csv file, an .xls file, or whatever spreadsheet format you like.

If you chose TSV or CSV as your export format, you can open the exported file in a spreadsheet program or save it on your computer.

If you chose to export the data in XML format, a browser window opens to display your file as a Web page, which looks something like Figure 3-20. From there, you can copy the file, paste it into a text file (like Wordpad), and save it as an XML file (give it a name like Tasks.xml). You can then import the XML file into a database program—follow the import instructions of whatever database program you use.

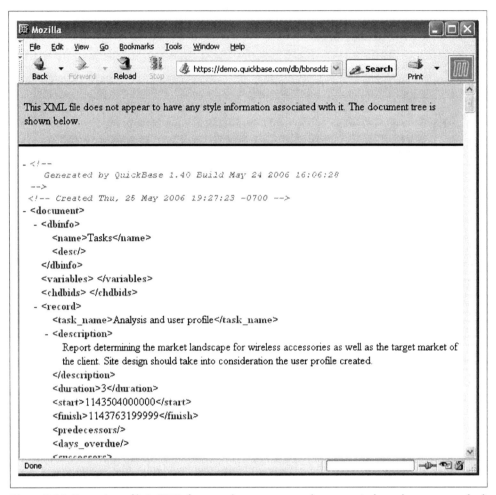

Figure 3-20. Exporting a file in XML format takes you to a new browser window whose contents look something like this. You can use this code to import your data into another database program.

Editing and Collaborating on Documents

Your team is working on a report that's due at the end of the week. Three people have revisions to make, and everyone else has to read and OK the changes. If you've ever tried doing this document dance by email, flinging one attachment after another through cyberspace, you know what a nightmare it can be. Is *this* file the most recent version? Has Elaine made her updates yet? Did Fred sign off on *this* version or the last one? (Maybe typewriters weren't so bad after all.)

Enter QuickBase, which gives you a centralized way to share, edit, and track your documents. You'll wonder how you ever produced a report without it. This section tells you everything you need to know when it's time to work with the documents...and other people.

Finding a Document

Before you can work on a document, you've got to find it. No problem. Just search for a document (or for any text *inside* a document) the way you'd search for any QuickBase data:

1. Open the application you want to search in and click the Find drop-down menu. The Find window opens.

2. Type in your search term, like a filename or the document's title. Click Find.

   QuickBase searches inside all documents stored in the application you're in and shows you a list of documents that match the term you're searching for. Links to matched documents appear in the File field.

3. Click the name of the document you want to open.

   QuickBase downloads the file so your computer can open it in the appropriate program—a .doc file, for example, opens in Word.

TIP

To make your search more precise, use Advanced Find, where you can specify plenty of other criteria, like Author, Category, Date Created, or Date Modified. You can even search for a word or phrase that's inside the document. For more on using Advanced Find, zip over to "Find an Existing Record" on page 42.

Reserving a Document

There's nothing more frustrating than spending hours editing a document only to find out someone else has undone all your hard work. QuickBase helps you avoid this snafu by letting you *reserve* documents. Reserving a document is like checking it out of the library—while you're working on it, no one else can. When you reserve a document, everyone else who has access to that document sees it as locked (there's an icon that looks like a closed padlock), and they can't upload any changes to it until you release your reservation. With QuickBase, no two team members will ever again try to upload the same document at the same time.

Even better, QuickBase automatically saves up to three versions of a document—a new version of JulySalesReport.doc *doesn't* overwrite all the previous versions of JulySales-Report.doc. (After three versions have been uploaded, QuickBase deletes the oldest one each time someone uploads a new version.) So if you need to undo someone else's

—ahem—"improvements" to your work, you can easily find the version *you* uploaded before they got their mitts on it.

Here's how to reserve a document for your exclusive working pleasure:

1. Open a report that contains a record with the document you want to reserve. Then click the Edit button for that record. (The Edit button may say EDIT or E, depending on how you've set your User Preferences.)

   The Edit Document page, shown in Figure 3-21, appears.

2. In the File section, find the document you want to revise. To its right is an icon that looks like an open padlock. The open lock indicates that the document isn't reserved. Click the lock.

   The Document Reservation window opens. This window has a text box where you can type in a comment that describes the revisions you're making.

3. If you want to display a comment with your reservation, type it into the text box. For example, you might type *Updating sales figures* or *Adding minutes of last meeting*. (Adding a comment is optional.) Click Reserve Document.

   QuickBase reserves the document for you and changes the icon to a locked padlock. If you see a green lock, it means you're the one who reserved the document. A pink lock means somebody else has reserved it. As long as you have the document reserved, no one else can upload changes to it. (They can download it, though.)

After you've made your changes, upload the revised document into QuickBase ("Adding Documents" on page 121). Don't forget to release the reservation (described next) so someone else can work on the document.

Release a reservation

No fair putting a lock on a document and never letting anyone else work on it. When you've reserved a document to revise, update, or edit it, at some point you've got to let others have their turn. Here's how to release a reservation:

1. Open or create a report that shows the record containing the document you've reserved. Click that record's Edit button.

   The Edit Document page appears. It looks like the one in Figure 3-21, except the icon is a green padlock, which means that you've reserved that document.

2. Click the green padlock next to the document you're ready to release.

   The Document Reservation window opens.

3. Click Release Reservation.

   Now your colleagues can revise and upload the document.

What happens if you reserve a document, win the lottery, and then take off on the next plane to Tahiti? Does that mean your coworkers are permanently locked out of the

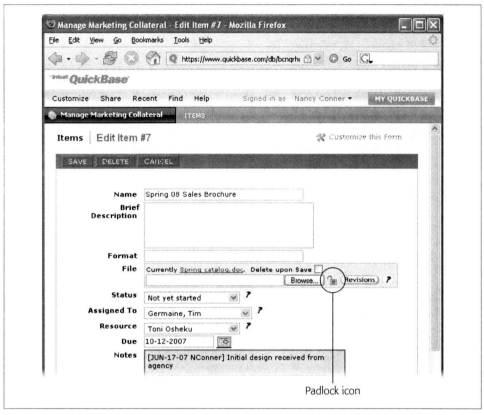

Padlock icon

Figure 3-21. When you want to reserve a document, click the open padlock icon. If the padlock is closed, it means someone has reserved the document—and if the closed padlock is green, that someone was you.

document? Not to worry. An application's administrator can release the reservation on any file in the application. Sit back, sip your Mai Tai, and enjoy your flight.

Viewing a Document's Revision History

When you want to know who's done what to a document, or when you need to find an earlier version of a particular document (QuickBase automatically saves up to three), check out the revision history:

1. Open or create a report containing the record that's got the document you're interested in. Find the record and click its Display button (a button labeled either VIEW or V, depending on how you've set your User Preferences).

   A page containing the details for the record opens, as shown in Figure 3-22.

2. In the File field, click the Revisions button.

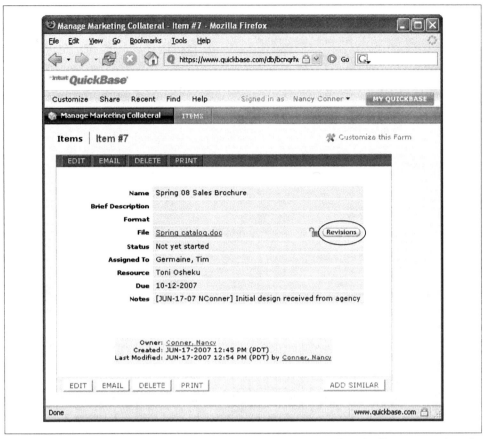

Figure 3-22. When you want to check a document's revision history, find the file you're looking for and click the Revisions button.

The Revision History window opens, giving details about who's revised the document and when they made their changes.

NOTE

If there's no Revisions button, it means the application's administrator has restricted access to that field's revision history.

Restoring a Previous Version

Oops! Somebody updated the report on the Henderson account with figures from the Hankerman account. You don't have to redo the whole report; you can *restore* the previous, pre-Hankerman version.

NOTE

To restore a previous version of a document, you must have permission to modify a field. If you don't have this permission and think you need it, talk to the application's manager (see Figure 3-18).

It only takes a few steps to restore a previous version of a document:

1. Open or create a report containing the record that has the problem document. Click the Edit button (or pencil-point icon) for the appropriate record.

   The Edit Document page opens.

2. Find the document you're interested in and click Revisions.

   The Revision History window opens.

3. Find the document version you want to restore and turn on the checkbox to its left. Click Restore.

   A confirmation window asks if you're sure you want to restore that file.

4. Click OK.

   QuickBase restores the document you checked.

Managing the Revisions List

Ever worked on a project where everyone on the team wanted to edit everybody else's writing? Maybe Joe is busy reuniting split infinitives while Susan is on the hunt for comma splices—and the meaning of the document gets lost in all that tinkering. Sometimes, revisions fly faster and thicker than snowflakes in a blizzard. If you've got administrative privileges, you can control how many versions of a revised document QuickBase stores—so an important revision won't get shoved into oblivion by newer versions.

Managing an application's revisions list is easy:

1. Open the application that holds the documents and select Customize→Tables.

   The Tables page opens with the Fields tab selected. (If you're in a multi-table application, choose the table you want from the left-hand menu.)

2. Find the field that holds documents (look for File Attachment in the Fields tab's Type column) and click its name.

   QuickBase takes you to the Properties page for that field. About halfway down the page is the Revisions section, shown in Figure 3-23. Here, you can set the number of revisions QuickBase keeps—from one to all. You can also let end-users see the revision history or make the revision history off limits (so Joe can stop worrying about split infinitives and get back to work).

3. Make your selections and click Save.

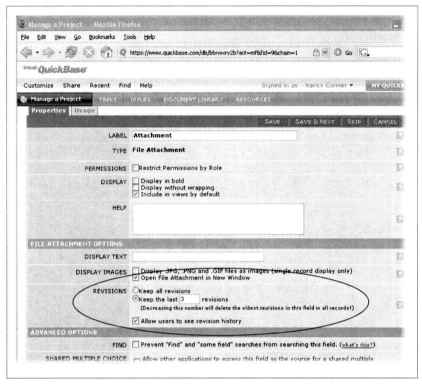

Figure 3-23. Manage a document's revisions from the Properties page of the field in which QuickBase stores the document. In the Revisions section (circled), you can tell QuickBase how many versions to store when the document is revised. The default is three, but you can change that number by turning on the "Keep the last ___ revisions" radio button and typing in whatever number you want. If you're the packrat type, save ALL revisions by turning on the "Keep all revisions" radio button. Turn on or off the "Allow users to see revision history" checkbox, depending on your preference.

QuickBase puts your instructions to work.

NOTE

When you lower the number of revisions QuickBase stores—for example, maybe there are half a dozen revisions hanging around and you think two would be plenty —QuickBase deletes the oldest versions. So before you switch from six to two versions in the revision history, make sure that you can do without the four oldest versions. You don't want to accidentally delete a version that someone, somewhere, still needs.

Deleting a Version of a Document

Of course, if someone contaminated the Henderson report with Hankerman data, you probably want to get rid of the messed-up version once and for all. If you're the application's administrator, you can banish any version of a document for good. Simply follow the steps you'd take to restore a previous version, but when you get to step 3, turn on the checkbox next to the version you want to delete. Then click Delete (and OK to confirm). The version you deleted is gone for good.

NOTE

Only an application's administrator can delete a version of a document. If you don't manage the application, you won't see a Delete button on the Revision History page.

CHAPTER 4

Report Sharing, Change Notifications, and Reminders

As you've learned by now, QuickBase is an amazingly flexible information container. You can stuff it with almost endless amounts of addresses, milestones, tasks, documents, whatever, and never once will you hear it complain, "Hey, buddy, I'm tired." But sometimes you *want* your super-powered database to speak up. Sometimes you want to share with others the sleek and info-rich reports you learned about in Chapter 2. Or perhaps certain people need to know when certain records have changed. And maybe everyone—you, your colleagues, definitely the boss's shiftless nephew—needs a little nudge now and again to remember when something's due. No problem.

This chapter shows you how to turn QuickBase from quiet recipient to bold communicator. You'll learn, for example, how to share reports with anyone who needs to see them. Even better, QuickBase is happy to send off recurring reports that get automatically dispatched. For the folks in the trenches who need to know about small-scale changes, just a few mouse clicks let you make sure they're notified whenever a record changes. And for those in need of a nudge, QuickBase is ready to keep the team on target: Email reminders are quick and easy to program.

Sending Reports to Yourself and Others

The reports you learned about in Chapter 2 are a great way to get a filtered look at just the data you're interested in. A well-designed report—whether it's a table, chart, calendar, timeline, or spreadsheet—helps visually summarize the key info you've been packing into your QuickBase applications.

QuickBase reports (like the example in Figure 4-1) serve up a selection of your data in a visually pleasing and easy-to-digest format. Sounds like the sort of info you'd want to share with everyone—not just you and your fellow QuickBase users, but anyone you work with, like vendors, suppliers, and maybe even your proud parents. Good news: QuickBase makes it easy to distribute your reports far and wide. You can email or print

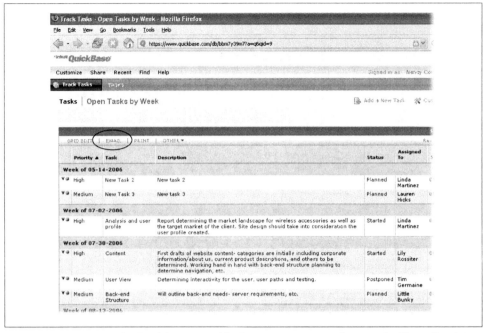

Figure 4-1. You can email a QuickBase report like this one to anyone with an email address. QuickBase sends a copy of the report and a link to the same report in QuickBase. To get started, click the report's Email link (circled).

individual reports, or you can set up *subscriptions,* recurring reports that QuickBase automatically sends out for you.

Quickly Emailing Individual Reports

When you want to email a report (to another QuickBase user or to anyone with an email address), you can do so right from QuickBase. It's fast and easy—just follow these steps:

1. Open or create the report you want to email (see Chapter 2 for all you ever wanted to know about reports). In the header at the top of the report, click the Email link.

   QuickBase opens a page that looks like Figure 4-2.

2. In the top text box, type in the email addresses of whomever you want to receive the report. You can type in a bunch of addresses; be sure to separate them with a comma, a semicolon, or by hitting Enter after each address.

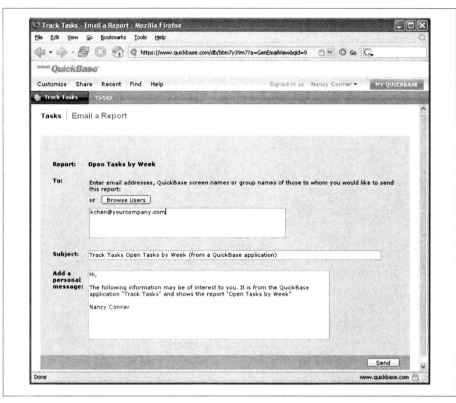

Figure 4-2. When you want to send a report via email, type recipients' names into the topmost box, or click Browse Users to choose from QuickBase users with access to the application. In the other boxes, you can write your own subject line and a custom email message. When everything looks good, click Send to zip the report off to everyone on your recipient list.

TIP

To speed up the process of entering email addresses, click Browse Users. The Select a User window opens, showing users who have access to this application. You can pick the ones you want, select them all, or search for a specific user or group to add to your email list.

---

3. QuickBase starts you off with a suggested subject line and some text for your email message. If you want, you can edit these. Just click in the appropriate text box and type away. When you're done, click Send.

The email you send contains a copy of the report itself plus a link to the report in QuickBase, as shown in Figure 4-3. QuickBase also sends an email to your registered email address, letting you know that the email went out in your name. (That way, if anyone else is using your QuickBase account to send out emails, you know about it.)

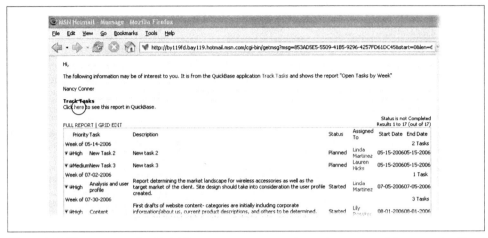

Figure 4-3. When you email a QuickBase report, your email contains a copy of the report itself and also a link (circled) to the report in QuickBase. (Users have to be signed in to QuickBase to follow the link. If the recipient of your email hasn't registered with QuickBase, they can do so on the sign-in page.)

Printing Reports

When you need a hard copy of a report to pass around the table at a meeting or include in a printed document, you can print right from QuickBase. Here's how:

1. **Open the report you want to print. In the dark blue bar that appears above the records, click Print.**

    The Print Options box opens.

2. **Choose one of these options:**

    • To print the records exactly as they look on your screen, choose "Print the report," and then click OK.

    • To print each record on its own individual page, choose "Print all records displayed (one per page)." QuickBase calls this "form view" format (a form contains selected fields, rather than all the fields, for each record; to learn how to create custom forms, see "Creating a Custom Form" on page 441). If there's more than one form available for this table, a drop-down list of forms appears; choose the one you want (or "All fields"), and then click OK.

    QuickBase shows you a print preview Web page and opens your browser's Print dialog box.

3. **If everything looks OK, click Print.**

    QuickBase sends the report to your printer.

If you want to print whatever's on your screen at the moment, you can do so from the Customize menu. Just click Customize→"Print this page". QuickBase opens a window showing you exactly what will print (if part of your report is cut off here, it will be in the printed document, too) and a Print window. In the Print window, select the number of copies and click OK to send the page to your printer. This fast, simple way to print is useful when you want to print a list of fields or user screens that don't have a Print button of their own.

Getting QuickBase Charts into Office Files

I've got a QuickBase pie chart that would look great in the report I'm handing out at the next meeting. How do I get a copy of it into Word or PowerPoint?

QuickBase generates charts using Flash technology, which lets you interact with the chart when viewing it in your Web browser (to see details about the underlying data, for instance). When you want to put a copy of a chart into a Word document or a PowerPoint presentation, you first have to tell QuickBase to change the chart from the Flash format to an image that you can copy. Here's how:

1. Open the Chart report you want to copy. Right-click somewhere in the white space that surrounds the chart itself, and then select Copy Image.

   Your computer copies the chart to the clipboard.

2. Open the document or presentation you want to paste the chart into. Position the cursor where you want the chart to appear, and then select Edit→Paste (or click Ctrl+V).

Word or PowerPoint then inserts the QuickBase chart into your document. Unfortunately, charts are the only report type that you can copy to the clipboard.

Printing Address Labels

When a table holds lots of info about your contacts, it makes sense to use that table to print address labels for a mailing. For example, say you've got a table that holds all kinds of data about your customers: name, job title, contact info, product interest, recent orders, and so on. When it's time to mail out the quarterly newsletter or a new catalog, how do you get the names and addresses out of that table and onto address labels?

QuickBase has a wizard that makes it easy for you print labels from a table. The wizard extracts names and addresses and formats them to fit onto a standard sheet of labels: three labels across and ten labels down. All you have to do is run the wizard and then print the labels directly from Internet Explorer.

NOTE

Sorry, Firefox fans: QuickBase's Address Label Wizard works only in Internet Explorer version 5.0 or higher.

Before you begin, make sure your browser is set up to print the labels properly. In Internet Explorer, select File→Page Setup. In the Page Setup dialog box, clear the Header and Footer boxes so that they're blank. In the Margins section, set all margins (Left, Right, Top, and Bottom) to 0.25 inches, and then click OK. (And remember to put mailing label sheets in your printer!)

Now you're ready to run the wizard. Point your Web browser to *http://tinyurl.com/ d2h84*. (Bookmark the page so you can easily find the wizard again, or keep reading to learn how to create a report that gives you—and, if you want, anyone else who uses your application—one-click access to the wizard.)

When you first go to the wizard's page, it asks you to sign in with your QuickBase username and password. (Even if you're already signed in to QuickBase in another window or tab, you need to sign in here, too.) Type in the requested info, and then click the "Login to QuickBase" button.

QuickBase opens the Address Label Wizard. This wizard has two steps:

1. From the drop-down list, choose the table that holds the names and addresses you want to print. In a multi-table application, look for the name of the application, followed by a colon, followed by the name of the table. For example, if you want the Customers table from the Customer Orders application, choose Customer Orders: Customers from the drop-down list. When you've selected the table you want, click Next.

    QuickBase opens a page like the one shown in Figure 4-4. The fields you see will vary depending on what's in your table; QuickBase guesses which fields you want to print based on the names of the table's fields. It selects fields like Title, First Name, Last Name, Address, and so on.

2. Check that the displayed fields are the ones you want to print and that they're in the order you want them to appear. If a drop-down displays the name of a field, that field's contents will print on the label; if a drop-down says Leave Blank, it means QuickBase is skipping a field from the table. Use the drop-down lists to make adjustments to what will appear on the labels, and then click Next.

    QuickBase displays the labels based on the contents of your table. If the addresses don't look right, click your browser's Back button to return to step 1 of the wizard.

NOTE

When you select Leave Blank to hide a field, don't worry about extra spaces or lines showing up on your labels. QuickBase closes up any white space left by blank fields.

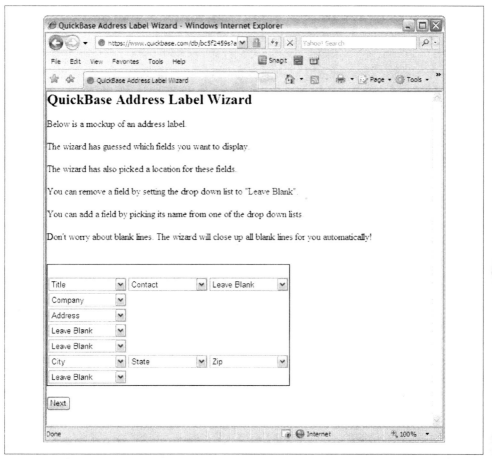

Figure 4-4. Use the QuickBase Address Label Wizard's drop-down lists to select the fields you want to display in the order you want them to appear. To remove a field, choose Leave Blank.

When the labels look good, you're ready to print them. In Internet Explorer, click File→Print to open the Print box. Click the Print button to print the names and addresses on your labels.

To make it easy to get to the Address Label Wizard right from an application, you can create a report that takes you directly to the wizard. Open the application and create a Table report for the table that holds the names and addresses. In Report Builder, follow these steps:

1. In the Columns To Display section, turn on the "Custom columns" radio button.

   The section expands to let you select the columns you want.

2. Select the fields you want to appear on your labels (they can be in any order), such as Contact Name, Company, Street Address, City, State, and Zip. In Report Builder's Additional Options section, turn on the "Custom options" radio button.

The section expands to show you more options.

3. From the Format drop-down list, pick "XML (structured)".

A new box appears, labeled "Associated XSL document".

4. Type or paste the following line into the "Associated XSL document" box: *6mztyxu8?act=dbpage^pagename=addresslabels.xsl*. (Don't include the period at the end.) Click Save.

QuickBase opens the Save Report As dialog box.

5. Give your report a name (like Address Labels) and specify who can see the report, and then click OK.

QuickBase creates the report and adds it to the application's left-hand Reports menu.

Now, when you choose this report from the application's Reports menu, QuickBase opens the Address Label Wizard, so you can easily print mailing labels. Opening the wizard this way saves you a couple of steps: There's no need to sign in again or choose a table. In the wizard, just check that the fields are set up the way you want them, click Next, and print the labels from Internet Explorer.

WARNING

The Address Label Wizard doesn't work for any application that requires tokens.

Creating Report Subscriptions

If you have a report that needs to go out regularly, like a monthly sales report or a weekly project update, you can create a *scheduled report subscription*, which automatically emails a particular report on a periodic basis—you decide whether the report goes out monthly, weekly, or daily.

NOTE

QuickBase limits the number of subscriptions and reminders you can send based on the size of your billing plan. For each table in an application, the daily limit is three times the number of users your billing plan allows, with a hard upper limit of 500. For example, the QuickBase 100+ User Monthly Plan allows up to 100 users. If that's your plan, each table in your application can send up to 300 subscriptions and reminders (combined) per day. If you have a bigger plan that allows more users, though, the daily limit of subscriptions and reminders for each table is 500. What if you go over the limit? QuickBase still emails everyone who's supposed to get a subscription or a reminder, but those emails contain a *link* to the report rather than the report itself. And the application manager gets a notification telling her that the application's subscriptions and reminders exceeded the limit.

Subscribing to reports for yourself

If you're an ordinary user without administrator-level access to an application, you're limited to creating subscriptions only for yourself. That's still a handy way of keeping up to date on what's happening with the applications you regularly use. For example, is Marcia still topping all the other sales reps on cold calling this month?

NOTE
Administrators get much broader sending privileges, as explained in the next section.

Subscribing to a report is a piece of cake:

1. Open the application you're interested in subscribing to. Click Customize→Personal Automated Emails.

   The Personal Automated Emails page opens. If you have any current subscriptions, you'll see them in a table on this page. (If you're in a multi-table application, look in the far-left Table column to see which subscription belongs to which table in your application.)

2. Click Create a New Email.

   The "Choose a new email type to create" box appears. This box has three choices: Email Notification, Subscription, and Reminders ("Stay on Top of Things with Email Notifications" on page 44).

3. Turn on the Subscription radio button. If you're in a multi-table application, choose a table from the Table drop-down list. Click the Create button.

   The Emails: New Subscription page, shown in Figure 4-5, appears.

4. Use the Select Report drop-down menu to choose the report you want. Specify how often you want to receive the report: daily, weekly (you choose which day of the week), or monthly (on the first day of each month).

   "Me" already appears as the choice in the "Deliver to" drop-down menu. In fact, if you don't have administrative privileges, it's your *only* choice.

5. When you're done, click Save.

   QuickBase takes you back to the Personal Automated Emails page, with your new subscription listed. See "Modifying Report Subscriptions" on page 159 for info on how to delete your subscription or put it on hold (if you're going away on vacation, for example).

Sending subscriptions to others

It may sound like something straight out of Publishers Clearing House, but if you're an administrator, then you have the power to send subscriptions to anyone associated with your application—any viewer, team member, or manager—whatever their role.

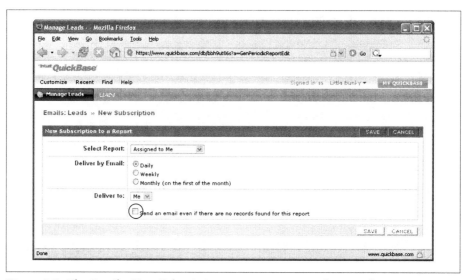

Figure 4-5. The Emails: New Subscription page is your control center for setting up new subscriptions. QuickBase presents a drop-down list of the available reports you can subscribe to. Select the report you want and how often you want to receive it (daily, weekly, or on the first day of each month). Turn on the "Send an email even if there are no records found for this report" checkbox (circled) if you want to get the report—whether there's data in it or not.

So if you want to make sure that everyone on your team has a list of open issues before the next meeting, you can create a report of open issues, and then set up a report subscription and sign your team up to receive that report via email.

If you're an application's administrator, you have some extra options on the Customize menu. Select Customize→Create a new→Email Subscription from the menu bar. If you're in a multi-table application, QuickBase asks you to choose a table. Do that, and then QuickBase takes you to the Emails: New Subscription page, which looks pretty much like the page in Figure 4-4, except that, as an administrator, you have more decisions to make. (Ain't that always the way?) For administrators, the "Deliver to" drop-down menu is loaded with all kinds of choices (not just Me). Click the "Deliver to" drop-down menu to choose from a list of users to subscribe to this report, as shown in Figure 4-6. You can subscribe all users who have access to the application or subscribe users based on their roles. There's also a new section: Mail Options. So if you want to add your own subject line or message, click the plus sign next to Mail Options and type in your text, as shown in Figure 4-7.

NOTE

When you choose to send a subscription from QuickBase, the From address says *notify@quickbase.com*. If you want it to come from you, the From address looks like something along these lines: *charlesatlas@globehoisting.com (via QuickBase) <notify@quickbase.com>*.

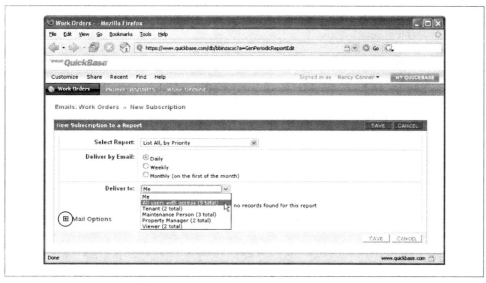

Figure 4-6. This Email Subscription page lets administrators pick and choose report recipients. Choose the lucky people from the drop-down list shown here. To select a From address or create a custom subject line or message, click the plus sign next to Mail Options (circled) and take a look at the next figure.

Modifying Report Subscriptions

Unlike magazine publishers, QuickBase won't make you wait 6 to 8 weeks to change your subscription. You can edit, temporarily hold, or completely cancel any subscription in just a few steps, as explained in the following sections.

Editing a Subscription

If you want to edit your report subscription—perhaps daily emails are cluttering up your inbox and you only need to see the updated report once a week—follow the first two steps for creating a new subscription ("Subscribing to reports for yourself" on page 157): Open the application, and in the menu bar click Customize→Personal Automated Emails to get to the Personal Automated Emails page.

If you're an administrator, select Customize→Tables to get to the Tables page, shown in Figure 4-8. If you're in a multi-table application, select the table you want the left-hand Tables list, and then click the Emails tab.

Whichever route you take, you'll see a list of the automated emails for this application. Find the subscription you want to change and click its name. This opens a page like the one back inFigure 4-5, where you can make whatever changes you want. Click Save when you're done.

Figure 4-7. When you click the plus sign next to Mail Options on the Email Subscription page, QuickBase lets you add some personal touches to the emails that go out. For example, you can select a From address (normally, the email comes from QuickBase, but you can choose to have it come from the application manager). If you want, add a custom subject line, email message, or both, to accompany the emailed report.

Temporarily Disabling a Subscription

When you go on vacation, you don't want newspapers piling up on your doorstep and letters spilling out of your mailbox, so you suspend newspaper delivery and tell the Post Office to hold your mail. In the same way, you can suspend your QuickBase report subscriptions—QuickBase calls it *disabling* your subscription.

Start by going to the Email Notifications, Reminders and Subscriptions page: from any page in the application, click Customize→Personal Automated Emails. (Application administrators click Customize→Tables, choose the table you want if you're in a multi-table application, and click the Emails tab.) Turn on the left-hand checkbox next to the subscription you want to suspend, and then click the Disable Checked button.

Disabled subscriptions remain visible in your subscriptions list, marked Disabled in big, bold, red letters—you can't miss 'em.

When you're back from vacation and done showing off your tan, you can re-enable any subscriptions you've suspended. On the Personal Automated Emails page (for personal subscriptions) or the Emails tab of the Tables page (if you're an administrator), turn on the checkbox next to any and all disabled subscriptions you want to reactivate, and then click Enable Checked. QuickBase restores the subscriptions, and you're back on schedule.

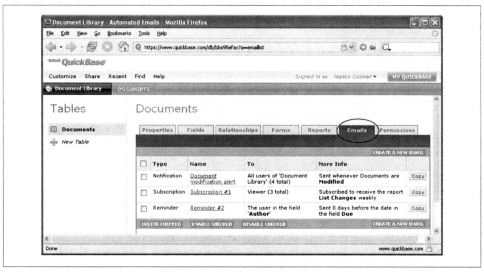

Figure 4-8. The Emails tab (circled) of the Tables page is all about email: It lists all the subscriptions, notifications, and reminders you've created for this application. Use this page as a central hub for managing automatic emails: You can edit, copy, enable/disable, or delete any email on the list. You can even create a new automated email from this page; simply click one of the "Create a New Email" buttons on the right-hand side of the screen.

NOTE

Administrators can disable and enable subscriptions for all subscribers. Users who aren't administrators can do this only for themselves.

Deleting a Subscription

When a subscription has run its course (for example, when your team has successfully completed a project and you've finished popping champagne corks), you won't need regular updates anymore. To delete a subscription, go to your Personal Automated Emails page: From any page in the application, click Customize→Personal Automated Emails. If you're an administrator who's deleting a subscription for a bunch of people, go to the Emails tab of the Tables page by clicking Customize→Tables, making sure you've got the right table (in a multi-table application), then clicking the Emails tab. Turn on the checkbox to the left of the subscription you want to delete, and then click Delete Checked. QuickBase asks you to confirm the deletion; click OK and it's gone forever.

Triggering Change Notification Emails

You can keep everyone on the same page with notifications about the latest data coming into or out of your applications. Whenever someone adds, deletes, or changes a record, QuickBase can send out an email notification of the change to everyone on the application's notification list.

Setting up notification emails is different for application administrators than it is for users who don't have administrative privileges. The next two sections take you through both procedures.

Signing Up for Emails for Yourself

Ever have someone create a new work order for you…and then forget to tell you about it? Or maybe you're a manager who wants to keep an eye on purchase orders as they're coming in (do those clowns in Marketing *really* need 5,000 red rubber noses?). If you want to be the first to know when someone adds, changes, or deletes a record, follow these steps:

1. Open the application you want and then click Customize→Personal Automated Emails.

   The familiar Personal Automated Emails page appears. If you currently have any email notifications set up for that application, you see them on this page.

2. Click Create a New Email.

   The "Choose a new email type to create" box appears.

3. Turn on the Email Notification radio button. If you see a Table drop-down list (which means you're in a multi-table application), then select the table you want. Click Create.

   The Emails: New Notification page, shown in Figure 4-9, opens.

4. You've got a bunch of choices to make here:

   • If you want to give this notification a name (making it easy to find later on), type that name into the Notification Name text box. It's always a good idea to give a notification a descriptive name; two months from now, you don't want to be looking thought a long list of emails trying to remember whether the notification you want to delete is the one named Notification #15 (or Notification #16 or Notification #17…).

   • The Notify When drop-down menu lets you specify what kind of change you're interested in: when someone adds, modifies, or deletes a record—or any combination of those changes. So you can get a notification only when someone modifies a record; when someone adds a new record or modifies an existing one; when someone changes or deletes a record; when any addition, change, or deletion happens; and so on.

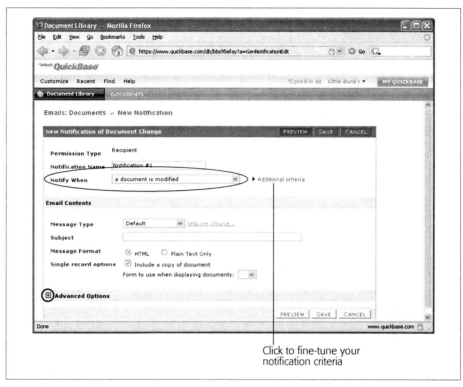

Click to fine-tune your
notification criteria

*Figure 4-9. The Notify When drop-down list (circled) lets you select whether you want
notification when a record is added, modified, or deleted (or any combination of those actions).
You can fine-tune your notification criteria by specifying that certain fields or conditions will
trigger a notification email: Click the "Additional criteria" link to do so. Click the plus sign
(circled) next to Advanced Options if you want notification only of either single record changes
or batch record changes (as in an import), or to change the From address on your notification
emails (usually email comes from notify@quickbase.com, but you can also have it sent from the
application manager's address.)*

- Click the "Additional criteria" link to narrow your notification criteria, so you
  receive only the emails you need to see. You can set a specific field or fields to
  trigger a notification (so you get an email, for example, when someone uploads
  a new version of a document but not when someone tweaks its title) or a certain
  kind of change, such as when a task becomes three days overdue or its priority
  changes to High.

- The Message Type drop-down menu gives you two choices about the body of
  the notification email: You can receive a QuickBase-authored default message
  or a custom email message that you write. (Since you're just sending notifications to yourself, something like this always sounds good: *Hi, Gorgeous! Looking
  good today. Oh, by the way, there's been a change in a Project Issues record.*)

- The Subject text box is where you type the subject line you want for notification emails. Something like *New sales lead added* or *Document edited* will clue you in to the kind of change as soon as a notification hits your inbox.

- If you like pictures in your email, make sure the HTML radio button is turned on. If you're more the plain-vanilla type—no pictures, no graphics, no buttons, just the (text-based) facts, ma'am—turn on the Plain Text Only radio button.

- If you want a copy of the new or changed record included in the email, turn on the "Include a copy of record" checkbox (the name of the checkbox reflects the kind of record you're working with in this particular application: document, issue, lead, timecard, and so on).

- If you've created your own custom forms—for example, you want records to show different fields to users who are assigned different roles—you can select the custom form you want from the "Form to use when displaying documents" drop-down menu.

- You can also fine-tune your notifications using the Advanced Options. You've got two choices under Advanced Options. First, you can choose to trigger notifications only for one-at-a-time record changes or for all-at-once multiple changes (as in an import). Second, you can receive your notifications with a QuickBase From address (emails will arrive from *notify@quickbase.com*) or, if seeing the boss's name makes you sit up and pay attention, you can receive notifications with the application administrator's email address in the From line. If you choose that option, the From address of your notifications will look something like this: *thebigboss@yourcompany.com (via QuickBase) <notify@quickbase.com>*

5. When you've made your selections, click Preview if you want to see what your notification email will look like. When everything looks good, click Save.

The Email Notification Preview page opens, displaying your new notification. Now, whenever someone adds, changes, or deletes a record (depending on your selections), QuickBase shoots you an email that tells you about the record and contains a link to that record in QuickBase.

Sending Notification Emails to Others

If you're an application's administrator, you've got a few more options when you're setting up email notifications. These options relate to *who* can receive the notification emails: Depending on how you set this up, QuickBase will notify you alone, a specific user or group of users, or anyone in the world with an email address.

To set up email notification as an administrator, choose Customize→Create a new→Email Notification. If you're in a multi-table application, pick the table you want to create the notification for. The Emails: New Notification page for administrators looks a little different than it does for other users, as you can see in Figure 4-10.

Fill out the fields in the way you want. There are a couple of administrator-only options to consider:

- **Permission Type.** You can set Permission Type to Recipient, which means that QuickBase sends notification emails only to QuickBase users who have access to this application, or to Open, which means that QuickBase sends notification emails to the email addresses you specify—whether or not the people with those addresses are QuickBase users. Which should you choose? The box in "Choosing a Permission Type" on page 167 gives some tips for making your decision.
- **Notify Whom.** QuickBase lets you fine-tune your list of notification recipients. If you set Permission Type to Open, Notify Whom presents a text box—just type in the email addresses of whomever you want to get notification emails (you can separate addresses with commas or by hitting Enter). If you set Permission Type to Recipient, QuickBase shows you a drop-down list next to Notify Whom that includes the following options:
  —**Yourself.**
  —**All users with access to this application.**
  —**A specific list of users.** When you choose this option, QuickBase lets you browse users or type in the email addresses, screen names, or group names of a specific set of users.
  —**Yourself when you are listed in a specific field.** For example, you can send yourself a notification when your name appears in the Requested By or Record Owner field.

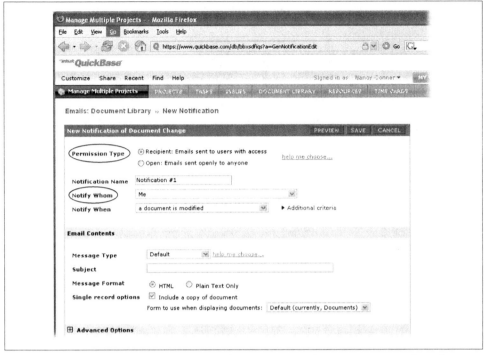

Figure 4-10. Administrators have a couple of extra options when setting up email notifications. Permission Type (circled) lets you choose whether QuickBase sends notification emails to QuickBase users who have access to this application, or to anyone at all. (For advice on making the choice, see the box in "Turning Text into a Link" on page 175.) The Notify Whom drop-down menu (also circled) is where you configure more precisely who gets the notification emails: It might be you alone, all users with access to the application, or a select group. When you choose the Open permission type, the Notify Whom drop-down menu changes to a text box; type in the email addresses you want QuickBase to notify.

> — **The user whose name is listed in a specific field.** If you want to make sure that Joe Green knows when you've assigned him a new work order, for example, you can choose to send a notification to the user whose name appears in the Assigned To field.

After you've filled out all the information, click Preview to take a peek at how the email notification will look. When everything looks good, click Save.

When you copy an application ("When Copying Won't Work" on page 252), you can also copy that application's list of users. When you do this, however, QuickBase disables the email notifications in the copy. If you want to enable them, navigate to the Emails tab of the Tables page (Customize→Tables, choose a table if you're in a multi-table application, and then click the Emails tab), turn on the checkbox next to any notifications you want QuickBase to send, and then click the Enable Checked button.

Choosing a Permission Type

What's the difference between the Recipient and Open permission types? How do I know which one to choose?

When you're an administrator setting up email notifications for an application, you have to decide whether to send notifications only to registered QuickBase users who have access to this application or to anyone with an email address, whether they're a QuickBase user or not.

The Recipient permission type is more secure, because the information that QuickBase sends in the notification email depends on the recipient's role. In other words, Quick-Base won't send sensitive information to a recipient whose role doesn't allow him or her to see that information. (You can set a role's permissions so that people assigned to that role can view or modify only the records their own group creates—so, for example, the Northwest sales staff can't tinker with the records belonging to the Southeast sales staff, or vice versa.) And if multi-record changes, like Search & Replace or an import, trigger this kind of notification, QuickBase won't include the actual records in the email—just a link to the affected records. So users viewing the changed records will see the same report they always see, according to the permissions set for their role. When you use the Recipient permission type, individual users' roles determine what they see.

If the Recipient permission type is more *secure,* the Open permission type is more *flexible.* You can send a notification of a record change to anyone who has an email address, even if they're not a registered QuickBase user. So if you need to share data with someone outside your organization, such as a consultant or a vendor, you can do so without actually inviting them to join an application. With Open permission, the tricky part is making sure that you don't send someone data you don't want them to see. Unlike Recipient permission, where QuickBase constructs the email according to the recipient's role, QuickBase can't check the permission levels of someone who isn't even registered with the site. So it's up to you to make sure that sensitive information doesn't go out to the wrong people.

There are two ways you can do this:

- Create a custom form containing only those fields you don't mind sharing with the world. Use that form as the basis for your Open permission notifications.

- Create a custom message for your notification email. In a custom message, you can specify which fields to include in the email. Include only those fields you want outside people to see, and your notifications won't give away anything you don't want them to.

TIP

When you create an Open notification, you can send a notification to email addresses that appear in your data and are stored in an Email Address field. Here's how: When you're creating the notification, click the Notify Whom drop-down menu and then select "The email addresses listed in the field: Email." Notifications will go to all email addresses listed in the email field of the different records in the application.

Editing, Disabling, and Deleting Email Notifications

After you've created an email notification, you can tinker with it in the following ways:

- **Edit.** If you want to change anything about a notification, you can—the kind of change that triggers a notification, the fields of interest, the list of recipients, whatever. To edit a personal change notification (which you created just for yourself), get to the Personal Automated Emails page: Open the application and click Customize→Personal Automated Emails. If you're an administrator and you're going to edit a notification you created for others, open the application, click Customize→Tables, select the table you want from the left-hand list (for multi-table applications), and then click the Emails tab. From there, the steps are the same whether you're editing a personal or administrator-created notification: Click the name of the notification you want to change, make your changes, click Save, and you're done.

- **Disable.** To put notifications on hold while you're away from the office, open the application and then select Customize→Personal Automated Emails. This lands you on the Personal Automated Emails page. (Administrators see the notifications they've created by clicking Customize→Tables, making sure they've got the right table, and then clicking the Emails tab.) Either way, you see a table listing all your notifications for this application. The left-hand column of that table holds checkboxes; turn on the checkbox for any notification you want to disable. Click Disable Checked, and QuickBase will quit sending you those notifications until you enable them again.

- **Enable.** When you're ready to start getting notifications again, follow the steps for disabling a notification. All disabled notifications have Disabled next to their name. To re-enable a notification, turn on the left-hand checkbox and then click Enable Checked. Then watch your inbox for those notifications to start flying back in.

- **Delete.** The process for deleting a notification is almost identical to the process for disabling one. After you've turned on the checkbox of the notification you want to delete, though, click Delete Checked. To make sure you didn't click the wrong button, QuickBase asks for confirmation that you really, really want to delete this notification. Click OK to confirm, and wave bye-bye to that notification.

TIP

To save time, you might want to set up a notification that's similar to one that already exists—for example, an administrator might want to notify one set of people when a new purchase request comes in and another set of people when it's approved. It's easy to copy an existing notification. If it's a personal notification for your eyes only, navigate to the Personal Automated Emails page (Customize→Personal Automated Emails). If you're an administrator, choose Customize→Tables and then click the Emails tab. Whichever route you take, you'll see a table of notifications in the application. Find the notification you want, and then click its Copy button in the far-right column. QuickBase creates an exact copy of the notification. If you've copied the New Purchase Order notification, for example, the copy's name will be (imaginatively) "Copy of New Purchase Order." You can then edit (and rename) the copied notification however you'd like.

Sending Reminders

When it's up to you to make sure that everyone on your team meets their deadlines, sending a reminder can be an effective way to keep people on task. You can set Quick-Base up to send automatic reminders by email before a task is due. If you habitually need to chase someone down for overdue tasks, you can also send an automatic reminder *after* the task's due date.

Creating Reminders

To have QuickBase give someone an automatic nudge, follow these steps:

NOTE

Only application administrators can create email reminders. So if you're a user without administrative privileges, feel free to skip this section. If you're a user who *wants* administrative privileges, contact the application's manager.

---

1. Open the application you want to create the reminder for. Select Customize→Create a new→Email Reminder (choose a table if you're in a multi-table application). Or you can take the scenic route: Customize→Personal Automated Emails→Create a New Email→Reminders→Create. (If you don't have permission to create reminders, here's where you find out: QuickBase tells you so and offers you a chance to email the application's manager to request that permission.)

Whether you took the long way or the short way, QuickBase lands you on the Emails: New Reminder page, shown in Figure 4-11.

2. **Fill in the appropriate info. When you're done, click Preview to see what the reminder will look like; click Save to create the reminder.** Here are the different fields you can set for a reminder:

   - In the Remind Whom drop-down menu, choose the person or people you want to notify. For example, for an upcoming work order, you'd want to remind the person named in the Assigned To field. Or you might want to send a reminder to the last person who modified a record.

   - The Remind When field is where you specify when you want the reminder sent. Pick the number of days and whether you want the reminder to go out before or after the date field you choose, which might be, for example, the date a task is scheduled or the date the record was created or modified. You can send out a reminder to update a record one week after the record was created, for example, or you can send out a reminder that a task is due five days before the scheduled deadline.

   - Under Additional Criteria, you can tweak when a reminder goes out. This gives you a lot of control so that you're not inundating your people with more reminders than they can handle. For example, you might choose to send out reminders only for those tasks assigned a Priority of High. The options QuickBase provides here relate to the fields in the particular application you've chosen.

   - If you want, customize the reminder's subject line and contents.

   QuickBase saves your reminder and sends out an email at the time you specified.

Editing, Disabling, and Deleting Reminders

As with report subscriptions and email notifications, you can edit, suspend, or delete reminders. To do so, first get to the Emails tab of the Tables page: Open the application that contains the reminder and select Customize→Tables (if you're in a multi-table application, choose the table you want from left-hand list), and then click Emails. The Emails tab shows a table containing all the reminders, subscriptions, and notifications for this table. Look in the Type column of the Emails table for the Reminders you've created. When you find the one you want, you can perform any of the following actions:

- **Edit.** To edit a reminder, find the reminder you want to modify and click its name. This opens the Reminder Email page (shown back in Figure 4-11). Make whatever changes you want, and then click Save when you're finished.

- **Copy.** When you need a new reminder that's similar to an existing one, click the reminder's far-right Copy button. QuickBase copies the reminder, with "Copy of" in front of the name. You can then edit the copy (see above) to make whatever changes you'd like the new reminder to have.

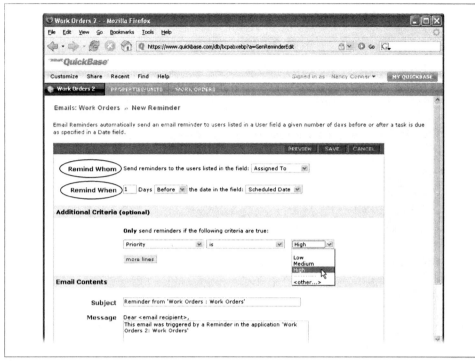

Figure 4-11. Who, what, and when: Reminders let you notify the right people about what's going on exactly when they need to know. In the top section of the Reminder Email page, select who gets the reminder and when you want them to get it. In this example, whoever's assigned a work order will receiver a reminder of their work orders on the day before they're scheduled to do the job. If you want, you can be selective about the reminders you send, such as sending a reminder only about high-priority work orders. So if you want a reminder sent only when certain conditions apply, choose the field and its contents that will trigger the reminder. You can also customize the subject header and email message to suit your needs.

- **Disable.** If someone's on vacation, they probably don't need reminders of what's going on back at the office. To suspend reminders while someone's away from their job, go to the Reminders page. Find the left-hand checkbox for the reminder you want to put on hold. Turn on the checkbox, and then click Disable Checked. QuickBase won't send that reminder unless you re-enable it.

- **Enable.** To get a disabled reminder going again, go to the Reminders page and find the reminder you want. (All disabled reminders say Disabled in big red letters after their name.) Turn on the left-hand checkbox and click Enable Checked. The reminder's good to go.

- **Delete.** If the person you've been reminding no longer needs an occasional nudge from QuickBase, you can delete a reminder. It's just like disabling: Go to the Reminders page and turn on the checkbox for the reminder you want to delete. Click Delete Checked, and then click OK to confirm.

Customizing Your QuickBase Emails

QuickBase takes a load off your mind by remembering to send out important notification emails. But what if those emails, with their terse wording and generic look, are just so not you? You can add interest to the emails QuickBase sends on your behalf by customizing your notification emails' text, look, or both.

Customizing the Text of Your Notification Emails

You don't have to go with QuickBase's generic (read: *boring*) message for email notifications. You can create a custom message that calls attention to a particular field within the changed record or that offers instructions or commentary to people who receive the notification.

Start by choosing "Custom message" in the Message Type drop-down menu shown in Figure 4-12. As soon as you make that choice, the text box shown in Figure 4-12 appears. When you click in either the Subject or the Custom Message text box, the Fields & Markers menu appears. This menu is where you'll *embed* various fields into the body of your email. That means that the contents of the embedded field, such as a phone number or modification date, appear in the body of the email. (The contents of the Fields & Markers menu are specific to the application you're working with. So a purchase request application has fields like PO Number and Priority; a time-tracking application has fields like Billing Rate or Total Time for Week; a property management application has Unit Number, and so on.)

If all this feels a bit theoretical, here's an example to help you understand just how handy this customization tool can be: Say you need to keep your people aware when a contact's name changes. You don't just want to tell them there's a new contact—you want to supply the contact's actual name. So if the lead at Weasel Systems, Philip Collier, has left the business to become a haberdashery consultant (Phil always did wear nice hats), you want QuickBase to notify people ASAP that Phil is gone and that Ernestine Woolgar has replaced him. To trigger an email notification like that, type *The lead has changed from [old.FirstName] [old.LastName] to [FirstName] [LastName]* into the Custom Message text box. From now on, QuickBase emails name changes to your team as soon as someone modifies the first or last name field in a record in that application. In the case of the Weasel Systems example, the email would read *The lead has changed from Philip Collier to Ernestine Woolgar.*

To make sure that the previous notification goes out only in the case of a name change, click the "Additional criteria" link next to the Notify When drop-down menu (see Figure 4-11), turn on "When specific fields change," and then turn on the First Name and Last Name checkboxes. Otherwise, recipients will get the email when someone makes *any* kind of change to the record.

When you tell QuickBase to send out a notification for each record change (as in the example), QuickBase sends out an email every time someone adds, modifies, or deletes

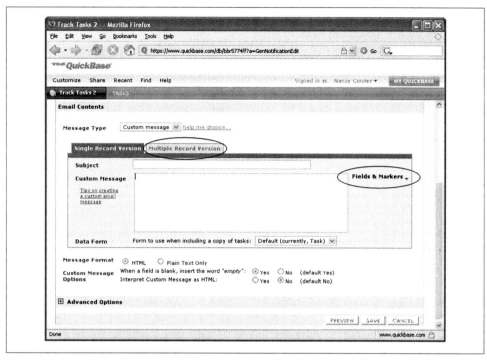

Figure 4-12. When you choose "Custom message" from the Message Type drop-down menu, and then click inside the Subject or Custom Message text box, the Fields & Markers drop-down menu (circled) appears. Click Fields & Markers to insert codes into your custom email that will show the recipient what's changed in the record. For custom messages in the case of multi-record changes (like an import), click the Multiple Record Version tab (also circled) for a slightly different set of options—the main difference, of course, is that you want to send just one email for the entire import, not one email for each record that changed as the result of an import (which could change dozens or hundreds of records).

a record (depending on how you've set up the notification). What if someone adds or changes a whole bunch of records at once, by importing a client list, for example? If there are 100 names on the list, you don't want to flood your team's inboxes with 100 separate emails.

For this kind of multi-record change, click the Multiple Record Version tab of the Custom Message box, to send one email with a notification of a whole bunch of record changes. When you click this tab and then click in either the Subject or the Custom Message text box, QuickBase displays a Markers drop-down menu. Click Markers to see what kinds of markers are available for your custom email. For example, you can have your email display the name of the application with all the changes and a link to the table that's changed, the table itself, or a summary of the changes. When you make a choice from the Markers drop-down menu, the marker magically appears in the text box, so you don't have to remember the names of all the different markers.

When QuickBase sends a notification about multiple changes, the email consists of a *heading* (which appears only once at the beginning of the email) and a *body* (which contains each individual record change). You can embed some markers in the heading only, some in the body only, and some in either—keep reading to find out which values are which.

There's one marker that can go only in the heading section of your notification email: *%SummaryReport%* . This marker presents a summary report of all the records that have changed. So if someone has added 100 new names to the Sales Leads application, this marker sends a summary table, giving an overview of the new leads.

Here's a list of what you can embed in the body (only) of an email, followed by the marker you use to embed it (some of these markers appear in the handy Fields & Markers menu mentioned earlier):

- **Field value.** To embed a field value, type the name of the field inside square brackets. So if the field value is *price,* you'd type *[price]* (or select [price] from the Fields & Markers drop-down menu). QuickBase inserts the contents of that field into the notification email.

- **What a field's value used to be.** When you want to include what the field used to hold—you might want to show, for example, a change in price—type *old* and a period, then the name of the field, inside square brackets. So to show the old price (a good idea if you're running a sale), you'd type *[old.price]*.

- **The changed record.** To include the whole record that's changed, type this: *%RecData%*.

- **A link to the changed record.** If you want to insert a link to the record that's changed, type *%RecLink%*.

- **The changed record's label.** In QuickBase, a record's *label* has nothing to do with pop stars or music companies; instead, it's the value of its key field. To include this info in your email, type *%RecLabel%*.

- **The changed record's ID.** QuickBase assigns each record its very own, built-in identification number. The marker to include this ID in your email is *%RecID%*.

You can embed the following info in either the body or the heading of an email:

- **The name of the application that contains the changed record.** This one's particularly useful when you have a bunch of applications to keep track of. Put the application's name right in the email to make sure everyone's straight about what changed where. Type *%AppName%*.

- **A link to the application.** To include a link to the application that holds the changed record, use this marker: *%AppLink%*.

- **The name of the table that holds the changed record.** This can be good information to share when the changed record is part of a multi-table application. Type *%dbname%*.

- **The table's ID.** Just like individual records, tables have ID numbers. To include the ID in notification emails, type *%dbid%*.

Customizing the Look of Your Notification Emails

When it comes to sending out up-to-the-moment information, you couldn't ask for a better personal assistant than QuickBase. But, truth be told, the emails themselves can look a bit dull. How about snazzing up the emails QuickBase sends on your behalf, maybe with the corporate logo, the slogan of the moment, or a link to your company's Web page? Customizing QuickBase's emails is a particularly good idea if QuickBase sends emails to your customers or clients, making it clear that the emails come from your organization.

To put your personal stamp on the notification emails QuickBase sends from your application, start by opening the application. Click Customize→Application to get to the page shown in Figure 4-13. Make sure the Settings tab is selected, and then click Branding in the left-hand menu. Turn on the Customize Emails checkbox.

Type the custom text you want your emails to display in the Upper Left Element text box. What you type in here appears in the top-left part of emails QuickBase sends from this application. You can also link to an image file (see "Using an Image as a Hyperlink") or to a Web site (see the box "Turning Text into a Link" that follows).

NOTE

Don't see Application on the Customize menu? That means you don't have permission to make application-wide changes. If you think you should have such permission, talk to the application's administrator: to find the administrator's name, go to your My QuickBase page and look at the application in Details format. The name you want is in the Manager column.

> **GEM IN THE ROUGH**
>
> ## Turning Text into a Link
>
> If you want to put a link to a Web site into the email messages QuickBase sends, don't just type the address as you'd type it into your Web browser. If you do, it just appears as text, not as a link. Instead, type it like this: *<a href="http://www.yourcompany.com/">Visit Our Site</a>*, replacing *yourcompany.com* with your company's actual Web address and the words *Visit Our Site* with whatever text you want to display as a link.
>
> Also, to ensure that the link appears in the email, make sure that the email notification you've created uses HTML as its format. To check, go to Customize→Email and click

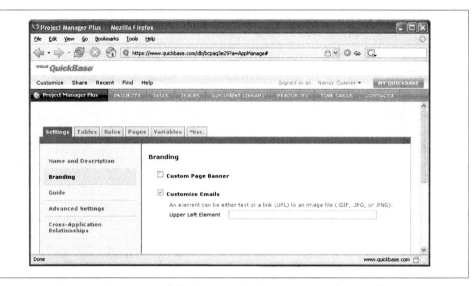

Figure 4-13. The Branding section of the Settings tab (Customize→Application) lets you customize the emails QuickBase sends on your behalf, giving emails a look and feel that expresses your corporate identity. The Upper Left Element text box lets you add text or an image to the upper-left corner of all the emails QuickBase sends from this application.

the name of the notification you want. In the Message Format section, make sure that the HTML radio button is turned on.

Using vCard and iCalendar with QuickBase

You've probably wished from time to time that there was an easy way to get contact info and appointment details out of QuickBase records and into an email, address book, or calendar program. In the past, your options were either copying and pasting, or typing until your fingertips got sore. Now, QuickBase works with vCard and iCalendar, two industry-standard formats that let you exchange data with other programs: vCard is for exchanging contact information (think of it as an electronic business card), and iCalendar works with calendar data, letting users easily download appointments, meeting invitations, and task information. Once you've set up a vCard or iCalendar field in your application, users can download, store, or send contact and calendar information as easily as clicking a button.

Here's how vCard and iCalendar work: When an application has a vCard field (for contact info) or an iCalendar field (for tasks and appointment info), QuickBase displays an icon with the records in that application, as shown in Figure 4-14. A user who sees that icon can click it to download the fields you've associated with the vCard or the iCalendar field. For example, Sharon Choe might click the vCard icon to download information about a sales lead—name, phone number, email (whatever fields you've

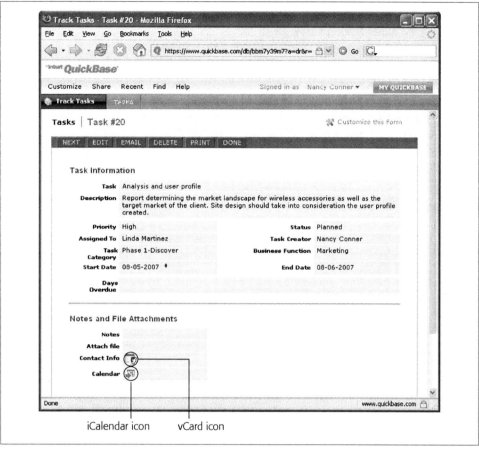

iCalendar icon   vCard icon

Figure 4-14. When users view a record, they can easily download certain information stored with that record by clicking the vCard or iCalendar icon (circled). vCard stores contact information; iCalendar holds time-related information.

chosen). Once she's downloaded the info, Sharon can open it in Outlook (and many other email programs) and then email or store it. iCalendar works the same way, except it bundles information that you might find on a calendar: start date, end date, appointment time, and so on.

Sound good? Here's how to add vCard and iCalendar fields to an application:

1. Open the application to which you want to add a vCard or iCalendar field. If you're adding vCard, choose a table that holds contact information, like Sales Leads or Customers. If you're adding iCalendar, choose a table that holds time-related records, like Tasks or Projects. Then select Customize→Create a New→Field. (Or, you can click your way to the Fields tab of the Tables page: Customize→Tables→Fields, and then click the upper-right Create New Fields button; for more on using the Tables page to add fields, see "Add a field" on page 219.)

The Add Fields page opens.

2. Type in a name for your new field. For vCard, you might name the field *Contact Info*; for iCalendar, something like *Calendar* works well. From the Type drop-down menu to the right of the name, choose either vCard or iCalendar as the field type. Click Add Fields.

    QuickBase creates the new field and asks whether you'd like to add it to any custom forms in the application.

3. Choose either Yes or "Not right now." You can always add the field to custom forms later, but it's a good idea to do it now, to give your users wide access to this feature.

    QuickBase returns you to the Fields tab of the Tables page, where your new field appears in the list of fields with a black arrow pointing to it. But you're not done yet, as QuickBase reminds you. In the Fields table's Info column, your new field shows Incomplete Settings, marked in red to get your attention. What QuickBase is telling you is that you need to let the vCard or iCalendar field know which fields to bundle up in its info packet for users to download.

4. To complete the settings for your vCard or iCalendar field, click its name.

    The Field Properties page opens. On this page, adjust the properties—like the name of the field or how it displays its contents—of whatever field you choose. The Field Properties page relates to the specific field you chose. vCard and iCalendar fields have a special section all their own, as Figure 4-15 shows.

5. In the vCard Options or iCalendar Options section, select the fields you want your vCard or iCalendar field to hold.

    Because these two field types hold different information, there are some differences in what you'll select here:

    - **vCard.** For a vCard field, you must specify a Name field—contact info at its most basic—and in some cases an email field. You can also include job title, business and cell phone numbers, fax number, address, notes, and company.

    - **iCalendar.** For an iCalendar field, you need to select a Subject field (the field whose contents will serve as the subject for the iCalendar event, like Task), Starting Time and End Time fields, and an Organizer field (a User field, like Task Creator, that indicates who's setting up the meeting or event). The Location and Description fields are optional.

NOTE

The Starting Time and End Time fields must be of the field type Date/Time, Date, or Work Date for iCalendar to work with them. (If you use a Date or a Work Date field here, their values show up in Outlook as all-day events, because these fields have no time of day info.) Time of Day fields won't cut it here, because iCalendar needs to know the date—not just the time—of the scheduled event.

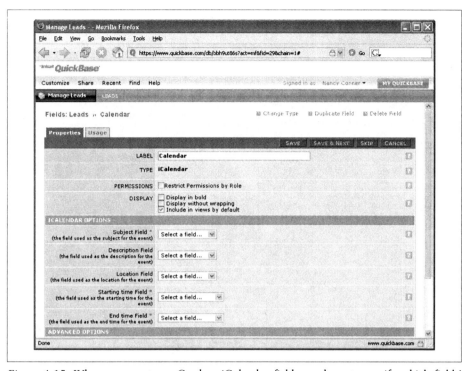

Figure 4-15. When you create a vCard or iCalendar field, you have to specify which fields' information the new field will hold. This example is for an iCalendar field. Fields marked with an asterisk are necessary for iCalendar to work; other fields are optional.

6. When you've chosen your fields, click Save.

   QuickBase saves your settings and returns you to the Tables page.

Now, when someone opens a record in your application, they'll see the vCard or iCalendar icon (as you saw back in Figure 4-14). When they click the icon, they download the information in the vCard or iCalendar field (which contains the fields you just selected) for that record. They can store it on their computer or open it with a program like Outlook—from there, they can store contact info in their address book or add meeting details to a Calendar program.

CHAPTER 5

Planning Your QuickBase Solution

QuickBase is flexible enough to match the way you work. After all, you don't want to change the way you do things to fit some programmer's idea of how to organize your data. But that also means that, in order to get the most out of QuickBase, you need to have a clear picture of what you're trying to accomplish.

So before you jump in and start creating tables and applications, take some time to define the problem you want QuickBase's help with: Analyze your organization's *workflow* (the steps you and your colleagues follow while doing your collective job), decide what kinds of information you need to track, and determine who needs to know what to keep things running smoothly. Defining and refining your problem now saves time down the road.

Defining the Problem

If you don't understand a problem, you can't solve it. So start by defining the problem you want to solve. Try writing it down as a broad statement—something like, "Having too many different versions of the budget is driving everyone nuts!" or "Sales reps in the field don't have access to the most recent promotions," or "Client requests keep getting lost; clients getting angry." Maybe your whole team's drowning in too much information and you want a better way to distribute information efficiently. Whatever the problem, you can solve it only if you identify the specifics.

Clarifying Your Problem

To clarify your problem, it helps to ask yourself questions like the ones below. As an example, imagine you're a human resources (HR) manager for a big company and you need to track mountains of hiring requests and candidate résumés. Here are the kinds of questions you may start asking:

- **What's the problem?** It's hard to coordinate the hiring needs of different offices around the country. Documents, like interview notes and résumés, get misplaced or attached to the wrong file. Promising candidates with specialized skills sometimes get overlooked and then are snatched up by another company. So my department's problem is organizing and coordinating information that's stored in a number of different locations.

- **Is it my problem or someone else's? If it's a shared problem, what part of it is mine?** Because I'm the HR manager, it's my problem. But *my* problem can also create problems for other hiring managers throughout the company. Solving this problem can save time for my fellow managers and maybe even result in better hiring decisions.

- **Is it a new problem or an old one? If it's an old problem, how have we tried to solve it? What's wrong with the old solution?** Recent, fast growth has made this a new problem. Old methods for tracking applicants no longer work because the company now has offices across the nation.

- **What do I want to accomplish in solving the problem?** I want to match up good candidates with job openings as quickly and efficiently as possible. I want to make it easy to find information about candidates—for instance, searching a candidate's résumé for specific information (like level of education) or filtering candidates by specific criteria (like years of experience). I want to keep all our regional offices informed and coordinated. I also want to be able to share appropriate information easily. For example, candidates should be able to chart the progress of their application, hiring managers should be able to read all the details about a candidate, and clerical staff should be able to easily update everything.

- **How will I know that the problem has been solved? In other words, what conditions must the solution satisfy?** When a hiring requisition's approved, managers will automatically get a list of prioritized, qualified candidates. All data and documents related to the hiring process will be easy to find in a central, accessible location. Separate offices will all have access to the same candidate pool.

Again, putting it all in writing before you start to work in QuickBase is a big help. And it doesn't have to look like a list of questions and answers. You could get a whole task force to brainstorm on a whiteboard, use an email list to gather ideas, or scribble away in a dimly lit café with a pencil stump if that's more your style. You can even use mind-mapping software (these are programs that help you capture and organize bursts of related ideas; search Google for a list of popular options). The point is to think through your problem thoroughly and have all your thoughts, ideas, and concerns in one place.

The whole point of defining your problem is to clarify your *objectives*—the end results you want your solution to accomplish.

Identifying Your Objectives

Exploring a problem helps you clarify your objectives. For example, the HR manager from the previous example might come up with this list of objectives:

- Centralize information so it's easy to find.

- Coordinate offices around the country.
- Create different ways of viewing positions and candidates, based on the viewer's role.
- Automate such tasks as sending managers a list of qualified candidates when a position is approved.

To show you how to evaluate the challenges that your team faces, the rest of this chapter walks you through two different kinds of problems faced by two different kinds of companies.

Exploring Your Workflow

To see what problems QuickBase can help you solve, try breaking down your organization's workflow into the steps that represent a typical day of doing business. When you distill a large or complex process into a series of steps, you can identify bottlenecks to get rid of, events to automate, and information to record. QuickBase can track every step of the process. It can even let the various players know when it's their turn to step up and do their thing to move the work along.

A Typical Day in the Life of a Task

To get a sense of your organization's workflow, think about a typical workday. Take a look at what sort of information comes in, who receives it, who gets it next, and what they do with it. Figure out all the steps that lead to the final outcome.

Example 1: Distribution company

Say you work for a distribution company that specializes in novelties, from squirting lapel flowers and dribble glasses to rubber chickens and whoopee cushions. When a new joke shop places a big order, a cascade of events follows from the time the order comes in to the time your delivery driver unloads the boxes.

A customer calls in and places an order with a customer service rep (CSR). The CSR passes the order on to Madge, fulfillment specialist extraordinaire, who pulls items from their shelves: a case of exploding cigars, a couple dozen bald head wigs in assorted skin tones, some of that new super-realistic fake vomit. Madge puts the items in boxes, along with a packing slip. When the order's all packed, Madge tells Ron, the dispatcher, that the order's ready to go. Ron assigns the order to a driver, and the driver loads the boxes into his truck and delivers them.

Figure 5-1 sketches out this workflow: An order passes through the hands of a CSR, a fulfillment specialist, a dispatcher, and a driver, who delivers everything to the customer. Each person in the chain has to do his or her job before the process can continue, and so each person needs notification before taking that next step.

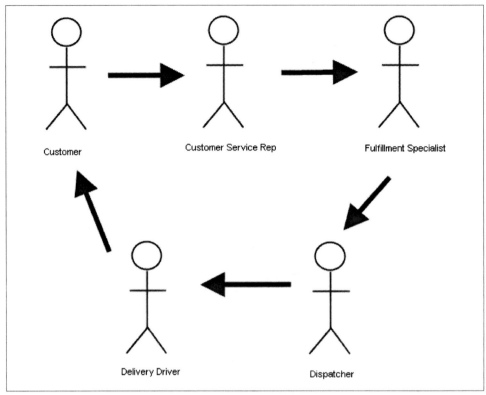

Figure 5-1. When an order comes in to a distribution company, it travels through a clear chain of steps. A series of people each do a specific job, and then pass the order on to the next person in the chain. Start with a simple workflow; you can always add extra steps and alternative paths later on. Here, for example, customers may place an order over the Internet rather than talking to a sales rep, but these variations don't change the flow once an order enters the system.

TIP

When you lay out your own workflow, you can sketch it out on paper (stick figures optional), or use a computer program like Microsoft Visio or the open-source JBoss jBPM program (www.jboss.com (*http://www.jboss.com*)).

Example 2: IT department

This time, imagine that you work in the IT department of a large corporation. Fellow employees who use the software you develop call you to report software bugs. When a new bug comes in, you enter it into a tracking system and assign it to one of the developers (Lauren, say), who'll investigate and fix the problem. After Lauren has fixed the bug, Simon from Quality Assurance tests the fix to make sure everything's working as it should. If the fix doesn't work, then Simon sends it back to Lauren with a description of the problem. Lauren tries again and sends it back to Simon for more testing.

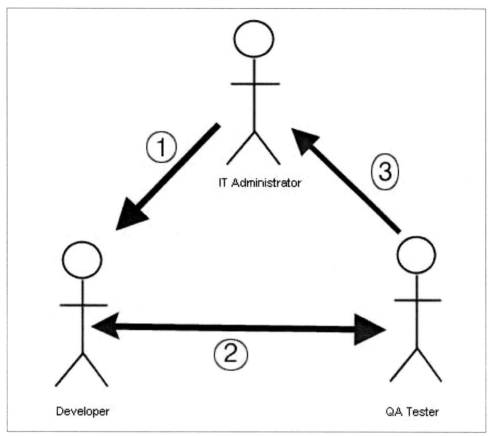

Figure 5-2. A workflow doesn't always move sequentially from person #1 to person #2 to person #3; sometimes it branches. This workflow shows how the administrator assigns a bug to the developer (1), who then passes the bug fix back and forth with the QA tester until everything's working (2). Finally, the QA tester reports back to the administrator (3).

When Simon gives the fix a green light, you can let the original caller know the bug's been fixed.

Again, there's a clear workflow here, as Figure 5-2 illustrates: You receive the bug and assign it to a developer (who fixes the problem) and a tester (who makes sure the fix works). The developer can't fix a bug until you tell her about it, and the tester can't test it until he gets the fix from the developer.

NOTE

Chapter 6 has other examples of business processes and problems, and shows you how to use QuickBase's prebuilt applications to streamline and automate workflow.

Tracking Information

Of course there's more to workflow than getting a package to a customer or tracking software fixes. Sometimes you need to track the status of different parts of your workflow. For example, when an order or job's status changes, a problem comes up, or a deadline passes, you've got a new piece of information to deal with. QuickBase can capture and track all the information along your entire workflow (as well as for each individual player). So, first take a look at what information you need to track, and then break that information down by job role.

What Information Do You Need to Track?

Once you have a sense of the workflow, you can identify the information that comes into play (and changes) at each stage of the process. Think about the kinds of information that you need to track: things you already track routinely, things you wish *somebody* would keep track of, and information that lands between those two extremes.

Example 1: Distribution company

The novelty distribution company has a lot of information to track. For example:

- What's the customer's account status?
- Are any special promotions going on?
- Are there enough items in stock to fill the order?
- What items are in a package?
- How many of each item are in a package?
- Now that the order's packed, how are inventory levels? Is it time to place an order with a supplier?
- Where's the package now?
- When is the package scheduled to arrive at its destination?

As Figure 5-3 shows, the daily workflow generates information that goes into company records—and vice versa. For example, if Madge starts packing an order for three dozen rubber chickens, but there are only 27 in stock, what happens then? Or when a customer calls in demanding to know, "Where's that carton of trick golf balls I ordered two weeks ago?" can the customer service rep find the answer quickly?

Above and beyond the daily information shuffle, most managers want to track data at a higher level, showing a bigger picture. They need information that answers questions like these:

- What are our most popular items?
- Which fulfillment specialists pack the most orders?
- Which drivers deliver fastest?

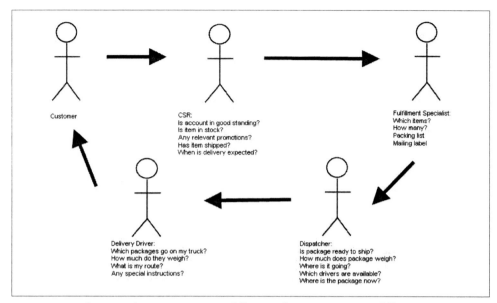

Figure 5-3. Each step in the process requires different information or raises different questions. Not all team members need the same information.

- Which promotions get the best customer response?
- What are seasonal and regional buying patterns?

Finally, although the company needs to keep track of all this information *somewhere*, you don't want to overwhelm team members with lots of data that has nothing to do with their jobs. Madge, for example, doesn't know or care whether a customer's account is in good standing or whether a box she packed yesterday is halfway to Kalamazoo or still on the loading dock. And Ron doesn't care whether the shipment he's assigning is a hot seller or a slow mover. So it's a good idea to have a way to show individual team members only the info they need. The next section breaks down the general information the company tracks into the specific information that each team member needs to get the job done.

Example 2: IT department

The IT department also has lots of information to track, like:

- **Problem status:** Unassigned, Open, In Development, On Hold, QA, Resolved.
- **Priority:** Low, Medium, High, Flashing-Lights-and-Sirens.
- **Dependencies:** Will fixing this bug affect other programs or functions?
- **Frequency:** Is this a one-time problem or does it pop up all over the place?
- **Time:** How long will it take to fix this bug?

- **Assigned to:** Who's dealing with it now? Also, which developers and testers are overloaded and which can handle another assignment?

In addition to this information regarding each individual bug, you'll want to get a high-level overview, perhaps for a monthly or quarterly report. Just for starters, here are a few (you can probably come up with even more):

- How many high-priority fixes do we deal with?
- Which developers get the job done fastest (or, to flip it around, which developers work slowly and don't meet deadlines)?
- How long is IT taking, on average, to fix reported bugs?
- How many open versus closed issues are there?

As in the distribution company example, not everyone needs all this info to do her job. Lauren the developer, for example, may not care which tester will check her fix. Simon, on the other hand, *does* need to know whose fix he's testing, in case he needs to ask that developer a question. And even though a little healthy competition is a good thing, you don't necessarily want Lauren eyeing the cubicle of another developer who's been a little slow on the job lately. You'd prefer she focus on her own work quality instead of keeping tabs on her co-workers.

What Information Do People Need?

QuickBase lets you track tons of information. But the point is to give your team members only the information they need to do their jobs. You're not helping anyone by swamping them with data they don't need. And in some cases, you don't want them poking their noses around in info that's really none of their business.

Think about each player's role in the workflow and what each person needs to know (or be able to look up) in order to move that process along.

Example 1: Distribution company

The workflow for the novelty distribution company is pretty straightforward. As the order passes from one team member to the next, it starts as information (an order), becomes actual goods, and then becomes information again (a completed order).

Here are the key players in the process, along with what each person needs to know:

- **Customer Service Rep.** When someone calls to place an order, the CSR must have access to the customer's account standing. (No whoopee cushions for you if your last invoice is six months past due.) Also, the CSR needs to know about any current promotions. For example, if there's a promotion offering a free pair of fuzzy dice with every $100 order, then the CSR can use that information to increase sales. Because CSRs at this company also handle customer inquiries and complaints, each rep also needs to see information about order status and location.

- **Fulfillment specialists.** Madge and her colleagues need to know which items are in an order. Fulfillment specialists also need to know where an order is going, so they can label the box. Finally, they need to know when an order has been packed, so you don't get three different packers boxing up the same order three times.
- **Dispatcher.** Ron needs to know when an order is ready to ship and where it's going. He needs to know (or create) the drivers' routes. Although Ron doesn't necessarily care about the contents of a package, he needs to know its weight. If a driver runs into a problem en route that affects delivery schedules (a flat tire, for example), then Ron wants to know that, too.
- **Drivers.** Drivers must know when a shipment's ready to hit the road. They also need to know where they're going, which packages get delivered where, and whether any packages require special handling. Special instructions are also helpful, like "Deliveries go to back door" or "Try to ignore vicious dog." The driver completes the process by collecting the customer's signature. When the driver submits that signature back to the organization, the process is complete, and the order is closed.

As you can see, each team member needs to know only a part of all the total information the company tracks. As you'll see in the next section, QuickBase lets you restrict the information people can view depending on their role in the company. For example, fulfillment specialists might see open orders but not delivery schedules.

Example 2: IT department

In the IT example, the players needs to know when it's their turn to go to work, and they need some info about the bugs they're working on:

- **Administrator.** This person, who's in charge of assigning and tracking bugs, cares less about the specifics of any given problem than about its priority and status. The administrator is also responsible for making sure that bugs, once assigned, move through the pipeline in a timely manner. So she needs to know each bug's status, who's working on it and for how long, and which bugs are still unassigned (something the developer and tester don't need to worry about yet).
- **Developer.** To organize her workload, Lauren needs to know the nature of the problem, its priority, and the expected time frame for fixing it. She also wants to know the affected computer platform, the problem's frequency, and any *dependencies* (that is, which system activities depend on other activities). If you're changing the invoicing system, for example, then changes you make to that system may affect Accounts Receivable.
- **Tester.** Over in QA, Simon needs to know when a fix is ready for testing. He wants to know which developer fixed the bug, in case he has questions. Dependencies are vital info for Simon, because if a fix affects other software or other parts of the same program, then he needs to test those, too. Priority and time frame are also

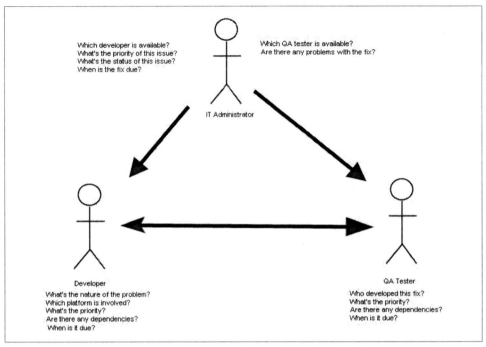

Figure 5-4. Although they're all dealing with bugs, the people in this small IT department need different information at different times. The administrator needs to keep a high-level overview of the process, while the developer and the tester both focus on the nuts-and-bolts details of individual bugs.

important, because he can't afford to let a high-priority issue sit there for a week awaiting testing.

Figure 5-4 shows how these pieces of information fit into the IT department's workflow.

Keeping the Team on Track

Think of QuickBase as a virtual manager—or, perhaps, the best assistant manager you never had. It can tell team members when it's time for them to do something, and it can let you know when the work's been completed.

How Does Your Team Know What to Do and When?

Do people on your team waste time waiting for someone to tell them it's their turn? Any dinky little spreadsheet can hold information, but QuickBase can let people know as soon as everything's in place for them to get to work.

Example 1: Distribution company

Relying on people to pass on information can only slow down the workflow. If Madge has to walk over and tell Ron when a shipment's ready to go, or if Ron has to print out a manifest and route for each driver and put it in an inbox, then problems are bound to pop up. If someone forgets to make a call or send an email, a customer's important order can get delayed unnecessarily. Papers can get buried under other papers or slip down behind filing cabinets.

Here's how QuickBase can help a distribution company stay on track:

- **Automatic notifications.** When someone adds, modifies, or deletes part of an order, QuickBase can automatically send an email to the person who needs to know about it. You can even specify the kind of change that triggers an email: when a new order's received, when the status of an order changes, when a shipment is assigned to a particular driver, and so on. "Stay on Top of Things with Email Notifications" on page 44 tells you how to set up and fine tune automatic notifications.

- **Roles.** In QuickBase, a *role* lets you control the level of access a person has in your application. You can set different roles for each job function, and then decide what information people in each role can see and what they can do with that information. For example, you may want the dispatcher to be able to see—but not change—the contents or destination of an order.

- **Reports.** As Chapter 2 explains in detail, a report is a way to display an application's data. You can sort, filter, and group the information any way you like, creating a report to display it. Reports are *dynamic*; that is, their content changes as the data changes. So, for example, you can create a report called Orders In Transit, which shows all orders with status fields that say "in transit."

Here's how these features would play out in the workflow: When a customer service rep creates a new order record, QuickBase adds it to the Open Tasks report for fulfillment specialists. Madge works her way down the list of open tasks, packing up orders. When an order's packed, she changes its status from "processing" to "ready to ship." That change in status triggers an email to Ron and adds the order to his My Open Tasks report. (You can even create a special report ["Creating a Report from Scratch" on page 61] called something like Unassigned Shipments, letting Ron focus on orders that are packed but not yet assigned to a driver.)

When Ron assigns the package to a driver and changes the order's status to "in transit," QuickBase adds the order to the driver's manifest and fires off an email notification to the customer who placed the order, saying that the package is on its way. As the order works its way through the pipeline, you don't have to worry about whether Madge gets sidetracked on the way to Ron's desk, or whether Ron skips over a customer when he sends out a batch of notification emails.

You can even create a role for customers, so they can view what's in their own order and see when it'll be delivered.
_____

Example 2: IT department

The IT example has similar opportunities for automating the workflow and passing along necessary information. Say you assign a bug to Lauren, the developer. When you make the assignment, QuickBase can send Lauren an email notification that she's got a new problem to fix and add the bug to her My Open Issues report. You can even put the My Open Issues report on the developers' Dashboard page ("Creating Different Dashboard Pages for Different Roles" on page 361), so it's the first thing Lauren sees when she opens the Feature and Bug Tracker application, as shown in Figure 5-5.

When Lauren fixes the bug, she changes the status to "QA," indicating that it's time for the tester, Simon, to take a look. As application administrator, you can set things up so that Simon gets an automatic email notification that the fix is ready for him and has been added to his My Open Issues report. This way, you don't have to send blizzards of emails to make sure that everyone knows what's going on. Once you understand your process—and what QuickBase can do—you can use QuickBase to keep the work flowing right along.

How Do You Know When the Work's Done?

By defining your workflow and all the information it produces and modifies, you get a clear picture of what has to be in place so you know the work's been done. In the distribution company example, a job begins when an order comes in and ends when the customer who placed the order gets the package. Also, each step in the process has a clear endpoint. The customer service rep's job ends when the order is passed on to the fulfillment specialists; Madge's job ends when she's packed the order and changed its status; Ron's job ends when he's scheduled the package for delivery; and the driver's job ends when the customer accepts delivery.

As the person in charge, you want to keep an eye on the workflow and make sure orders are flowing smoothly. But you may not need (or want) to be informed of every single status change. If you got an email every time Madge packed a box or every time Ron assigned a delivery, then your inbox would soon be flooded. It doesn't hurt for you to have that information, but it's overkill. So you can set up your QuickBase application to highlight what you need to know—in short, that people are getting their jobs done. For example, you may want a simple report at the end of the day showing completed vs. open orders.

Similarly, you can set up QuickBase to make sure an IT team is on track. To see who's fixed which bugs, you can open the Bug Tracker application and view closed issues by

Figure 5-5. When Lauren the developer opens the bug-tracking application, her Dashboard displays a report of all the open issues assigned to her, with their priority, status, and other information. To find out how to set up a custom Dashboard for different roles, see "Creating Different Dashboard Pages for Different Roles" on page 361.

type or by assigned person (both these reports are built into the application). To see who's slacking, you can view *open* bugs by assigned person. And if your main concern is to make sure that your team addresses software problems quickly and efficiently, then you can subscribe to daily or weekly reports, showing important info like all high-priority bugs that remain unresolved.

From Planning to Application

With your objectives, workflow, and information in hand, you can create and tailor your QuickBase application to solve your specific problems and make your life oh so much easier.

Start from a Prebuilt Application

Start by looking at QuickBase's prebuilt applications ("A Tour of QuickBase's Application Templates" on page 195). You may find one that fits your situation perfectly. After all, Intuit created these applications after analyzing typical business problems and getting suggestions from QuickBase fans. Because QuickBase applications are so flexible, you can always customize them to better fit your needs. For example, you can edit prebuilt drop-down list items. (Maybe your IT department says a bug is *in testing* instead of saying *QA*.) You can even add a whole new table to a multi-table application. Chapter 6 explains all your choices.

TIP

You can also browse through QuickBase's application library, which holds more than a hundred applications designed by QuickBase staff and customers alike. It's a great place to find ideas about designing applications and using QuickBase to the max. To get there, start in My QuickBase, then click Create a New Application. Toward the bottom of the page, click the Visit the QuickBase Application Library link.

Design Your Own Application

On the other hand, you may prefer to build your application from the ground up. If you run a really unique small business, you may find it faster to start from scratch than try to adapt one of QuickBase's built-in applications. Or maybe you've already been tracking data in a spreadsheet and just want to share it with your team via QuickBase. You can simply import what you've got rather than try to contort it into a prebuilt design. Chapter 7 is all about do-it-yourself applications. With the work you've done in this chapter—identifying the problem, objectives, workflow, and data to be tracked —you've got everything you need to create an application that gets the job done.

Consider the QuickBase Enterprise Edition

As you ponder your company's workflow—especially if your organization is really big —you might realize that you're going to need several corporate-level QuickBase accounts. But will those accounts get out of hand? How will you know what's going on in all of them? And how can you be sure that company policies about security and access are followed across the board?

To address these concerns, consider purchasing the QuickBase Enterprise Edition ("QuickBase Enterprise Edition" on page 27), which lets you gather multiple accounts into one or more master account, or *realm*. As a realm administrator, you can monitor costs and usage statistics, set consistent password and access policies, control user access, and more. It's a high-level administrative tool for organizations with complex needs. To find out more, go to www.quickbase.com (*http://www.quickbase.com/p/ home.asp*), and then click Enterprise.

Using QuickBase's Prebuilt Applications

Ready-made things always seem like cheating somehow—not quite as good as the real thing. Well, that may be true of clip-on neckties and store-bought brownies, but it's definitely not the case with QuickBase. The next chapter shows you how to create your own application from scratch, but that's not always the best way to go.

Many business functions and processes share common ground, no matter what organization you're with—like tracking time, assigning leads, or managing contacts. Quick-Base comes with dozens of prebuilt solutions—called *templates*—that already handle those tasks perfectly. Not only is starting with a ready-made application faster than designing a whole new one, it takes advantage of the design and programming work done by QuickBase developers who've spent countless hours polishing these templates. Your time is much better spent figuring out what you need in a solution, as described in Chapter 5, so you can tweak the template to meet your needs.

There are templates for managing purchase requests, creating a knowledge base, running a Web-based survey, tracking time and billing, sharing documents, managing leads or work orders—and more. All you have to do is choose the template you want, click a button or two to create an application, and then enter, upload, or import your data. This chapter takes you on a tour of QuickBase's template gallery and shows you how to create and adapt an application from a template.

A Tour of QuickBase's Application Templates

To see a list of the templates QuickBase offers, start from your My QuickBase page. Click the Create a New Application button. This opens the Create a New QuickBase Application page, shown in Figure 6-1. On the left is a list of categories targeting different business types (Legal, Real Estate, and so on) and business activities (Project Management, HR & Back Office, and so on). Click any category to see the templates it holds.

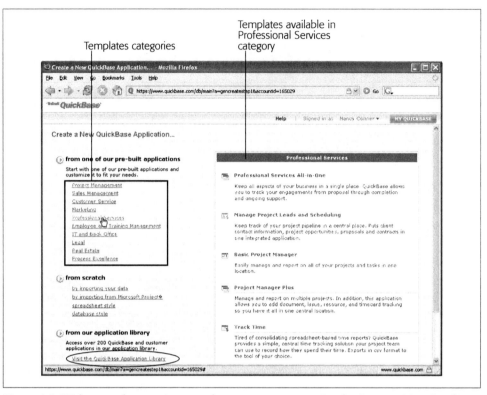

Templates categories

Templates available in
Professional Services
category

Figure 6-1. With a template, you're up and running in minutes. On the Create a New QuickBase Application page, check out the category list on the left. When you click a category name, the templates available for that category appear on the right side of the screen. Click any template name to explore that application and see whether it meets your needs. (You can also browse QuickBase's application library, which contains over 200 applications designed by QuickBase developers and real-world users. Click the "Visit the QuickBase Application Library" at the bottom of the page [circled]—and prepare to be inspired.)

When you browse a category looking for one kind of application, you may find another that'll come in handy, too. For example, if you're a human resource manager looking for a way to keep track of job applicants' résumés, you may also want to explore the Recruiting Requisitions template to help you organize hiring requests coming in from across your company.

QuickBase's templates include both single table and multi-table applications. And each template has a number of different reports ("QuickBase's Report Formats" on page 51) already built in. You can put any of these reports to work for you as soon as you've added some records. For example, the Develop Press Releases template (listed under Marketing) includes a calendar report that tracks due dates, and table reports that list all your records (by description or by resource). The following sections give you a quick tour of QuickBase's different template categories.

Project Management

Managing a project involves tons of responsibility: Planning the project, keeping the team on task and on track throughout the project's life cycle, and making sure the project ultimately meets its initial objectives. Meanwhile, managers need to keep an eye on both the calendar and the bottom line. Some project managers describe their jobs as being just a bit trickier than juggling chainsaws.

QuickBase offers three prebuilt applications related to all phases of a typical project life cycle:

- **Project Manager.** As any project manager knows, project management is a complex series of interrelated activities. And it's not just your own work you're responsible for—you've got an entire team to manage. This multi-table application lets you keep your data organized, keep an eye on progress and approaching deadlines, create status reports, and more. The Project Manager application template contains two tables: Projects and Tasks. These two powerful tables will let you make sure that the projects you're managing and the tasks they involve stay on target.

- **Project Manager Plus.** When you need a high-powered tool to help you keep track of all the facets of numerous projects, choose this template. In addition to the two tables included in Project Manager, this template adds five more: Issues (or as people in the real world like to more frankly call them: "problems"); Documents, so you can create a library of all the primary and supporting documents for your projects; Resources, so you can keep tabs on your project team, their contact info, and other relevant data; Timecards, so you know how much time your team members are spending on various projects; and Contacts—when you're managing several projects at once, you need to keep all your contact info straight. No more mistaking Lisa Nickell for the Finance Director of Amalgamated Seafood Products when she's actually the CEO of Multinational Produce, Inc.

TIP

Does seven tables sound like too much to manage? (Kind of like Snow White trying to keep track of all those dwarfs.) You can still use the Project Manager Plus template to get started with your project management application. After you've created the application, simply delete any tables you don't need.

- **Project Manager Plus (Microsoft Project Starter).** If you use Microsoft Project as your desktop project management tool, use this prebuilt application to import data from MS Project into QuickBase, preserving the task dependencies you've already set up. A real advantage of this application is that it lets you manage projects in MS Project and QuickBase simultaneously. Your team can update project and task status in QuickBase, and you can then import updates back to your original MS Project file. (Then again, QuickBase is so flexible and easy to use, you might decide it's everything you need for managing your projects.) Besides its ability to synchronize with MS Project, this application comes preloaded with five tables: Projects, Tasks, Issues, Documents, and Resources.

Sales Management

Sales management is all about helping your sales team to do their job: chase down opportunities, track and manage contacts, close the deal—and develop long-term relationships with happy customers. QuickBase makes it easy to organize your sales team and sales-related documents. Sales management templates include the following powerful applications:

- **Track Team Pipeline.** This multi-table application has two tables: Opportunities and Activities. As sales manager, you can help your reps stay on top of their opportunities, while the Activities table tracks how your team follows up on those opportunities.

- **Manage Your Sales Team.** This template includes five tables—Companies, Contacts, Opportunities, Activities, and Sales Reps—for centralized management of a far-flung sales force.

- **Sales Force Automation.** This is a monster application for serious sales managers. It has seven—count 'em, seven—tables: Opportunities, Activities, Contacts, Companies, Renewals, Lead Tracking, and Sales Library. With that kind of organized info at your fingertips, you can keep miles ahead of the competition.

Customer Management

Business guru Peter F. Drucker wrote, "The result of a business is a satisfied customer." The applications in this section help you to make sure your business produces the satisfied customers it needs to thrive. QuickBase helps you support your customers with a high level of service by offering these customer management templates:

- **Support Customers.** Ever had an irate customer call up because an order, special request, or inquiry got lost? Such calls are a thing of the past when you use this template to track customer requests and make sure someone gets back to your customers quickly and efficiently.

- **Knowledge Base.** They say that the only stupid question is the one that goes unasked—but that doesn't mean you want to spend your time answering the same questions over and over again. Instead, use the Knowledge Base application to create an in-house FAQ. It's fully searchable and a snap to update.

Marketing

These days, it seems like everyone's trying to sell *something*. Generating buzz about your company's products is a challenge—even if you manufacture the best darn deluxe whoopee cushions ever produced. Let QuickBase streamline the workload with these templates:

- **Manage Marketing Programs.** If you're a marketing manager, this application helps you orchestrate your marketing campaigns. You can prioritize and budget marketing programs, store and organize materials (from banner ads to press releases), and keep track of start and end dates. Use Calendar reports to easily keep track of the launch dates and end dates of multiple programs.

- **Manage Marketing Collateral.** As your marketing materials make their way through the review cycle, you can see at a glance whether Legal has approved the new sales letter or management is still dickering with (er, "reviewing") the latest product brochure. Keeping all your marketing collateral in a central location also means that sales reps have access to the latest materials when they're on the road. That way, the minute everyone's okayed that brochure, your sales force can start using it, whether they're in Anchorage, Topeka, or Miami.

- **Organize Customer References.** Need to let your team know who are the best customers to serve as references or contacts for the press? Looking for customers to involve in case studies or give testimonials about your product's features? This application makes it easy to store and, more importantly, *use* information about your customers.

- **Develop Press Releases.** Instead of trying to manage the review process by sending out dozens of press releases in various stages of development to a whole bunch of different people, get organized by keeping press releases in one place. You can track the status of each release and see at a glance who's signed off on it. Use the Calendar report to keep an eye on due dates and make sure the news gets out while it's still news.

- **Run a Survey.** Use this template to create a Web-based survey, and then read and analyze responses as they come in.

- **Marketing All-in-One.** This multi-table application lets you do it all. It rolls the first four tables of this section into one application, which means you can manage your programs and collateral, track customer data, and develop press releases all from one central application.

Professional Services

Whatever kind of professional service your company provides—from accounting to architectural design, from janitorial services to training—you want to manage clients and projects smoothly. You can adapt the prebuilt applications in this category to almost any kind of service industry. Here's what's available:

- **Professional Services All-in-One.** With multiple tables for clients, projects, tasks, and issues, this application lets you keep track of leads, manage clients and the services you provide to them, assign individual tasks, and deal with problems as they arise. One application covers the entire professional-services life cycle: from initial contact with a potential client, to providing the service, to following up.

- **Manage Project Leads and Scheduling.** This multi-table template contains both a Clients table and a Projects table, so you can manage both from one application.

- **Track Time.** To record how much time employees spend on a project, use this single-table application to create and manage timecards.

- **Share Documents with Clients.** This template's the same as the Document library template ("Project Management" on page 197).

NOTE

The Professional Services category also gives you access to the Project Manager and Project Manager Plus templates described in the Project Management section.

Employee and Training Management

When you're in charge of people, you need to do a whole lot more than remember who's assigned to which cubicle. You need to make sure your people have up-to-the-minute training for their jobs and to keep track of how well they're doing those jobs. If you're in HR, you're used to the daily risk of drowning in job requisitions and new batches of résumés. Let QuickBase toss you a life preserver with these templates:

- **Training Management.** If you're in charge of training in your organization, your life just got easier. QuickBase's prebuilt Training Management application is a powerhouse made up of five tables: Students, Classes, Course Catalog, Venues, and Instructors. Create, schedule, and manage classes—and make sure that everyone knows when and where each class will take place. (There's even a cool directions feature that works with Google Maps, so no one can use getting lost as an excuse for showing up late.)

- **Manage Performance Reviews.** Whether they're quarterly, semi-annual, or annual, it seems like it's always time to start another performance review cycle, and this template makes sure you're on top of it. With four table—Employees, Reviews, Self-Reviews, and Peer Feedback—this application helps you gather and organize all the information you need to do fair and timely reviews.

- **Job Candidate Tracker.** Companies both large and small can get flooded with résumés from eager job seekers. This template makes it easy to keep them organized. You can store and search resumes and other candidate info, prioritize applicants and keep track of their status, and record interview notes. And when it's time to send out decision letters, you can print mailing labels right from your Web browser.

- **Recruiting Requisitions.** The flip side of tracking candidates is dealing with the hiring requests that come in from managers. This template tames the hiring process, letting you organize open job requisitions by position, manager, and department. You can prioritize requests and track them throughout the candidate search.

NOTE

This category also has the "Run a Survey" template described in the Marketing category.

IT and Back Office

If you're the go-to person for all things IT, then you've got more balancing acts going on than a three-ring circus. You've got to field questions, manage development cycles, handle change requests, and fix bugs all while poised on a high wire over a pit of hungry crocodiles. (OK, so some days it just *feels* like there's a pit of hungry crocodiles.)

And because it's the people behind the scenes who make a company work, this category also includes goodies for back-office staff.

QuickBase can help you manage all that information and keep deadlines on target with these templates:

- **Purchase Request.** Managing the purchase approval process involves a lot more than rubber-stamping requests. This template gets rid of paper purchase order forms and gives you a centralized location to process POs, from the moment they come in until they're approved or denied. You can prioritize purchase requests and track them through the approval process, so you can find requests still awaiting approval before they slip through the cracks.

- **Request Manager.** When requests come flooding into the IT department like water over Niagara Falls, you need a way to organize, prioritize, and assign them, and then keep track of their status. You have the option of letting co-workers create their own requests. Also, QuickBase can send out automatic email when a new request is assigned or an existing one resolved. And if you're sick of picking up the phone or shooting off an email to answer questions about status, you can opt to let the people who've made a request view its status.

NOTE

The IT and Back Office category also has the Knowledge Base template described in the Customer Management section.

- **Project Portfolio Manager.** Got about a million projects and about that many people clamoring to get theirs done *now?* This application helps you get organized. You can manage, sort, and prioritize your projects, track costs and risk, and keep an eye on project schedules. And if you share your project portfolio with your colleagues, those clamorers will understand just how much work you're dealing with.

- **Feature and Bug Tracker.** It's impossible to manage requests for features and reported bugs that come in via email, phone calls, meeting notes, conversations by the coffee pot, notes on napkins dropped on your desk after lunch, and so on. This application collects change requests in one place, where it's easy to prioritize, assign, and manage them.

- **Asset Tracker.** If you're in charge of equipment and other resources, this application helps you keep track of what you've got, where it is, and what it's worth. Whether you're upgrading existing computers or unloading worn-out office furniture, Asset Tracker keeps you on top of the resources you're responsible for.

- **Run the Spec Review Process.** When different people from various departments are reviewing specifications, it's tough to keep track of who's seen which version. With this application, you can keep all your specifications in a central location, notify participants of changes, see who's reviewed a document (and who needs a nudge or two) and who has (or hasn't) signed off on it.

Legal

With a centralized location to track staff time and expenses, store and share documents and contracts, and make contact information easy to find, QuickBase helps law firms and legal departments run smoothly. Here are some of the templates for legal professionals:

- **Time and Billing.** QuickBase offers this application to meet the specific needs of law firms, but you can adapt it for any organization that bills by time and expenses. This application includes tables for cases, time, expenses, and resources.

- **Multi-Party Litigation.** When your law firm is involved in joint litigation, this application lets you easily share motions, discovery documents, and other information among those who need to know. It has tables for documents, dates (to monitor the litigation timeline), and people (so you can capture contact information for attorneys, witnesses, and other parties).

- **Contract Management.** Keep your contracts in a centralized place, where you can find them easily and keep track of when they're about to expire.

- **Document Library.** A QuickBase document library doesn't have any bookcases, leather chairs, or shushing librarians. Instead, it's a centralized repository for documents you need to share with others. With this template, you can categorize your documents; search for documents by category, author, or creation date; track revisions; and notify team members when someone has edited or added a document.

Real Estate

Managing properties means keeping track of a mountain of information—tenant leases (and when they expire), lease applications, maintenance requests, work orders, info about tenants, and more. Make it easy to stay on top of all the paperwork by organizing it in one centralized place. QuickBase offers these templates for property managers:

- **Work Order Management.** This application lets you prioritize, assign, and track work orders, so that everyone—from the tenant who called in a maintenance request to office staff to the worker who'll do the job—is on the same page. It has two tables: Properties/Units and Work Orders, so you can keep track of the work being done and the properties you manage.

- **Lease Management.** When you manage many properties, it's all too easy to lose track of when a lease is about to expire, leading to unnecessary vacancies and costing the company money. This multi-table application (its tables hold data about properties/units, leases, and tenants/prospects) lets you stay on top of managing leases so you can secure renewals and minimize vacancies. QuickBase can even email you a reminder when a lease is about to expire.

- **Commercial Property Management.** This application boils down the complex task of commercial property management into three tables: Properties/Units, Tenants, and Work Orders. Use the application to keep track of leases and work orders, no matter how many units you manage. Be aware of vacancies and know when leases are about to end. Make sure that high-priority repairs get taken care of ASAP, and that your maintenance staff stays busy.

- **Residential Property Management.** A multi-table application similar to the one for commercial property management, QuickBase tailors this application to the needs of folks who manage residential real estate.

Process Excellence (Six Sigma)

The whole point of that geeky endeavor known as *process excellence* is to make your business more efficient—and better at serving customers—than your competition. QuickBase's process excellence templates use the principles of *Six Sigma,* an approach that applies statistical methods to business processes to improve efficiency and reduce defects. Six Sigma began at Motorola in the 1980s, when engineers there devised a quality-measurement method that measured defects per million units; the goal was to produce no more than 3.4 defects per million items. And that's where the name *Six Sigma* comes from: sigma is the mathematical term for a standard deviation, and six sigma means that process quality is no more than six standard deviations of the process spread. In plain English, that means a process succeeds 99.9997 percent of the time.

NOTE

If your business doesn't use the Six Sigma methodology, then do your eyeballs a favor and jump ahead to the next section.

Over time, Six Sigma has evolved into a methodology that tries to eliminate defects from *any* process—not just manufacturing but also service procedures, IT processes, and transactions of any kind. If you've got a process, Six Sigma aficionados claim, then Six Sigma can improve it.

TIP

For more information on Six Sigma, surf on over to www.isixsigma.com (*http://www .isixsigma.com*), or check out *Process Improvement Essentials* by James R. Persse (O'Reilly).

To optimize your business's processes, check out these templates:

- **Prioritize and Schedule Projects.** Don't get overwhelmed by suggestions for projects. As project ideas come in, you can assign them a priority and put them through a structured and open approval process. After an idea wins approval, add it to the schedule and track its progress.

- **Manage Tasks.** The Task Manager shows the tasks to be done, who's supposed to do them, and when they're due. You can send automatic notifications ("Stay on Top of Things with Email Notifications" on page 44) when a deadline's approaching or has passed, and generate status reports ("Sending Reports to Yourself and Others" on page 149) as often as you need them.

- **Track Resources.** Even the best people don't do you much good unless you know what their skills and experience levels are. Keep track of your organization's employees and their Six Sigma level with this application.

- **Share Tools & Knowledge.** To make sure that everyone on the same team is also on the same page, use this application to give team members access to training materials, project templates, curricula, planning documents, and more.

- **Process Excellence All-in-One.** The application brings together three process excellence tables—Process, Roster, and Tools—so you can prioritize and schedule projects, manage tasks, track resources, and share tools and knowledge, all from one place.

Templates in Action: Three Examples

QuickBase lets you start with a template and then modify it to meet your organization's information-management needs. In this section, read stories of how prebuilt applications provide fast, easy solutions to the real-world (albeit fictionalized) problems of busy professionals.

National Sales Management

Carl oversees a nationwide sales force of 150 reps, plus managers and support staff. His main problem is capturing and sharing information—keeping everyone on the same page, whatever their local office, current on-the-road location, or time zone. In particular, he wants to make sure that sales reps get the most current information about pricing, products, and promotions. When salespeople travel, it's tough for them to keep up with the flood of information generated at headquarters. Back in the home office, the staff may add new procedures, update price lists, change credit policies, and so on. Even if they remember to notify the sales force by email, somebody's laptop may miss or eat the message. A solution that gives the sales force access to the corporate information they need, wherever they happen to be and whenever they're looking for it, would be ideal.

Meanwhile, Carl wants to be sure that he and his staff have access to all the daily details that each and every sales rep carries around—whether in a cell phone, Blackberry, or between the ears—like contact names, preferred products, best time to call, and names of customers' family members. That way, if a sales rep gets transferred or runs off to join the circus (same amount of traveling, but the work clothes are cuter), then the new rep can get up to speed fast.

QuickBase's Manage Your Sales Team template can simplify Carl's life in a big way. This prebuilt application has five tables, as you can see in Figure 6-2:

- **Companies.** Carl's sales force does business with a lot of other companies. This table helps make sure everyone's list is up to date. The Companies table is linked to the Opportunities table; with a single click, anyone viewing this table can see the details of previous leads with this company (and how those leads turned out).

- **Contacts.** It's not enough, of course, to know which companies you've done business with—Carl and his team also need up-to-the-minute information about who to call at each company when it's time to spread the news about a great new product or inquire about reordering supplies. And when contacts change—someone gets promoted, transfers to another department, or leaves the company—they need to know that, too. The Contacts table tracks everything to do with the decision-makers at the companies Carl sells to.

- **Opportunities.** When opportunity knocks, Carl wants to be sure he has a rep in place to open the door. This table lets his staff capture opportunities as they arise and estimate the probability that the opportunity will turn into a done deal. With this table, Carl's staff can upload relevant proposals and contracts. Preloaded reports include opportunities that are about to close, closed sales by account, and a breakdown of the most valuable accounts.

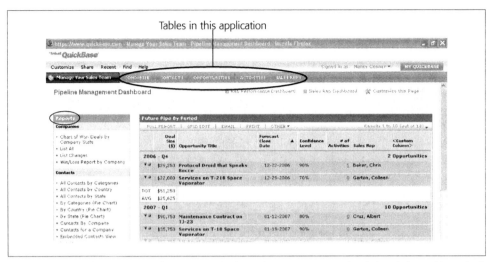

Tables in this application

Figure 6-2. The Manage Your Sales Team prebuilt application comes preloaded with five tables, which you can see circled across the top of the Dashboard page. Click a table's name to add records, search for data, or see the current reports for that table. You can see all the reports at a glance in the left-hand Reports menu (circled). One of the cool features about this prebuilt application is that it has different Dashboards for different roles—so a sales rep who opens the application, for example, sees a different Dashboard page than a manager. And because you created the application (which makes you its administrator), you can see these different Dashboards by clicking the links at the top of the page: Rep Performance Dashboard (which lets managers see their team's performance at a glance) and Sales Rep Dashboard (where each rep sees his or her pertinent info—My Activity List, My Pipeline, My Chart of Closed Deals, and so on).

NOTE

Thanks to QuickBase's customizable roles (which you can read about in "Creating a Brand-New Role" on page 356), Carl can make it so each sales reps sees only those opportunities assigned to him or her.

- **Activities.** This table is where sales reps report on what they did to follow up on opportunities—what kind of contact they made and what the result was.
- **Sales Reps.** Carl uses this table to keep tabs on his sales reps: what their targets are and whether their meeting those targets, as well as office and cell phone numbers. A vCard field ("Using vCard and iCalendar with QuickBase" on page 176) bundles each rep's contact info into an electronic package that Carl can easily download and open in Outlook.

Now Carl feels confident about two-way communication between his office and the field. The information he captures from his reps helps him perform analysis to identify top-performing and potentially high-growth accounts. And he doesn't have to worry that the information he sends out will get lost within a matter of days. Instead of trying to recall a half-remembered email from last week, reps can go to QuickBase and easily latch on to the information they need.

Residential Property Management

Russ manages two dozen apartment buildings in a medium-sized city that's home to a major research university. His job involves diverse tasks, like showing apartments and checking out prospective tenants, collecting security deposits and rent, managing leases, scheduling maintenance and landscaping work, and dealing with emergencies and tenant complaints.

Because Russ works in a college town, certain times of year are crazy busy—especially late summer, when hoards of students are moving in, and late spring, when those hoards move out again. And graduation weekend can be full of surprises, like the time a party ran out of beer, so the guests tossed the empty refrigerator out the window.

Russ needs a centralized solution that will help him track leases (and notify him when they're due to expire), organize information about his tenants, and keep his maintenance staff informed of both routine and high-priority jobs.

QuickBase's Manage Residential Property application, shown in Figure 6-3, offers three tables:

- **Properties/Units.** Russ uses this table to gather together all the info about each apartment: location, rent, square footage, number of bedrooms/bathrooms, appliances, and amenities (like high-speed Internet), current status (occupied, vacant, or about to become vacant), condition (refrigerator on front lawn, for example), and more. One feature he likes is a text box where he can paste the advertising copy he uses when he's looking for tenants, so he doesn't have to search for an old ad or write a whole new one every time a tenant moves out.

- **Work Orders.** With this table, Russ creates, prioritizes, and schedules work orders, so that the maintenance staff is always ready for the next job. With one central, online location for work orders and automatic email reminders, Russ is confident that his staff will take care of important repairs and necessary maintenance.

- **Tenants.** Tenants can be the hardest part of managing property, whether they pay their rent a few days late or punch holes in the wall for fun. The Tenants table keeps tabs on tenants from the time they submit a lease application to the time they move out. Russ records credit and employment information, references, deposit amounts, a copy of the lease, move-in/move-out dates—even car registration info for buildings with tight parking lots.

Using roles, Russ lets tenants view work orders that relate to their apartment, so they can see scheduled maintenance and repairs. Similarly, the owners of the buildings Russ

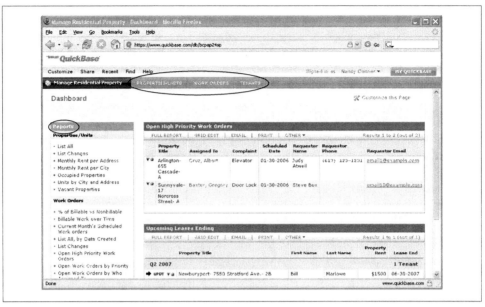

Figure 6-3. The Manage Residential Property prebuilt application includes three tables (circled): Properties/Units, Work Orders, and Tenants. Click the name of any table to see its data or add new records. Each prebuilt application has a number of reports created and ready to go. On the left side of the screen, click the Reports tab (also circled) to see what they are. (In a multi-table application like this one, reports are organized by table.)

manages have access to information about the properties, work orders, and tenants. Maintenance staff can view, add, and modify work orders, but don't have access to tenants' sensitive financial information. Russ likes the way he can keep all his property management information in one place, while keeping control over who sees and works with that information. So even when a refrigerator sails out a window, Russ can take it all in stride.

Project Management

As a project manager who serves as a link between her company's business and IT sides, Veronica sometimes feels like she has all the responsibility and none of the authority for making sure software development projects succeed. She has to make sure that end-users and corporate sponsors on the business side get their needs across to developers and testers on the IT side—and that the costs, risks, and limitations of developing software features are clear to the business folks. Communication, which should be the glue that holds her team together, frequently breaks down: people overlook emails, come to meetings with outdated documents, and waste time by duplicating data in different reports. As a result, no one's clear about who's supposed to be doing what by when.

QuickBase's Project Manager Plus template can help Veronica get her team on the right track by offering a centralized, easy-to-access location to record and assign tasks, share documents, identify and prioritize project issues, and keep an eye on deadlines. The application, shown in Figure 6-4, contains these tables:

- **Projects.** If you only manage one project at a time, you live a luxurious life. But when you've got multiple projects happening all at once, this table can help you keep track of them all. Veronica likes the way she can easily organize her projects: by company or by priority, for example. She can also create a timeline that shows all her projects in relation to each other, so she can watch for—and avoid—bottlenecks.

- **Tasks.** Even a small project includes many individual tasks. And just one overlooked or overdue task can wreak havoc with the cost, schedule, and ultimately the success of the project. With this table, Veronica records and assigns each step of the project, giving it a priority and start and end dates. Because each task in a complex project depends on other tasks, Veronica links tasks to their relevant predecessors and successors, so if there's a hold-up on one task, she can see at a glance how this may affect other tasks down the road. She particularly likes the graphic reports that offer an at-a-glance overview of what's happening with tasks: a calendar report that shows approaching due dates, a pie chart that breaks down tasks by status, and a timeline that shows all tasks by project phase. And she uses QuickBase to send weekly and monthly status reports automatically.

- **Issues.** Problems happen—the trick is dealing with them when they rear their ugly heads. Using the Issues table, Veronica captures issues as they arise, and then assigns them a priority and someone to deal with the problem. Automatic emails let team members know what issues they need to work on—and when resolving an issue is overdue.

- **Document Library.** A centralized repository for all of a project's documents keeps everyone on the same page. Team members easily find the most up-to-date version of a document, and they can reserve a document ("Reserving a Document" on page 141) when they're working on it to make sure that no one accidentally overwrites their changes.

- **Resources.** A team's only as good as the people who are on it. The Resources table is where Veronica keeps track of her team's names, roles, and contact information. When she adds a team member to the Resources table, QuickBase automatically includes that person in other parts of the application—for example, when Veronica adds Linda Martinez to the Resources table, Linda's name appears on the Assigned To drop-down menu for the Tasks and Issues tables.

- **Time Cards.** Veronica knows that time is money, so she uses this table to keep track not just of person-hours on a given project, but also of how much time each project has eaten up so far. A summary table displays how many hours a particular project has taken so far.

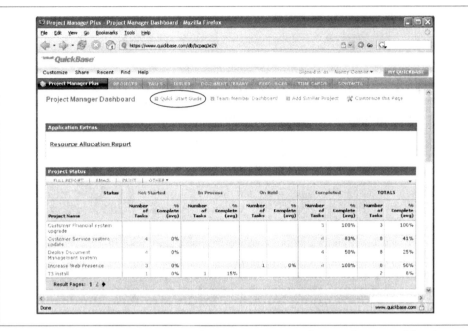

Figure 6-4. With seven tables to store your data, Project Manager Plus is one big, powerful application. But all those tables might seem a little overwhelming at first—where do you begin? QuickBase answers that question with its Quick Start Guide, which helps you get up to speed fast with your new application. When you create a new Project Manager Plus application, the Dashboard page shows a Quick Start Guide link (circled); click it for a tutorial that breaks down the complex process of creating a project management application into a series of steps. The Quick Start Guide covers some of the most popular things you can do with QuickBase, such as adding and assigning Tasks, creating reports, sending automatic emails, inviting users, and creating roles.

- **Contacts.** As projects grow and multiply, Veronica uses this table to keep all the relevant information for internal and external contacts in one central, easy-to-find location.

The Project Manager Plus application has four predefined roles: Viewer, Team Member, Project Manager, and Executive. As you'll see in Chapter 9, Veronica can customize these roles in any way she wants—or even create new roles with their own permissions. For example, she may want to create roles for business subject matter experts, project sponsors, and developers, each with different abilities to view, add, modify, or delete records. Using the tables, roles, and automatic notifications in the Project Manager Plus template—and customizing them to meet the exact needs of her project—Veronica's confident her team will stick together and stay up to date, informed, and on task.

Creating an Application from a Template

After you've browsed the templates and found one that looks like it'll meet your needs, you're just a couple of clicks away from creating your very own application from that template. Here's how:

1. On your My QuickBase page, click Create a New Application. When the Create a New QuickBase Application page opens, click the category that best describes what you want to do.

   The categories, and the templates in each, are listed in "A Tour of QuickBase's Application Templates" on page 195.

2. Click the name of the template you want to use.

   A box appears with a description of what the template does.

3. Click Create Application.

   Another box opens, asking you to name the application. There's a name already filled in, but you probably want to give your application an easy-to-spot name.

TIP

When you create a new application from a template, QuickBase assigns the application a name, like Manage Your Sales Team or Purchase Requests or Run the Spec Review Process. If you create two different applications using the same template, QuickBase gives them both the exact same name (you're allowed to have multiple applications with the same name). To avoid confusion later on—trying to remember, for example, which Knowledge Base application is for Project CHAOS and which is for Project DOOM—make sure each application you create has a unique name.

---

4. Type the application's name (if you're changing it), and then click OK.

   QuickBase creates your new application and takes you to its Dashboard page. Your new application is ready for you to start adding records or documents.

The Getting Started Guide

For some prebuilt applications (that is, the big, complicated ones), it can be easy to get lost roaming through all those tables. So QuickBase offers you some guidance to help you find your way around. For example, QuickBase's prebuilt Training Management template is a powerful, remarkably flexible multi-table application that can be used in different ways by students, their department managers, instructors, training managers, and more. But to get the most out of everything it can do, you could use a guided tour . You want it? You got it. Look for a Getting Started Guide link near the top of the page, like the one shown in Figure 6-5. Click the link to start learning the ropes of your new application.

The Getting Started Guide puts relevant Help information at your fingertips. It's packed with popular Help topics that relate to that application. Read through the guide from

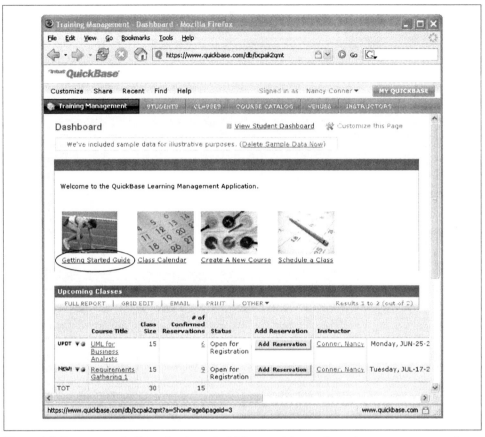

Figure 6-5. For some prebuilt applications, QuickBase anticipates the topics you may want to know more about. Click the Getting Started link (circled) to open a page of application-specific help, hints, and tips.

top to bottom, or click a link to jump to a specific topic. You don't have to read the guide right away—the link will appear on your application's Dashboard page unless you remove it. (To find out how to remove an element from your Dashboard, see Chapter 8's section on customizing your dashboard.)

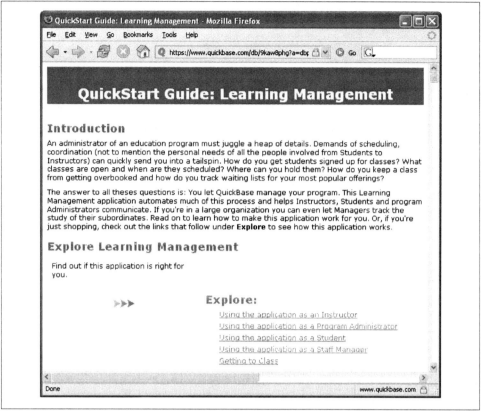

Figure 6-6. The Getting Started Guide takes you for a spin around your new application. It's like having a knowledgeable QuickBase guru give you your own personal tour of the new application. The folks at Intuit have anticipated your most likely questions and packed the answers into a single, easy-to-find, easy-to-read Help page written specifically for this application.

NOTE

Not all prebuilt applications have a Getting Started Guide. If you have questions about a new application you've created and you *don't* see a link to a guide, your best bet is to keep reading this book. In the unlikely event that you still need help, try the QuickBase Support Center (Help→QuickBase Support Center), where you can browse through frequently asked questions (and their answers), click KnowledgeBase for troubleshooting tips, or get help from QuickBase users who've been there by clicking Community Forum.

Don't like the guide that QuickBase has provided? Or maybe you love the guide and want to provide something similar for people who'll use your application in a particular role. You can write your own guide and put a link to it on the Help menu. For all the details, see "Creating a User Guide for Your Application."

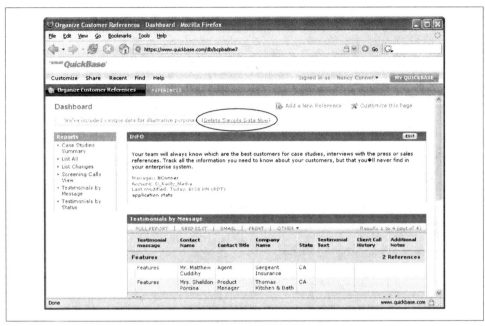

Figure 6-7. QuickBase starts you off with some sample data to help familiarize you with the fields and the kinds of records your new application holds. Here, all the records in the "Testimonials by Message" table are examples supplied by QuickBase. But once you start adding records of your own, you won't want QuickBase's examples cluttering up your tables. To get rid of the sample data, click the Delete Sample Data Now link (circled).

The Dashboard Page

To help you see what the new application will look like with some data in it, QuickBase displays sample data on the Dashboard page (as you can see in Figure 6-7) and in some of the reports. Seeing sample data's helpful in visualizing what you can do with the application, but you don't want those phony records hanging around forever. To delete the data QuickBase shows you as an example, click Delete Sample Data Now, and then click OK to confirm.

TIP

Already started adding records? It's still safe to click Delete Sample Data Now. Doing so deletes just the sample data that was already in the template when you created the application; it won't touch any of the new data you've added.

To begin adding records to a single-table application, the quickest way is to click the upper-right "Add a New Record" link. (Depending on the kind of table you're working with, the actual name of this link reflects the kind of records you can add: Add a New Task, Add a New Issue, Add a New Document, Add a New Timecard, and so on.) In a multi-table application, look in the blue Table bar and click the name of the table you want (the name will be the same as the kind of record you want to add), then choose "Add a New Record". Or you can import your data in a big batch of records.

Now that you've used a template to get your new application up and running, you can do everything that you'd do with any other QuickBase application. In the chapters ahead you can read about these topics:

- Sharing the application.
- Managing roles and groups.
- Creating dependencies.
- Managing tables.

TIP

If you've read a template's description and you're not quite sure it's what you want, go ahead and create an application from it. Take a look at the application, try displaying the sample data in a few different reports, and add a record or two to see how things look. If the application isn't what you want, you can modify some fields ("Modify a field" on page 223) or just delete the application. You can always try a different template (or build your own custom application as described in the next chapter).

Adapting a Template to Suit Your Needs

QuickBase templates get you up to speed fast, but you don't have to settle for a one-size-fits-all solution to your organization's needs. All QuickBase applications, including the prebuilt ones, are designed so that you can adapt them, tailoring them to do precisely what you require—like starting with an off-the-rack suit and ending up with a Saville Row fit. The sections that follow show you how to customize your prebuilt application's overall appearance as well as its fields and tables.

TIP

If you want to adapt an application—add a new table for example, or tweak its appearance to reflect your organization's culture—but you're worried that making changes to the application will mess it up, never fear. Just copy the application and play around with the copy. If you like the changes, you can make them permanent. If not, your original application's still safe and sound.

Customizing an Application's Appearance

QuickBase has designed attractive, easy-to-use application pages. But sometimes you want to make an application reflect your company's image. For example, when you share an application with people outside of your organization (vendors, clients, con-

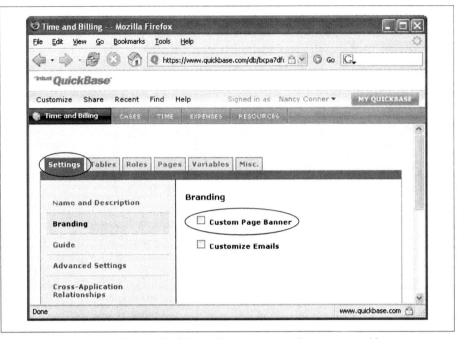

Figure 6-8. The Settings tab (circled) of the Application page is where you can add your company's own stamp to QuickBase application pages. Turn on the Customize Page Banner checkbox (also circled) to see the options available for tweaking an application's look and feel.

sultants, and so on), you probably want each page to display your company's name, logo, and maybe a link to your Web site.

NOTE

Only the application manager can customize a QuickBase page.

You can't completely redesign an application's appearance, but you can edit the colors of its header and text and add your own elements (text, an image, a hyperlink) to the upper-left, upper-right, and lower-right corners of any application page. To individualize a QuickBase application, follow these steps:

1. Open the application you want to customize.

   As the administrator, you can customize any QuickBase application, not just one you created from a template.

   In the menu bar, choose Customize→Application.

   The Application page opens, with the Settings tab selected. From the left-hand menu, click Branding. The page should look something like the one shown in Figure 6-8.

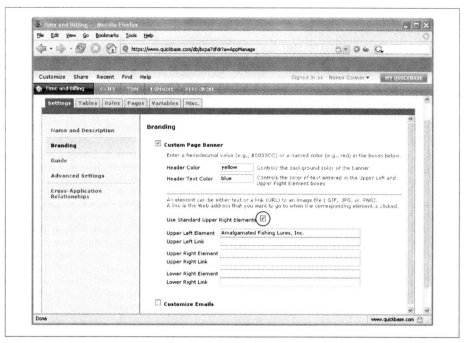

Figure 6-9. You can change both the background color and the text of your QuickBase application's header. Just type a color name or code into the Header Color and Header Text Color boxes. (For a listing of color codes, see www.w3schools.com/html/html_colors.asp.) If you want the upper-right links ("Signed in as" and the My QuickBase button) to stay as they are, turn on the Use Standard Upper Right Elements checkbox (circled). You can still type in an element of your own, such as a link, to appear above those standard QuickBase elements—just type what you want in the Upper Right Element boxes.

2. Turn on the Customize Page Banner checkbox.

   You see some new options that let you edit aspects of the application's appearance. You can change the background color and text color for the header at the top of the window.

   As described in Figure 6-9, you can also substitute your own text—or an image—for the links at the header's right, and make that text or image a link. You can also add your own text or image (with or without a hyperlink) to the window's upper-left and lower-right corners.

NOTE

When you turn off the Use Standard Upper Right Elements checkbox, you make the useful "Signed in as" and My QuickBase buttons go bye-bye. If your end-users need these to navigate the application, leave that checkbox turned on.

---

3. If you want to change colors in the header, then type either a color name or a hexadecimal color code.

   QuickBase understands common color names: *red, blue, yellow, green, purple*, and so on.

   Hexadecimal values give you a broader palette of millions of colors to play with. To use these colors, you must type a six-character code consisting of numbers, letters, or both. They tell the Web browser what color to displays when showing your application's page. You can see a chart of hexadecimal codes and colors at Webmonkey (www.webmonkey.com/webmonkey/reference/color_codes/ (*http://www.webmonkey.com/webmonkey/reference/color_codes/*)) or W3 schools (www.w3schools.com/tags/ref_colornames.asp (*http://www.w3schools.com/tags/ref_colornames.asp*)).

4. To add your own text, like your company's name, type it into any of the Element boxes.

   If you want to plop an image or logo of your choice in the application's upper-left or upper- or lower-right corner, instead of text, then see the box in "Using an Image as a Hyperlink" on page 219.

5. If you'd like users to be able to click this text (or image) to jump to a Web site outside of QuickBase (like your company's home page), then just type the Web address into a Link box.

   Easier still, open a browser window that shows the page you want, select the address, right-click, and select Copy. Back in the Custom Page Banner section, click in the Link box, and then right-click and select Paste.

6. When you're finished making changes, click Save Changes.

   QuickBase applies your changes. You can see them right away; just look at the top or bottom of the page. If you want to tweak your choices—maybe the text color you chose for the header doesn't show up vividly enough against the background —type any changes into the appropriate boxes.

7. When you're entirely finished, click Save & Done.

   Your application has a look and feel all its own.

TIP

You can customize any application's Dashboard page to emphasize the tables and reports you want to call to users' attention. "Creating Different Dashboard Pages for Different Roles" on page 361 shows you how.

Using an Image as a Hyperlink

You can link to your company's Web site or another off-QuickBase Web page with boring old text, like *Click here!* or *My Company's Name.* But wouldn't it be snazzier to whisk users off to the company site by clicking the company logo?

To use an image as a link, you have to make sure that Web browsers can find and display the image. That means it has to be on a Web server somewhere. It's easiest if you store the image right in QuickBase. You can store it on any Web server, of course —just paste its URL into one of the Element boxes on the Application Properties page. But if the Web page that holds the image isn't a secure site, viewers' browsers may flash a warning message like this one: *This page displays both secure and nonsecure items. Do you want to display the nonsecure items?* With all the viruses and worms slithering through cyberspace, a warning like that's apt to make users nervous, and some won't proceed.

If you link to an image that's stored inside QuickBase, however, your application page will load quickly and there won't be any security questions to scare users away from your application. Just upload the image to QuickBase as an attachment. Then, with that record onscreen in front of you, click the attachment to open it in a new browser window. Copy the file's location from the address box of the window displaying the image. On the Application Properties page, paste the address into an Element box. (For example, if you want the image to appear in the upper-left corner, paste the address into the box labeled Upper Left Element.) Click Save, and your image appears where you've told QuickBase to display it—the upper-left, upper-right, or lower-right corner of your application.

Customizing Fields and Tables

The folks at Intuit designed QuickBase's prebuilt applications by looking at common business problems and coming up with smart solutions. They've already taken the first giant steps described in the previous chapter: analyze the problem, define an objective, and design a viable solution. All you have to do is apply that solution to your own situation. But no one could anticipate the myriad procedures and information needs of every organization out there. That's why QuickBase templates are flexible, letting you add or modify fields to meet your organization's precise needs. So, for example, if QuickBase's prebuilt timecards don't allow for your company's tradition of paying everyone double overtime on the boss's birthday (yeah, right), you can change the template to make sure nobody misses out on their Boss's Birthday Bonus.

Add a field

To create a brand-new field that can hold whatever information you want, do the following:

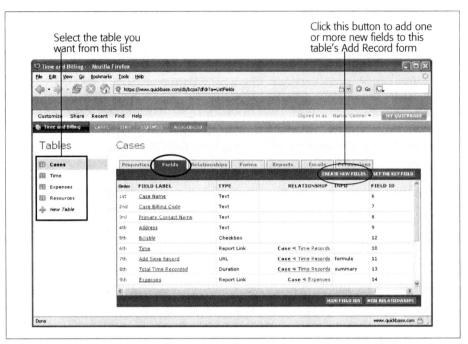

Figure 6-10. The Tables page offers one-stop shopping for everything you need to customize tables in your application. In a multi-table application, the tables are listed on the left-hand side of the page. Click the Fields tab (circled) to see all the fields a table holds. From this tab, you can add, modify, or delete any field in a table. To add one or more fields, click the upper-right Create New Fields button (also circled).

1. Open the application you want to customize. From the menu bar, choose Customize→Create a new→Field. If you're in a multi-table application, tell QuickBase which table you want to add the field to. (You can also add a new field from the Tables page, shown in Figure 6-10. To get there, click Customize→Tables; for a multi-table application, choose the table you want from the left-hand list. Click the Fields tab if necessary, then click the upper-right Create New Fields button.)

   The Add Fields page, shown in Figure 6-11, opens.

2. Type in a name for the field, like *Job type* or *Billing code*.

   A descriptive name that will be clear to the end-users who'll add and modify data works best.

3. Next to the name, choose from the "Select a field type" drop-down list.

   Choose a type that matches the type of information the field will hold: Date, E-mail Address, File Attachment, and so on. QuickBase can accommodate a wide range of information types, not all of which are as self-explanatory as, say, Phone Number. See "Assigning field types" on page 235 for full descriptions.

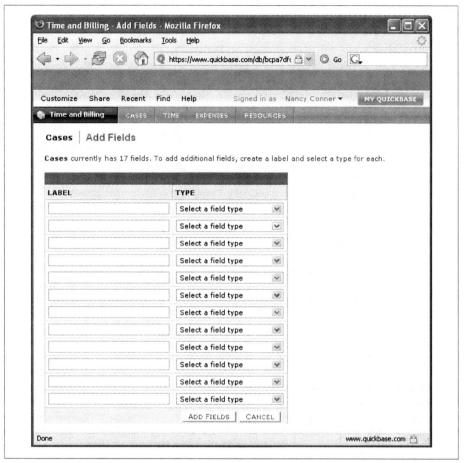

Figure 6-11. The Add Fields page is where you create new fields for any QuickBase application. Type the name of the field into a text box, and then click the drop-down menu to choose the type of field you want: text, numeric, date, checkbox, user, and so on. (For a complete list of field types, see "Assigning field types" on page 235 in the next chapter.) When you're done, click Add Fields.

NOTE

If you forget to select a field type, QuickBase prompts you to make your choice.

---

4. When you've entered as many fields as you want to add, click Add Fields.

   If QuickBase needs more information about a field, such as what choices to include in a multiple-choice field, then you see the Create Choices page.

5. If the Create Choices page opens, type the information QuickBase asks you for (such as the specific choices you want to appear on a multiple-choice list), and then click Next.

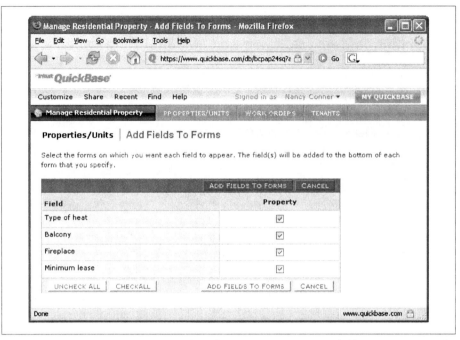

Figure 6-12. QuickBase may ask you which form you want your new fields to appear in. Make sure the correct checkboxes are turned on, and then click Save.

If your application has custom forms, a prompt pops up and asks whether you want to add fields to the custom form. Many prebuilt applications include custom forms, because custom forms can do a lot of cool things, like associate a form with a role or make certain fields required. If there's no custom form involved, you're done.

6. Click yes. (Or, if you don't want to worry about that for the moment, click Not Right Now—you can add them later.)

   The Add Fields To Forms page opens, where QuickBase shows you a list of forms related to the table to which you're adding the new field, as shown in Figure 6-12. (Remember, the Add Fields To Forms page is for applications with custom forms, so you may not see this page when you add a field.)

7. If you see the Add Fields To Forms page, make sure that the appropriate checkboxes are turned on, and then click Save.

   QuickBase creates your new fields and takes you to the application's Tables page. Any new fields you've added show up in the Fields table.

Now, when you open the form (for example, if you click the "Add a New Property" link in the example shown in Figure 6-12), your new fields appear at the bottom of the form.

Add a field in a specific spot

When you add new fields by starting from the Fields tab of the Tables page, QuickBase automatically tacks those new fields onto the bottom of the form. But you may not want them there. You want the fields in each record organized into logical segments of information, not scattered all over the place. For example, if you're managing residential property, you probably want information about a unit—number of bedrooms and so on—to appear in the Property Description section of the Add Property form rather than way down at the bottom of the page.

You can add a new field wherever you want it. Just open the form you want to add the field to, and then right-click an existing field that's close to where you want the new field to be. Up pops the shortcut menu shown in Figure 6-13.

Select "Add a field before this one" or "Add a field after this one." The Add a Field to a Form page opens. Scroll down to the bottom of its drop-down menu and select <Create a New Field>. The Create a New Field section magically appears on the page. Give your field a name and a type (see "Assigning field types" on page 235 for a full description of field types), then click Done. QuickBase slots in your new field, right where you specified.

Modify a field

You can change the properties of the fields in your QuickBase application. For example, you may want to change the width of a text box or, in a multiple-choice list of priorities, you may want to add *Red Alert!* to the current choices of High, Medium, and Low.

To modify a field, just follow these steps:

1. Choose Customize→Tables.

    The Tables page appears, as shown back in Figure 6-10. If you're in a multi-table application, choose the table you want from the left-hand list. If it's not already selected, click the Fields tab to see a list of the fields in the table you've chosen.

2. Find the name of the field you want to change and click it.

    The Fields page opens, with the Properties tab selected. Its options are specific to the field you're modifying, so your page may look different from the example in Figure 6-14.

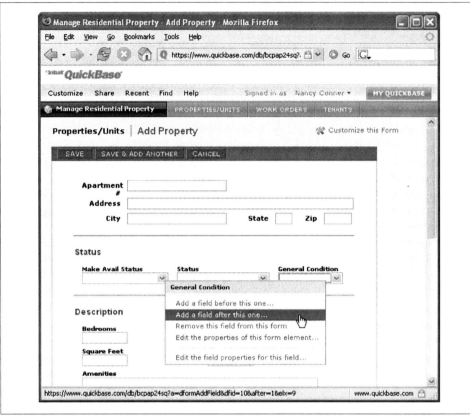

Figure 6-13. Add a new field wherever you like on an existing form by right-clicking a field either before or after where you want the new field to appear. You can also right-click any field to remove or modify it. (See "Modify a field" on page 223 for more on modifying an existing field.)

TIP

Looking for a speedier route to the Field Properties page? If you're looking at a Table report, just click the column heading of the field you want to change, then select "Edit this field's properties".

---

3. **Make your desired changes to the field.**

   You can change display options, restrict which roles can view or modify the data in the field, require unique values for the field, give Help directions, change the size of a text box or the options in a multiple-choice field, hide this field from searches, and more. The modifications you can make depend on the field.

4. **When you've finished making your changes, click Save (or Save & Next if you're modifying a bunch of fields).**

   QuickBase saves your changes and takes you back to the Tables page. If you want to see how the new form looks, then click the Add a New Record button.

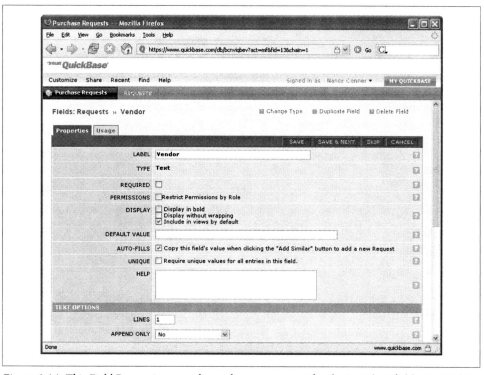

Figure 6-14. This Field Properties page shows the current setup for the "vendor" field in a purchase request application. (You may see different properties—like estimated cost or approval date—depending on the field.) A vendor name is a text field, and right now the field is multiple-choice. Users select from a list of vendors when adding a new record. You can make changes to any field properties on this page. If you have a question about a property, click the question mark at far right for instant help.

NOTE

You can't change a field's type—for example, you can't change from text to numeric or vice versa—in the form shown in Figure 6-14. To change a field's type, click the Change Type link at the top of the page.

Delete a field

When you want to get rid of a field, you have two choices:

- You can remove the field from the *form*. Although the field no longer appears in the form, it still exists, along with all the data it holds.

- You can delete the field from the *application*. This zaps the field into oblivion—completely, entirely, once and for all. It also deletes any data that was in the field. And when it's gone, it's gone.

To *remove* a field from a particular form (but still keep the field and its data in existence), open the form. You can open a form by clicking the upper-right Add a New Record link (such as Add a New Task or Add a New Document) or by selecting a table from the Table bar and choosing Add a New Record. Right-click the field you want to remove; doing so opens the shortcut menu shown back in Figure 6-13. Select "Remove this field from this form". QuickBase banishes the field (but it still appears on the Fields tab of the application's Tables page).

NOTE

Some forms are *built-in all-fields forms,* which means the form always displays all the fields it contains. If you try to remove a field from a built-in all-fields form, QuickBase opens a box explaining it can't remove fields from this type of form. If you still want to get rid of the field, then you'll have to delete it.

To *delete* a field, get to the Fields tab of the Tables page (Customize→Tables). Find the field you want to delete. In the far-right column is the Delete button; click it. QuickBase displays the usage statistics for that field. (And a good thing, too—if you find, for example, that more reports use the field than you'd thought, you may change your mind about getting rid of it.) On the Usage tab of the Fields page, click the upper-right Delete this Field button. A box appears, asking for confirmation. When you delete a field, you also delete all the data it holds, so be sure that's what you want to do. If you are, click "Yes, delete the field."

WARNING

When you delete a field and all its data, that stuff is really gone. You can't get it back after you've confirmed the deletion.

Add a table

Just because QuickBase built a template as a single-table application doesn't mean you have to keep it that way. In a matter seconds, you can add another table to an application by taking these steps:

1. With the application open, choose Customize→Tables.

   The Tables page opens.

2. On Tables page, click New Table (it's on the left-hand side, at the bottom of the list of existing tables).

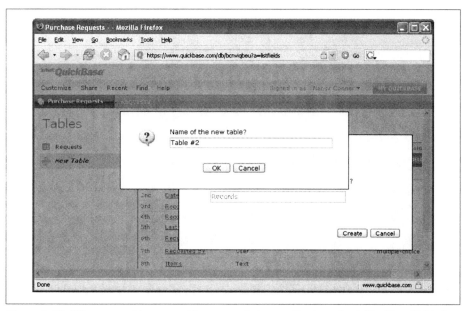

Figure 6-15. When you add a new table to an existing application, the Add a New Table box asks you to name the table and specify the type of records it will hold. Records might be work orders, purchase requests, timecards, sales leads, documents, and so on.

The Tables page grays out, and the Add a New Table box, shown in Figure 6-15, appears.

3. Type the name you want for records in that table.

Be specific: Purchase Orders, Requests, Issues—whatever best describes the kinds of records this table will hold.

4. Click Create.

QuickBase pops up another box, asking you to name the table itself. Type in the table's name. (To make things clear, give the table the same name as the records it holds: the Work Orders table holds work orders, the Timecards table holds timecards, the Ice Cream Flavors table holds—well, you get the idea.)

5. When you're satisfied with the names you've given a table and its records, click OK.

QuickBase creates the new table, giving it the built-in fields common to all Quick-Base tables—Date Created, Date Modified, Record ID#, Record Owner, and Last Modified By—and takes you back to the Tables page. Now you can work with the new table as you would any other, adding fields and records.

TIP

You can also specify who has access to this table. Click the Permissions tab to see which roles come built-in with your new table (usually Viewer, Team Member, and Manager) and to specify which roles can work with your new table. "Managing Roles" on page 351 tells you all about the different roles and how to set their privileges.

CHAPTER 7

Creating Your Own Application

Even though QuickBase offers many well-designed application templates (Chapter 6), there are a bunch of reasons why you might want to create your own application from scratch. You may be building an application for something unusual. Say you need to catalog a museum's rare butterfly collection and none of QuickBase's templates quite fits. Or maybe you have a spreadsheet that you want to convert into a QuickBase application. You like the way the spreadsheet is set up, and you don't want to spend time trying to make it fit into an application whose fields and records have already been defined. Or maybe you've decided to go from Microsoft Project to QuickBase for your project management needs, and you want to make the switch in the most painless way possible. Then again, you might want to design your own application just because you're a do-it-yourselfer. Whatever your reason, designing and creating a QuickBase application is easy, even if you've never thought about how databases work. (And if you're not quite sure what a database *is*, read the box in "Databasics" on page 230.)

This chapter shows you how to create single- and multi-table applications from scratch, and how to import data from other programs. (QuickBase can use data created in word processing, spreadsheet, and database programs. It can also pull in data from Microsoft Project.)

TIP

If you haven't already, take a look at Chapter 5. It helps you analyze what you need in an application so you'll have a clear sense of direction when you start working in QuickBase. Otherwise, you might end up heading down blind alleys or making mistakes that will take a long time to fix later on.

Building a New Application

QuickBase walks you through creating an application, one step at a time. You'll never get lost or confused as you create tables and define fields. Not only that, but you'll dazzle yourself (and your coworkers) with the results. Along the way, be prepared to answer the following questions:

- Should the application have several tables, or is one enough?
- What kind of records will a table hold?
- What fields will make up each record?
- What type of data will each field hold?

The first, and most important, decision you need to make is whether your application needs one table or several. The next section explains how to decide.

UP TO SPEED

Databasics

Before you jump in and start designing a brand-new QuickBase application, it helps to have some idea of what you're actually doing: creating a database. So if "database" is one of those words you throw around at parties without quite knowing what it means, read on (and try to get invited to more exciting parties).

A *database* is an organized collection of information. Strictly speaking, a database can be either paper or electronic. Technically, an album of baseball cards and a file cabinet stuffed with newspaper clippings are both databases, but nowadays the term usually refers to data stored on a computer in some systematic way. Databases hold their information in tables and can contain one table or many. A *table* is made up of records and fields. Each *record* (which represents a table row) holds information about one individual item, which can be a person, an object, a transaction, an issue, and so on. Each field holds a particular kind of information about each thing. So in a table whose records are people, the fields may be first name, last name, street, city, phone number, and so on. If you read down a column in a table, you're looking at just one field. So, for example, a column would show you all the telephone numbers of all the different registered customers. When you read across a row, on the other hand, you get the complete picture of a given customer.

The whole point of storing information in a database is that databases are *searchable*. You can instruct a computer to find records that match certain criteria in one or more fields to answer various questions: What did Shirley Krepinksi order on August 3? How many customers do we have in Idaho? What's our top-selling product in Zip code 02115?

Another important database feature is the *primary key*—a unique identifier (usually assigned automatically) to keep the records straight. Every record in a table has a primary key field. In a customer database, the primary key is probably the customer number. You might have two John Smiths buying from you, but only one of them is Cust594773. Primary keys keep your computer from getting confused when it searches a database.

As mentioned, a database can have more than one table (and if it does, each table needs its own, unique name). Usually, however, the tables don't just sit there in the same database. Their information's connected or interdependent in some way. A well-designed database maps out the *relationships* between tables. This cuts way back on duplicate information, because when tables are related, records from one table (like customer info or product details) can populate a field in another (like the Orders table), so you don't have to type in the same details over and over again.

Single-Table or Multi-Table?

The first step in building your own application is to pick whether you want the application to be single-table or multi-table. If you can store all your data in one spreadsheet, go with a single-table application. If you'd need several different spreadsheets to hold all your information, then you want a multi-table application.

Suppose, for example, you sell jewelry through online auctions. All you need to keep track of is the items you sell. You'd just need a single table with one record per item, containing information like price, minimum bid, description, ship date, and so on. Now suppose you add a different kind of information to the mix. You decide you want to keep track of your customers and store their contact information, with little nuggets like birthday reminders. Storing your customer info in the same table as your auction items doesn't make sense. People have names, Zip codes, and birthdays, not minimum bids and ship dates. So right away, you need to make the leap to a multi-table application.

TIP

If you're not sure whether to build a single- or multi-table application, start with a single-table. You can always add more tables later—see "Adding a Table to an Application" on page 318. On the flip side, if you find you've created tables you don't use or need, you can delete them ("Delete or Expel?" on page 258).

QuickBase wants to know whether you want a single- or multi-table application as soon as you start to create a new database. In the My QuickBase window, click the upper-right Create a New Application button. This takes you to the Create a New QuickBase Application page, shown in Figure 7-1. From there, you can create a single-table application, a multi-table application, or import data from a spreadsheet or Microsoft Project. (If your database information's already in another program, flip to "Creating an Application by Importing Data" on page 245.)

Creating a Single-Table Application: Spreadsheet Style

Your jewelry collection has grown to the point that you decide to sell some of it on eBay, and you're going to use QuickBase to keep track of it all. A Jewelry Collection application needs only one table, so you set out to create a new single-table application.

1. On the Create a New QuickBase Application page (My QuickBase→Create a New Application), click the "spreadsheet style" link.

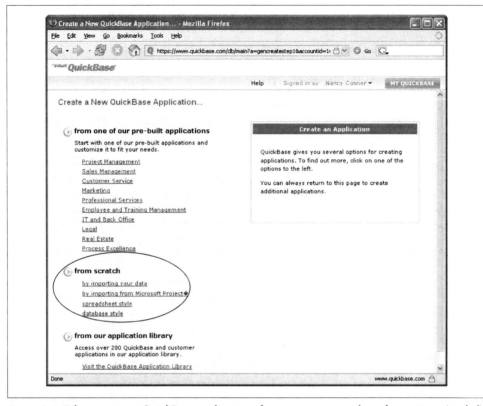

Figure 7-1. When creating a QuickBase application of your very own, you have four options (circled). If you want to start with data from another program—like Microsoft Project or an Excel spreadsheet —you can import that data and use it as the basis of your new application. If you want to design the application first and then enter data, choose spreadsheet style for a single-table application or database style for a multi-table application. To get a peek at applications others have designed, click the "Visit the QuickBase Application Library" link at the bottom of the page.

The Create an Application box on the right side of the window changes to display a Spreadsheet Style link. Click it, and a Create From Scratch page like the one in Figure 7-2 opens.

2. **In the "Name for this application" box, give your new application a descriptive name.**

You don't *have* to give it a name—as far as QuickBase is concerned, *Untitled Application* is a perfectly fine name. (But good luck finding your jewelry collection among 15 different Untitled Applications on your My QuickBase page.) For this example, *Jewelry Collection* fits the bill.

3. **In the second text box, tell QuickBase what you want to call records in this application.**

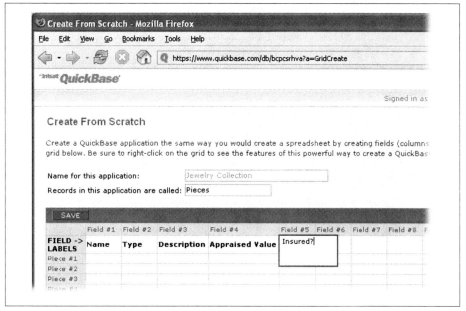

Figure 7-2. When you create a new spreadsheet-style application, you can tell QuickBase what to call records in the new application (the default is Records). Field Labels (the spreadsheet's top row) become the column headers. You can start entering information about individual records now (Piece #1, Piece #2, and so on) or just create the fields and enter data later.

This word will appear on the Add a New Record link in the new application. If you don't specify anything here, QuickBase calls records *Records*, which is fine and not at all confusing—just a little generic and bland. Depending on the application, you may want to call records *receipts, employees, orders, contacts, issues, tasks, requisitions*—whatever word best describes the kind of record the application holds. For the Jewelry Collection application, where each record describes one piece of jewelry, it makes sense to call a record a *piece*.

The Create From Scratch page is also where you define the fields in your QuickBase table.

4. Create Field Labels.

Fields are the different bits of information a record contains (think of them as columns in a spreadsheet). For example, each piece of jewelry in your collection might have a name, a type (earrings, bracelet, necklace), a detailed description (setting, number of carats), and an appraised value—each of these represents one field.

To create fields, click the cell just below Field #1. When a black outline appears around the cell you've selected, enter the Field Label you want to use. The bold black outline changes to red, and the letters you type appear inside the cell.

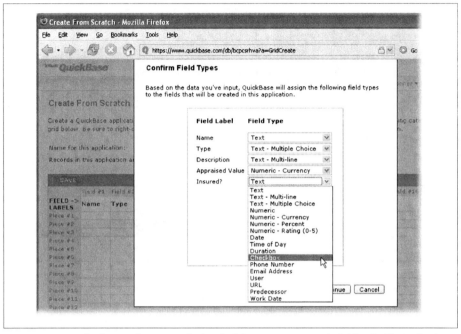

Figure 7-3. Use this box to determine the kind of data you want each field to hold. As the drop-down menu shows, you have a lot of choices. Most are self-explanatory—for a field that holds only monetary values, for example, choose Numeric – Currency. (For the full scoop on field types, see "Assigning field types" on page 235.)

5. To move to the next cell and create another Field Label, hit the Tab key or select the next cell with the cursor.

   After you've named some fields, you can start adding records if you want. You add records the same way you created the Field Labels: select a cell and start typing. You don't have to add records now, however.

6. When you've created all the Field Labels you want (you can always add or delete fields later; see "Customizing Fields and Tables" on page 219), click Save. (It's at the far right, in both the header and footer of the spreadsheet.)

   The Confirm Field Types box, shown in Figure 7-3, appears. This box has two columns:

   Field Label contains the names you've given the fields in your new application.

   Field Type contains drop-down menus that list data type options for each field. All fields start out as text fields. You may want to change some of them (to Numeric – Currency for the "Appraised value" field, say). If so, click the down arrow and make your selection. (See "Assigning field types" on page 235 to learn all about the different field types).

---

7. When you've assigned field types, click Continue.

   QuickBase creates your application and takes you to its Dashboard page. Even if you haven't entered any data yet, your new application has two reports built in: List All and List Changes. (You can find them in the Reports menu on the left side of the Dashboard). Some new applications will have more than these two reports; QuickBase is pretty clever at figuring out how you might want to view the data in your application.

From your new application's Dashboard, you can add records using a form, as shown in Figure 7-4. You can also create a new report, customize the Dashboard, or do any of the other cool things you can do with any QuickBase application.

Assigning field types

When you're creating a brand-new application, not only do you have to create its different fields, you have to tell QuickBase what kinds of fields to create. The field type determines what sort of information the field will hold, and whether the field requires a particular format. Some field types are open-ended, so a user can type in anything at all; others are restricted in some way, as in a multiple-choice list.

You can change an existing field's type from the Fields tab of the Tables page (Customize→Tables). Click the name of the field you want to change. On the page that opens, click the Change Type link at the top of the form to get to the Change Field Type page. From the drop-down menu, select the new field type you want. Click Convert Data to change the field type.

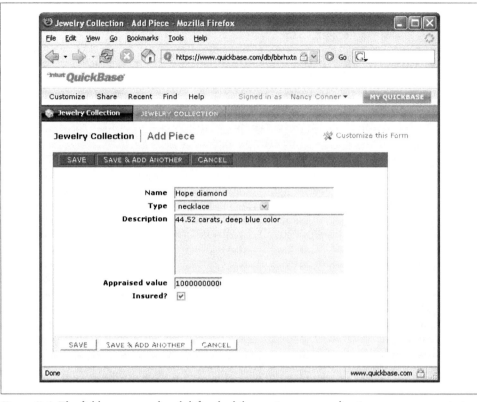

Figure 7-4. The fields you named and defined while creating your application now appear—just as you set them up—on the application's Add Record page. This figure shows how the field types chosen in Figure 7-3 display on the page when you add a new record.

WARNING

When you change a field type, the change may affect the data that the field holds. For example, if you have a Cost field that holds numbers in the form of currency and you change that field to Numeric—Rating, it'll mess up your data, changing a $100 cost into a five-star rating. So be careful. QuickBase does try to head off any mistakes you might make in choosing a field type; if you specify an invalid field type on the Change Field Type page, QuickBase returns an error message and takes no action to change the field type.

Of course, whether you're creating a new field or changing an existing one, you need to understand what kind of data a particular field type holds—when you do, you can have a field day with field types. Your application works most smoothly and efficiently when each field type matches the kind of information it contains. Here are your choices:

- **Text** is the most versatile and common field type. Despite the name, a text field isn't restricted to letters. It can hold letters, numbers, symbols—any character you can type. The box you get is the familiar long rectangle. Users can type in more characters than that rectangle can hold—an unlimited number of characters, in fact—but if they do, they can't easily see what they've typed. If users are likely to enter lots of text, choose the next field type: Text—Multi-line.

- **Text—Multi-line** is the same as a Text field, but with a little more room. As its name suggests, this field displays a box containing several lines (rather than just one). Use it when you want to give your users room to expand on the data in a field. For example, it's good for fields like Notes, Comments, or Detailed Description.

TIP

Sometimes, people can go on and on, filling up a Comments field with pages of information or opinions, for example. If you want a comment—not a book—you can restrict a text field's length to a specific number of characters. After you've created a text field, edit its properties, using the Maximum Length field to specify the maximum number of characters people can enter in that field.

- **Text—Multiple Choice** takes the form of one of those nifty drop-down lists, but you get to specify the choices. So you may use it for a field like Priority (Low, Medium, High) or Contacts (with a list of names). Multiple choice is the way to go when you need choices to be restricted (as in, you don't want some joker typing *Mickey Mouse* into the Contacts field), but you want users to be able to add a new choice to the list (<Add New Choice> appears as an option in the multiple-choice list). That way, when a new contact named Michael Mauss appears, you don't necessarily have to be the one who remembers to add him to the list of contact names. (To learn more about creating and editing multiple-choice text fields, see "Shared Multiple-Choice Fields" on page 402.)

TIP

You can write form rules to nest subfields in multiple-choice fields. For example, you might have a multiple-choice list that displays states. When someone clicks a state, another multiple-choice list displays the counties in that state. "Using Form Rules to Create Nested Multiple-Choice Lists" on page 453 tells you how to nest multiple-choice lists.

- **Numeric** can contain only numbers. If someone types in any other kind of character, like a letter or the @ symbol, QuickBase displays an error message, telling them to try again using numbers.
- **Numeric—Currency** tracks money to help you keep an eye on the bottom line. You can even specify the currency symbol displayed with the amount—$, £, or ¥, for example—by editing the field's properties ("Editing a field's properties" on page 299).

- **Numeric—Percent** accepts only numbers and displays its contents as a percent. So if you type 72, the field displays 72%.

- **Numeric—Rating (0–5)** is a multiple-choice field that lets users rank something on a scale of zero to five. (Even if you tweak the numbers by editing the field's properties ["Editing a field's properties" on page 299], this field won't display numbers higher than five). Of course, you could use a multiple-choice Text field to present a list from zero to five, but the cool thing about this field is that it displays the selections using stars instead of a number. If someone were rating your job performance, wouldn't you rather have five shining stars than a boring old number 5?

- **Date** holds a date—nothing else. When you make a field a Date field, QuickBase displays a calendar button next to the field in forms, making it easy for people to find and enter the right date. Usually, dates appear in MM-DD-YYYY format (12-22-2007, for example). By editing this field's properties, you can change the format to display the month by name, add the day of the week, drop the year if it's the current one, and so on.

- **Date/Time** is like a Date field, only better. You get the calendar button and can type a time, as well.

- **Time of Day** holds the time of day in one of two formats: 12-hour (2:27 PM) or 24-hour (14:27).

- **Duration.** As its name suggests, this field holds a period of time: weeks, days, hours, minutes, even seconds. You can measure time in whatever format makes most sense to you. For example, if you're estimating the time it will take to complete a certain task, you can show that estimate as 6 hours, .25 days, or 06:00.

NOTE

This field has a feature called Smart Units, which displays duration in the easiest-to-understand unit. For example, with Smart Units turned on, if you type *180 min*, QuickBase displays *3 hours*, and *168 h* as *1 week*.

- **Checkbox.** A checkbox lets you collect two possible pieces of information—Yes or No. To indicate Yes, users turn on a checkbox by clicking inside it. To indicate No, users leave the checkbox alone (or, if there's already a check in the box, click in the box to turn it off). For example, a checkbox labeled "OK to call at home?" lets salespeople keep track of customers who don't like to be interrupted during dinner.

- **Phone Number.** As the name implies, this numeric field displays its numbers in phone-number format, with or without extensions. If you type in *5559478*, the record displays *555-9478*. And if you type in *8005559478*, the record looks like this: *(800) 555-9478*. If you put a 1 in front of a long-distance number, you get this: *1 (800) 555-9478*. QuickBase applies phone number formatting from right to left, so it recognizes the last seven digits as the local phone number. Because it's a numeric field, a Phone Number field won't accept letters. So if you type *1-800-CALL-NOW* into a Phone Number field, QuickBase displays just *1800*.

- **Email Address.** When someone types an email address into this field, QuickBase displays the address as an email link. If you want to send an email to that address, click it. QuickBase launches your email program (if necessary) and opens a new, blank email with the address already filled in.

- **User.** This field stores info about a QuickBase user. It's useful for fields like Assigned To, when you want the User field to hold info about people who have access to the application—there's not much point in assigning a task to someone who'll never see it. This field displays the user names you've selected in a drop-down list. (This can be useful when you want QuickBase to send a reminder to a person in the Assigned To field, for example.) You also have the option of letting users add new choices to that list.

- **File Attachment.** Many applications need supporting documents. Use this field to let users attach a file—like a Word document or an image—to a record. When someone attaches a file, QuickBase copies the file and displays a link users can click to open the file.

- **URL.** A URL (which stands for *uniform resource locator*) is the address you type into your Web browser to get to a Web page, like www.quickbase.com (*http://www.quickbase.com*). You can display the URL as a link or as a button with text, like *Click here!* You can also direct QuickBase to open a new browser window when someone clicks the link, so folks don't surf away from the application in pursuit of more info.

- **Report Link.** This field lets you link records in one table with records in another table. (For more on linking tables, see "Linking Tables" on page 387.)

- **iCalendar.** iCalendar is an industry-standard data format that allows the exchange of calendar information. As a field type, it bundles up certain information from time-related records (such as tasks) and keeps them in a portable format. For example, you might have an important meeting listed in the Tasks table—iCalendar can store the name of the task (say, Strategy Meeting), its date, start and end times, and so on, all in one packet. Users click the iCalendar icon to download the info. From there, they can store it or open it in Outlook—and many other programs—to add it to their own calendars.

- **vCard.** Like iCalendar, vCard is a widely used format that makes information portable; vCard's specialty is contact information. Store items like somebody's name, email address, phone and fax numbers—the stuff you'd put on a business card—in a vCard field. Then users can click the vCard icon and download that virtual business card. From there it's easy to open the info in Outlook or most other email programs and store it in the address book.

NOTE

For more about using iCalendar and vCard, see "Using vCard and iCalendar with QuickBase" on page 176.

- **Predecessor.** In an application that tracks tasks, very often one task must be completed before the next can begin. For example, your team has to gather requirements before they can write the requirements specification, and they have to write the specification before the review process can begin. The whole process is like a chain, where each element depends on the one before it. The Predecessor field shows these dependencies as a list of tasks that must be finished before a subsequent task can begin.

- **Work Date.** Like a regular Date field, this field holds a date and displays it in the format you choose. When you use it together with a Predecessor field, however, a Work Date field is much smarter than a plain ol' Date field. Work Date helps you keep precise track of predecessor tasks and how much time they need. In this kind of field, QuickBase can use parts of days in computations (regular Date fields work only with full days). For example, if you initially estimate that a predecessor task is going to take three days, and then, later on, tack on another day and a half, QuickBase automatically advances the date for the followup task by *two* days—because if you extend a three-day job by a day and a half, that job finishes not on the fourth day but on the fifth.

- **Formula fields.** Formulas are how tables get smart—instead of just holding data, formulas tell QuickBase to perform some sort of calculation on the field. There are many kinds of formula fields: Text, Numeric, Date, Time of Day, Duration, Checkbox, Phone Number, Email Address, URL, and Work Date. To find out how to get fancy with formulas, skip to "Writing Formulas" on page 417.

NOTE

There are a few kinds of fields that apply only to related tables in multi-table applications. To learn about those, see "Linking Tables" on page 387.

Creating a Multi-Table Application: Database Style

Sometimes one isn't enough—a bicycle with just one wheel, sunglasses with just one lens, a wristwatch with just one hand. And when it comes to storing and tracking data, sometimes you need more than a single spreadsheet or table. You need an application with multiple tables to store different—but related—kinds of information.

Here's an example. Say it's your job to plan company events. In that case your multi-table application might have the following three tables:

- **Venues.** In this table you'd track location, facilities, available square footage, prices, cancellation policy, and so on. Different events require different kinds of ven-

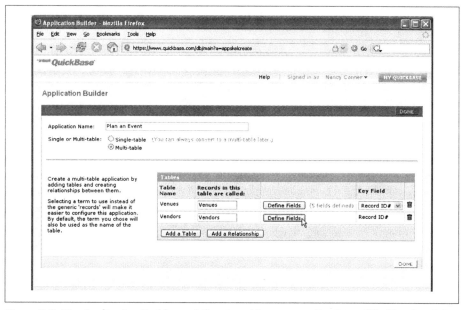

Figure 7-5. Use Application Builder to define the tables your application will hold and to define the fields that make up the records in each table. You can link tables by creating a relationship between them. (For more on linking, see "Linking Tables" on page 387.) And if you change your mind about a table, just click the far-right trash can icon to delete it.

ues. You wouldn't want to hold the annual shareholders' meeting at a state park or the softball tournament in a ballroom.

- **Vendors.** Track caterers, entertainment, florists, printers, equipment rental companies, and so on. Which caterer made those hot wings everyone loved at last year's company picnic? What was the name of the string quartet the boss said sounded like prowling alley cats? You'd keep vendors in a separate table from venues so you can easily search for what you need, and so you don't have to retype vendor info for each event.

- **Tasks.** Planning an event takes a huge number of steps. Making reservations, touring facilities, sending in deposits, choosing a menu, mailing invitations, putting up fliers—the list goes on and on. Even if you've got the process down to a science, it's helpful to track what you've done and what you still have to do.

1. To create a multi-table application, head to the Create a New QuickBase Application page (My QuickBase→Create a New Application) and then click the "database style" link. When a Database Style link appears in the upper-right Create an Application box, click it.

   Application Builder opens (shown in Figure 7-5).

2. In the Application Name box, name your new application so you can find it easily on your My QuickBase page.

Plan an Event would be a good name for an application that holds information related to setting up the annual company picnic or holiday party.

3. Tell QuickBase that you want to create an application with more than one table by turning on the Multi-table radio button.

   The current page changes to explain a bit about multi-table applications and to display the Tables table, where you create the first table in your new application. There's also an Add a Table button, for when you're ready to create a second (or third, or fourth) table.

TIP

You can use Application Builder to build either a single- or a multi-table application. If you're comfortable working with spreadsheets, though, you may find spreadsheet-style ("Creating a Single-Table Application: Spreadsheet Style" on page 231) the easier route to creating a single-table application. Not only can you see the columns and rows as you design the application, you can add data at the same time. With Application Builder, you design the application first, adding data only *after* the application has been created.

---

4. Next, tell Application Builder what you want to call the records in your first table.

   QuickBase gives the table the same name.

5. Click the Define Fields button to name and define the fields that the table will hold, as Figure 7-6 shows. In the box that opens, give a name and assign a field type to each field in the new table.

   Don't worry if you haven't figured out all the fields yet; you can always add more later ("Add a field" on page 219). When you're done adding fields, click OK.

TIP

Note: You don't *have* to define any fields right now—QuickBase will happily create empty tables or even a blank application. But if you know at least some of the fields, you might as well set them up now.

---

6. If you want to designate a field you've created as the table's *key field,* select it from the drop-down list in the Key Field column of the Tables table.

   Every record in a database has a key field (sometimes called a *primary key*) to identify it as a unique record, so that, for example, if you've got two different vendors named Mary Johnson, you can remember which Mary is the caterer and which Mary does the juggling-and-sword-swallowing act. Usually, a key field is an ID number automatically assigned by QuickBase when someone creates a new record. Most of the time, using this Record ID # for the key field is exactly what you want. Occasionally, though, you may want to use some other unique identifier for the key field, like an Employee ID number or a Customer number. After you've defined some fields within a table, you can change that table's key field. When you

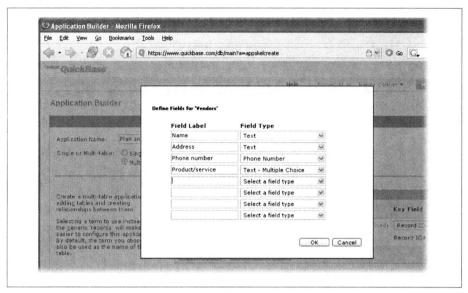

Figure 7-6. When you create a table, you have to give a name and assign a type to each field in the table.

define some fields for a new table in Application Builder, QuickBase adds those fields to the Key Field drop-down list.

7. To add the next table, click Application Builder's Add a Table button.

QuickBase adds a row to the Tables table, letting you name another table and define its fields. Keep going until you've defined all the tables you want in the application —at least for now. You can always add ("Adding a Table to an Application" on page 318) or delete ("Delete or Expel?" on page 258) tables later.

TIP

In the far-right column of the Tables table is a picture of a trash can. If you decide you don't need one of the tables you've created, click the trash can icon to dump it.

After you've created at least two tables, you can create a relationship, as described next, to link them. If you don't want to do that now (you can always do it later), click Done. QuickBase creates your new multi-table application and displays its Dashboard page.

Creating relationships between tables

In a multi-table application, relationships between tables save you a lot of time, effort, and typing. Simply put, a *relationship* links two tables. In QuickBase, when you create a relationship, you're telling QuickBase to take a record from one table and make that record a field in another table.

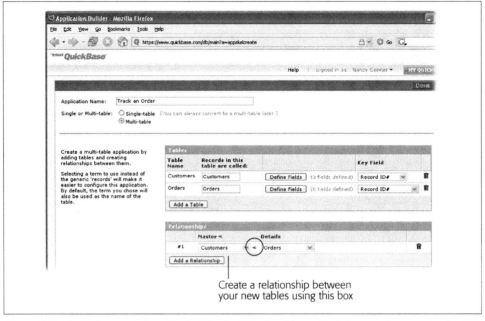

Create a relationship between
your new tables using this box

Figure 7-7. The little crow's foot (circled) in the Relationships table helps you keep track of which table's the master table and which is the details table in a relationship. One record in the master table can relate to many records in the details table.

If the concept sounds a bit abstract, it's easy to grasp when you apply it. Imagine that you're creating an application to track customer orders. When an existing customer places a new order, you don't want to have to type in all the information you already know about the customer: name, address, phone number, credit card number, and all that jazz. So you create two tables: Orders and Customers. By creating a relationship between these tables, you can set things up so that someone entering a new order can use a drop-down list to select the customer who placed the order, rather than typing in all the customer's info.

NOTE

This section barely scratches the surface about QuickBase relationships and what you can do with them. For the full scoop, check out Chapter 10.

In Application Builder, when you click the Add a Relationship button, Application Builder displays a Relationship table, as shown in Figure 7-7.

QuickBase uses the concept of *one-to-many* relationships to define which table's the so-called master table and which is the details table. One-to-many simply means that *one* record in the master table can be associated with *many* records in the details table, but not vice versa. Put another way, a single customer can place many different orders, but a single order can't belong to many different customers—each order's associated with only one customer. So in defining the one-to-many relationship, the one thing (customer) that can have many different things associated with it (orders) is the master table.

In Application Builder, choose the master table and the details table. QuickBase helps you remember which is which by showing a little crow's foot that begins at *one* point and grows into *many* branches. To the left of the crow's foot, next to the one point, is the master table; to the right, where it branches out, is the details table. Click Add a Relationship to create another relationship or Done to create the application.

NOTE

You don't have to define relationships when you're creating a new application; you can create relationships between tables—even across applications—in applications that already exist. Chapter 10 tells you everything you need to know about relationships (the kind involving tables, that is—if you've got questions about your love life, try Dear Abby instead).

Creating an Application by Importing Data

Chapter 3 tells you all about how to import data into an existing QuickBase application. But you can also create a whole new application by importing data from another program, such as Microsoft Word, Excel, or Project. So if you've been emailing spreadsheets around to everyone on your team, you can simplify your life greatly by using that spreadsheet to create a QuickBase application—giving everyone easy, centralized, up-to-the-minute access to data.

To create a new application using data from another program, you can copy and paste the data, import it as a file, or import from Microsoft Project. Whichever method you choose, start from the Create a New QuickBase Application page (My Quick-Base→Create a New Application).

Copying and Pasting

If your data's currently in a Word table or an Excel spreadsheet, you can simply copy the data and paste it into QuickBase. QuickBase analyzes the data and suggests a table structure, which you can then adjust as needed.

Say you've been keeping records about your jewelry collection in a Word table and decide you want to create a QuickBase application instead. You may start off with a table that looks like the one in Figure 7-8.

To create a new application by copying data from another program and pasting it into QuickBase, follow these steps:

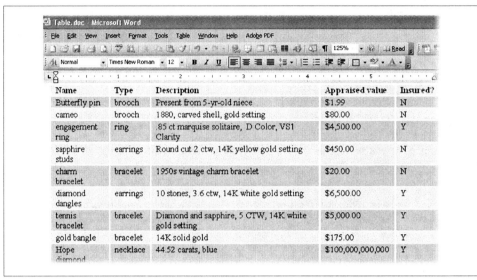

Name	Type	Description	Appraised value	Insured?
Butterfly pin	brooch	Present from 5-yr-old niece	$1.99	N
cameo	brooch	1880, carved shell, gold setting	$80.00	N
engagement ring	ring	.85 ct marquise solitaire, D Color, VS1 Clarity	$4,500.00	Y
sapphire studs	earrings	Round cut 2 ctw, 14K yellow gold setting	$450.00	N
charm bracelet	bracelet	1950s vintage charm bracelet	$20.00	N
diamond dangles	earrings	10 stones, 3.6 ctw, 14K white gold setting	$6,500.00	Y
tennis bracelet	bracelet	Diamond and sapphire, 5 CTW, 14K white gold setting	$5,000.00	Y
gold bangle	bracelet	14K solid gold	$175.00	Y
Hope diamond	necklace	44.52 carats, blue	$100,000,000,000	Y

Figure 7-8. Even if your Word table has a lot of fancy formatting, you can copy and paste it right into QuickBase. QuickBase strips out the formatting (which it can't use) and converts your data into a QuickBase-style table.

1. On the Create a New QuickBase Application page, click the "by importing your data" link.

   The upper-right Create an Application box changes to display information about importing data.

2. Click the Create Now link.

   QuickBase opens the Creating Via Import—Step 1 page, shown in Figure 7-9.

3. In your original document or spreadsheet, select the data you want to paste. Then copy your selection to the Clipboard by choosing Edit→Copy from the menu bar or by typing Ctrl+C (in Windows) or ⌘-C (on a Mac).

   Any selection method will do. In Word, for example, you can select an entire table by clicking in it and choosing Table→Select→Table. To select data in a spreadsheet program, you can drag across cells to select them, and then let go of the mouse button when you've highlighted what you want.

4. After choosing the Copy command, go back to QuickBase's Creating Via Import —Step 1 page. Click in the "Paste into here" text box and select Edit→Paste (or press Ctrl+V in Windows; ⌘-V on a Mac).

   Your data appears in the text box.

5. Click Next.

   QuickBase opens the Import page, looking something like the one shown in Figure 7-10. This page shows how QuickBase has analyzed your data to name its fields (using the headings from the columns in your table) and assign field types.

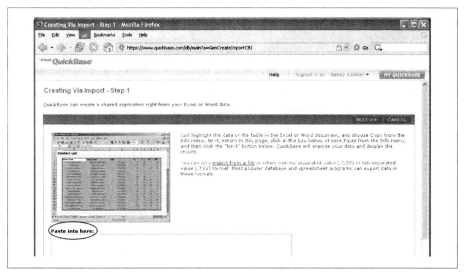

Figure 7-9. Paste your data into the "Paste into here" box (circled).

6. Look at the field types and make sure they're what you want.

   For example, even though Description is a text field, you may want to change it to Text—Multi-line to give yourself a little more typing room when entering data. Or you might want a text field to be a multiple-choice field. If you choose the multiple-choice field type, QuickBase automatically makes the contents of that field the different choices.

7. When everything looks OK, click Import.

   QuickBase pops up a box where you can name your application and its records—it's a good idea to call them something more interesting than *Records* (like *Tasks, Work Orders, Timecards,* or whatever).

8. Type in the name of your new application and what QuickBase should call its records, and then click OK.

   QuickBase creates the application and opens its Dashboard page. Figure 7-11 shows an example.

Importing a File

Copying and pasting isn't the only way to get your spreadsheet data into QuickBase. If you can save a spreadsheet as either a .csv (comma-separated values) or a .tsv (tab-separated values) file, you can import that file into QuickBase. Doing so is a snap—and is probably the fastest way to create a database on the fly.

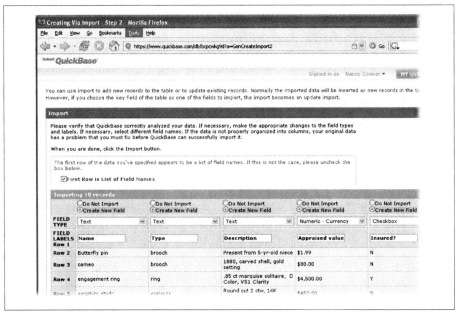

Figure 7-10. When you paste in data to create a new application, QuickBase analyzes that data to create Field Labels (column headings) and assign field types. For example, QuickBase sees the data in the Insured? column is always Y or N and interprets this as a checkbox field. You can modify these field types now, or just click Import and change them later.

TIP

Before you begin, make sure you've saved the spreadsheet you want to import as a .csv or .tsv file. (Excel, for example, offers the .csv format.) And remember where you saved it, because you'll have to tell QuickBase where to get it.

When you're ready to import the file, follow these steps:

1. Go to the Create a New QuickBase Application page, and then click the "by importing your data" link.

   The upper-right text box displays a Create Now link.

2. Click Create Now.

   The Creating Via Import—Step 1 page opens.

3. Click the "import from a file" link.

   A different version of the Creating Via Import—Step 1 page opens. Figure 7-12 shows you what this one looks like.

4. Click the Browse button.

   A File Upload window opens.

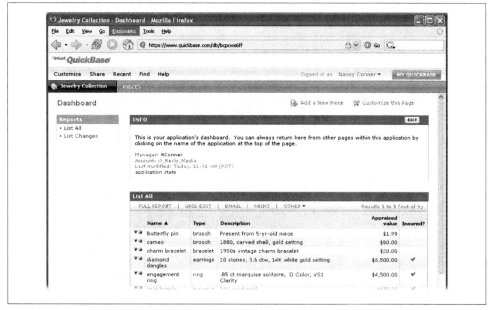

Figure 7-11. The simple table from Figure 7-8 becomes a powerful and versatile QuickBase application. QuickBase also analyzes the data you imported and the field types you assigned to create some helpful reports in your new application.

5. Find the file you want to upload. Click the file name, and then click Open.

   The name and path of the file you selected appear in the Creating Via Import—Step 1 page.

6. Click Next.

   The Import page opens (the same one you saw back in Figure 7-10). From here, the steps are the same as steps 6–8 in the previous section for copying and pasting a file. Confirm that the field labels and types are what you want, and then name the application and its records.

Importing from Microsoft Project

Microsoft Project is one of the world's most popular project management programs. QuickBase has created a synchronization tool to get your Project files and your Quick-Base applications on the same page. You can use this synchronization tool if you want to switch from Project to QuickBase for project management, or if you want to use both Project and QuickBase at the same time. For example, you may want your Project files formatted as QuickBase applications so that your team can easily share and update project management data. Whenever you like, you can export QuickBase info back into Project, updating your original Project file.

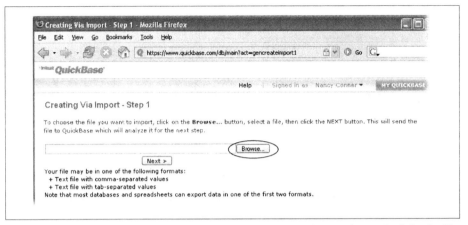

Figure 7-12. Importing a .csv or .tsv file is as easy as telling QuickBase where to look for the file. Use the Browse button (circled) to find and select the file you want to import.

To get QuickBase and Project in sync, start from your My QuickBase and click Create a New Application. On the page that opens, click the "by importing from Microsoft Project" link. Then, in the upper-right Create an Application box, click Import from MS Project.

This opens the Converting a Microsoft Project File into a QuickBase Application page, which gives you step-by-step instructions for using a Project file as the basis for a new application. Here are those steps in a nutshell:

1. Download the synchronization tool to your computer. (Obviously, this has to be the same computer on which you've got Project installed.)

   On the Converting a Microsoft Project File into a QuickBase Application page, right-click the QuickBase/Microsoft Project Synchronization Tool link. You can't miss it: It's in big blue letters near the top of the page. From the shortcut menu that pops up, select Save Target As or Save Link As (or even Save Link Target As).

   A Save As box opens, asking where you want your computer to save the file.

2. Indicate where you want to save the synchronization tool. Desktop is a good choice because the file's easy to find after the download's complete. Click Save.

   Your computer downloads the file and saves it where you specified.

3. Find the file (it's called QuickBaseProject.mpp) and double-click it.

   MS Project starts up and opens the file.

TIP

If Project starts yelling about macros and safety problems, turn on the "Always trust macros from this publisher" checkbox and click Enable Macros.

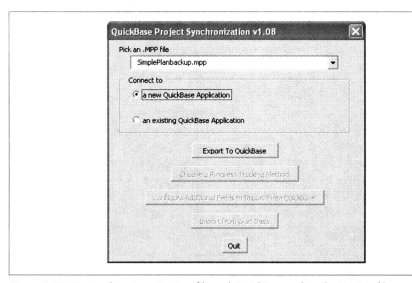

Figure 7-13. To synchronize a Project file and QuickBase, select the Project file you want from the drop-down list. If you're creating a brand-new QuickBase application, your only choices are to export the Project file or quit. If you're importing data to an existing application, the other buttons allow you to synchronize Project and the existing QuickBase application, as well as tell QuickBase whether you want to move data from Project to QuickBase or vice versa.

4. In Project, open whatever project or projects you want to use to create your new QuickBase application. Make sure all files are open, and then make QuickBase-Project.mpp the active window in Project. Finally, type Ctrl+Q.

   A box appears, asking for your QuickBase sign-in info.

5. Type in your QuickBase ID and password, and then click the Sign In button.

   A dialog box like the one shown in Figure 7-13 opens.

6. From the "Pick an .MPP file" drop-down menu (at the top of the box), select the Project file you want to convert to a QuickBase application. Just below the menu, in the "Connect to" section, turn on the "a new QuickBase application" radio button. Then click Export to QuickBase.

   QuickBase creates your new application and shows you a message box to let you know it succeeded. The message tells you when the application was created and how many records were added.

7. Click OK to acknowledge the message and close the box.

   QuickBase takes you to your My QuickBase page, where your new application appears in your Applications list.

When Copying Won't Work

Why can't I copy my application?

When you try to copy an application, QuickBase may tell you that it can't make a copy. Several things can trigger this message:

- You don't have permission to create applications. Talk to the person who manages your billing account to request this permission.

- You're not an administrator of the application you want to copy, and the person who created the application has turned off copying for non-administrators. Talk to the application's manager.

- At least one table in the application holds more than 20 MB of data.

- The application has more than 75 MB of attachments.

The size restrictions mentioned in the last two items above are there to make sure QuickBase *stays* quick—copying huge applications with tons of data could slow it way down, and no one wants that. When an application is too big to copy, you've got two choices: You can copy the application without its data (so you get the application's structure but none of the information it holds), or go back and delete obsolete data and attachments from the application before copying. Just make sure you're not getting rid of anything you—or someone else—might need later!

Copying an Existing Application

You don't have to reinvent the wheel each time you build a new application. Besides using QuickBase's prebuilt templates (explained in Chapter 6), you can copy an existing application, with or without its data, and use it as the starting point for a new application. Doing so can be helpful when you've spent time building and tweaking an application and you need a similar structure for a new application. Copying an application also comes in handy when you're considering a change to an existing application (maybe you want to add a table, but you're not sure how the addition would work out in practice). Copying lets you try the change on for size before you commit to it. If the change works out, great. If not, you can delete the copy and keep the original as it was.

Copying an existing application is so easy your three-year-old nephew could do it:

1. Open the application you want to copy. Then select Customize→Import/Export. The Import/Export page opens.

2. Turn on the "Copy this application" radio button, and then click the Copy This Application link. (If "Copy this application" is grayed out, the application's administrator hasn't given you permission to copy the application. And if you try to turn on that radio button, anyway, QuickBase reminds you that, for your role, copying this application is a no-no.)

The Table Properties page opens. This is where you define the new application you're creating. On this page, the application's name is already filled in, starting with "Copy of." If you're copying an application called *Manage Project CHAOS* , for example, the name here will read *Copy of Manage Project CHAOS*.

3. If you want, change the application's name (or you can change it later) and write a description of the application. After that, you've got two choices to make:

   - **Data.** You can copy the application with all its current data, or you can copy it without data to get the application's structure but leave behind the information it holds. If you're experimenting with making a change to a working application, copy the application *with* its data so you can get a feel for how the change will work. (For an application that has attachments you want to copy, as well, turn on the "including file attchments" checkbox.) If you're using the application as a model for a brand-new application, copy it *without* the data so you can fill in the new application with fresh data all its own.

   - **Users & Roles.** You can copy over all the current users with or without the roles they have in the application you're copying. Copying users *with* their roles is helpful when the same team is starting a new project—QuickBase automatically assigns everyone the roles they had in the previous project. If you're going to be adding new team members or changing roles (or if you simply don't want any of the users to have access to the copied application just yet), turn on "Copy users and roles separately (don't assign roles)."

4. After you've made your choices, click Copy Application.

   QuickBase creates your new application and takes you to its Dashboard page. From there, you can work with the copy as you would any other application.

Keep in mind that, after you've made a copy, the copy is a whole new application. If you've copied an application so you can experiment without messing up the working application (you might want to try adding a new table or creating some custom Dashboards, for example), the application you copied is completely separate from the original. As you experiment, users are adding, modifying, and deleting records in the original application. So even if you start out with an exact copy, by the end of the day, the original will probably hold different data from the copy you made.

By the way, if the thought of other QuickBase users copying and messing with *your* application makes you feel protective (let 'em design their own darn application!), you can limit others' ability to copy an application you manage. Here's how:

1. Open the application you want to stay one-of-a-kind and then select Customize→Application.

   QuickBase opens the Application page (take a peek at this page in Figure 7-14).

2. If it's not selected already, click the Settings tab, and then click Advanced Settings from the left-hand menu.

   QuickBase shows you a variety of advanced options for managing your application.

3. In the Options section, make sure that the checkbox labeled "Allow users who are not administrators to copy" is turned *off*. Then click Save Changes.

   The application is yours, all yours. Only users with administrative-level privileges in this application can copy it.

Modifying an Application's Properties

Once you've created a new application, you'll probably want to take some time perfecting it, tweaking it, and adding those finishing touches that make all the difference. QuickBase's versatility means that when you build an application, whether from scratch or using a template, it's never set in stone. For any application, you (and other administrators) can:

- Add or modify fields
- Customize the Dashboard
- Create and save different reports
- Add or delete tables
- Create relationships between tables or applications
- Invite others to come over and play with your application ("Sharing an Application" on page 280)
- Create and assign roles to control levels of access

You can also change the properties of an existing application, putting the final touches on your magnum opus of data storage and sharing. To see what properties you can change, open the application and, from the menu bar, select Customize→Application to open the page shown in Figure 7-14.

When you click Customize→Application, you see the following tabs:

- **Settings.** The Settings tab is your control center for a variety of look and feel options in your application. The left-hand menu shows you what you can tweak on this tab:

  —**Name and Description.** This section has text boxes where you can change the name and the description of the application. It also shows you who the application's manager is. (If that's you, and you want someone else to take over, click the "transfer" link and fill in the screen name or email address of your lucky successor.)

  —**Branding.** Click Branding to customize the appearance ("Customizing an Application's Appearance" on page 215) of the pages in your application or to add a logo or link to emails that QuickBase sends from this application on your behalf.

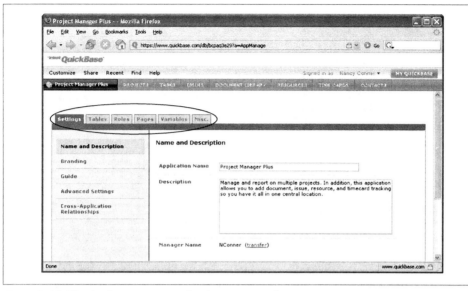

Figure 7-14. The Application page is the place to start when you want to customize various parts of your application. The tabs across the top of the page (circled) let you zero in on which aspects of the application you want to change or manage. On some tabs, such as the Settings tab shown here, there's a menu on the left-hand side, from which you can select various options.

—**Guide.** You've gone to all the trouble to design your new application; now help the people who'll use it find their way around. Here's where you can write your very own custom guide to your application. (For more on how to do that, see "Creating a User Guide for Your Application" on page 263)

—**Advanced Settings.** This section deals with specific things that users can or can't do with your application:

—Set the Find menu to **Default to "All Tables"** (as opposed to the table a user is in when he clicks FInd). This option, for multi-table applications, is usually turned off.

—**Allow users who are not administrators to copy** the application. Imitation is the sincerest form of flattery. Even so, you may not want users without administrative privileges to copy your application. Normally, this checkbox is turned off, which means that copycats will have to look elsewhere.

—**Allow users who are not administrators to export data**. This box is usually turned on, meaning that anyone working with your application can download data from it. (It's a good thing when employees take work home with them, right?) But if you don't want anyone who doesn't have administrator-level privileges to export data from this application, turn off this checkbox.

—**Allow non-SSL access via API**. If this option brings to mind a nice, hot bowl of alphabet soup, you probably just want to leave it turned off, the way it comes. This option has to do with security—for the highest level of security, leave this checkbox turned off. If you want to know what SSL stands for and why someone might want to turn this option on, see the box in "SSL Spells Security" on page 256.

SSL Spells Security

SSL, which stands for *secure sockets layer*, is a privacy-protecting way of sending documents and data over the Internet. SSL encrypts data so that third parties (read: people who shouldn't see it) can't peek at your data when it's traveling over the Internet. In most cases, you want the highest level of security for your QuickBase data, so you want SSL access only.

In some cases, though, you might want to allow non-SSL access to your application. For example, say you have a program, such as a test browser for your organization, that you want to let interact with QuickBase, but that program doesn't support SSL. If *all* QuickBase applications *always* required SSL access, you'd be stuck. But you have the option to go to the Application Properties page and allow non-SSL access to your application. Be aware, though, that when you allow non-SSL access, it weakens your application's security. To protect your data, stick with SSL if at all possible.

—**Hide from public application searches**. If you've shared an application with everyone in your organization or everyone on the Internet, turning on this checkbox means that the application *won't* appear in the results of an application search. You might use this option when you create a survey that you want to offer to a randomly selected group of people, for example; turn on this checkbox, and then email the application's Web address only to those people you're inviting to complete the survey.

—The **QuickBase User Picker** (Figure 8-8) shows up when you need to select a QuickBase user or group of users—for instance, when you're sharing an application with your team. Usually, any QuickBase user with access to the application can see a list of all of that application's other users. But sometimes you might not want everyone seeing everyone else—for example, if you share an application with clients, you probably don't want every client peering at all the other clients. In a case like that, turn this checkbox on to keep the user list private.

—**Cross-Application Relationships.** A relationship creates a link between tables, but the linked tables don't necessarily have to be in the same application. You can link applications so that users of another application have access to information in this one. For example, you may want to link your Plan an Event

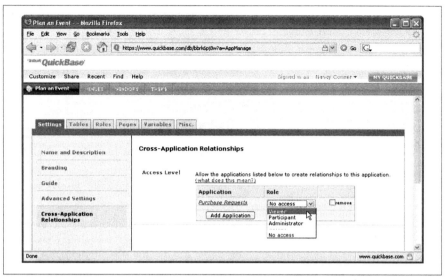

Figure 7-15. When you create a relationship between applications, the role you grant the application determines the level of access users of the other application will have to data in your application.

application with a Purchase Request application so that staff working with purchase orders can see more details about the vendors you choose.

To create a relationship between applications, click the Add Application button. The Select an Application window opens, listing other QuickBase applications to which you have access. Select the one you want, and then click OK. The application you selected appears on the Cross-Application Relationships section, as shown in Figure 7-15. From there, you can assign the application a role, just as you'd do with a new user you were adding to the application. Whatever role you assign to the application applies to everyone who uses that application. For example, assigning the role of *Viewer* lets users of the Purchase Request application act as Viewers when accessing data (such as through a lookup field) in your Plan an Event application. (For more on cross-application relationships, see "Creating a Relationship Across Applications" on page 389.)

NOTE

When you create a relationship between your application and another, users in the other application don't have *direct* access to your application unless you've put them on your application's permission list ("Permissions tab" on page 31). So someone who uses the Purchase Request application, for example, can't come poking around your Plan an Event application unless you give them explicit permission to do so (or another administrator in Plan an Event does).

- **Tables.** On the Tables tab, you'll see a list of all the tables in a multi-table application. From here, you can create a new table, change the order of the tables in the Table bar, get an overview of tables' fields and relationships, and delete or expel a table from the application.

FREQUENTLY ASKED QUESTION

Delete or Expel?

The event I planned is over and done with, so I don't need its Tasks table any more. What's the best way to get rid of an obsolete table?

When you're finished with a table, you have two options for getting rid of it:

— **Delete** the table, which obliterates the table and all its data.

— **Expel** the table, which removes the table from its current application but preserves both the table and the info it holds.

If you're in the mood to unleash your inner Godzilla, destroying table and data alike as you ravage the countryside, stomp through these steps:

1. Open the application that contains the table you want to delete. Select Customize→Application, and then click the Tables tab.

   The Tables tab opens, showing a list of all the tables in your application.

2. Find the table you want to delete. To the right of it, click the Delete button.

   A box appear, warning you that once you've deleted a table, you can't change your mind and get it back.

3. If you're sure you want to delete the table type *YES* in the box. (Use all capital letters, or QuickBase will ignore your request.) Click OK.

   QuickBase destroys the table and all its data and returns you to the Tables tab.

Just keep this in mind: When you delete a table, you remove that table and everything in it from QuickBase—permanently. After you've deleted a table, you can't undo the delete or get the data back. So be really, really sure that deleting the table is what you want to do before you shout *YES* in the confirmation box and click OK.

If you're in a kinder, gentler mood—or if you simply think that the table's data might come in handy some day—you can *expel* a table from the application. Expelling removes the table from its current application (so it's no longer crowding the other tables there) and places it in a new application of its own. When you expel a table, you know where to find the table if a need for it pops up later on. Or, if you find that you never, ever visit the table in its new application, you can simply delete that application ("Deleting an Application" on page 315) once you're sure don't need it.

To expel a table, begin by following the same steps you'd take to delete the table: In the application you want to expel the table from, click your way to the Tables tab (Customize→Application→Tables). Find the table you want to expel. At its far right, sitting next to the Delete button, is a button labeled More. Click it, and then click "Expel this table". A box pops up, explaining that the table you're expelling will find a new home in its very own single-table application and asking if you want to proceed. Click "Yes, expel it" if you do.

QuickBase removes the table from the current application and, at the same time, creates a new application holding just that table. When you return to My Quick-Base, the new application (which has the same name as the table it holds) appears in your Applications section.

Later, if you have a change of heart and want to restore the table you expelled, you can absorb it back into its original application.

- **Roles.** Get an overview of the roles that exist in this application and what they can do. You can create a new role, determine which role takes precedence if there's a conflict between roles (often, the same user gets assigned a couple of roles in an application), and see—and adjust—which roles have access to which reports in the application. The Roles tab also lets you manage permissions for each role, edit the Dashboard (here called the Home Page) associated with each role, and decide which tables each role does (or doesn't) get to see.

NOTE
To learn everything you ever wanted to know about roles (and possibly a bit more), see "Managing Roles" on page 351.

- **Pages.** Look on this tab to see the special pages in the application—Dashboards, Getting Started Guides, and so on. You can edit or delete such pages from this tab.
- **Variables.** Simply put, an *application variable* is some piece of information that applies to the entire application, as opposed to a particular table or record. For example, a project management application is likely to have a project launch date that affects multiple tasks and issues within the application. In that case, you can create a variable that contains the launch date, and then use it in different places throughout the application. If the launch date changes (that never happens, right?), you don't have to hunt it down in every place it appears throughout the application —just edit it once by editing the variable (you can do it from the Variables tab). You can use variables as XML output, but unless you're a developer, you'll most likely use it in formulas.

To create a variable, click the "Create a new variable" link on the Variables tab. In the box that opens, shown in Figure 7-16, give your variable a name (such as *Launch Date*) and a value (such as the launch date; variables can also be numbers or text). Click OK, and QuickBase adds the new variable to a list of variables on this page.

When you want to use a variable in a custom formula, throw a pair of brackets around the name, like this: *[Launch Date]*. Then insert it into your formula. If you're not sure what you're doing with custom formulas, skip over to "Writing Formulas" on page 417. You'll be creating formulas like a mad scientist in no time.

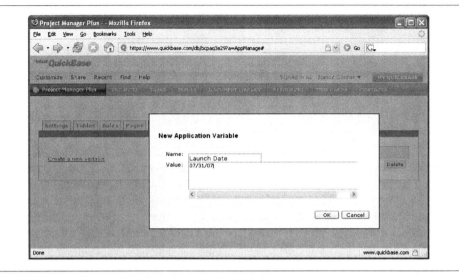

Figure 7-16. Variables simplify formulas writing when there's a common element that you want to use in formulas across the application.

- **Misc.** This Miscellaneous tab offers a variety of options for working with your application, as shown in Figure 7-17. Here's a rundown of what you'll find there:

  —**Show application statistics.** Click this link to open a new window showing a rundown of each table in the application: its size, who owns it, when it was created and last modified, and how often its been visited (total and today).

  —**Copy application.** When you want to make a quick-as-a-wink copy of the whole application, with or without its data, you can start here. (See the box in "When Copying Won't Work" on page 252 for reasons why you might want to copy an application.)

  —**Transfer application.** Counting down the days until your gold watch and retirement party—or just wishing you were? When you're ready to pass on the ownership torch of an application, click this link. QuickBase asks you for the screen name or email address of the next lucky owner; type it in and click Next. Confirm that you've selected the right person by clicking Next again. QuickBase asks whether you want to transfer management (power to administer the application), ownership (responsibility for the billing account), or both. Make your selection and click Next, and then Authorize Transfer.

  But don't get out the golf clubs just yet: The person you transferred the application to has to accept the transfer before QuickBase actually makes the switch. Until then, you're still in charge.

  —**Delete application.** When an application has run its course (perhaps a project you've been managing has successfully completed), you can delete the application from QuickBase here. Because deleting is an application is a serious thing

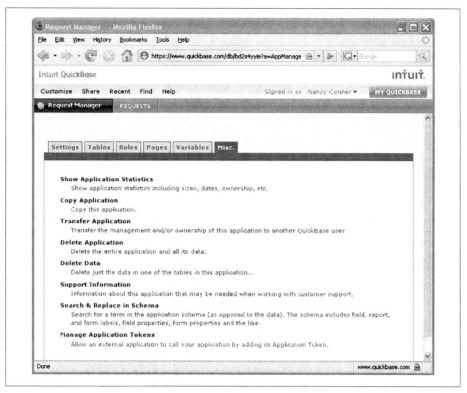

Figure 7-17. The Misc. tab gathers together various options for working with your QuickBase application. But these aren't just odds and ends; these are powerful application-management tools: You can see how much an application is being used, search for and replace a term throughout the application's schema on page 262, delete an application you no longer need, and more.

(when you delete an application, it's gone forever), you have to confirm your deletion request twice.

— **Delete data.** This link strips out the data from one table in the application (so in a multi-table application, you have to choose the table that's losing its data). Confirm to QuickBase that you really don't want that data any more, and it's gone.

— **Support information.** QuickBase is so easy to use and so reliable that there's a good chance you'll never have to contact its support team. But in the unlikely event that you do, this is a good section of the application to visit first. It gives you the table number and dbid (that stands for *database identifier*) for each table in the application.

— **Search & replace in schema.** When you use the Find button to search an application, you're searching its data, the records it contains. You can also search an application's *schema,* the structure that holds that data. Data is like the furniture in the rooms of a house; the schema is like the beams, walls, and floors that make up the house itself. Why would you want to search for and replace a term in the schema? Maybe you created a prebuilt application to track work orders, but your company calls work orders "tickets"—and it'd be easier to change the term throughout the application than to try to get everyone to change the local lingo.

When you click this link, the Replace Term in Schema page opens, asking for your search term. Type it in, and then click Search. QuickBase shows you all occurrences of that term in the schema, as shown in Figure 7-18, and puts up a new box asking for the replacement term. Type it in, click Replace in Selected Items, and then click OK to confirm. Now, QuickBase is speaking your language.

— **Manage Application Tokens.** Application tokens are a security feature that make sure any API calls sent to your application are legitimate. The token is a string of characters that has to be added to any API call made to the application; if the token isn't in the API call, the call gets blocked. To find out how to generate tokens and assign them to your applications, see "Enhancing an Application's Security with Tokens" on page 347.

Give Your Application's Users a Guided Tour

After you've done all that hard work to create your application (well, okay, it *wasn't* hard, but no one will know that when they ooh and ahh over your creation), you want to make sure that the people who'll load it up with data and work with it on a daily basis know what they're doing. You designed the application, and you want to make sure people use it as you intended.

You can't hold each person's hand every time they open your application, but you can do the next best thing: Write a guide that offers instructions, tips, and helpful hints. You store the guide right inside the application, so it's always accessible, right there on the Help menu.

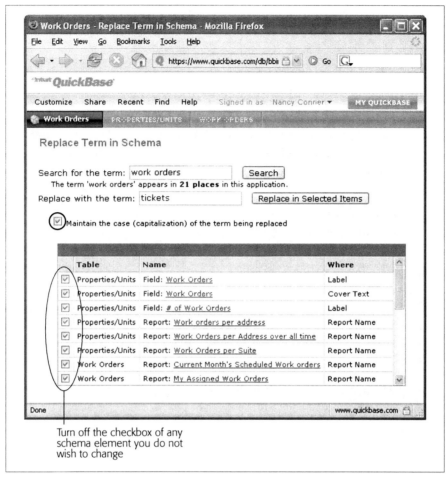

Turn off the checkbox of any
schema element you do not
wish to change

*Figure 7-18. When you search for and replace a term in the application's schema, you change
the names of its fields and reports. To keep the case of the replacement term the same as the
previous term (meaning capital letters stay capitalized and lowercase letters stay lowercase),
turn on the "Maintain the case..." checkbox (circled). If there are some elements in the schema
that you don't want to change, you can deselect them by turning off the checkbox in the left
column.*

Creating a User Guide for Your Application

There are two parts to writing a guide to your QuickBase application: First, write the
guide, and then link it to the application's Help menu so users can find it when they
need it.

Write your guide right inside the application. Your guide must be a *rich text page*, which
is a document that uses simple HTML, so Web browsers can display it. Even if "HTML"
is one of those techy acronyms that set off that little twitch under your eye, you can

write a rich text page. That's because QuickBase offers an HTML editor that makes writing a rich text page as easy as typing up tomorrow's to-do list.

To add a rich text page to your QuickBase application, start from any page in the application and follow these steps:

1. From the menu bar, select Customize→Application.

   QuickBase opens the page you saw back in Figure 7-14.

2. Click the Pages tab. Then click the left-hand "Create a new Page" link.

   QuickBase asks what kind of page you want to create: Dashboard, text, or rich text.

3. Turn on the "Create a new rich text page" radio button and click OK.

   QuickBase creates the page and adds it to the Page table of the Pages tab, giving it the imaginative name Untitled Page.

4. To the left of your new Untitled Page, click the Edit link.

   QuickBase opens its supercharged text editor, shown in Figure 7-19. This looks a lot like a word processor, with a generous text box for typing and familiar buttons for formatting text.

5. Write your masterpiece in the text editor. Besides paragraphs of text, you can insert links to Web sites or to pages within QuickBase, create bulleted and numbered lists, add tables, and more. When you're done, give your guide a name in the Page Name box. This must be a filename, ending with the file extension *.html*, so Web browsers can read and display your guide—it's *not* the name end-users will click in the Help menu. (You'll write that name in the next set of steps). When everything looks good, click Save & Done.

   QuickBase saves your guide and returns you to the Pages tab.

TIP

Looking for a shortcut to get to the page where you write your guide? Start with the Help menu. Click Help→"Create a Guide". A dialog box appears that outlines the steps for writing a guide: Create a rich text page inside the application and then add the guide to your application's Help menu. In the dialog box, click Create, and QuickBase whisks you straight over to the application's Pages tab. From there, click "Create a new Page" and then jump into the preceding list of instructions at step 3.

Writing the guide is nine-tenths of the battle. It takes only a few mouse clicks to add your shiny new guide to the application's Help menu. If you're still on the Pages tab, click the Settings tab. If you've navigated somewhere else in the application, select Customize→Application.

1. On the Settings tab, click Guide in the left-hand menu.

   The "Guide to" page, shown in Figure 7-20 opens.

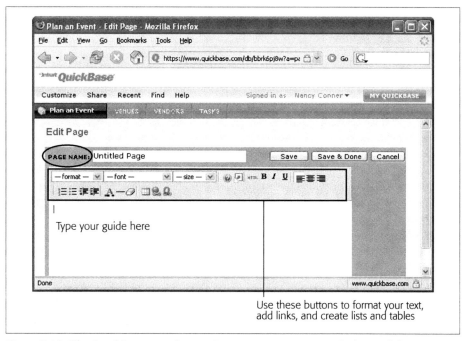

Use these buttons to format your text,
add links, and create lists and tables

Figure 7-19. The QuickBase text editor makes it easy to create a guide that Web browsers can display. Just click in the large text box and start typing. The buttons across the top of the text editor let you select a font, color, size, and other formatting for your text—and more (hover your cursor over a button to see what that button does). Click the Save button to save your work as you're creating the guide. When you're finished, give your guide a name in the circled Page Name box (this must be a filename ending in .html), and then click Save & Done. You can always come back and edit your page later by clicking Customize→Application→Pages→Edit.

2. Fill in the appropriate info so people can find your guide.

   In the Title box, type the name of your guide as you want it to appear on the application's Help menu. (You can create up to three guides. For example, you might want to create a guide for each role in the application. So in a sales management application, you might have "Guide for Sales Reps" and "Guide for Sales Managers," each addressing the different things those users can do.)

   The "Links to" drop-down menu shows existing pages that QuickBase can display. If you've created and saved your guide (see the previous set of steps), your rich text page will show up in this list. Find your guide (remember, its filen ame must end in .html) and select it.

   Creating a description in the Description box is optional. But it's a good idea, particularly if you're creating more than one guide. The description you write here appears beneath the link to your guide on the Help menu, so a few words describing your guide will help users know which guide to select.

3. When you're done, click Save Changes.

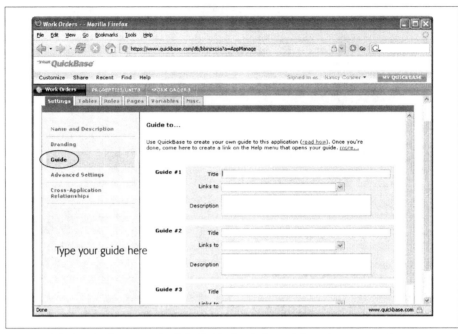

Figure 7-20. On the Settings tab, click Guide (circled), and then give your guide a name and description. Then, from the "Links to" drop-down menu, select the HTML file you created. You can create up to three guides to add to an application's Help menu.

QuickBase adds your guide to the Help menu.

Now, when someone using your application clicks Help, the guide you just created appears in the Help menu, just below Help & Support. When that person chooses your guide from the Help menu, QuickBase opens a new window that shows your custom help page.

And if your guide has run its course (maybe you had special instructions for an out-of-the-ordinary project that's now finished), you can delete it. Select Customize→Application and click the Pages tab. Find the guide you want to delete, and click its far-right Delete button. Confirm once, and the guide is gone.

Tips and Tricks for Working with User Guides

Writing a guide and making it available through your application's Help menu is so easy that the toughest part about the whole process is deciding what to write. Once you've created your guide, you can spiff it up by adding images. You can even make sure your application's users have all the help they need despite QuickBase's limit of three guides per application. Read on to learn how.

Adding Images to a Guide

If a picture is worth a thousand words (or even a few hundred), then you can save yourself a lot of typing by including screenshots or other images in your user guides. Instead of simply using words to describe where to look for a button, link, or field, for example, show your readers a screenshot so they can see that button, link, or field for themselves. Adding an image or two will save your users a lot of confusion—and save you a lot of headaches.

As you may have already noticed, however, the QuickBase text editor (Figure 7-19) you use to create user guides doesn't have a button for inserting an image, as nice as that would be. And you can't copy and paste an image into the text editor, either. Your best option is put *links* to images in your guide. When a reader clicks the link, voilà—a new window opens, showing an image that illustrates the guide's content.

To link to an image from a user guide, first make sure that the image you want to link to lives somewhere on the Web. It's probably best to store the image inside your QuickBase account (if you store it on a Web site that isn't secure, users may get a "nonsecure items" warning that could scare them off from viewing the image). For example, you can create a Document Library application to hold all your images. (Here's the fastest way to create this kind of application: Start on your My QuickBase page and click "Create a New Application"→Legal→Document Library→Create Application.) Each image you upload becomes a record in your document library with its very own Web address. Open the image you want to link to and copy that Web address from your browser's address bar.

When you've got the Web address of your image, follow these steps to link to it in your guide:

1. In the application that contains your user guide, click Customize→Application→Pages.

   The application's Pages tab opens, displaying specialized pages for this application: any dashboards and rich text pages you've created.

2. Find the guide you want and click its Edit link.

   QuickBase opens the text editor shown in Figure 7-19.

3. Find or add some text that refers to the image you're going to link to. For example, say you're linking to a screenshot of a form for adding accounts; you'll want to include text that refers to the "Add New Account form"" Or you might add a new sentence that says "Click here for an example." In either case, select the text that you want to link to the image (that is, the text readers will click to see the image), and then click the Insert Web Link button—it looks like a globe sitting on some links of chain.

   The Insert/Modify Link box, shown in Figure 7-21, opens.

4. Type or paste the image's Web address into the URL box. If you want a tip balloon to appear when a reader hovers her cursor over the link (something like "Screenshot

of Add New Account form"), type it into the "Title (tooltip)" field. From the Target drop-down list, select "New window (_blank)" to make the image open in its own window when a reader clicks the link. Click OK.

QuickBase inserts the link into your text.

5. When you're done adding links and writing or editing your guide, click Save & Done.

QuickBase saves your user guide and takes you back to the Pages tab. Now, anyone who reads the guide can see your lovely images.

TIP

After you add images to your user guide, it's a good idea to take a look at the guide to double-check that the links work the way you want them to. If an image file is really big, QuickBase may have trouble displaying it. In that case, you may have to reduce the image's size or upload the image to a Web site outside of QuickBase and link to it there.

Creating More than Three Guides

QuickBase lets you create up to three user guides and add them to your application's Help menu. Most of the time, you'll probably find that three custom guides is plenty. But if you have a complex application with a lot of tables or user roles, you might find you need more than three. Similarly, some organizations like to make in-house procedures available inside their QuickBase applications—and there could be dozens of procedures. Although you can't add more than three guides to the application's Help menu, this section teaches you a couple of workarounds that let you give users all the guidance they need.

If you've played with QuickBase, you know that an application's tables can hold a lot of info. One way to offer an exhaustive list of Help topics is to whip up a Help table that holds all the tips and instructions the application's users may need. Doing so is a snap. Start by adding a table to your application (click Customize→"Create a new"→Table). QuickBase asks you what to call the table's records; you can stick with Records (QuickBase's suggestion) or call them something like Tips or Help Topics. Name your table ("Help" is a nice straightforward name) and then click OK to create it.

After you create the table, you need to add fields to it: in this case, you'll add just two. On the Tables page (QuickBase takes you there as soon as you save your new table; you can also get there by clicking Customize→Tables and then selecting your table from the left-hand menu), click the Fields tab, and then click the upper-right Create New Fields button to open the Add Fields page. Here, you'll add two fields:

- **Topic.** Make this a Text field. You'll use it to identify each help topic in the table.

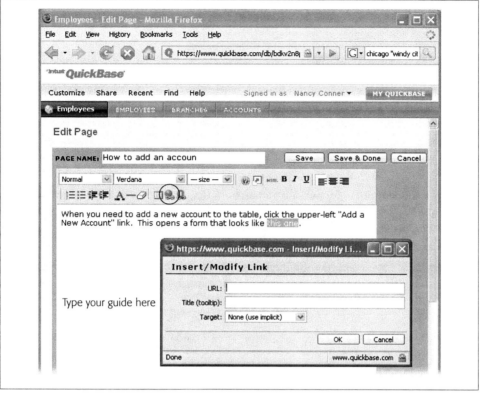

Figure 7-21. To link to an image, highlight the text that will hold the link, and then click the Insert Web Link button (circled). This opens the Insert/Modify Link box, where you tell QuickBase where to find the image (URL) and how to display it (select "New window (_blank)" from the Target drop-down list).

- **Instructions.** Make this a Text-Multi-line field to give yourself plenty of room to type your explanation.

When you're done, click Add Fields.

Now you've got a table where you can add and update Help topics whenever you need to. Simply open your Help table, click "Add a New Record" (or whatever you've decided to call the records), and write your guide to that topic.

To make the table easy to read, customize the List All report to display only the Topics column. View List All, and then click the upper-right "Customize this Report" link to open Report Builder. There, use the "Customs to Display" section to show only Topics, and then save the edited report.

Another option for giving your application's users lots of guidance is to make your user guide a table of contents that links to as many other documents as needed. For example, if you have documents about company policies and procedures that you want to make available to the people using your application, you can do so right through the Help menu. There's virtually no limit to the number of documents or Web pages you can link to.

The process is simple. First, make sure that your documents are accessible on the Web, either on a Web site of their own or within QuickBase. (Chapter 3 tells you how to get documents into a QuickBase application.)

Next, create a user guide and call it something like "Help for this Application." Make its text a list of topics that you'lll link to the relevant documents. For each topic, select the text that will hold the link and then click the Insert Web Link button. Next, in the Insert/Modify Link box (Figure 7-21), tell QuickBase where to find the linked document or Web page. When you're finished, click Save & Done.

Now when someone clicks Help and selects your guide, they'll see a list of topics they can click to get the full scoop.

CHAPTER 8

Managing Applications

Creating an application is only half the battle—and way less than half the fun. Once you've set up your QuickBase application, it's time to put it to work for you. And no matter how brilliantly you designed your design, as you start using QuickBase in your day-to-day workflow, you'll probably want to tweak things a bit. This chapter covers the ins and outs of managing a QuickBase application: customizing your Dashboard, sharing your application with your team, adding a new field (or a whole new table)—and more.

The Administrator's Dashboard

Just as its name suggests, the Dashboard is an application's control center. It's the first page you see when you open an application, and it puts all the controls and at-a-glance information you need in one place. From it, you can search, add records, create or look at reports, pick a table in a multi-table application, and more. As an administrator, you've got a few more things you can do with the Dashboard. As Figure 8-1 shows, some extra links and menu options appear on an administrator's Dashboard page (compare this figure with Figure 1-12 to get a sense of the difference).

Customizing Your Dashboard

The Dashboard page is amazingly customizable—as it should be. As the master of this application, you can set up your Dashboard just the way you want it. You can customize the Dashboard to give you easy access to important documents, records, and other information. You can move sections around, add buttons, edit headings, embed or hide reports, and more. To give your Dashboard a custom overhaul, click the upper-right Customize this Page link to open the Edit Dashboard page, shown in Figure 8-2.

The following sections explain the changes you can make to customize each part of your Dashboard.

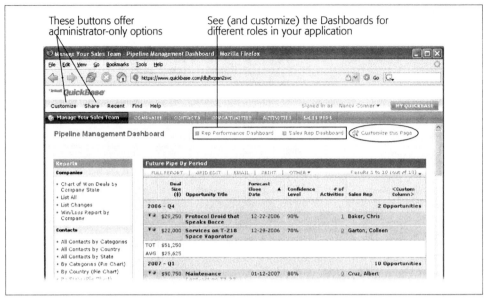

These buttons offer administrator-only options

See (and customize) the Dashboards for different roles in your application

Figure 8-1. When you're an application's administrator, you can customize the Dashboard for yourself or for different roles within the application. Click the right-hand Customize this Page link (circled) to set up your own Dashboard page just the way you want it. You can also create, view, and edit specialized Dashboards and assign them to different roles (more on that in the next chapter). The menu bar's Customize and Share menus give administrators some extra options that end-users don't have: tweaking the application as a whole, its tables, or its roles; inviting users; and creating and assigning roles.

Heading

All applications start out with a home page named the Dashboard—no matter what the application's called. If you forget which application you're in (which isn't hard to do when you're working with a bunch of different applications), you have to look all the way up to the upper-left corner to see its name.

Make life easier by customizing the Dashboard's heading to reflect the application you're in. On the Edit Dashboard page, find the Heading text box. (In a new application, this box is blank.) Type a good descriptive name, like *CHAOS Project Dashboard* or *Southwest Realty Property Management Dashboard*. Click Preview to see how the new name looks. When you click Preview, a pop-up window opens, showing your Dashboard with its new name. (If you've turned off pop-ups in your Web browser, you won't see this preview.) Click Save to rename the Dashboard for this application.

Buttons

You can add buttons to the upper-right part of the Dashboard page, making it a matter of one quick click to find, for example, a particular report. On the Edit Dashboard page, go to the Buttons section (at upper-right) and click Add New. QuickBase displays a

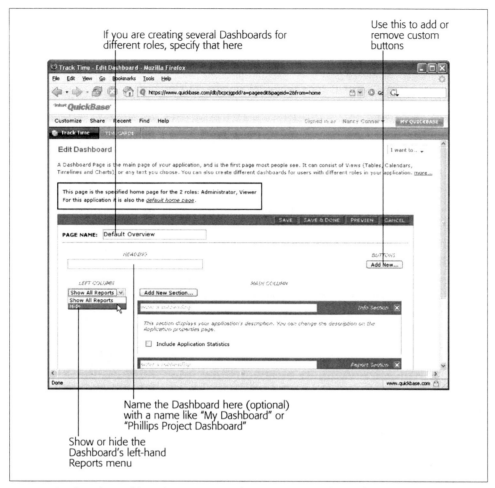

If you are creating several Dashboards for different roles, specify that here

Use this to add or remove custom buttons

Name the Dashboard here (optional) with a name like "My Dashboard" or "Phillips Project Dashboard"

Show or hide the Dashboard's left-hand Reports menu

Figure 8-2. The Edit Dashboard page contains four sections: Heading (where you can rename your Dashboard page); Left Column (show or hide its Reports menu); Main Column (modify main sections like Info boxes and reports); and Buttons (customize your Dashboard's navigation buttons).

button to the left of Add New (Figure 8-2). This new button is labeled Untitled, followed by a QuickBase link icon, and an X.

First, define what the new button will link to. Click the QuickBase link icon (it's a fat blue Q sitting on some links of chain; you can see it in Figure 8-3). The Select Link Type menu pops up, giving you these choices:

- **Add.** Puts a button on the Dashboard that takes you to the Add Record page for one of the tables in the application. When you choose Add from the Select Link Type menu, QuickBase shows you a list of all the tables in the application. Choose the one you want. Add buttons are especially useful when you're adding various task types in a multi-table application.

NOTE

Creating a Dashboard page button to add records makes sense only in a multi-table application; for example, you might want to make it super easy to add a new document to a project management application that tracks documents, tasks, issues, and resources. (Single-table applications already have an Add a New Record link on the Dashboard page.)

- **Go to page.** When you select this option, QuickBase shows you all the pages within the application you can link to. For example, if you've created a text page, you can choose that page from the list of pages, letting you create a button that takes the reader right to that text page. Linking to a text page is really helpful when you want everyone on your team to have easy access to important information: the latest promotions in a sales application, for example, or the vision and scope document for a software development project.
- **Show report.** Choosing this option from the Select Link Type menu shows you a list of all the reports in the application. Pick whichever one you want the button to link to.

After you've decided what the new Dashboard page button will link to, you need to give the button a descriptive name. Right now, the new button's name is Untitled—not terribly helpful. Click the word *Untitled* next to the QuickBase link icon, and the word appears in a text box. Now you can change it to whatever you like.

To see what your new button will look like, click Preview. To add it to your Dashboard, click Save.

TIP

If you decide you don't want the new button after all, you can click Cancel to discard the button instead of saving it. But if you've made a number of changes on the Edit Dashboard page and you don't want to get rid of them all—just the button you don't want—click the X to the right of the QuickBase link icon on the offending button. Click OK at the prompt, and the button is no more. Clicking the button's X on the Edit Dashboard page also banishes an existing button you created a while ago but no longer need.

Left Column

The Left Column section (on the left side of the Edit Dashboard page, as shown in Figure 8-2) governs the Reports menu on the Dashboard's left side. It gives folks a quick way to find and open any of the reports associated with this application. (Clicking a table's name in the Table bar and selecting a report from the menu is the other way.)

If your Dashboard feels crowded and you don't want to display the left-side Reports menu, choose Hide from the drop-down menu in the Left Column section. When you're done, click Save. (You can always bring the Reports menu back choosing Show All Reports from the same menu.)

Main Column

The Dashboard page can display a lot of information: one or more info boxes, text descriptions, and reports that you want to see up front when you open the application. A Dashboard page can have up to six sections, three of which can be reports. To add a new section, go to the Edit Dashboard page and look in the middle of the page for the Main Column section (Figure 8-2 shows an example).

The Main Column section already contains info about whatever your Dashboard currently displays in the main part of the page. For example, you'll probably see an Info section there (labeled on the right), which tells you what's in the application's Info box on page 275. Usually, an Info box holds a description of the application and some statistics about it. There also might be a report or two visible on your Dashboard page —if so, you'll see Report Section boxes in the Main Column section.

If you want to add a new section to your Dashboard page, click the Add New Section button, which gives you these options:

- **Text.** A text section is simply a box with some text in it. It's a great way to give yourself a front-and-center reminder, announce an upcoming meeting, or focus your team's attention on a new document everyone should read. When you select this option, QuickBase opens a Text Section box like the one in Figure 8-3. Type a heading and your text. You can format the text to change the font, create lists, center or indent text, and so on using the formatting buttons or—if you're an HTML whiz—by typing the tags yourself. You can add a hyperlink to another page in QuickBase or anywhere on the Web. When you're finished, click Preview to see what your text box will look like. (Figure 8-4 shows the text box that results from Figure 8-3.)

- **Report.** A *report* is a way of displaying some of an application's data—like sales figures by region or a timeline of project tasks. If you find yourself looking for the same report over and over, you can put it on your Dashboard page, so it's there when you open the application. Click the Add New Section button and select Report. The Main Column section expands as shown in Figure 8-5. Give the report a name, and then choose the report you want from the drop-down menu, and adjust other options as explained in the figure.

- **Info/Description.** This is how you create an Info box, which describes the application and contains statistics about it: the application manager's name, the billing account, the last time someone modified the application, and a link to further statistics, including usage statistics like the size of the application (in terms of both number of records and number of bytes), the size of any attachments (in bytes),

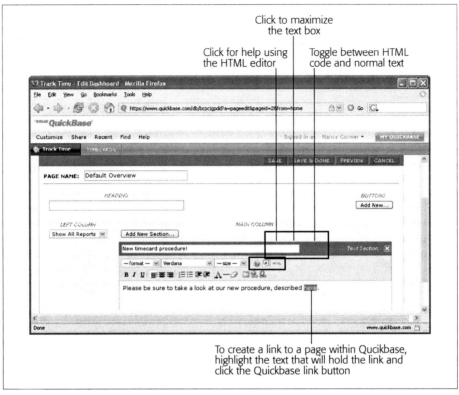

Figure 8-3. Edit Dashboard's Text Section box contains an HTML editor so you can add some pizazz to the notice on your Dashboard page, whether or not you know what an HTML tag looks like. You can get help using the editor, make the box you're working in bigger, or see the HTML you're magically creating by clicking one of the three top buttons (circled). To add a link, highlight the text you want to contain the link, and then click one of the link buttons. The globe icon is for Web links; the Q is for linking inside QuickBase.

and the total number of hits. There's not much you can do with an Info box on the Edit Dashboard page, because the actual description comes from the Application Properties page. You can give the Info box a header (or change its current header). And you can tell QuickBase whether or not to display the application statistics; if you don't want to display those statistics, turn off the Include Application Statistics checkbox.

NOTE

To create or edit the description that appears in an Info box, you use the Application Properties page. To get there, choose Customize→Application and select the Settings tab. (Or, if you're on the Dashboard, just click the Info box's upper-right Edit button.) On the Settings tab, type in the Description box to add (or edit) a description for your application. Don't forget to click Save Changes when you're finished.

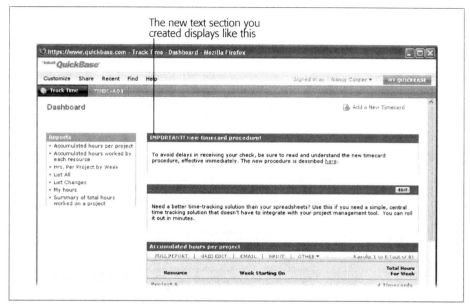

The new text section you created displays like this

Figure 8-4. This Dashboard displays a newly created Text Section, complete with a hyperlink. The new section appears at the top of the Dashboard page because it's the first section in the Main Column area of the Edit Dashboard page. If you want, you can move the Dashboard sections around (see "Rearranging Dashboard sections" on page 277).

When you click the Add New Section button, QuickBase adds the new section to the top of the Main Columns area of the Edit Dashboard page. It also adds the newly created section to the top of your Dashboard page, but that may not be where you want it. For example, it makes sense to have the Info box at the top of the page, where it provides an introduction to and overview of your application. But after you've added a couple of new reports, the Info box gets pushed way down the page, where it isn't doing a bit of good. Next you'll learn how to fix that.

Rearranging Dashboard sections

You can rearrange the sections on your Dashboard to suit your needs, whether you want the report you use most right at the top or whether your aesthetic sense simply demands a different arrangement. Moving sections around is easy and kind of fun. To reorder sections on the Dashboard, follow these steps:

1. Open the Edit Dashboard page (from the application's Dashboard, click the Customize this Page link). Find the section you want to move, and hover your cursor over the section's dark-blue header.

   The cursor changes to a four-way arrow, as shown in Figure 8-6.

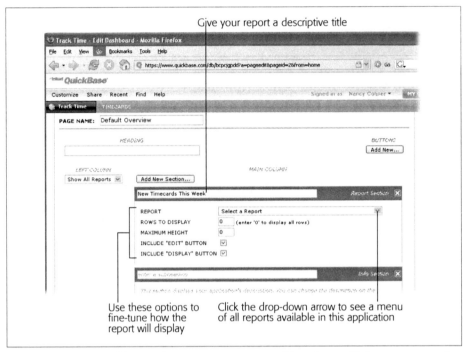

Figure 8-5. You can add up to three reports to your Dashboard page. If the report you select holds a huge table, you can control its size by limiting the number of rows displayed on the Dashboard or restricting its height (users can see the whole table by clicking a "more" link). You can also turn Edit and Display buttons on or off, depending on whether you want access to them from the Dashboard.

2. When the cursor changes to the four-way arrow, click and hold the left mouse button (Ctrl-click if you're using a Mac). Move your mouse to drag the section to where you want it to go.

   The section turns transparent as you move it around the screen.

3. Reposition the section where you want it to appear, and then release the mouse button.

   You've changed the order of the sections. The section you moved appears in its new home.

4. When you're done moving sections around, click Preview to see your Dashboard's new look (disable any pop-up blocking feature in your Web browser for Preview to work). Click Save when you're done.

   QuickBase takes you to your newly redecorated Dashboard page.

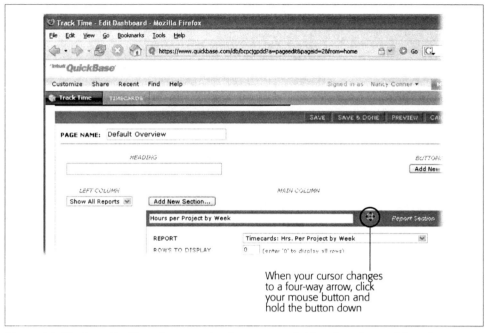

Figure 8-6. Moving a Dashboard page section is as easy as clicking, dragging, and dropping.

Deleting Dashboard sections

A Dashboard can hold six sections, max. So there might be times when you want to delete an old section you no longer need. For example, maybe you put up a text section with a reminder, and now that reminder is old news. Or your team has successfully made it through a project phase (hooray!), and you no longer need a timeline report for that phase on your Dashboard.

Deleting a section takes three simple steps:

1. Open the Edit Dashboard page (from the Dashboard, just click Customize this Page). In the Main Column part of the Edit Dashboard page, find the section you want to delete. Click the X in the upper-right corner.

   A confirmation box appears, making sure that you really want to delete the section.

2. Click OK.

   The section disappears from the Main Column area.

3. Click Save.

   QuickBase returns you to your Dashboard page, minus the deleted section.

Sharing an Application

Creating a QuickBase application can be so rewarding and produce such great results that you want to show off your application to your colleagues, your boss, your kids, maybe even your neighbors (hope you have understanding neighbors). If you actually plan to get any work done, though, you must bring your team members on board to work with the data in your application. Whether you're showing off a newborn application or putting people to work—or maybe a little of both—you do it by inviting folks to join your QuickBase application.

Sharing your application doesn't mean that everyone has the same level of access to it. In a property management application, for example, you might want tenants to be able to see when they're scheduled for maintenance or repairs, but not eyeball all the details about all your properties. (You want to avoid phone calls that begin, "How come I'm paying $1,500 a month and the guy across the hall is only paying $1,125?") With QuickBase, you can decide exactly who has access to what in an application—you can show or hide tables, records, and even individual fields.

TIP

You can also specify what a particular class of user (called a *role*) can do with your application's data: You might want some people to be able to add, change, or delete some fields, for example, while only viewing others. Specifying what users assigned to a certain role can do in your application is called setting *permissions*, and "Billing Account Administration" on page 25 tells you all about it.

Basic Sharing

Your first step in sharing a QuickBase application is to let QuickBase know who you want to share it with. You do that on the Users page. In the application you want to share, choose Share→"Manage users" to open the Users page, shown in Figure 8-7.

To bring new users into an application, click the Add Users tab. The User Picker, shown in Figure 8-8, opens.

Next, click the "Make a selection" drop-down menu at the top of the User Picker. This menu offers you some or all of the following choices:

- **Users in your company.** When you select this option, QuickBase presents you with all the registered QuickBase users with your company's email address.

- **Select from users in this application.** Choose this option to get a list of all users who already have access to the application. You won't use this option to invite new users—obviously—but there are other times when it's very handy, like when you're creating groups.

- **Search for a specific user.** When you think that the person you want to add already has a QuickBase account, you can use this option to find him or her. It

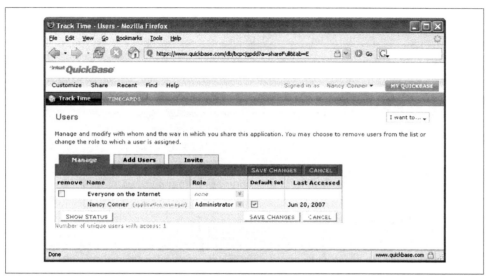

Figure 8-7. The three tabs of the Users page—Manage, Add Users, and Invite—give you easy access to the actions you can perform on your application's users. The table lists all users currently in your application. When you create a new application, there are two users: you (as application manager) and Everyone on the Internet (with no access yet).

opens a Search box where you can type in the screen name, full name, or email address of the QuickBase user you're looking for. QuickBase searches for that person based on the info you supply. And here's the cool part: If you search for someone's email address and that person doesn't have a QuickBase account, QuickBase creates a provisional account for that person and sends out an invitation (see the next section for more about inviting people).

TIP
To save a step in the search process, click the User Picker's lower-left Search button.

- **Create a new user.** If you can't find the person you want to invite, or if you know for sure that he or she isn't currently a QuickBase user, choose this option, which shows the Create a New User dialog box. Type the email address of the person you want to add into the dialog box. If the email address happens to belong to a registered user, that person's name appears in User Picker's Search Results box. If QuickBase doesn't find a current user with that email address, it shoots off an email invitation to the address and creates a provisional account.

- **Select a group.** As Chapter 9 describes, you can speed up user management by creating groups of users and applying permissions or roles to the whole group at once. If you've created a group and added users to it, you don't have to add new users to your application one at a time—instead, you can bring the whole team on

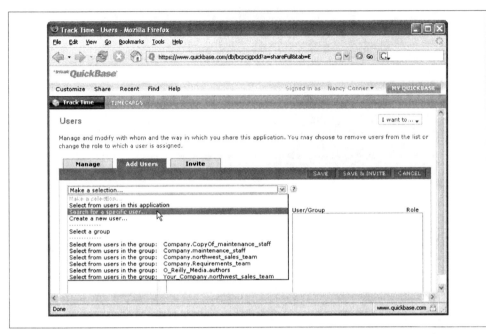

Figure 8-8. The User Picker, on the Users page's Add Users tab, lets you find existing QuickBase users and add them to your application—or even create new users. Use the drop-down list to choose how you want to find a user. You can search for an existing user or create a new one. When you select a user, his or her name appears in the left-hand box. Click the Add button (it's hidden under the drop-down list in this picture) to make the name jump over to the right-hand list box, which adds that person to your application.

board with just one click. You can also pick and choose from among members of the group, if you want.

NOTE

What you see on the User Picker drop-down list depends on your situation. For example, if anyone in your QuickBase billing account has created any groups, you'll see an option called "Select from users in the group: groupname" (the name of the actual group appears instead of *groupname*). Choose a group, and the User Picker displays a list of its members. From there, you can decide which members you want to add to your new application.

When you select a user or group from the drop-down list, the name appears in the left-hand list box, as shown in Figure 8-9. (If you find a user by searching, the box is called Search Results.) When you select a user's name, QuickBase highlights the name you've chosen in yellow and displays the information it has about that person: full name, email address (which might be private), and screen name (if the person has one). Check to

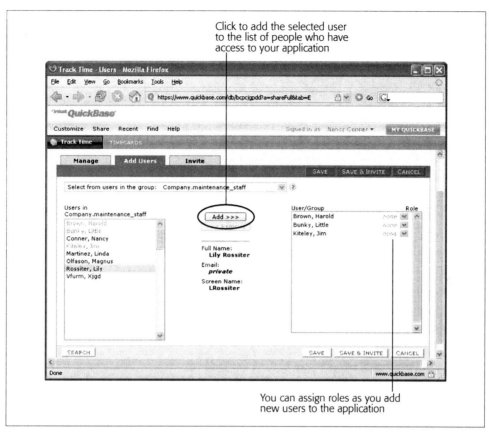

Click to add the selected user to the list of people who have access to your application

You can assign roles as you add new users to the application

Figure 8-9. When QuickBase finds a user or group of users that you can add to your application, their names appear in the left-hand list. (This box's name changes depending on what you select from the drop-down menu above it. In this case, it shows the results of a "Search for a specific user.") Select a name in the left-hand box, and then click Add. Users you've added appear in the right-hand list box. Next to each name is a drop-down list of all available roles in the application (Project Manager, Team Member, Administrator, and so on). You'll learn how to work with roles in the next chapter.

make sure you've got the right person (you wouldn't *believe* how many John Smiths already have QuickBase accounts), and then click Add. QuickBase transfers the name to the right-hand list box, which lists the people you're adding to the application.

TIP

To clear the names you've chosen so far but still stay in the User Picker, click Cancel (then OK at the confirmation prompt).

If you want, you can assign your new users roles when you add them. In the User Picker's right-hand box, next to each name, is a drop-down list. The list contains the roles associated with your application (the default is None, which means that you've added the person to your application, but they don't yet have any access to it). Choose whichever role you want for each user, or you can assign roles later.

When you've added all the users you want (for now), click Save. QuickBase adds these users to your application and takes you back to the Manage tab of the Users page.

TIP

In a hurry? Save yourself a step or two by using Quick Share. From the menu bar, select Share→"Share with a new user". On the Quick Share page, type or paste email addresses into the text box, assign a role (see Figure 8-9), click Next, and then click Confirm (or Confirm & Invite to send an email invitation)—and you're done!

FREQUENTLY ASKED QUESTION

Status Symbol

At the bottom of the Manage and Invite tabs on the Users page, there's a button that says Show Status or Hide Status. What's that about?

A QuickBase user's *status* indicates the state of his or her QuickBase account, and you can choose whether or not to display it as you prefer. Here are the different status levels that QuickBase users can have:

- **Verified.** Everyone who registers with QuickBase ("Creating an Account" on page 2) is a verified user. Since most QuickBase users eventually register, it's the most common status.

- **Provisional.** When you add people to your application who don't yet have a QuickBase account, their status is provisional. Provisional users aren't on probation—they just haven't registered yet. As soon as they complete the QuickBase registration process, their status changes from provisional to verified.

- **Unverified.** Unverified users are a step up from provisional. These people have begun the registration process but not yet completed it. They haven't replied to the verification email that QuickBase sends out. Unverified users can't sign in until they're fully registered. (And if you're a verified user and you change your email address, you might suddenly find yourself unverified.) If you're unverified, when you try to log in, you see a message telling you that you're unverified. To get in QuickBase's good graces, you've got to click a button that sends a new verification email—reply to it, and you're all set.

- **Denied.** A user with this status has no access to any application in your billing account. You might deny someone, for example, when they leave your company for a new job. To find out how to deny a user, see "Deny tab" on page 32

- **Deactivated.** A deactivated user has no access to QuickBase at all. The line between denied and deactivated can be a little fuzzy. To understand the difference, see "Deny? Deactivate? What's the Diff?" on page 33.

Because you can add users to an application even when they don't yet have a QuickBase account, the Users page is a good place to keep track of whether someone has accepted your invitation and registered. If you really need Nicole to get to work on the CHAOS project *now* and her status is still provisional, you know it's time to track her down and make sure she registers. On the other hand, if Nicole's status is deactivated, it's probably time to find out who moved into her cubicle.

NOTE

To enhance security, QuickBase puts a 60-minute time limit on the pages you use to manage access to your application. After 60 minutes, any changes you haven't saved are lost. So if you're making a lot of changes—or if you get called away from your desk—be sure to save those changes. You don't want to find out too late that the page has expired.

Inviting Users

When you're ready to send out invitations to your QuickBase party, you don't have to buy engraved stationery and a roll of stamps. Instead, just follow these steps:

1. You have to add folks to your application in order to invite them. So follow the instructions listed in "Basic Sharing" ("Basic Sharing" on page 280) to add invitees to the application. You end up back on the Users page (like the one shown back in Figure 8-7, but with your new users added). From there, click the Invite tab.

   The Invite tab of the Users page, shown in Figure 8-10, opens. This page lists the names of all the users in your application.

TIP

If you've already assigned users a role, it appears in the Role column. (Flip to "Assigning a Role" on page 357 to find out why it's a good idea to assign new users a role *before* you invite them in.)

---

2. Find the names of users you want to invite (there may be some users who you don't have to invite, like people who know from this morning's meeting that they've been added to the application). For each name, turn on the left-hand column's "select" checkbox. When you've selected all the users you want to invite, click the Invite button.

   QuickBase takes you to the Invite Users page, shown in Figure 8-11. This page shows the screen names or email addresses of your invitees and contains a one-sentence message about your application.

3. If you want, add some text to the email QuickBase will send (that single sentence is a little terse).

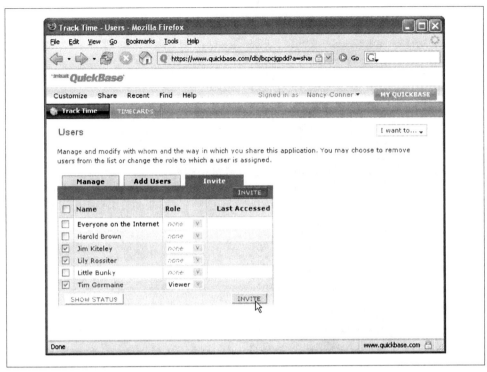

Figure 8-10. The Invite tab of the Users page lets you send out a formal invitation for users to join your application. When you click the Invite button, QuickBase fires off an email to everyone whose "select" checkbox is turned on, letting them know that they're in on the application.

You can, for example, explain what the application is about—if you wrote a description for the Info box on page 275, you could paste it in here—or what you want the invitee to work on. Signing your name is always a nice touch, too.

4. When the email's ready to go, click Send.

   QuickBase sends the email and takes you back to the User page's Manage tab.

TIP

You can save time by inviting users at the same time that you add them. The User Picker has a Save & Invite button—click it to send an invitation email to everyone you're adding.

Bulk Sharing

Adding users one at a time is fine when one or two new people join your team, but it's slow when you've created a new application and you want to get the whole team on board fast. If you've got a 100-person sales force, for example, it would take half a day

---

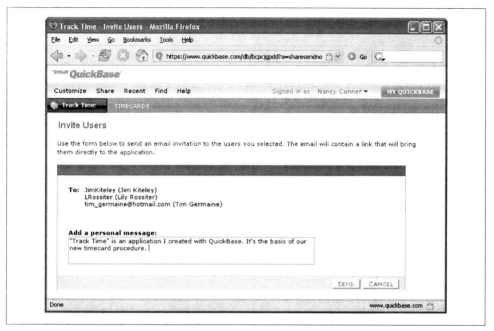

Figure 8-11. QuickBase's standard invitation email is to the point, but perhaps a little too brief. You can fill in some details by typing in the text box. When you click Send, QuickBase sends the email to everyone whose screen name or email address appears in the To list.

to add them to your Sales Leads application one by one. Never fear: Just as you can import a whole bunch of records all at once ("Importing Data into Quick-Base" on page 102), you can also import users, freeing up your time for more important things (like a coffee break).

Here's how to add users to a QuickBase application in bulk:

1. Open the application you're importing users to and find your way to the Users page (in the menu bar, choose Share→Manage users).

   The Users page opens right to the Manage tab.

2. Click the upper-right "I want to" button and choose Import Users.

   The Import Users page appears, as shown in Figure 8-12.

3. In the text box, type or paste email addresses of all the users you want to add. Separate each address by typing a comma or semicolon, or by hitting Enter.

   In most cases, you can type or paste email addresses right into the box. If your list of email addresses is super long—say, thousands of addresses—the box in "A Cast of Thousands" on page 289 tells you how to import addresses from a file.

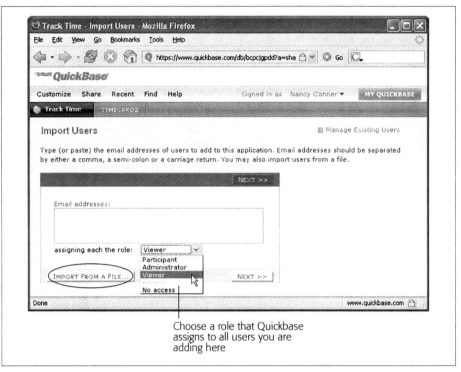

Choose a role that Quickbase
assigns to all users you are
adding here

Figure 8-12. You can add many users at once by typing or pasting their email addresses into the "Email addresses" text box. Note that when you add many users at once, QuickBase assigns them all the same role—so make sure that the role that appears in the drop-down list doesn't give away too much power. You probably don't want all 200 new users to have administrative privileges, for example. If you have a document or spreadsheet that holds a massive list of users and don't want to paste them in, click the Import From a File button (circled).

TIP

If you've ever sent out a regular email message to your entire team, then you've got an automatic way to save time. Open that message, and then copy the addresses from the "To:" field. If some of the addresses on the list are in their expanded form (like Irina Roskova <iroskova@kirovopera.com>), you don't have to edit them. Quick-Base is smart enough to recognize the part that's an email address.

---

4. If you wish, use the drop-down menu below the text box to assign a role to all these users at once.

The choices depend on the kind of application you're working with—a project management application will have roles like viewer, team member, project manager, and administrator; while an application to manage your sales team will have roles like viewer, sales rep, sales manager, and administrator. (You can also choose to assign No Access, which is useful when you want to add a bunch of people now and sort out their roles later.) When you're finished, click Next.

QuickBase takes you to a confirmation page, showing the email addresses that you put in the Import Users page's text box.

5. Click Confirm to add these users to your application or Confirm & Invite to add them and send each of them an email invitation ("Inviting Users" on page 285) at the same time.

QuickBase adds the list of users (complete with whatever role you assigned) to your application and takes you back to the Manage tab of the Users page.

WORKAROUND WORKSHOP

A Cast of Thousands

When you want to add a humongous list of users to your QuickBase application, trying to copy and paste them all in might be more of a pain than a pleasure. As long as you have those addresses in a file somewhere, you can import them en masse, saving yourself oodles of time and effort.

If you store email addresses in a spreadsheet all their own, the process is simple: Save the spreadsheet as a .csv file and follow these steps:

1. Open the QuickBase application you want to import users to, make your way to the Users page (Share → →Manage Users), and then click "I want to"→Import Users. The Import Users page (Figure 8-12) opens. Below the box where you enter email addresses is the Import From A File button.

2. Click Import From A File. The "Choose a file" dialog box pops up.

3. Click the Browse button and find the file you want to import. Click Open, and then click OK. QuickBase imports your list of addresses, which appear in the Email addresses box of the Import Users page.

4. From here, the steps are the same as steps 3 and 4 for bulk sharing ("Bulk Sharing" on page 286): Click Next, and then click Confirm (or Confirm & Invite).

QuickBase imports your massive list of users and adds them to your application.

If the email addresses you want to import exist as only one field in a spreadsheet, copy the column that holds the addresses and paste them into a new file—either a new spreadsheet that you save as a .csv file or into a text editor like Notepad (save the list as a .txt file). Then follow steps 1–4 above.

What about importing a list of email addresses from Microsoft Word? If you currently store your addresses in a list or a table in Word, you can't import directly from a Word .doc file because of all the formatting Word adds to a document. If you've got a list or table of email addresses in Word, follow these steps:

1. Convert the Word document to a text file. To do so, in Word select File→Save As. The Save As dialog box appears.

2. At the bottom of the Save As box is the "Save as type" drop-down menu. From that menu, select Plain Text (*.txt). Click Save. The File Conversion dialog box opens, warning you that converting the file will strip out all its formatting. (Word just can't believe that there might be times when you don't want all that behind-the-scenes formatting.) This box gives you various options—you don't have to mess with these; the defaults should work—and shows you how the file will look in its new format.

3. Click OK. Word saves the file as a text file. If the Word document was named *addresses.doc*, then the new file is called *addresses.txt*. (And addresses.doc still exists in its regular Word format.)

4. Now, you can import your list of users into QuickBase. Follow steps 1–4 above.

QuickBase imports your list.

Sharing with Everyone in Your Organization

Remember in kindergarten when they taught you that it's nice to share? Even though you've moved from the classroom to the workplace, it's still true. And in the spirit of sharing, QuickBase has made it super easy for you to share an application with everyone you work with, from Jimmy in the mail room to the CEO. As long as they've got a company email address, they can access your application. You might, for example, want to create an application to share information about benefits, upcoming meetings, and other company events, and then make that application available to everyone in the company.

Here's how to share an application with everyone in your organization:

1. In the application you want to share, choose Share→Manage users. On the Users page, click the Add Users tab.

   The User Picker window opens (Figure 8-8).

2. From the drop-down menu, select "Search for a specific user". Alternatively, you can click the lower-left Search button.

   The "Search for a User" dialog box pops up.

3. In the Search box, type in your organization's email domain (that's the part that starts with the @ symbol, like *@megamultinational.com* or *@savethewalla-bees.org*). Click OK.

   The email domain you searched for appears in the Search Results box.

4. Click Add.

   The email domain jumps over to User Picker's right-hand list box. Next to it is a drop-down list that lets you assign a role to everyone in the bunch (that is, everyone whose email address ends with, say, *@savethewallabees.org*).

5. From the drop-down menu next to the domain name, assign a role. (For an FYI-only application, Viewer is a good choice.) Then click Save.

   QuickBase adds this group of users to your application. Now, anyone whose registered QuickBase email address ends with your organization's email domain can view your application.

Converting Placeholders to Real People

You've probably attended a wedding reception or banquet where little cards sit on the tables to show who sits where. If your name is Sarah Greene, you're not going to sit down at George Osmond's spot, or vice versa. Place cards keep everyone in a large gathering organized—if you get stuck in traffic and arrive a little late, you know your seat is waiting for you, because your place card holds your seat until you get there.

Sometimes, QuickBase sets out a few place cards for people who'll be sitting at your application's table, creating a *placeholder* in a user field (a user field is a field that holds information about registered QuickBase users, such as "Created by" or "Assigned to"). QuickBase usually uses placeholders when you've imported some data into an application. For example, say you've got a spreadsheet that tracks tasks assigned to various people on your team. Because you know everyone on your team, you fill in the "Assigned to" field with first names and maybe a nickname or two. *You* know who Spike is, but when you import the data from your spreadsheet, QuickBase has no registered user by that name. QuickBase does know, however, that you've assigned that task to *somebody,* so rather than leaving the "Assigned to" field blank, QuickBase creates a placeholder in that user field. Placeholders have quotes around the name, like this: "Spike" (see Figure 8-13 for an example). Those quotes mean that QuickBase is holding the "Assigned to" seat in that record for somebody, but doesn't recognize the name as a QuickBase user.

At a banquet, you ultimately don't want to spend the evening with a bunch of cards marking empty seats; you want your guests to arrive, sit down, and dig in. And the same thing goes for your QuickBase application. You want QuickBase to convert placeholders to actual users, so that everyone on your team can dig in and get to work. When you assign Spike a task, for example, you want to make sure that Robert J. Spiketon (Spike's registered QuickBase name) gets an email notification about it.

To convert a placeholder into a real person, take these steps:

1. In an application that contains placeholders in one or more user fields, choose Share→"Manage users" to open the Users page. Click the "I want to" button and select Replace Placeholders. (Try saying *that* three times fast.)

   The Replace Placeholders page, shown in Figure 8-14, opens, showing all the placeholders QuickBase has inserted.

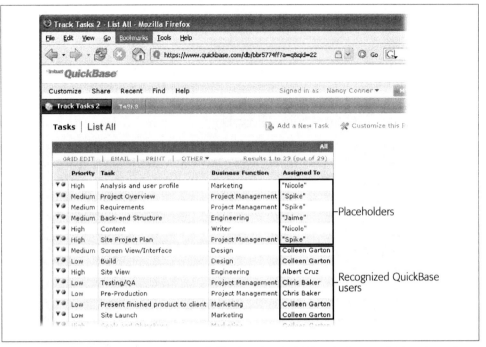

Figure 8-13. Placeholders appear in a user field only when QuickBase isn't sure which registered user belongs there. You can tell which names are placeholders because those names have double quotes around them.

NOTE

If the "I want to" button on your Users page doesn't have a Replace Placeholders option, that application doesn't have any placeholders—so you don't have to worry about replacing them.

---

2. At lower-left, click the Guess Replacements button to make QuickBase try to match each placeholder with a screen name.

   If QuickBase finds an exact match, it returns that screen name in the Replace With column. If you have a lot of placeholders to deal with, the Guess Replacements button can be a real timesaver. You may have to replace some of them by hand—but only the ones QuickBase guesses wrong.

3. To tell QuickBase which user to replace with (if QuickBase guesses wrong, for example), click the Pick New User button.

4. The User Picker opens, where you can easily find the coworkers you're looking for.

   Whether you tell QuickBase to guess who the placeholders really are or select the replacements with the User Picker, QuickBase inserts actual user names into the Replace With column.

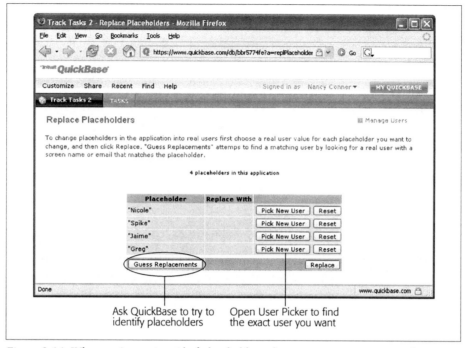

Figure 8-14. *When you're getting rid of placeholders, there are two ways to put real names in the Replace With column. Click the Guess Replacements button (circled) to have QuickBase search for a screen name that exactly matches the placeholder. Or, for a little more precision, click Pick New User to open the User Picker and select the users yourself. If you make a mistake and want to clear an entry in the Replace With column, click the Reset button next to the name you want to clear.*

5. When the right names for each placeholder appear in the Replace With column, click Replace.

QuickBase dumps the placeholders, replacing them with the matched-up users, and returns you to the Replace Placeholders page. If you have any placeholders left, they appear in the Placeholder table. If not, QuickBase tells you that you currently have 0 placeholders in the application.

Adding and Modifying Fields

As people use your QuickBase application, adding and working with data, you'll probably find that you (or they) want to make some adjustments to the application itself. For example, they might want to add a field to a form, move the fields around to make data entry easier, or change a field from text entry to multiple choice. QuickBase lets you adjust your applications so that they make sense to you, your team, and the way you all work.

Adding Fields

Whether you've created a form from scratch or found it in a prebuilt application, sometimes you wish it gave you more room to fill in details, for example, or had fields in a different order. With QuickBase, you can easily add new fields to any table in any application—even as you're entering data in a form. (Too bad you can't use QuickBase to add a Customer Feedback box to your income tax return.)

NOTE

Fields, explained in detail back in "Customizing Fields and Tables" on page 219, are the parts of a form or table that hold the little pieces of information that make up each record (if you were using an order form to buy a new sweater, the fields would be things like style, size, color, and so on).

To add a new field to a table in your QuickBase application, take these steps:

1. Open the application and select Customize→Tables from the menu bar.

   This gets you to Table Central—the Tables page—shown in Figure 8-15. The Fields tab, already selected, shows you a list of all the fields in the table.

2. If you're in a multi-table application, choose the table you want from the list on the left side of the page. The header and footer of the Fields table has a button called Create New Fields. Click this button.

   The Add Fields page opens. This page has a text box for field labels and, to the right, a drop-down menu full of field types.

3. For each field you want to create, type the field's name into a Label text box and then choose the type of field you want it to be.

   For example, if you want to create a field that shows how much something costs, label that field Price or Cost and choose Numeric—Currency for the field type. (For a rundown of all the different types of fields, see the box in "Assigning field types" on page 235.)

4. When you're finished, click Add Fields.

   QuickBase creates the field and takes you back to the Tables page.

If the application to which you're adding a field currently has any custom forms (forms designed by you that go above and beyond the normal call of duty), QuickBase shows you a prompt asking whether you want to add the new field to any of those custom forms. Your choices are Yes and Not Right Now. "Creating a Custom Form" on page 441 explains all about custom forms—and when you might want to add fields to them.

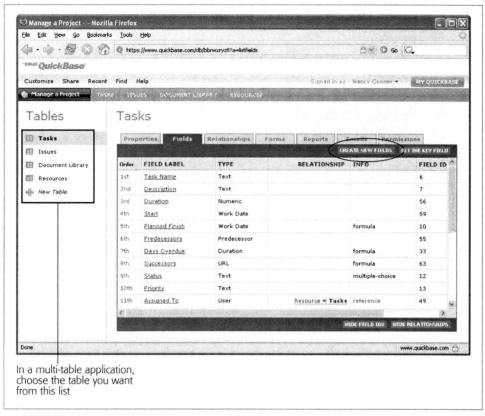

Figure 8-15. The Fields tab of the Tables page is your centralized location for managing a table's fields. The left-hand menu indicates that you're in a multi-table application—be sure you select the table whose fields you want to work with. To create new fields in a table, click the Create New Fields button (circled).

In a multi-table application, choose the table you want from this list

---

TIP

Here's a shortcut when you're adding a field. Click Customize→Create a new→Field. (If you're in a multi-table application, tell QuickBase which table you're adding the field to.) This route skips the Tables page, landing you right on the Add Fields page.

If you're in the process of entering data and you suddenly think, "Boy, it would be nice to have a field here to enter the names of clients' family members," you can create a field right then and there, without even leaving the form. Here's how:

1. Right-click a field in the neighborhood of the field you want to create.

   A context menu pops up.

2. From the context menu, select "Add a field before this one" or "Add a field after this one," depending on where you want the new field to appear.

Figure 8-16. When you add a new field to a form you're working with, just name the field and define its type—then go right back to the form and start entering data into the new field.

The Add a Field to a Form page, shown in Figure 8-16, opens.

3. In the Select a Field box (at left), scroll down to the bottom of the list, where you'll find <Create a New Field>. Select that, and then give your new field a label and select its type. Click Done.

QuickBase returns you to the form you were working in, with the new field in place. You can start entering data in it immediately.

Modifying Fields

Even if your table has all the fields you could ever want or need, you might want to fiddle with them a bit: change their order around, change a field's name (from Misc. to Comments, for example), tinker with its properties (such as making it an auto-fill field), change its type, or delete a field you don't use. You can customize a table's fields to your heart's content.

Whatever you're changing about an application's fields, start from the Fields tab of the Tables page: Open the application you want, then select Customize→Tables from the menu bar (to save your clicking finger, the Fields tab is already selected).

Renaming a field

From the Fields tab of the Tables page, click the name of the field you want to rename. The Properties page for that field opens (shown in Figure 8-17). The field's current name appears in the Label box. To change it, click inside the Label box and enter the new name. Click Save to save the new name.

Reordering fields in the default report

In any QuickBase application, there's a default report that determines the settings for List All and List Changes reports, as well as any new report you want to create. When

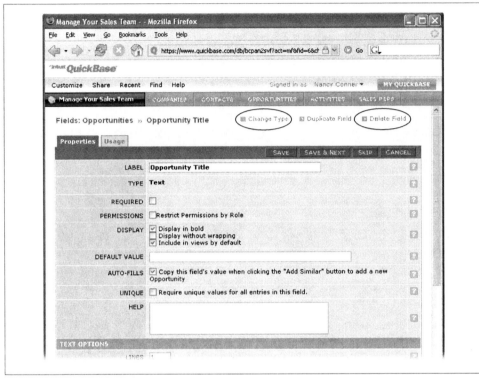

Figure 8-17. To change an existing QuickBase field, use the field's Properties page. If you want to change the field's type, click the upper-right Change Type link (circled). You can delete a field from this page by clicking the upper-right Delete Field button (also circled), or from the Fields tab of the Tables page.

you use Find to do a search, the default report also sets up the order of fields in the results. You can change the order of fields in a table's default report.

On Tables page, click the Reports tab. There you see a list of reports for that table. Right at the top of the list is one called Default Report; click its name. This opens the Default Report page, shown in Figure 8-18, which lists fields in the order they appear in the default view. Select the field you want to move, and then click the arrow on its right to change its position in the list. When you've got the list looking good, click Save.

NOTE

Don't reorder fields in an application's default report unless you have a good reason for doing so, such as minimizing the number of columns to display. The default report affects a variety of things in an application (such as search results), so unless you're careful, messing with the default report can mess up your application. To be safe, reorder the fields in an existing report (next section), not the default.

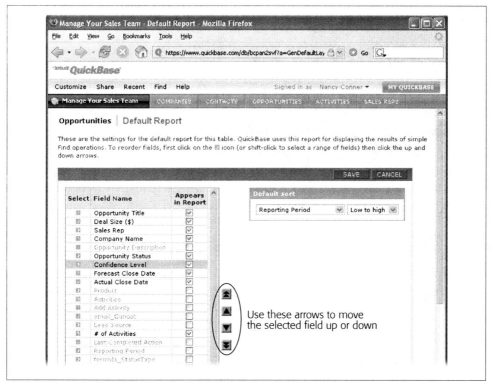

Figure 8-18. On the Default Report page, select one or more fields from the list, and then use the arrows (circled) to change their order. The single arrows move the selected field up or down one place in the list; the double arrows move the field up or down five places.

Reordering fields in an existing Table report

To reorder fields in just one particular Table report (rather than affecting the whole table by changing the default report), open the application that holds the report you want and click Customize→Table, and then click the Reports tab. (If you're in a multi-table application, select the table that holds the report you want to change.) On the Reports tab, click the name of the report you want. This opens Report Builder for that report. Scroll down to the Columns to Display section. Next to the Your Columns box is a set of arrows like the ones shown in Figure 8-18. Use these arrows to rearrange the fields in this report, and this report only. Don't forget to click Save when you're done.

Editing a field's properties

On the Fields tab of the Tables page, click the name of any field to work with that field's properties. There's a lot you can do with field properties. Look back at Figure 8-17 to get an idea of all the different possibilities. Some properties are specific to the type of field you're looking at (text, numeric, date, and so on), but the following properties apply to all fields:

- **Label.** As mentioned earlier, this is where you change a field's name.
- **Type.** This item informs you of the type assigned to this field. You can't change a field's type from the Field Properties page. (To change it, click the upper-right Change Type button and flip ahead to "Changing a field's type" on page 301 for details.)
- **Required.** Turn on this checkbox to require this field when users add a record.
- **Permissions.** Sensitive info? Turn on this checkbox to restrict the data in this field to roles you select.

NOTE

If the field you're editing is a formula, summary, lookup, or snapshot field, that field gets its value from other fields, called *subfields*. For example, a summary field called Total might add up the Price, Tax, and Shipping subfields to get its value. In Quick-Base, when a field gets its content from one or more subfields, it inherits the most restrictive subfield's permission level. So if for some reason a viewer didn't have permission to see the Tax field, that viewer couldn't see the Total, either. In many cases, this won't do. To make sure that a role can see a formula, summary, lookup, or snapshot field, regardless of the permissions of any subfields, turn on the "Override permissions of sub-fields" checkbox in this section.

- **Display.** These checkboxes give you some options about how this field displays, like whether you want its contents in bold or to display without wrapping. You can also specify if you want this field included in reports by default.
- **Default value.** If you want the field to show a default value that users can change (if appropriate), type it in here. For example, you might type in *Medium* here as a default for a Priority field.
- **Auto-fills.** Save your team tons of time entering data by turning on this checkbox. *Auto-fill* means that when someone is adding new leads and they click the Add Similar button, the new record will open with this field pre-populated.
- **Unique.** If there's a field that requires a different value for each record—like a Social Security number or an Employee ID number—turn on this box.

TIP

Don't turn on the Auto-fills and Unique checkboxes for the same field. You'll just create extra work for your team—when they click Add Similar to add a new record, the field that's supposed to have a unique value will be prepopulated with info from the previous record. So they'll have to clear the field and *then* enter a unique value.

- **Help.** This is where you can type in information to define what a field's all about. When a user clicks the little question mark to the right of the field, what you type in this box pops up in a Help box.

NOTE

The Field Properties page also has an Advanced Options section. Chapter 10 gives you the scoop on working with advanced fields. To learn about advanced field properties, jump ahead to "Working with Advanced Fields" on page 399.

Changing a field's type

Say that the Comments field in an application is currently a text box, but that's not big enough for the comments people want to type in. You might want to change the Text field to a Text—Multi-line field, or maybe you'd rather people kept their opinions to themselves, so you want to change it to a nice, terse multiple-choice field.

When you navigate your way to a field's Properties page (Customize→Tables, and then, on the Fields tab, click the name of the field you want to change), you can see the field type, but you can't change it from the Properties page. To do that, click the upper-right Change Type link.

This opens the Change Field Type page, which shows you the field label and its current type and has a drop-down menu from which you can choose a new field type. Click Convert Data when you're done.

The Change Field Type page displays a red-letter warning that changing a field type can mess up your data. Pay attention. If the field whose type you're changing has data in it, QuickBase modifies all that data to fit the new field type. If QuickBase can't convert the information, it throws it out completely. So make sure you're not trying to convert, say, a Numeric—Currency field into a Date field, or someone will have to reenter all those lost dollar amounts.

TIP

If you're not sure whether changing a field type will harm your data, create a guinea pig to experiment on before you change the field type for real. Copy the field you want to change (click the Duplicate Field link on the Properties page) and see what happens when you change the copy's field type.

Seeing how much use a field is getting

Not sure how useful a field is? Maybe you don't use it much, but before you chuck it, see whether others who use your application need that field more than you think they do.

To check a field's usage statistics, go to the Fields tab of the Tables page (Customize→Tables), and then click the name of the field you're checking out. On the field's Properties page, click the Usage tab (you can see this tab back in Figure 8-17). The Usage tab gives you a breakdown of how many reports, forms, relationships, roles, other fields, and notifications currently use this field.

Hiding a field from Quick Find searches

Once in a while, you might create a field inside a table that nobody else needs to see. Say you want to know when records are created or modified, but no one else on your team really cares about that information. Or you may have your very own private rating scale for your co-workers: from "Why did I hire this clown?" to "Almost as good as I am." You can create a field and hide it, so that it doesn't show up in any Quick Find searchers your co-workers may do.

NOTE

Following the steps described here hides the field from Quick Find only. A user who's searching with Advanced Find or creating a report can still stumble upon your field. So maybe you'd better rethink that rating scale.

To keep QuickBase from searching a particular field during Quick Find searches, do this:

1. Open the application you want and select Customize→Tables.

   The Tables page (Figure 8-15) opens, with the Fields tab selected.

2. In a multi-table application, click the name of the table you want. Find the field you want to hide, and click its name.

   The Field Properties page for that field opens. (Flip back to Figure 8-17 to see an example.)

3. In the Advanced Options section of the Field Properties page, turn on the checkbox next to "Prevent 'Find' and 'some field' searches from searching this field." Click Save.

   QuickBase omits this field from Quick Find searches.

Duplicating a field

Who says you can have too much of a good thing? In QuickBase, if you've got a field you really, really like, you can duplicate that field and all the data it holds. You might want to duplicate a field, for example, if your company is changing the names of various products. To avoid confusion between old and new names, you can duplicate the Product Name field (and all its contents), calling the duplicate field something like Old Product Name. That way, as product names get updated, users can still find products by their previous names. So nobody will get frustrated trying to find "Men's Hawaiian

Shirt, Blue Hibiscus" after that product's name has changed to "Luau Extravaganza" —searches will turn up both the old and new names.

Here's how to duplicate a field and its contents:

1. In the application that holds the field you want to copy, navigate to the Fields tab of the Tables page (Customize→Tables). If you're in a multi-table application, select the table you want from the left-hand list. Find and click the name of the field you want to copy.

   The Properties tab for that field opens. In the upper-right part of the page is a Duplicate Field link.

2. Click Duplicate Field.

   The Duplicate Field page opens, showing you the name of the field you're about to copy and asking you to name the new field (whose contents will be an exact copy, at this moment in time, of the field you're duplicating).

3. Check that the field name in the "Field to duplicate" drop-down list is the field you want. If not, click the drop-down arrow and select the right field. Type in a name for the new, duplicate field. When everything's all set, click OK.

   QuickBase creates the duplicate field and returns you to the Fields tab of the Tables page. Your new field is now in the list of fields, identified by a fat black arrow.

Your duplicate field is a field of its own, separate from the field you used to create it. So when someone edits the Product Name field, for example, the changes apply to that field only; the contents of the Old Product Name field remain unchanged.

Deleting a field

To delete a field, head for the Fields tab of the Tables page (Customize→Tables). There, the far-right column holds a Delete button. Select the field you want to get rid of, and then click Delete. QuickBase takes you to the Fields Usage page, so you can double-check whether the field's getting a lot of use. If you still think the field has to go, click the Delete this Field button. A confirmation box appears (QuickBase doesn't take this field deletion thing lightly). Click "Yes, delete the field." QuickBase takes you back to the Tables page, and the field you deleted has disappeared from the list.

WARNING

QuickBase's caution is well founded. When you delete a field, you also delete any and all data that the field holds. Once that data's gone, you can't get it back. So, when you delete a field, be extra certain that you're not obliterating data you might need .

You can also delete a field from the field's Properties page. Click the upper-right Delete Field link and review the field's usage stats. If the field's gotta go, click Delete this Field, and then confirm your decision.

Working with Fields in Table Reports

If you're looking at a table that's not quite up to snuff and want to make some changes to its fields, you can make those changes right from the report. You can add, hide, or move a column without having to go to the Report Builder. You can also change how a column looks or open its Field Properties page right from a Table report. Here's how:

- **To add an existing field to this table,** click the heading of the column to the left of where you want the new column to appear. A context menu appears, as shown in Figure 8-19. From the menu, select "Add a column." QuickBase opens a box that presents all the fields that currently exist in this application. Select the field you want, then click OK. QuickBase adds the field you chose to the right of the column you clicked.

- **To hide a field that currently appears in the table,** click the heading of the column you want to hide, and then select "Hide this column" from the context menu. QuickBase makes the column disappear.

- **To move a column within a table,** click the heading of the column you want to move, and then select "Move this column" from the context menu. The column heading turns red, and when you hover your cursor over the column, the cursor becomes a four-way arrow, as shown in Figure 8-20. While your cursor is on the heading of the column you want to move, click, and then drag the column to its new position. Keep your mouse button down as you drag, and then release the button when you've got the column in place. QuickBase jumps the column over to its new spot.

- **To change the column's properties**—that is, to change the way the table displays a particular column—click a column's heading, and then select "Set column properties". A box appears that lets you tell QuickBase how you want to change the look of the column in this table, such as changing the heading text, setting the column's width, and indicating whether to wrap text in this column.

Whenever you make one of the preceding changes, QuickBase needs to know whether the change is permanent or just a temporary whim. After you've made a change to a table's fields, three choices appear at the top of the report: Save, Save As, and Revert, as you can see in Figure 8-20. Here's what each choice lets you do:

- **Save.** This option overwrites the current settings for this report. (A user who doesn't have permission to save reports won't see this option.) When you select Save, QuickBase asks for confirmation. Choose "Yes, overwrite it" if you want to save the report with its new look; choose "No, cancel" if you've changed your mind.

- **Save As.** This option lets you save your changes as a new report with a new name. When you select Save As, a box pops up and asks you to name the report and to indicate whether QuickBase should save this report as a Personal Report (for your eyes only) or a Shared Report (that anyone with access to the application can see). Users who don't have permission to save reports can only save their changes as a

Figure 8-19. When you click the heading of any column in a table, this context menu appears. In addition to letting your sort and group the column's data, this menu lets you make changes to the table right from a Table report. You can move or hide any column in the current report, or you can add an existing field as a new column. If your table is part of a relationship and this field participates in the relationship, you can add a related field. This menu also lets you perform the neat trick of turning a field into a whole new table (see "Customizing Fields and Tables" on page 219), change the column's properties, or go to the Properties page for this field.

Personal Report. When you've given the report a name and chosen to make it Personal or Shared, click OK to save the report.

- **Revert.** This option discards your changes and goes back to the report as it was before you started playing with it.

TIP

You can also click a column's heading to convert that field into a brand-new table (as "Turn a Field into a Table" on page 319 explains in detail). Or, if you want to zip over to the field's Properties page, click the field's column heading and select "Edit this field's properties".

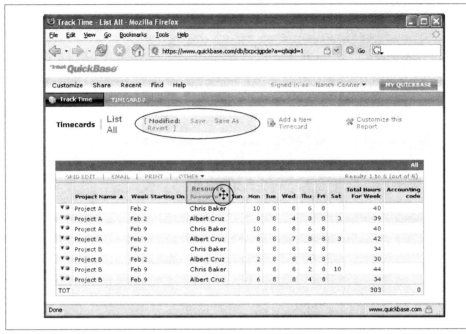

Figure 8-20. To move a column within a table, click and drag the four-way arrow (circled) across the column headings until you have it in position, and then release the mouse button to drop the column into its new spot. When you're done playing with the table, choose Save, Save As, or (if you don't like the changes) Revert at the top of the screen (also circled).

Creating Conditional Drop-Down Lists

Multiple-choice fields can hold lots of options—sometimes too many. For example, say your company has six different districts and each district has two or three dozen branch offices. When you add a new employee to a Human Resources application, you don't want to scroll through a long list of hundreds of options in the Branch Office field; it'd be much easier to select the district first, and then choose from a menu that lists only the branches in that district.

Enter *conditional drop-down lists*, which make data entry faster and cut down on mistakes. Conditional drop-downs let you create two related fields; what you choose in the first field determines the options available in the second field.

To create conditional drop-downs, you first need to set up two tables to hold the related information and then create a relationship between those tables. For the example, in the Human Resources example, in addition to an Employees table, you'd want two other tables: Districts and Branches.

Make sure that the Districts and Branches tables contain a record for each district and each branch—respectively—that you want to appear in the conditional drop-downs. ("Add or Modify a Record" on page 40 tells you how to add records.)

Next, create a one-to-many relationships between the District and Branch tables. One district can have many branches, so you'd make the District table the "one" side of the relationship (QuickBase calls this the master table) and the Branches table the "many" side of the relationship (the details table in QuickBase-speak).

After you've set up the relationship between the Districts and Branches tables, a new multiple-choice field appears in the Branches table: Related District. Edit the Branches records to make sure that each branch has the appropriate district in its Related District field. For example, for the Boston, New York, and Providence branches, you'd select Northeast as the Related District; for the Miami, Atlanta, and Charlotte branches, you'd selet Southeast as the Related District; and so on.

You've created one relationship, and you've got two more to go. Set up these one-to-many relationships in the application:

- Districts (one) and Employees (many).
- Branches (one) and Employees (many).

If you take a moment to think about it, these relationships make sense:

- One district has many employees.
- One branch has many employees.

The new relationships you've created change the Employees table's Add Employee form so it looks like the one in Figure 8-21. The three new relationships you created automatically added two new drop-down fields to the form: Related District and Related Branch. But those two drop-downs aren't conditional just yet. If you add a record

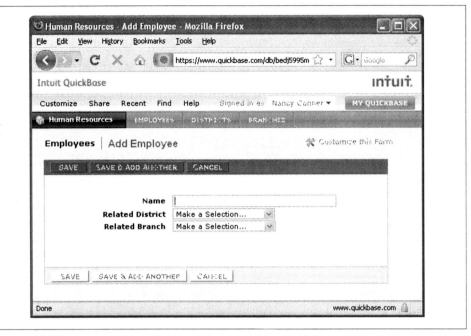

Figure 8-21. When you create a relationship between tables, QuickBase automatically adds related fields to the details table's Add Record form.

to the Employees table at this point, each drop-down still lists *all* the multiple-choice options for that field.

To make the Related Branch drop-down conditional on what you've selected for Related District, you need to edit the Related Branch field in your Employees table. To do that, follow these steps:

1. Select Customize→Table.

   The Tables page opens.

2. If it's not already selected, choose the Employees table from the left-hand list of tables. Then click the Fields tab.

   The screen changes to list all the fields in the Employees table.

3. Find the Related Branch field and click its name.

   The field's Properties page opens.

4. On the Properties page, find the Reference Field Options section. Turn on the checkbox labeled "Filter choices by selecting another field first."

   The section expands as shown in Figure 8-22.

5. From the After drop-down list, choose the field you want Branch options to depend on: Employees: Related District. Then, from the "Show only choices where" drop-

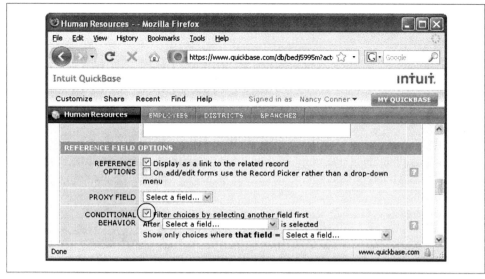

Figure 8-22. Turn on the "Filter choices by selecting another field first" checkbox (circled), and then set the conditions for your conditional drop-down.

down, choose the same field (Related District) in your Branches table. Finally, click Save.

In the Employees table's Add Employee form, QuickBase makes the options presented in Related Branch conditional on what you've selected for Related District.

That's it! Now, when you add new records to the Employees table, what you choose in the Related District field determines the choices that the Related Branch field displays.

TIP

You can write a form rule that makes the form hide the conditional drop-down (Related Branch, in this example) until you make a selection in the drop-down on which it depends (the Related District field, in this case). "Using Form Rules to Create Nested Multiple-Choice Lists" on page 453 tells you how.

Applying Field Restrictions

Many applications hold sensitive data that not everyone in the office needs to see. People in HR, for example, need access to your salary and benefits information. The guy two desks over, however, certainly doesn't need to know how much more you make than he does.

Because some information needs to be stored and shared—just not shared with everybody—QuickBase lets you restrict access to fields. These restrictions are based on roles, so you have to have some roles set up and decide which roles to restrict before you apply field restrictions.

There are a few things to know about restricted fields before you start limiting access:

- There are three permission levels for any field: View, View/Modify, and No Access. No Access means the field doesn't appear in any reports, forms, or record change notifications for the role assigned No Access, and users in that role can't import data into that field.

- Just because you're the application manager doesn't mean you have automatic access to all fields in your application. If you want access to a particular field, make sure that whatever role you assign yourself has permission to view or work with that field.

- The permission you set for a field on its Properties page doesn't override permissions you give at the record level. Here's an example: If you grant a role permission to View records, you can't set the permission to View/Modify for just one field within that record. If you tried, users in that role would be able to see—but not modify—that field (just like all the other fields in that record.)

- Some fields rely on other fields, called *subfields*, to get their values. Such fields include formula, summary, lookup, and snapshot fields. For example, a summary field holds the sum of two or more other fields, and a lookup field holds the contents of a field in a master table. In the normal course of things, a field inherits the permission level of its most restrictive subfield. In other words, if a summary field's subfield is set to No Access for a particular role, users in that role won't have any access to the summary field, either. When you want users to be able to view or modify a formula, summary, lookup, or snapshot field—whatever the permission levels its subfields—take this route: Select Customize→Tables, and then click the name of the field you want. On the Properties tab of the Fields page, find the Permissions section. Turn on the "Override permissions of sub-fields" check box. Now, restricted subfields won't affect the permission level of this one.

- When you restrict access to a field, users who don't have access to that field may still see its name around the application (in drop-down lists, for example). But even if they can see the field's name, they can't see what's in the restricted field itself.

There are two ways to go about restricting access to a field: You can start from the Fields tab of the Tables page or from the Customize Roles page.

Restricting access from the Fields tab of the Tables page

To restrict roles from the Tables page, follow these steps:

1. From any page in the application, click Customize→Tables. When the Tables page opens (Figure 8-15) with the Fields tab selected, click the name of the field you want to restrict. (If you're in a multi-table application, make sure you're looking at the right table.)

The field's Properties page opens. (Figure 8-17 shows an example of this page.)

2. In the Permissions section, turn on the Restrict Permissions by Role checkbox.

   The section changes to show current permissions. (If you just see a plus sign next to the words Show Permissions, click the plus sign to see the field's permissions in detail.)

3. For each role listed, click the drop-down menu to set the access level for that role. To hide the contents of the field from people in a particular role, click No Access. When you're done, click Save.

   QuickBase applies the access restrictions you set.

Restricting access from the Roles page

Here's how to restrict roles if you're starting from the application's Roles page:

1. Open the application you want and click Customize→Roles.

   The Roles page opens, with the Permissions tab selected, as you can see in Figure 8-23.

2. On the far left side of the page, select the role whose access permissions you want to restrict. Then, find the table name you want in the Permissions tab (in a multi-table application, you may have to scroll down a bit). Click the Fields drop-down list and select Custom Access, and then click the "edit" link.

   QuickBase displays that application's fields and their current access levels for this role in the Permission tab's right-hand pane.

3. Find the fields you want to restrict; click the drop-down list to the right of each field to set that field's permission level. After you've set permissions, click Save.

   QuickBase applies the new permissions and returns you to the Roles page.

TIP

When you're changing the access permissions for just one field, start from the Fields tab of the Tables page. If you're restricting a number of fields, start from the Roles page.

Creating Dependencies

A project never happens all at once, like *poof!* and everything's done. It takes place in stages. And usually, steps in one stage must be complete before the next stage can begin. In the software development life cycle, for example, one team must gather business rules and user requirements before they can write a business requirements specification, and the business requirements have to be spelled out before the system specs can be

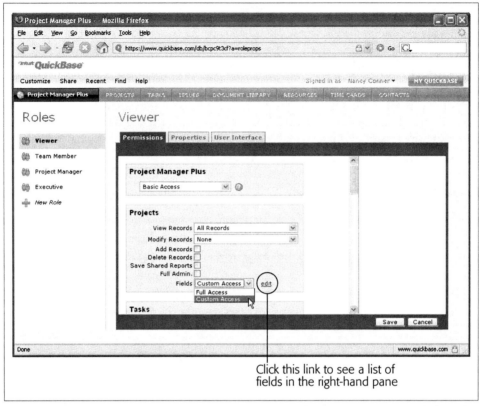

Click this link to see a list of
fields in the right-hand pane

Figure 8-23. The Roles page lets you manage an application's roles in numerous ways, including what records people assigned that role can see and how they can work with a table's data—even down to the individual fields a role has access to. When you assign custom access to a table's fields, click the edit link (circled) to see all the fields in the chosen table, so you can pick and choose which fields a given role can work with.

written. It doesn't make sense to move on to Phase II before Phase I's completed. That's because Phase II *depends* on Phase I.

If you're involved in planning and tracking tasks over time, QuickBase can make your life a whole lot easier, because you can define *dependencies* between tasks that make up your project. How does that make your life easier? When you define a dependency, any changes to predecessor tasks will automatically update the start date of the tasks that depend on them. And, as everyone knows, change happens. So updating the dependencies is one less thing for you to worry about.

TIP

Want to get a feel for working with dependencies? Check out QuickBase's Project Manager Plus template ("Project Management" on page 197). It comes with this feature already built in.

In creating dependencies, QuickBase relies on two field types:

- **Predecessor.** This field type holds the list of tasks that have to be completed before the dependent task can begin.
- **Work date.** Unlike a regular date field, which starts at midnight and counts whole days only, work date fields support computations that use some part of a day. For example, if a predecessor task takes three and a half days to complete, a work date field understands that the task ends in the middle of the fourth day.

NOTE

If you (or someone) manually types a date into a dependent task's Start Date field, QuickBase interprets this as the earliest start date. So if a predecessor task finishes early, it doesn't affect the dependent task's specified start date. When this happens, QuickBase displays a blue dot next to the date to indicate that someone manually changed the date that QuickBase has calculated based on a predecessor.

Adding dependencies to a project management application takes some effort, but the end result is well worth it—a few extra steps now will save you lots of time later on. Here's what to do:

1. Open the project management application for which you want to create dependencies. From the menu bar, select Customize→Tables.

   The Tables page opens, with the Fields tab preselected.

2. If you're in a multi-table project management application, select the table you want (such as Tasks). In the upper-right part of the Fields table, click the Create New Fields button.

   The Add Fields page opens.

3. In the Label text box, type the name you want for a predecessor field (such as *Predecessor Task*). To the right of the name, click the "Select a field type" drop-down menu and select Predecessor. Click the Add Fields button.

   QuickBase asks whether you want to add this new field to any existing custom forms.

4. If you do, select Yes and flip over to "Creating a Custom Form" on page 441 to read about adding fields to custom forms. Otherwise, click "Not right now."

   QuickBase takes you back to the Fields tab of the Tables page. Now, you've got a predecessor field, but no work date fields to go with it. You want to change the current Start Date field (which is a plain vanilla date field) into a work date field —for any task that has a predecessor, its start date will depend on when the predecessor gets done.

5. Find the Start Date field in the Fields table and click its name.

   The Properties page for that field opens.

6. Click the Change Type link.

   The Change Field Type page opens. This page warns you that changing the field type can sometimes mean that you lose data. In this case, because you're converting from a date field to a work date field, you don't have to worry about that.

7. From the "to" drop-down list, select Work Date, and then click Convert Data.

   QuickBase changes the field type and returns you to the field's Properties page.

8. Make your way back to the Tables page (Customize→Tables). In the Fields tab, look for a Task Duration field. If you see this field on the list, click its name to open its Properties page; check to make sure that the Task Duration field type is numeric and its units are days. If you don't see a Task Duration field, you need to add one ("Add a field" on page 219). When you create your Task Duration field, make its field type numeric and specify days as the units it uses. When your Task Duration field is all set, click the name of End Date field.

   The Properties page for End Date opens.

9. Click the Change Type button (as you did back in step 6).

   The Change Field Type page opens.

10. This time, select Formula—Work Date from the drop-down list, and then click Convert Data.

    QuickBase takes you back to the Field Properties page for the End Date field.

11. Find the Formula Options section of the Field Properties page and turn on the End Date Formula Builder radio button.

    The page changes to display the Formula Builder, shown in Figure 8-24.

12. From the "Start field" drop-down menu, select Start Date. From the "Time span" drop-down menu, select Task Duration. If your organization uses a seven-day week, turn off the "Work week is weekdays only..." checkbox. (If you leave it turned on, QuickBase counts business days but not weekends in calculating durations.) Click Save.

    QuickBase saves your changes and returns you to the Fields tab of the Tables page.

13. You're almost done. Click the name of your predecessor field (Predecessor Task in this example).

    You're whisked to the Properties page for this field.

14. Find the Predecessor Options section. This section contains two drop-down menus: Start Date Field and End Date field. For your Start Date Field, select Start Date. For your End Date Field, select End Date. Click Save. (If you've given your Start Date and End Date fields different names, like Launch and Planned Finish, choose those fields for the Start Date Field and the End Date Field.)

    You did it! Now, when you add a new task or edit an existing one, you can tell QuickBase its predecessor, and QuickBase will calculate its start date for you.

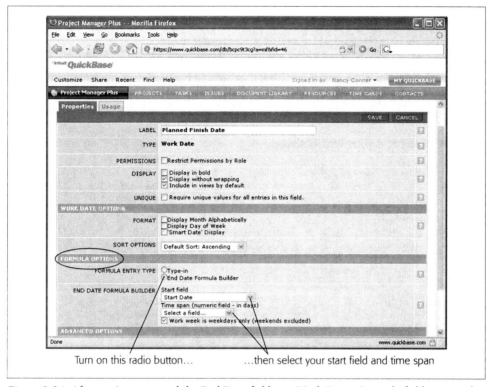

Turn on this radio button...   ...then select your start field and time span

Figure 8-24. After you've converted the End Date field to a Work Date - Formula field, you need to tell QuickBase the fields to use in its calculations. Formula Builder appears on the Field Properties page's Formula Options section (circled).

Deleting an Application

After the party's over—your team has successfully completed a project, for example—an old application can become obsolete. Of course, not just anyone can delete an application (that might be disastrous if a data-entry clerk were having a bad day). You need to have administrative privileges in the application or be a billing account administrator to give an application the ax.

Before you delete an application, ask yourself whether you'll ever need its data. Because when an application is gone, it's gone for good—along with all its records.

When you don't need an application anymore, there are three ways you can delete it:

From the My QuickBase page

If you're deleting an application from My QuickBase, make sure that your Applications list is in Details display mode, which looks like a table instead of a bunch of little pictures. (If you're seeing enough database icons to make your head spin, click Display→Details.)

Look over your Applications list to find the application you want (or *don't* want, in this case). Click the row in which the application appears to highlight that row, and then right-click. A shortcut menu pops up. Choose "Delete this application," and then confirm by clicking OK.

From the application you're deleting

Open the application you want to get rid of. On the menu bar, click Customize→Application, and then click the Misc. tab. Find the Delete Application link and click it. In the confirmation box, click "Yes, delete this application." You get another confirmation box, asking whether you're absolutely, positively sure you want to delete the application (after all, deleting an application also deletes all its data, so it's a good thing QuickBase asks you to think twice). Click OK, and the application is gone.

TIP

If you'd rather recycle an application than destroy it altogether, go to the Miscellaneous tab and select Delete Data. Doing so leaves your application intact; it just clears out all the current data. So you've got a fresh, clean application all ready for the next project.

From your Billing Account page (billing account administrators only)

If you're the person (or one of the people) in charge of your organization's QuickBase billing account ("Managing Your Billing Account" on page 23), you can delete an unwanted application from your Manage Billing Account page.

TIP

This method is fastest if you're deleting a number of applications at once.

---

1. From My QuickBase, click Manage your billing account. (If you're an administrator of more than one billing account, choose the account you want.)

   The Manage Billing Account page opens.

2. Click the Applications tab to display the applications in this billing account. Find the application you want to delete and turn on the checkbox to the left of its name. (If you want to delete more applications, keep turning on checkboxes until you've got them all.) Click the Delete Selected button.

   QuickBase opens a confirmation page, listing the application (or applications) you selected.

3. Click "Yes, delete checked applications."

WARNING

This route doesn't pop up another confirmation box, so make sure that you really want to delete all the applications in the list.

---

4. QuickBase returns you to your Manage Billing Account page and confirms the number of tables it deleted.

Managing Tables

If you're planning a large event, like an awards banquet, you need lots of tables, each holding related groups of people. You might seat guests by company or by department, for example. You'd think about who sits where so that the people at each table have something in common.

Managing tables in your QuickBase application isn't all that different from planning seating at a banquet. Some applications need only one table to hold all your data; other, more complex applications require a number of tables and some thought about what each table will hold. Chapter 7 helps you decide whether to go single-table or multi-table when you're creating a brand-new application. Sometimes, though, as an existing application grows more complex, you might find that adding another table makes your data easier to manage. QuickBase lets you create a new table from scratch or absorb an existing table from another application.

FREQUENTLY ASKED QUESTION

How Many Tables?

As my QuickBase application grows, it's getting a little harder to find the information I need. Do I need to add another table? How do I know how many tables I need?

In QuickBase, even a single-table application can hold a ton of information. And it's so easy to change tables as you work with them, adding new fields as the need arises, that you may reach a point where you're collecting so much data in one table that it simply makes sense to break out a second table and redistribute your data.

If you're not sure whether you need a new table in an existing QuickBase application, take a look at the following situations where adding another table makes sense:

- **Duplication.** If your fingers are getting cramped from typing the same information over and over again, you might want to reorganize your data into two tables. For example, say you've created an application to store information about inventory, organized by product. But you buy many different products from the same manufacturer, so each time you list a new product, you have to type details about the manufacturer that you've typed a million times before. When a manufacturer's phone number springs to mind more readily than your own, it makes sense to create two tables, one containing product information and the other containing

---

manufacturer information. Then create a relationship ("Creating a Relationship" on page 385) to link them.

- **One table, two purposes.** It can be frustrating if you're relying on one table to do two different things. For example, in an inventory tracking application like the one just mentioned, you're going to have some data that changes moment-to-moment (as customers place orders, your supply of a product decreases, for example) and other data that rarely changes (like manufacturers' addresses). Instead of cramming all this info into one table, separate it into two so you can focus on the stuff that actively changes.

- **Too many fields.** If your table has too many fields, it gets cluttered with information. For example, maybe somebody got the idea somewhere along the line that a sales application would be a great place to capture customer feedback. Now, instead of holding data related to who's buying what, the application has a whole set of fields gauging customer satisfaction with the product, with service, and so on. Not only are you making the sales table do double duty, you're making the form unnecessarily long and the table unnecessarily crowded. You can streamline your sales table by creating a second table (perhaps in the form of an online survey application ["Add a new table" on page 318]) to capture customer feedback.

- **Totals don't add up the way you want to see them.** Even though your table holds all the necessary data to show you the totals or averages you need to see, you might have trouble getting it to show just the right summary-level info you want. For example, say you store information about your sales force in one table. Of course, some territories are hot, hot, hot in terms of overall sales, while in others it's tougher to close the deal. So when you look at the total sales for your reps, you also want to see the average sales in each person's territory to get a clearer sense of how each sales rep is doing in context. Good idea—but it's impossible to display the totals in this way if you store all your data in one table. You can, however, create a second table to sum up and group your data in ways that one table can't handle on its own. (In this case, you'd create a new table to hold sales by territory, then average territory sales in that table. By creating a relationship to link the new table to an "average by territory" field in the original sales table, you can see how each rep's sales relate to average sales for that area. To find out more about linking tables, see "Linking Tables" on page 387.)

Adding a Table to an Application

Need another table? Adding a table to a QuickBase application is a whole lot easier and faster than dragging the old card table out of the attic and figuring out how to unfold the legs. There are two ways you can expand your application to include another table: add a new table or absorb an existing one from a different application.

Add a new table

To add a shiny new table to your QuickBase application, follow these steps:

1. Open the application that needs a new table. From the menu bar, click Customize→Tables.

   QuickBase opens the Tables page, which you saw back in Figure 8-15. On the left-hand side of the page is a big green plus sign and the words New Table.

2. Click New Table.

   The Tables page grays out, and the Create a New Table box, shown in Figure 8-25, appears.

3. Tell QuickBase what you want to call records in this table (purchase orders, time-cards, territories, invoices—whatever the table will hold), then click Create.

   Another box opens, asking for the name of your new table. Give the table a good, descriptive name to make it easy to find. Usually, naming the table the same thing as the records it holds works well—the Invoices table, for example, holds invoices.

   If you want the table to be a sub-table, click the drop-down menu and select the table you want to link to.

4. After you've named your new table, click OK.

   QuickBase creates your new table and adds it to the list on the left-hand side of the Tables page. Now you can work with the new table—grant access, add records, and so on.

TIP

When you add a table to an application, whether by creating a new table or absorbing an existing one, be sure to give the new table's records a unique name. If you have two different tables in an application and both tables hold records called Issues, for example, users will get confused when they try to add new records.

POWER USERS' CLINIC

Turn a Field into a Table

Sometimes, you're working away on a table and suddenly realize that life would be a whole lot easier if that one table could magically morph into two. For example, say you have a Customer field in your Orders table, and you'd like to break out a separate table to store information about your customers—transferring all the info you've already collected about customers from the Orders table.

When you want to turn an existing field into a whole new table, open a Table report that shows the field you want to convert. Click the column name, and a context menu appears, as shown in Figure 8-26. From that menu, select "Convert this field into a table."

QuickBase opens a box that shows the name of the column and the info it contains. If you select the Customer column, for example, you see the names of all the customers that column holds. Click the Additional Fields button (Figure 8-27) to add other fields

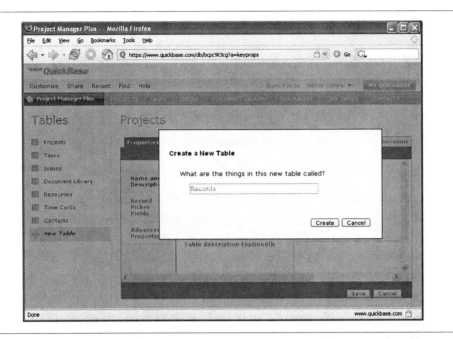

Figure 8-25. When you add a new table to an existing application, you have to give the table a name and tell QuickBase what to call records in that table.

from this table to your new one—in the example, you'd want to add the Address, Email, and Phone fields to your new table. When you're finished adding fields, click OK, and then click Next.

A confirmation box appears, explaining that QuickBase is about to remove the data from the old table and place it in the new one. What this means is that the field in the current table will become a lookup field in relation to the new table; the field, as it exists in the table now, will cease to exist in the old table once you've used it to create a new table. (If you're unsure what a lookup field is, see "Lookup Fields" on page 399.) In the example, when brand-new customer Jack Wolfmann calls up to place an order, you won't be able to add his customer info directly to the Orders table, as you used to. Instead, you'll add Jack to the Customers table first. After you've done that, Jack's name will automatically appear as a multiple-choice option in the Customer Name field.

If you want to proceed—and make sure you do, because you can't undo the conversion once QuickBase has completed it—click Continue. QuickBase asks you to name the new table and its records, making a guess at these names based on the name of the field you chose to create the table. Adjust if necessary, and then click OK.

QuickBase converts your field (or fields) into a table and adds that table to your application.

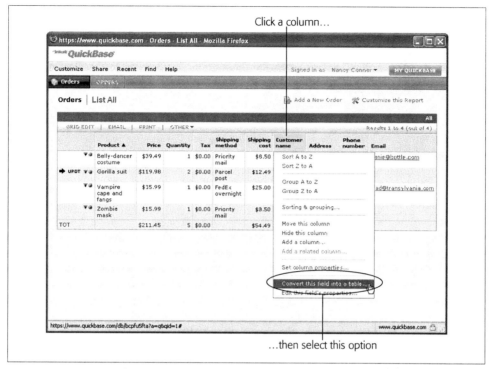

Click a column...

...then select this option

Figure 8-26. To turn a field into a table, click the column heading of the field you want to convert. From the context menu that appears, select "Convert this field into a table," and QuickBase begins the transformation process. You don't even have to wave a magic wand.

> When you convert a field into a table, QuickBase automatically creates a relationship between the old table and the new one. Chapter 10 is all about relationships, so flip ahead to that chapter if you want to learn more about working with related tables.

Absorb an existing table

Occasionally, a table living in one application would be more helpful in a different application. For example, even though a project has ended, some of the data in the old project would be handy to have in the new one. Or, if you manage a lot of applications, you might want to consolidate info from several applications into one. In such situations, you don't have to go through all the trouble of exporting data from the old application and importing it into the new one. You can simply transfer the table itself from one application to another, which QuickBase calls *absorbing* a table.

When you absorb a table from one application into another, you remove the table from its previous application and transfer it completely into the new one. If you don't want

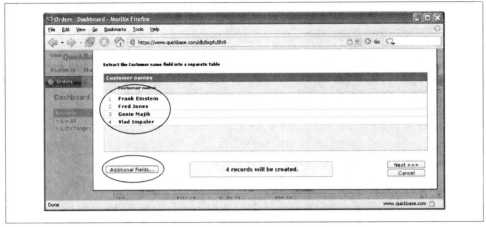

Figure 8-27. When you convert a field into a table of its own, QuickBase shows you both the field you're converting (in this case, "Customer name") and its contents (circled). When you click the Additional Fields button (also circled), QuickBase shows you other fields you can transfer to the new table; turn on the checkbox next to any field you want to come along for the ride.

to uproot the table, don't absorb it. Instead, you can link tables across applications ("Linking Tables" on page 387 tells you how).

Here's how to absorb a table into an application:

1. In the application you want to absorb the table into, choose Help→Application Site Map from the menu bar.

   The Site Map for your application opens.

2. In the Tables section on the left side of the page, click "Absorb a Table." When the Absorb Table page opens, click the "Select a Table" button.

   The "Select an Application" window opens, listing all the applications to which you have management-level access. You can't absorb a table from an application where you have, for example, view-only access.

3. Turn on the radio button of the application you want to absorb the table from, and then click OK.

   In the "Select a Table" window, QuickBase displays all the tables in the application you selected. If it's a single-table application, you see just one table. If it's a multi-table application, you see a list of tables.

4. Turn on the radio button of the table you want to absorb and then click OK.

   Back on the Absorb Table page, QuickBase shows you the name of the table you're about to absorb and the application you're absorbing it from. QuickBase also tells you that you'll have full administrative privileges for the absorbed table and lets you select an access level ("Restricting access from the Fields tab of the Tables page" on page 310) for other roles.

5. Assign an access level, and then click OK.

QuickBase absorbs the table and returns you to the Tables page.

TIP

If your absorbed table's records have the same name as records in another table in the application, be sure to rename the records in one table to avoid confusion. For example, if you're going to absorb a table listing the names of last year's customers into a new application that already has a Customers table, you might rename last year's records Former Customers. To change the name of a table's records, go to the Tables page (Customize→Tables) and click the Properties tab.

Absorbing vs. Copying a Table

When you absorb a table into a different QuickBase application, you transfer the table from one application to the other, moving the table from its old home into a new one. As part of the absorption process, QuickBase breaks any relationships (links to other tables) the old table may have had. But what if you change your mind and want to move the table back to its previous application—but its relationships are gone?

Here's a trick that lets you avoid that problem: Copy the table, and then absorb the copy. Start by copying the entire application that contains the table:

1. Open the application you want to copy. From the menu bar, select Customize→Application, and then click the Misc. tab. From there, click Copy Application.

   The Table Properties page opens. Here, you can give the copy a name (or just stick with QuickBase's suggested *Copy of [application name]*—for example, Copy of Work Orders or Copy of Sales Leads). In the Copy Options section, turn on one of these radio buttons: "Copy this application with data" (if you want the copy to contain the current application's records) or "Copy this application without data" (if you want the application's tables without any records in them). Similarly, decide whether you want your copy of the application to assign users the same roles they currently have.

2. When you've made your choices, click Copy Application.

   QuickBase copies the application and takes you to the new copy's Dashboard.

After you've copied the application, follow the steps in "Absorb an existing table" on page 321 to absorb the table from the copy into the application where you want that table to appear. (Then, if you wish, delete the copied application ["Deleting an Application" on page 315] so it doesn't clutter up your My QuickBase page.) Now, your table is intact—with all its relationships—in its original application *and* a table in the application you absorbed it into. Of course, these tables are now two separate tables in two separate applications, so *don't* assume that data you enter in one application shows up in the other.

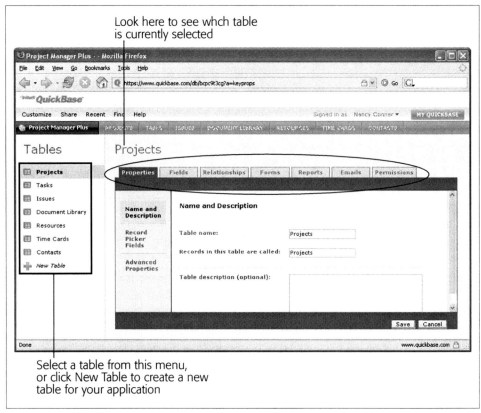

Look here to see whch table
is currently selected

Select a table from this menu,
or click New Table to create a new
table for your application

Figure 8-28. The Tables page, with its seven—count 'em—tabs (circled), offers one-stop shopping for managing the tables in an application. The name above the tabs tells you which table you're currently working with. To switch to another table, select its name from the left-hand list of tables. From the same list, you can click New Table to add a brand-new table to your application.

Managing an Application's Tables

For the most part, working with tables means adding, modifying, and deleting records, and then displaying those records in various ways. You got the basics on how to do those things way back in Chapters 1 and 2. But you can also apply changes to the tables that hold those records. For example, QuickBase lets you rename tables and adjust their properties. You can manage emails, roles and permissions, reports, and forms on a table-by-table basis. (To get even fancier with tables—creating relationships or working with formulas and advanced fields—skip ahead to Chapter 10.)

To manage the tables in your application, head to Table Central—the Tables page, shown in Figure 8-28. Wherever you are in an application, you can get there by clicking Customize→Tables.

Properties tab

The Properties tab is where you go to adjust a table's *properties*—the characteristics of a given table. Whatever changes you make in this section, be sure to click Save when you're done.

- **Name and Description.** Maybe you were in a hurry and didn't name a table when you created it, and now it's annoying (not to mention confusing) to see tables named *Vendors, Venues, Tasks,* and *Table #4* spanning the top of your multi-table application. Renaming a table is about as easy as easy gets. Click the Properties tab of the Tables page (you can see this tab in Figure 8-26). The tab opens to the Name and Description section. (If your screen doesn't look like the one in Figure 8-26, click Name and Description on the left.) Type in the table's new name in the "Table name" text box. If you want to rename the table's records, there's a box for that, too. And if the names of the table and its records don't sufficiently describe what the table holds, you can elaborate in the optional "Table description" box. When you're done, click Save, and QuickBase applies your changes.

- **Record Picker Fields.** When you're looking for a record you worked with recently, you probably click Find and check the bottom of the menu that opens, under the Recent section. QuickBase displays partial records in the Find menu—not the whole scoop, but just enough so you can find the particular record you're looking for. This partial display is thanks to *Record Picker*, which is how QuickBase lets you find a specific record fast, without having to go through all the details of every record in a table.

   This section of the Tables page's Properties tab, shown in Figure 8-29, tells Quick-Base which info to display in Record Picker. Record Picker is set up to display what's in a table's key field, but that information doesn't always mean much to end-users—if you're looking for a document, for example, which would be more helpful: the document's record ID number or its title? The Record Picker Fields section shows you which fields Record Picker currently displays for that table. Use the drop-down lists to change the fields. (If you don't want three fields to show up in Record Picker, choose "Select a field" in one or more of the drop-down menus.) Click Preview to sneak a peek at how your records will display in Record Picker (see Figure 8-29 for an example). Click Save when you're finished.

- **Advanced Properties.** This section holds a smattering of other ways to tweak a table's properties. Usually, the checkboxes on this page are left turned off. But a power user like you might have a good reason to adjust one or more of the following properties:

   —**Prevent the Find menu from searching this table.** Occasionally, you might create a table that's nobody's business but yours—a table tracking your personal to-do list, for example, or your all-time favorite Dilbert strips. When someone searches the application, you don't necessarily want info from your personal table coming up in their results. You can prevent QuickBase's Quick Find fea-

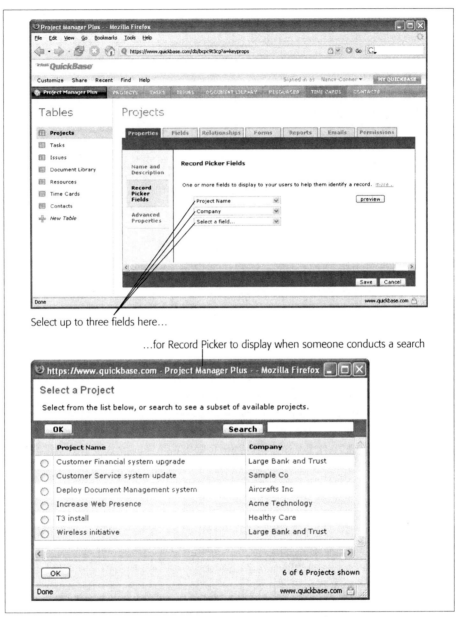

Select up to three fields here…

…for Record Picker to display when someone conducts a search

Figure 8-29. Top: Select the fields you want displayed in search results and then click the preview button. Bottom: QuickBase shows you how the fields you've selected will display in users' search results.

ture from searching a specific table in an application. A couple of things have to be true, though, for this trick to work:

1. You must be a manager of the application that holds the table.

2. The table you want to hide must be in a multi-table application (single-table applications are fair game for Quick Find searches).

If you've got those criteria in place, you can hide a table from Quick Find searches by turning on this checkbox.

NOTE

Hiding a table is a little like playing a game of hide-and-seek—your table might get found if someone's clever enough. When your table goes into hiding, users can't search your table using Quick Find. However, somebody using Advanced Find or creating a report can still select and search the table.

— **Hide from menu bar.** If you really want to keep a table top-secret, tell Quick-Base not to display it on the application's menu bar by turning on this checkbox.

TIP

You can also hide a table from certain roles. "Hiding tables or buttons" on page 364 gives you details and instructions.

— **Suppress edit button in reports.** If you don't want the reports for this table to show the Edit button (which displays as a button labeled with either the word Edit or the letter E, depending on the user's preference settings), turn on this checkbox.

— **Allow non-SSL access via API.** If you don't know what SSL or API stands for, it's probably best not to mess with this checkbox. SSL, which stands for secure sockets layer, is all about security. For the highest level of security, leave this checkbox turned off. To learn more about SSL, see the box in "SSL Spells Security" on page 256.

— **Alias.** This is an FYI section, telling you the alias for this particular table. Knowing a table's alias is a must for writing formulas ("Writing Formulas" on page 417).

— **Singular noun override.** QuickBase figures out whether the noun referring to the records in your application should be singular or plural. You can force QuickBase to always display a term of your choosing throughout the application. If you want to do this, type in your choice here and click Save. QuickBase opens a new window, telling the number of places where the current term appears and giving you three self-explanatory choices:

— Yes, replace all

— No, don't replace anything

— Show me more details

— **Menu heading override.** The application's Table bar (a blue bar across the top of the screen) displays the name of each table in the application. You can change a table's name on the Table bar (but nowhere else in the application) by typing the new name here.

Fields tab

The Fields tab of the Tables page (flip back to Figure 8-15 for a look) shows you all the fields a table holds, giving info about their type, any relationships they're involved in, and their individual ID numbers. Head to this tab when you want to do one of the following:

- Add a new field
- Set a table's key field
- Rename a field
- Reorder fields
- Edit a field's properties
- Change a field's type
- Check out how much use a field is getting
- Apply field restrictions
- Delete a field

Relationships tab

If you need help with your relationships, you'd better find a good counselor. But if you want to manage the relationships between tables in your QuickBase application, head to the Relationships tab of the Tables page. Figure 8-30 shows you what it looks like. From here, you can see all the table relationships in an application, click Edit to modify those relationships or create a whole new relationship—even faster than signing up with an online dating service.

NOTE

Chapter 10 reveals the ins and outs of table relationships.

Forms tab

The Forms tab (Figure 8-31) shows you how many forms currently exist for adding information to this table. This is where you can create and preview a new form for your a table, such as a data entry form available only to users assigned a certain role. For any form, you can edit its layout or create or edit its rules (which let forms change to fit the situation) and set permissions about who can see, modify, or add forms for this table. Forms are a powerful QuickBase tool, and you can read all about customizing them in "Customizing Forms" on page 439.

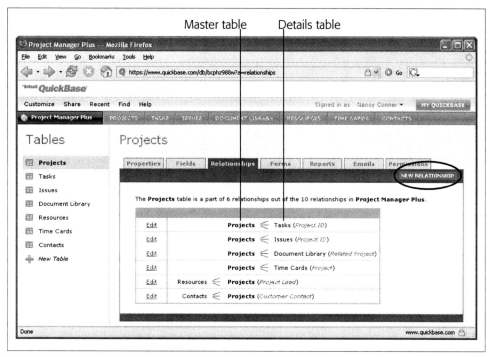

Figure 8-30. The Relationships tab of the Tables page shows you all the relationships in which the selected table participates. You can tell whether the table is a master table or a details table by which side of the crow's foot it's on: a master table (on the left) is the "one" in a one-to-many relationship, while the details table (on the right) is one of the "many." To create a new relationship, click the New Relationship button (circled).

Reports tab

QuickBase comes with a lot of built-in ways to display your data, and users can create and save reports of their own. Chapter 2 gave you an introduction to QuickBase reports. The Reports tab of the Tables page, shown in Figure 8-32, is where you go to manage the reports associated with any table in your application.

As you'd expect, the Reports tab shows you all the reports associated with the table you chose. The More Info column tells you whether there's anything special about this report—like that it's a pie chart instead of a table—and Last Used shows you whether a particular report is older than those cave paintings at Lascaux.

From the Reports tab you can do these nifty things:

- Create a new report from scratch by clicking the upper-right "Create a New Report" button.
- Click a report's name to zip over to Report Builder and give it a tweak.
- Display, copy, or delete a report (there's a button for each option).
- Reorder the fields in a table's default report.

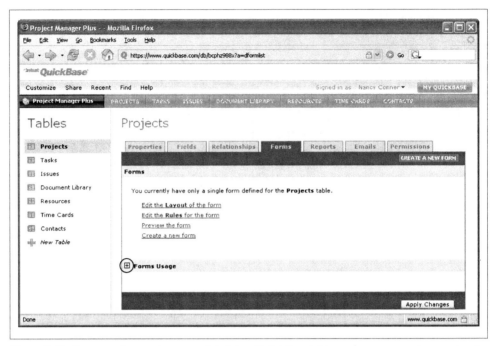

Figure 8-31. Forms are how you get your data into a QuickBase table, and you can create or customize them here. Click the plus sign (circled) next to Forms Usage to fine-tune which roles can display, edit, or add a form.

- Change the default settings for creating Calendar reports:

  In the upper-right part of the Reports tab, click More→Change the Default Calendar Properties to go to the Default Calendar Settings page. Then choose the settings you want to be standard whenever someone creates a new Calendar report. You can adjust the field that's the basis for the calendar (usually Start Date), tell Quick-Base what to display (durations, fields), specify the maximum number of characters or items that QuickBase can show for a date, show or hide an Add link, show or hide weekends, and display each record as a link to that record or as plain old text.

- Change the default settings for creating Timeline reports:

  When you click More→Change the Default Timeline Properties, QuickBase opens a Timeline Report Builder that looks just like the one you saw way back in Figure 2-34. Use it to adjust the resolution (Year/Month or Week/Day, for example), display milestones, and select the default starting and ending fields for new Timeline reports for this table.

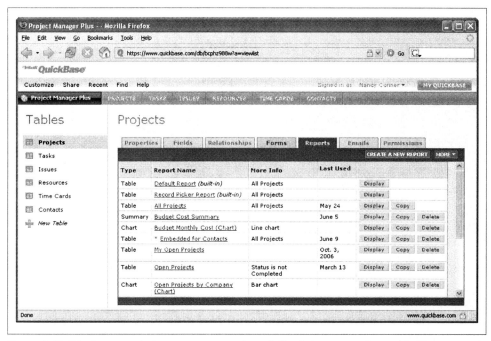

Figure 8-32. The Reports tab shows you an overview of all existing reports for a table. You can easily manage or create reports from this tab.

Emails tab

When a project is in full swing, there can be dozens of email notifications, subscriptions, and reminders flying through cyberspace on a daily—even hourly—basis. To manage all the automatic emails related to a table, click the Emails tab of the Tables page, shown in Figure 8-33. Chapter 4 explains all about the emails that QuickBase sends out on your behalf while you do other things—catch up on paperwork, sit through a meeting, even catch a few well-deserved zzzzs.

From the Emails tab, you can do just about anything related to QuickBase's automated emails:

- Create a new notification, subscription, or reminder.
- Disable a notification (when you head off on vacation, for example) or enable it (when you're back at your desk again).
- Modify a notification by clicking its name.
- Copy a notification (maybe you like it so much, you want to get it twice).
- Delete a notification when you don't need it anymore.

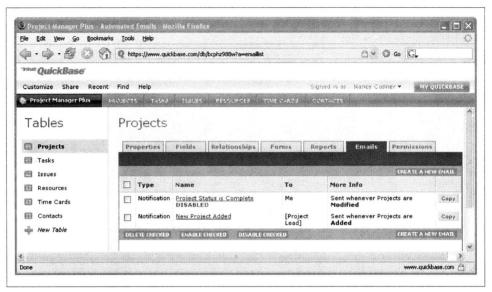

Figure 8-33. No matter how many—or how few—email notifications, subscriptions, and reminders QuickBase sends out for a table, you can see and manage them all from the Emails tab.

Permissions tab

In QuickBase permissions govern what users can or can't do in your application. Each user has a role, and each role has associated permissions. So nobody can go sticking their nose in places they're not supposed to. Chapter 9 talks about roles and permissions in detail. The Permissions tab, shown in Figure 8-34, lays out all the roles and permissions for the table you selected, letting you fine-tune the permissions of each role on a table-by-table basis.

Using QuickBase Enterprise Edition

If you're part of a large enterprise, your organization may have several—or several dozen—QuickBase applications up and running. That's great: QuickBase offers each division or workgroup the flexibility to create and use applications in ways that suit its working style. But as QuickBase applications multiply, you might start to wonder how to balance the needs of business users with those of upper management. People who use QuickBase on a day-to-day basis want flexibility, customization, and accessibility, and QuickBase gives them all three. At the same time, though, the people in IT need both visibility and centralized control, so they can administer security and other policies.

Fortunately, your enterprise can have the best of both worlds: Put QuickBase Enterprise Edition to work, and you'll give end-users flexibility *and* give IT centralized adminis-

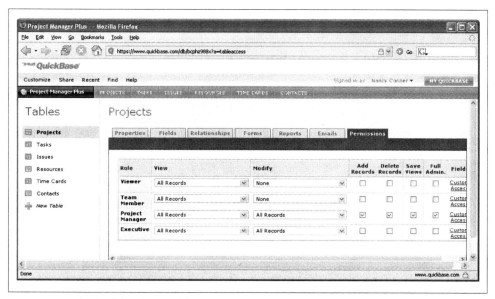

Figure 8-34. The far-left column of the Permissions tab lists the different roles that exist in relation to this table. As you look to the right, you see all the different permissions that role has for working with this table: the ability to view, modify, add, or delete records; save shared reports (which other users can see, too); or manage the table with full administrative privileges. Click Custom Access in the far-right column (and see "Applying Field Restrictions" on page 309) to learn about setting permissions for individual fields.

tration. With Enterprise Edition, your QuickBase applications all have a Web address that includes your company name, and you can set up a consistent look-and-feel (complete with corporate logo) on every QuickBase page. And administrators get a clear overview of usage, costs, and traffic. Everybody's happy—and the enterprise runs smoothly.

A Realm of One's Own

When your organization signs up for Enterprise Edition, QuickBase creates one or more *realms* based on your organization's needs. A realm is an umbrella for one or more accounts, and each of those accounts has one or more applications. Figure 8-35 gives an idea of how the structure works.

As realm administrator, you can keep an eye on all the accounts and applications in your realm, and you have a degree of control over them. You can approve or deny users, check usage stats, customize the look of applications in your realm, and more. Read on to find out how.

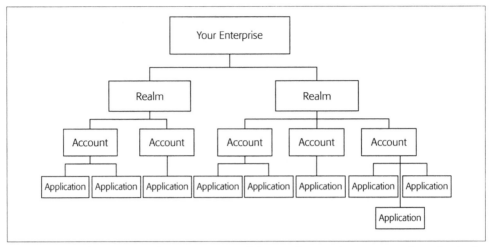

Figure 8-35. With Enterprise Edition, accounts and their applications become part of a realm. Realm administrators can set policies and view activity for all applications within the realm.

Establishing Your Realm

Creating a realm couldn't be easier—QuickBase does it for you. When your company decides it's time to upgrade to Enterprise Edition, taking advantage of all the cool features you'll read about here, simply call the helpful folks at QuickBase. They'll create your realm (or realms—you can have more than one). All you need to do is choose your URL—something along the lines of *mycompany.quickbase.com*—and QuickBase takes care of the rest.

What if your company already has a bunch of QuickBase applications when you upgrade to Enterprise Edition? No problem. When QuickBase creates your realm, it schedules a switchover to transfer all existing applications smoothly and painlessly to the new Enterprise Edition's account structure. (If only everything on your to-do list could be so easy!)

Once you've got a realm, you'll want to set it up just so. You manage your realms from the aptly named Manage Realm page. To get there, start from your My QuickBase page and click the right-hand "Manage the realm" link. This takes you to a page that looks like the one in Figure 8-36. The three tabs on the far right are where you go to manage your realm. The following sections explain how to use the Manage Realm page to set up your realm.

Setting access levels

Ask any emperor—a realm's not a realm unless you can protect its borders. With your QuickBase realms, you do that from the Directory tab of the Manage Realm page,

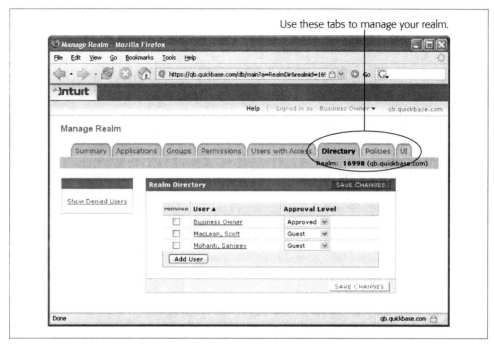

Use these tabs to manage your realm.

Figure 8-36. *The five tabs on the left probably look familiar—they're the ones you use to manage your QuickBase billing account. When you're a realm administrator, three new tabs appear on the right. (You can't tell from this figure, but the tabs for managing a realm are green instead of the usual blue.) The Directory tab shows who's in the realm (or out of it, if you've denied someone access). Use the Policies tab to set password and sign-in policies. And click the UI tab (that's short for "user interface") to customize pages within your realm.*

shown in Figure 8-34. To get there, start from your My QuickBase page, click "Manage the realm", and then click the Directory tab.

The Realm Directory shows you who's in the realm and which approval level each person has. Realms offer three levels of approval:

- **Guest.** This is the automatic approval setting for people who use the applications in your realm. A guest has access to individual applications they've been invited to join by the applications' managers.

- **Approved.** With Enterprise Edition, you can create applications that are for approved users only. So, for example, if you want only managers and other key employees to have access to the data in a human resources application, you can easily set that up using this approval setting. Users with Guest status can't get access to applications for approved users only. You have to grant Approved status by hand.

- **Denied.** Want to banish someone from your realm, such as an employee who's left the company? Assign that person Denied status. It's a fast, easy, and centralized way to make sure that a former user has no access to any of the applications in your realm. (Of course, if you want to make sure that the former employee can't *ever* use his or her now-defunct corporate email address to log in to QuickBase, you need to deactivate that person.)

Setting a person's access levels for a realm is simple:

1. First, go to the Realm Directory (My QuickBase→"Manage the realm"→Directory).

   This page shows you the users in the realm and their access levels.

2. In the list of users, find the person you want. To the right of the name is a drop-down list—click the arrow.

   The list opens to show you your options: Approved, Guest, and Denied.

3. Choose the access level you want.

   If you want to set access levels for several different people, just repeat steps 1 and 2 until you're finished.

4. When you're all done, click Save Changes.

   QuickBase applies the access levels you've assigned.

Setting password policies

These days, you can't pay too much attention to security. For most enterprises, that means you want a consistent password policy across your organization. To make things easier for your employees (and for your own peace of mind), you can apply the company's password policy to all QuickBase accounts in your realm.

To set a password policy for your realm, click your way to the Policies tab of the Manage Realm page (My QuickBase→"Manage the realm"→Policies). That gets you to the page shown in Figure 8-37, where you can tinker with these settings:

- **Minimum length.** Set the smallest number of characters a password can have. For security, it's a good idea to require at least eight characters.

- **Require Mixed Case.** When it comes to QuickBase passwords, case matters. If you want to make passwords harder to crack by requiring that they have a combination of upper- and lowercase letters, turn on this checkbox.

- **Require Mixed Alpha/Num.** Just as mixed-case passwords are harder to break, so are passwords that use a combination of letters and numbers. Turn on this checkbox for a high level of password security.

- **Passwords expire every ___ days.** An old password is a stale password—and a stale password can be an insecure one. To keep passwords fresh, have users reset them periodically. Your can choose to require a reset every 60, 90, 120, 180, or 350 days.

- **Size of password store.** Recycling old paper and aluminum cans is good. Recycling old passwords? Not so good, if you care about security. The *password store* keeps track of users' old passwords; the number you type here determines how many new passwords a user has to come up with before he can reuse an old one. For this setting, pick a number from 1 to 24, the range QuickBase offers.

After you've finished setting up your password policy, don't forget to click Save to apply the policy across the realm. (The next section discusses sign-in policies.)

TIP

You can have users sign in to QuickBase by logging in to your company's network. To find out how, contact QuickBase to set up LDAP authentication.

Setting sign-in policies

Busy people have a lot on their minds. And sometimes they forget stuff. When Fred boards the plane for his Orlando vacation, it's his business if he suddenly wonders whether he remembered to turn off the waffle iron at home. But it's *your* business to be sure that his browser's not open to a confidential QuickBase application while he's off zipping around Space Mountain. Fortunately, you don't have to stop by his desk to check. You can set policies that govern user sign-ins across the realm.

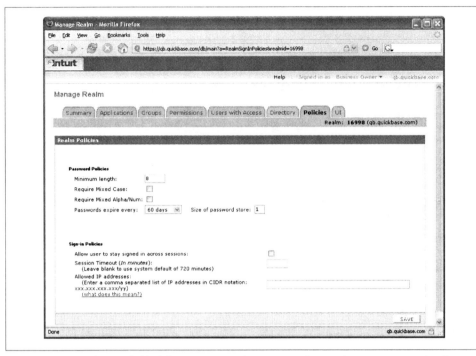

Figure 8-37. Use the top half of the Manage Realm page's Policies tab to set password policies, so users won't get lazy and rely on the same old, easy-to-guess passwords. The bottom half of the tab is where you control users' sessions: You can make people sign in for each new session, determine how frequently sessions time out (forcing folks to sign in again), and set up IP filtering.

The Policies tab of the Manage Realm page (My QuickBase→"Manage the realm"→Policies) lets you control people's QuickBase sessions. Your options (shown in Figure 8-37) are :

- **Allow user to stay signed in across sessions.** Turning on this checkbox means that users of applications in your realm don't have to sign in each time they access QuickBase. To beef up security, turn this checkbox off—this forces users to sign in every time they start a new QuickBase session.

- **Session Timeout (In minutes).** To make sure nobody stays logged in longer than they should, you can decree that a session will time out after a specific number of minutes. That doesn't mean *inactive* minutes; when the clock ticks over, a user has to sign back in, even if they're actively using QuickBase. So if you don't want to interrupt people's work (they can find enough excuses to do that), set the timeout to a long interval, like the length of a typical workday or every 24 hours. (In case you don't have a calculator handy, there are 1,440 minutes in a day.)

If you leave the Session Timeout box blank, QuickBase sessions will automatically time out every 720 minutes (that means every 12 hours).

- **Allowed IP addresses.** Nowadays, between branch offices, on-the-go users, telecommuting, outsourcing, and everything else that keeps business going around the clock, it can be hard to know who's getting access to your applications—and from where. IP filtering (see "IP Filtering" on page 339) lets you regulate who can get into your realm by specifying the IP addresses that can access QuickBase. To turn on IP filtering, enter all the IP addresses you deem acceptable, separated by commas. These might be, for example, all the IP addresses associated with your corporate domain.

NOTE

Specifying acceptable IP addresses is the first step toward IP filtering. After you've filled in the "Allowed IP addresses" box, make sure that the managers of high-security applications in your realm turn it on for their applications—you need both turned on for an application to be secure. If an application manager turns on the Realm IP Filter checkbox but you haven't specified IP addresses for the realm (or vice versa), QuickBase won't do any filtering for that application. To turn on IP filtering for an application within the realm, jump to "Turning on IP filtering" on page 346.

When you're done adjusting your sign-in policy settings, remember to click Save.

UP TO SPEED

IP Filtering

IP filtering adds an extra layer of security to your QuickBase applications by making sure that only computers and devices you've approved can get into a QuickBase application. Here's a quick primer on how it works:

IP stands for *Internet protocol,* and it's a way of identifying computers and other devices connected to a network. An IP address works kind of like a phone number: It lets one IP device, like a computer, find and interact with another IP device. (The phone number analogy only goes so far. Current technology lets different computers on the same network swap IP addresses.) An IP address consists four groups of numbers, with periods in between, and up to three digits in each group, like this: 123.45.678.901.

You probably think of computers by their domain name, like *www.quickbase.com*. Domain names are a nice, easy-to-remember, human-centric way to identify a computer or device, but they're not how computers identify each other on the network. When you type *www.quickbase.com* (or some other domain name) into your Web browser, that name gets translated into the appropriate IP address. The translation is done by a *domain name server* (DNS) using lookup tables for domain names and their associated IP numbers. When an organization applies for a domain name (like *www.yourcom-*

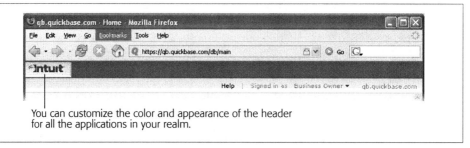

You can customize the color and appearance of the header
for all the applications in your realm.

Figure 8-38. Put your brand on your realm's QuickBase pages by displaying your organization's logo. (This page shows the logo for Intuit, QuickBase's parent company.) It's a nice way to standardize the appearance of all your realm's applications.

pany.com), it usually gets a whole range of IP addresses. The organization then assigns those numbers to different machines on its network.

IP filtering is a way to grant access only to certain, approved IP addresses. That way, unless someone is coming from inside your network, they can't get access to applications that filter by IP address. So use IP filtering when you need to keep an application ultra-secure—meaning no one gets in unless they're signed into your corporate network.

Customizing your realm

One of the advantages of Enterprise Edition is that you can customize the look and feel of your QuickBase pages to reflect your organization's brand. This keeps your applications consistent with the rest of the company's Web presence. If some of your applications are accessible to the public, branding those applications makes it clear that your company's QuickBase pages are *your company's* pages.

QuickBase lets you customize the header at the top of all the pages of all the applications in your realm. Instead of the familiar QuickBase logo, you can add your own. And you can match the color of the header to the color scheme your company uses. Figure 8-38 gives you an idea of what customization can do for your QuickBase pages.

NOTE

As you've probably already noticed, customizing a realm is a lot like customizing the appearance of an application. The difference, of course, is that customization at the realm level applies to *all* applications in the realm.

It's easy to put your brand on your realm's QuickBase pages. Start on the UI (user interface) tab of the Manage Realm page, shown in Figure 8-39. (To get there, start from your My QuickBase page, select "Manage the realm", and then click the UI tab).

After you've clicked the UI tab, follow these steps:

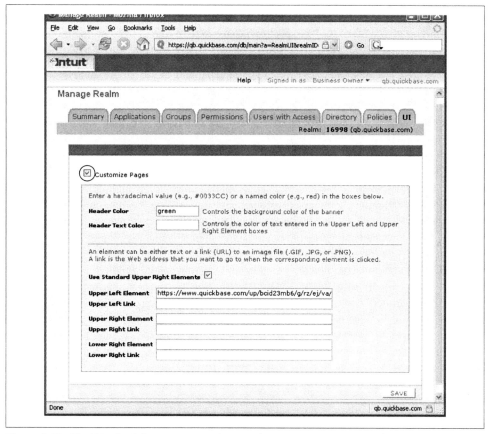

Figure 8-39. The UI tab of the Manage Realm page lets you customize pages for consistency across all the applications in your realm. Use the top part of the page to select a color for the header and any text that appears in it. The bottom part of the page lets you add images (like a logo), text, and links. To get started customizing your realm, turn on the Customize Pages checkbox (circled).

1. Turn on the Customize Pages checkbox.

   QuickBase unveils your customization options.

2. Add a little color to your pages.

   The colors your choose here apply to the header of your realm's pages: Header Color sets the background color; Header Text Color sets the color of any text in the header. To specify the colors you want, you can use either hexadecimal color values or plain ol' English words like "aqua" or "purple".

3. Add whatever text, images, or hyperlinks you want in the header. You might add your company's logo or text such as a slogan or a current promotion. Any images or text you add can contain a link to a relevant page on your organization's Web site. You can also add text or an image to the bottom-right part of QuickBase pages.

This is just like customizing an individual application. Type in any text you want to appear in the banner. If you want an image, you need to tell QuickBase where to find that image. (The best place to store it is in a QuickBase application; this makes it super-easy and super-fast for QuickBase to find and display.) For the lowdown on how to use an image as a hyperlink, see "Using an Image as a Hyperlink" on page 219.

4. When you've made your selections, click Save.

QuickBase applies the customization to your realm.

NOTE

Managers of individual applications can override the customization you apply at the realm level. So if you don't want anyone messing with the custom header you've created, send out a memo telling application managers to keep their mitts off your customization.

Mastering Your Realm

You've conquered your realm by setting everything up the way you want it. Now, master your realm by presiding over its day-to-day management. QuickBase makes it easy. Every realm comes with its own Operations Center. To find it, go to your My QuickBase page and click the application called Operations Center. Figure 8-40 shows the Operations Center Dashboard. From here, you can perform realm maintenance and adjust who has access.

Maintaining the realm

You can't be ruler of your realm if you don't have a clue what's going on in it. Who's wasting resources? Who's not pulling their weight? Which applications are getting unwieldy or being underutilized? The reports listed under Realm Maintenance on the Operation Center's Dashboard give you the information you need to keep things running smoothly—and on budget. The following sections explain what each report contains.

TIP

You can customize any of these reports to fine-tune the information it presents.

Budgeting and Controlling Expenses. The reports listed here let you establish and track a budget, so you can contain expensive applications before they get out of control. Here's what this section holds, report by report:

- **Assign applications to divisions/workgroups.** This Grid Edit report shows which applications belong to which group within your organization. From here,

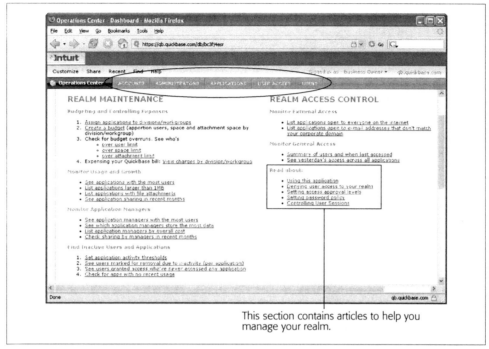

This section contains articles to help you manage your realm.

Figure 8-40. The Operations Center application offers one-stop shopping for managing your QuickBase realm. This application breaks down everything you need to know to keep an eye on what's happening in your realm. It consists of five tables (circled): Accounts, Administrators, Applications, User Access, and Users. A number of ready-made reports, which appear as links in the main part of the page, break down the info the tables hold. Reports in the left-hand column show info that helps you administer the realm, from expenses to usage to inactive users. Reports in the right-hand column help you monitor and control access. Get realm-administration how-tos in the "Read about" section (boxed).

you can assign or change the application's ownership (just find the application you want and click Edit).

- **Create a budget.** Is one application growing into a monster, eating up everything else in the realm? Rein it in with a budget. This Grid Edit report lets you set user and space limitations on any application in your realm.

- **Check for budget overruns.** Specialized reports let you check to see who's going over budget in terms of too many users, too much space, or too many attachments.

- **Expensing your QuickBase bill.** Running a realm can be expensive. This report breaks down QuickBase charges by division or workgroup, so you can see at a glance who accounts for which costs.

Monitor Usage and Growth. Some applications grow faster than others. Are some growing *too* fast? Are others stagnating? Discover the most-used and fastest-growingo applications by checking out these reports:

- **See applications with the most users.** Are any applications overflowing with users—and costing money you don't need to spend? This report will show you.

- **List applications larger than 1 MB.** Keep an eye on growing applications so you can rein them in before they challenge Godzilla to a fight.

- **List applications with file attachments.** Attached files can take up a lot of space. This report shows you applications that might benefit from trimming back on attachments.

- **See application sharing in recent months.** This report helps you keep tabs on which applications are being shared—and with whom.

Monitor Application Managers. The application managers in your realm are the ones out there on the front lines, creating and administering individual applications. Keep an eye on how they're doing with these reports, which can also help you control costs:

- **See application managers with the most users.** Are all those users necessary?

- **See which application managers store the most data.** Space is money. Don't let application managers waste it.

- **List application managers by overall cost.** If your budget is feeling a little strained, this report gives you an idea of which application managers might need to be invited to your office for a chat about good, old-fashioned values like frugality.

- **Check sharing by managers in recent months.** Who's been inviting the most users to their application party? This report tells you.

Find Inactive Users and Applications. Inactive users and applications don't just clutter up your realm—they cost money. You don't want to pay for users who never access an application or for obsolete applications that store unneeded data. Unearth the deadwood with these reports:

- **Set application activity thresholds.** Use this Grid Edit report to establish thresholds for what you consider acceptable activity for users of a particular application. If it's been two months since a user's last visit to an application, perhaps that user doesn't need access.

TIP

You can use automatic email notifications to find out when an activity threshold gets crossed.

- **See users marked for removal due to inactivity (per application).** Sleeping Beauty snoozed for a hundred years after she pricked her finger. This report reveals users who are on their way to beating her record.

- **See users granted access who've never accessed any application.** Sometimes people turn down an invitation—and they don't even send an RSVP. Check here for users you might want to clean out of an application.

- **Check for apps with no recent usage.** Do you really need old applications hanging around in your realm? Applications in this table may be good candidates for deletion.

TIP

Before you delete an application, export its data so you can store it outside of Quick-Base (see "Exporting Data" on page 137).

Controlling access to the realm

It would be really cool to have a moat, drawbridge, and portcullis to control who enters your realm. The reports in this section are the next best thing.

Monitor External Access. Are barbarians storming the gates? Well, okay, *barbarians* might be kind of a strong word. But if your realm includes applications that are accessible to people outside your organization, you might want to keep an eye on those applications. The reports in this section let you do just that:

- **List applications open to everyone on the Internet.** It's fine if this report lists things like customer surveys and other applications that let customers access their own information. What you *don't* want to see listed in this report is the application that includes the home addresses and phone numbers of everyone on the board of directors.

- **List applications open to e-mail addresses that don't match your corporate domain.** These applications are accessible to certain outsiders—people with email addresses outside your corporate domain. Such people might include consultants, outsourced staff, or temporary workers. Applications that appear on this list shouldn't contain any super-sensitive data.

Monitor General Access. These reports show you who's accessing which applications. Use them to make sure traffic flows smoothly throughout your realm:

- **Summary of users and when last accessed.** Get a bird's-eye view of user access.

- **See yesterday's access across all applications.** This report gives an application-by-application breakdown of the previous day's traffic.

Restricting an application to approved users

As realm administrator, you have the power to grant certain users special Approved status. Then, you can set up applications so they're available only to approved users. It's like putting these users on the guest list of an exclusive club—they won't have to deal with velvet ropes or bouncers that hold back the riffraff; they can just waltz right in.

If you're creating a new application for approved users only, read up on how to create an application, whether from scratch or from one of QuickBase's simple-to-use application templates. It's also possible to restrict an existing application to Approved users.

To limit an application to approved users, you (or the application's manager, if it's not you) need to follow only a few quick steps:

1. Open the application you want to restrict to users with Approved status. From the menu bar, select Customize→Application.

   The Customize page opens, with the Settings tab selected.

2. In the left-hand menu, click Advanced Settings.

   QuickBase shows you the different settings options shown in Figure 8-41.

3. In the Realm Approval section, turn on the checkbox labeled "Only 'approved' users may access this application", and then click Save Changes.

   Now, only users with Approved status can access the application.

If you want a currently restricted application to have broader access, you can change it. Follow the steps above, but in step 3, turn off the "Only 'approved' users may access this application" checkbox, and then click Save Changes. Doing so allows anyone with Guest status to have access to the application (as long as they've been added by the application manager).

Turning on IP filtering

IP filtering (see "IP Filtering" on page 339) keeps applications secure by preventing access to anyone who's not logged in to the corporate network. As a realm administrator, you can set up IP filtering. Once you've set it up, the managers of individual applications have to turn it on.

To turn on IP filtering for an application, you (or the application's manager, if that's not you) follow steps 1 and 2 for restricting an application to Approved users. In step 3, go to the Realm IP Filter checkbox shown in Figure 8-41 and turn on the checkbox labeled "Only users logging in from 'approved' IP addresses may access this application." Click Save Changes, and your application just got that much more secure.

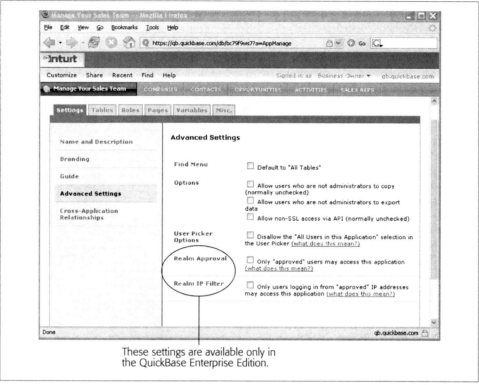

These settings are available only in
the QuickBase Enterprise Edition.

Figure 8-41. Enterprise Edition applications that are part of a realm show two new options on the Settings tab of the Customize Application page: Realm Approval and Realm IP Filter. Turning them on applies settings made at the realm level to an individual application. Application managers are the only ones who can turn them on or off.

Enhancing an Application's Security with Tokens

As Chapter 11 explains, QuickBase offers an API (application program interface) that lets developers create Web pages and programs that interact with QuickBase. This can be helpful if your organization wants to create a specialized program for interacting with its QuickBase applications, automate processes, or set up a central Web page for working with applications. But if you're security-minded (and these days, who isn't?), you want to make sure you allow only authorized API calls. (An *API call* is a programming function contained in a library. Programmers use API calls to interact with Quick-Base for a specific purpose, such as to get a record, add or delete a field, change a user's role, and so on.) To make sure that incoming API calls are legit, you can use tokens to beef up your application's security.

A *token* is like a watchdog for your application, letting allowed API calls through but keeping the bad guys out. It's a string of characters that gets inserted into an API call. That string of characters has to match the token you've assigned to the application, or the call gets blocked. As the application's manager, you decide whether the application requires tokens. Requiring tokens is a good idea simply for the added security it gives your data—this is especially important for applications that hold sensitive or confidential information, such as financial data or employee records. If an API call doesn't contain the token, it can't access your application.

NOTE

If your application has tokens enabled, you can't use exact forms. So if exact forms are essential to your workflow, don't enable tokens for that application. If you've already enabled tokens and you want to stop using them, open the application and click Customize→Application and click the Misc. tab. Click Manage Application Tokens, and then click the Disable Application Tokens button.

Setting up an application to use tokens involves two steps:

1. Create the token.

2. Assign the token to an application.

The next couple of sections explain how to do both those things.

Step 1: Create a Token

Before you can assign a token to protect an application, you need to create the token. Here's how:

1. On any page in your QuickBase account, go to the upper-right part of the page and click your name. Then select Edit User Profile.

   The User Profile page opens.

2. On the left side of the page, click Manage Application Tokens.

   The Manage Application Tokens page, shown in Figure 8-42, opens. If you've created any tokens, they appear here.

3. Click the lower-right Get New Token button.

   The Manage Application Tokens dialog box opens.

4. In the Manage Application Tokens dialog box, type in a description of the token so you can identify it later. A good choice is to type in the name of the application where you'll use this token. Click OK when you're done.

   QuickBase generates a token and adds it to your list of tokens. (You can see an example in Figure 8-42.)

Before you move on to step 2 (assigning the token to an application), copy the token: Select the token, right-click (Control-click on a Mac), and choose Copy from the context menu. You'll need it in the next step.

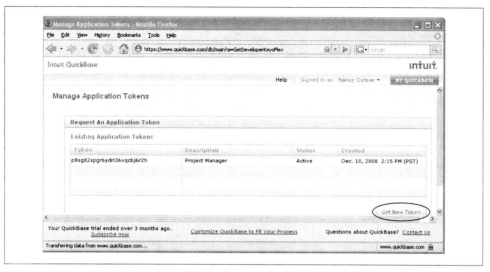

Figure 8-42. To create a new token, click the lower-right Get New Token button (circled). For each token you create, the list displays the token itself (a string of characters) and the token's description, status (active or inactive), and the date/time you created it.

Step 2: Assign the Token to an Application

Now that you've created a token, put it to work by following these steps:

1. Open the application you want to assign the token to. Then Click Customize→Application and click the Misc. tab.

    The Misc. tab opens.

2. Click the Manage Application Tokens link.

    The Manage Application Tokens page, shown in Figure 8-43, opens.

3. If you haven't enabled tokens in this application yet, click the Require Application Tokens button to turn them on. Then click the lower-right Assign Application Token button.

    QuickBase opens the Assign Application Tokens dialog box.

4. In the dialog box, paste or type in the token you copied in the last section. (This is the string of characters QuickBase generated in step 4 of the previous section.) You can include a description if you want (this could match the description you gave the token when you created it). If you'd like QuickBase to copy the token when it copies the application, turn on the "Ok to copy" checkbox. (Leaving it off enhances security, because there are fewer copies of the token floating around.) Then click OK.

    QuickBase assigns the token to the application.

The final step is to share the token with your trusted developers. They'll use it in creating programs and Web pages that work with your application.

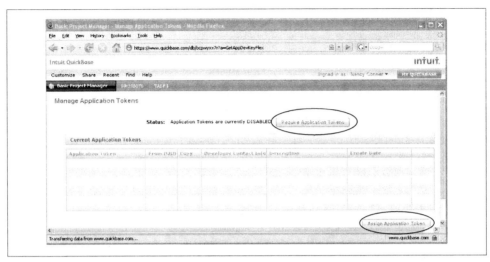

Figure 8-43. First, tell your application you want it to use tokens by clicking the Require Application Tokens button (circled, top). Then, click Assign Application Token (circled, bottom) to assign your token.

NOTE

Right now, tokens are optional; you choose whether to turn them on and use them to enhance an application's security. But in the future all QuickBase applications will require tokens. It's just that much more secure.

CHAPTER 9

Managing Roles and Groups

Managing QuickBase applications, as described in the previous chapter, is a breeze. Managing the people who work on an application is something else entirely. You want to make sure your team stays on track, with everyone doing their part to move the workflow along. But—as you know if you've ever caught someone playing Minesweeper on company time—people don't always perform the way you want them to. Although QuickBase can't do much about employees who shop on eBay, it can help ensure that everyone's looking at only what you want them to see.

When you add users to an application, you assign each one a role that determines his or her level of access to that application. Even better, you can define those roles in whatever way makes sense for your application. And when you're working with an application that has many users, you can save yourself a lot of time by creating *groups* of users. By assigning each group (and everyone in it) a role, you can manage people en masse instead of one by one. This chapter shows you how to use roles and groups to keep everyone organized.

Managing Roles

In most organizations the work gets done because people know their roles and understand the jobs associated with those roles. Take the circus, for example. You don't see the guy who mucks out the elephant stalls flying around on the trapeze—he doesn't have the skills or the training for that role. And if clowns take on the ringmaster's role, they're only doing it for laughs. To keep a circus running smoothly, the people in each role (ringmaster, acrobat, clown, whatever) have access only to certain areas (center ring, trapeze, the little trick car) so that they can perform their jobs. When people step out of their roles, chaos ensues.

Similarly, in a QuickBase application, people with different skills, training, and job functions need to use its data in different ways. *Roles,* which determine the level of access different people have to your QuickBase application, let you make sure that people use your application the way they're supposed to.

Roles let you control a number of things related to how people use your application:

- **What a user can see.** You can put limits on which records a user can see. For example, you may want people to see only those tasks or sales leads assigned to them. (You set limits by creating a custom access rule—see "Custom Access to Fields" on page 365.) In the same vein, you can hide certain fields and tables from a given role.

- **What a user can do.** Just as you can control which records a role can see, you can also control how users assigned that role can work with those records. Think of a professor who wants her students to be able to see grades, but not add, modify, or delete them. On the other hand, the college registrar may want professors to be able to modify course descriptions, but not add or delete them.

- **Which menu options a user can choose.** If you don't want users to have the ability to edit multiple records all at once (thereby reducing the possibility of multiple oopses), then you can remove that and other menu options. Restricting this ability means that a user in that role can't do a search and replace operation, import data, or use grid edit mode ("Grid Edit Reports" on page 52).

- **What a user's Dashboard shows.** Different roles call for different Dashboards. You can highlight the most important information that users in a role need to know by putting it front and center on their Dashboard. You can also remove the Dashboard's Add New Record button, show or hide its Info box, and customize it in other ways.

- **How a user works with reports.** Specify the reports that appear on a user's Dashboard or withhold permission to save reports.

Here's an example of how roles work. If you run a property management company, you want your office staff to be able to enter and modify information about individual properties, tenants, leases, and maintenance requests. You want tenants to see information about their own unit—like when maintenance is scheduled—but you certainly don't want them to have access to all the information about the other tenants and their units. Similarly, you want maintenance staff to know where to go and what to do each day, but there's no reason for the guy changing the light bulb in the hall outside apartment 103 to know how much 103's tenant earns or what her credit rating is. And you don't want maintenance staff or tenants to change or delete records. In this example, you'd set up a number of different roles:

- **Tenant.** Can view records related to his or her own unit. Cannot view any other records and cannot add, modify, or delete any records.

- **Maintenance staff.** Can view all work orders and physical details of properties. Can modify work orders (to close out a job) but not other records.

- **Office staff.** Can view, add, modify, and delete records.

- **You.** As administrator, you probably want complete control over your application: view and work with records, add users, assign roles, create groups, add tables, and so on.

This example also shows that there are clear groups that different employees belong to. You don't have to spend lots of time assigning roles one by one. You can put different QuickBase users into one group that you define—such as maintenance staff or office staff—and then assign that group (and everyone in it) a role.

QuickBase's Built-in Roles

When you create a new application, QuickBase creates at least three roles automatically. Usually, you'll see the generic ones listed below. In prebuilt applications, the names may be a little different, but the idea's the same—different levels of access and privilege.

- **Viewer.** A low-level role that can look at but not add, change, or delete records.
- **Participant.** A mid-level role that can work with records but not alter the application's properties or mess with other users.
- **Administrator.** A high-level role that has full administrative privileges.

For many applications, these three levels and their associated permissions meet your needs. However, you may want to tweak a role's permissions or even create a brand-new role. Before you start assigning roles, take a minute to think about the way your group works (Chapter 5). Can you customize QuickBase's existing, built-in roles to suit the process that your team follows? Modifying these built-in roles can mean less work, keeping your application cleaner.

Modify an existing role

Because applications have roles already built in, you may be able to fine-tune your application's existing roles to get your team working the way you want. Here's how to modify a role:

1. Open the application you want. In the menu bar, choose Share→Manage roles. (Alternatively, you can select Customize→Application and click the Roles tab.)

   The Roles tab, shown in Figure 9-1, opens. This page holds a table showing all the roles currently defined in your application.

2. Find the role you want to modify. To its right, click Permissions.

   The Roles page opens, as shown in Figure 9-2. Above the Permissions box, you can see the name of the role you're modifying (in this case, Viewer). The Permissions tab shows what this role currently can do in this application.

3. Use the drop-down menus to specify the role's access level to the application and which records this role can view or modify (or both).

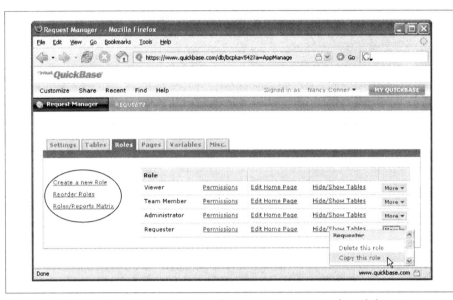

Figure 9-1. Click the Permissions link to see what permissions a particular role has. To customize a role's Dashboard, click Edit Home Page. To copy or delete a role, click the More button, and then make your choice. The menu on the left side of the page (circled) offers links to common actions involving roles. The Roles/Reports Matrix link takes you to a page that shows which roles can access the various reports in the application. To restrict the reports users in a particular role can see, click this link and see "Hiding buttons on the menu bar" on page 365.

In the top section, which shows the application's name (Request Manager in Figure 9-2), you have these options:

None. If you want to temporarily (or permanently) keep a role out of your application altogether, choose this option.

Basic Access. As its name implies, this is the lowest level of access a role can have within an application. It's useful when you want a role to be able to view and use your application but not to have administrative abilities. Users with basic access can't see the Share menu or customize the application itself. This is a good, safe level of access for most of your application's end-users—they can work with records and tables but can't make changes to the application as a whole.

Basic Access with Sharing. This offers all the basic abilities of Basic Access plus a bonus—user management rights. This access level gives users the ability to share with and manage other users. Use this option to let users create groups and invite other users to participate in the application, for example.

Full Administration. Administrators can customize an application's structure and access permissions. When you create a new application, you automatically have this level of access. Sometimes, you'll want to keep all that power all for yourself, but other times you might want to share it—for example, if you want to farm out some of your administrative duties to an assistant.

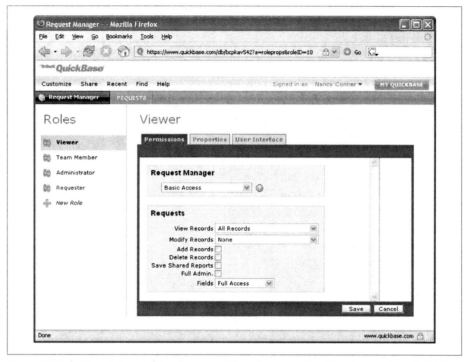

Figure 9-2. The Permissions tab is where you either okay or put the kibosh on various QuickBase activities. For example, under View Records, you might grant permission to view all records, none at all, records that belong to the user, or records with the user's name in a particular field. You can even create a custom rule to fine-tune this permission.

The lower section of this page is where you specify how a role can work with a table's records. In a single-table application, this section shows one set of choices (as in Figure 9-2, where it's labeled Requests). In a multi-table application, you get a set of options for each table in the application. Either way, these are your choices:

All Records. People in this role have permission to add and/or modify all records in the application.

Group's Records. Folks in this role can work with records created by someone who belongs to a group you specify.

Custom Rule. A custom rule is an access rule that you specify. For example, in a property management application, you might specify that a tenant can view a work order when that tenant's name matches the contents of the Tenant field. "Custom Access to Fields" on page 365 explains all about custom access rules.

None. Want people in this role to leave the data alone? Restrict their access by selecting None.

"When user is some field." For this option, a user in this role can add or modify records if his or her name appears in a specific field. The specific field depends on the table. For example, it might be Project Lead in a Projects table or "Assigned to" in a Sales Reps table.

"When user is 'Record Owner.'" When you create a record, QuickBase sees you as that record's owner (it's possible, though, to transfer ownership—see "Billing Account Administration" on page 25). If the current user's name appears in the Record Owner field, then that person can work with the record.

"When user is 'Last Modified by.'" If you want only the person who last modified a record to be able to view it or change it further, then select this option.

4. Use the checkboxes to fine-tune privileges.

   You can turn on (or off) four checkboxes to control the privileges of this role: Add Records, Delete Records, Save Reports, and Full Administration. The first three are self-explanatory; Full Administration means anyone assigned this role (like a manager) can edit field properties within a table.

5. Use the Fields drop-down menu to set access for specific fields.

   You can select Full Access to all fields in a table or Custom Access. When you select Custom Access, an "edit" link appears; click it, and QuickBase displays all the fields in the table. You can select access levels on a field-by-field basis.

6. Once you've set permissions the way you want them, click Save.

   QuickBase applies the changes you made.

Creating a Brand-New Role

Maybe you're already using the Viewer, Participant, and Administrator roles and you need a fourth role. Say you have two kinds of viewers—clients who need access to information that relates only to them, and executives who want to see *all* your application's data without getting their hands dirty actually working with it. Here's how to create a new role to reflect that there are viewers who look at different things in your application:

1. Choose Share→Manage roles (or Customize→Application→Roles) to get to the Roles tab. Click the Create a New Role link.

   QuickBase pops up a box that asks what you want to name the new role. The best name to choose here is one that describes the kind of user who'll be assigned this role, such as Client or Tenant or Maintenance Staff. (QuickBase suggests the not-exactly-imaginative name Untitled Role. If you're in a hurry, you can create a new role with that name. But, since you wouldn't be creating a new role if you didn't have a type of user in mind, it makes sense to name your new role when you create it.)

2. Give your new role a name and click OK.

   The Roles page opens. This page looks exactly like the Roles pages shown in Figure 9-2. The name of the new role appears at the top of the page, so if you're creating a new role for your clients, the page reads Client at the top. The new role has no permissions set yet, so it can't do anything in your application.

3. Set the permissions the way you want them, as described in the steps in "Modify an existing role" on page 353.

   If you want, you can also click the Properties tab and type a description of the role, but it's totally up to you.

4. When things look good, click Save.

   QuickBase creates your role and reopens the Customize Roles page.

Assigning a Role

By now you're probably feeling like a frustrated playwright—you've created all these great roles, but no one's acting in them yet. Unlike the playwright, all you have to do to bring your roles to life is assign them to QuickBase users.

You can assign roles to users as you share your QuickBase application with them. But sometimes you'll want to change a user's role—for instance, when they move from one job to another within the company. Or you might have assigned everyone a role of "none" or Viewer when you added new users and you want to assign them the correct role now.

When assigning roles, ask yourself two questions: What information does this person need to know to do the job? And how does the person need to be able to work with that information? The answers to these questions help you make sure that the role's permissions are broad enough to let the users do their jobs, but not so broad that they're getting into information they don't need.

Here's what to do to assign or change roles:

1. In the menu bar, click Share→Manage users.

   The Users page opens, showing the application's current users and their roles.

2. In the Role column, click the drop-down menu next to the role you want to assign or change.

   QuickBase lists the roles that exist for this application, as shown in Figure 9-3.

3. Select the role you want, and then move on to the next user (if you want to make more changes). When you're done, click Save Changes.

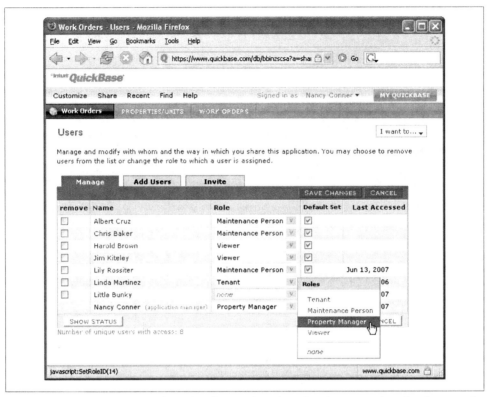

Figure 9-3. On the Users page, the Role column's drop-down list shows you the roles that exist for this application. To assign a role, just find the user you want, click the drop-down menu, and then choose the new role. Don't forget to click Save Changes when you're finished.

QuickBase applies the roles you've assigned and gives you a confirmation message.

NOTE

In a brand-new application, you won't have any users to assign roles to. Chapter 8 shows you how to add users to a new application; see "Sharing an Application" on page 280.

Prioritizing Roles

In real life, you play a number of different roles each and every day. As you go through a typical day, you probably wear one or more hats: parent, spouse, employee, boss, friend, and so on. Each of these roles has certain expectations, responsibilities, and privileges associated with it. Sometimes, it's a snap to keep all your different roles straight. Other times, though, roles can come into conflict, like when the boss wants you to work late to meet a deadline on the same night your spouse is planning a romantic

---

dinner and your teenager expects a ride to the mall. When roles conflict, you have to decide which has priority.

In QuickBase, roles can also come into conflict. It's possible for one QuickBase user to have more than one role in the same application. For example, Kevin might be a member of two different groups ("Managing Groups" on page 372). You've added both these groups to your application but assigned each group a different role—maybe you've designated one group as Viewer and the other as Participant. So what does that make Kevin—a Viewer who can see records but not work with them, or a Participant with broad abilities to work with the application's data?

The short answer is both. When a user like Kevin has two different roles, QuickBase grants him all the permissions available to either role. So because Kevin is both a Viewer and a Participant, he can do everything that a Viewer can do *and* everything that a Participant can do. He can see records like a Viewer and add, change, or delete records like a Participant. And if you've set things up so that Viewers can see only three different reports while Participants can see 12, then Kevin will be able to see all 12 reports, even though other Viewers can see only three. Since you want Kevin to be able to do all the things anyone in the Participant role can do, his roles don't conflict.

Now suppose you've set up a special Dashboard for each role. QuickBase needs a way to choose which Dashboard to display when Kevin opens the application. That's why the short answer isn't the end of the story. To control which role takes precedence when a user has two or more roles with conflicting permissions, QuickBase lets you *prioritize* an application's roles. Prioritizing sets up a hierarchy so that QuickBase knows which roles take precedence over others.

Here's how to prioritize roles in your QuickBase application:

1. In the menu bar, select Customize→Application, and then click the Roles tab. (Choosing Share→"Manage roles" offers another path to the same destination.)

   The Roles tab opens. (You saw this page back in Figure 9-1.)

2. On the left side of the page is a menu containing several links. Click the Reorder Roles link.

   QuickBase takes you to the Reorder Roles page, shown in Figure 9-4.

3. With roles, the lower the number, the higher the priority (just like you're the top dog when you're #1). Use the drop-down menu next to each role to set its priority.

   You don't have to change the number of each role by hand—if you reassign the #2 role to the #1 role, for example, QuickBase automatically drops the former #1 role down to the #2 slot when you click the Reorder Roles button.

4. When you're finished, click Reorder Roles.

   QuickBase shuffles the roles around and shows you the results.

If you want to make further changes, do so and then click Reorder Roles again when you're done. Otherwise, the roles are now in the priority shown.

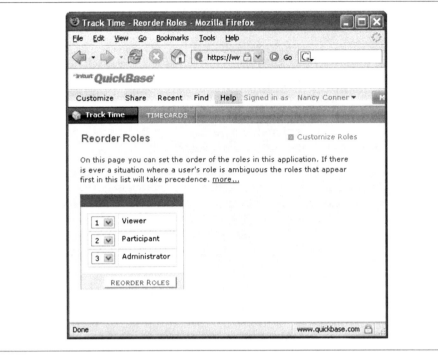

Figure 9-4. To assign roles a different priority, click the drop-down menu next to the role you want to reprioritize and choose its order—the lower the number, the higher the precedence. Another way to remember which role has precedence is to keep in mind that QuickBase always puts the highest precedence at the top of the heap, so whichever role appears at the top of the list is the one with the highest priority.

Using the example that opened this section, here's how you could reorder Kevin's roles: Since Kevin, who's both a Viewer and a Participant, needs to do all the things a Participant can do, you probably want Kevin to see the Participant's Dashboard page when he opens your application. But because Viewer currently has a higher priority, he'll see the Dashboard for Viewers instead. To make sure that Kevin sees the stuff that makes it easier for him to do his job, switch Participant to a higher priority than Viewer. That way, when Kevin's roles come into conflict, he'll land on the side of Participant.

POWER USERS' CLINIC

Trying Different Roles on for Size

It's one thing to create and assign a role. It's another thing entirely to know what it actually feels like to work with a QuickBase application in that role. Maybe its Dashboard doesn't show the reports that would be most helpful to Team Members. Or maybe it wasn't such a good idea to restrict the Participant role's ability to edit multiple records—wasting time and lowering productivity. As an application's administrator, you can wear the hat of any role in your application. So for each role, you can try out

---

the application and understand its look, feel, and workflow from your co-worker's point of view.

In the upper-right corner of any application (next to the bright orange My QuickBase button) are the words "Signed in as," followed by your name and a drop-down arrow. When you click that arrow, you can sign out, edit your User Profile, and see your current role. In most applications you create, your role is Administrator (or its equivalent—in a prebuilt project management application, for example, your default role is Project Manager). But you can change to a different role to see how the other half lives.

Next to your current role is a "change" link. Click it to open a box that displays all the roles in the application. Select the role you want, and then click OK. QuickBase switches you to that role and takes you to its Dashboard. So if you're a Project Manager and you select Viewer, then you can experience your QuickBase application in exactly the way a user assigned the Viewer role sees and works with it. You'll see the same buttons on the menu bar and the same reports in the Reports menu, and you'll have the same permissions as any Viewer.

Just don't forget that you can't tweak the application while you're experiencing it as a Viewer. If you find something you want to change for that role—maybe it would be helpful for Viewers to create shared reports, for example—click the drop-down arrow next to your name, click "change," and switch back to your rightful role as Administrator. From there, you can make whatever changes you want.

Creating Different Dashboard Pages for Different Roles

The whole point of creating and assigning different roles is to make it easier for people to do their jobs. So start them off with a Dashboard that puts the reports and info they need right in front of them. You can create a different Dashboard page for each role in your application, so that every time someone opens your application, the very first page they see (the Dashboard) shows them what they need to know. A sales rep might see a list of leads, for example, or a maintenance person a list of open work orders. Most important, customizing Dashboards to roles means that nobody wastes time digging around to find the information they need to get their job done.

In the previous chapter, you saw how to customize your own Dashboard. Creating custom Dashboards for the roles in your application is a similar process that involves two steps: First you create a Dashboard, and then you associate that Dashboard with a role.

Here's how to create a brand-new custom Dashboard:

1. Open the application for which you're creating new Dashboards. From the menu bar, select Customize→Application, then click the Pages tab.

   QuickBase opens the application's Pages tab, which lists any existing Dashboards in your application. (Many new applications come with just one built-in Dashboard.)

2. Choose a Dashboard, and then (on the right side of its row) click More→Copy this page.

   QuickBase copies the page you selected and adds it to the table, with the name "Copy of ..." So if you copied the Default Overview Dashboard, then your new page is "Copy of Default Overview." A fat black arrow points to your new copy.

3. Click the Edit link to the left of your new copy.

   The Edit Dashboard page opens. (You saw this page way back in Figure 8-2.)

4. Before you do anything else, give your new Dashboard a descriptive name.

   Something like Viewer Dashboard or Team Member Dashboard is a lot more helpful than Copy of Default Overview. Then edit the Dashboard in any way you like (jump back to "Customizing Your Dashboard" on page 271 to read all about editing Dashboards).

5. When you're done, click Preview to see how the new Dashboard looks; click Save to save it.

   QuickBase saves your new Dashboard and returns you to the Pages tab.

Assigning a Dashboard to a role

Now that you've got a custom Dashboard to assign, here's how to associate it with a role:

1. On the Roles page (Customize→Roles), find the role you want and click its name.

   QuickBase shows you the permissions for the role you selected (Figure 9-2).

2. Click the User Interface tab.

   The User Interface tab of the Roles page opens, as shown in Figure 9-5.

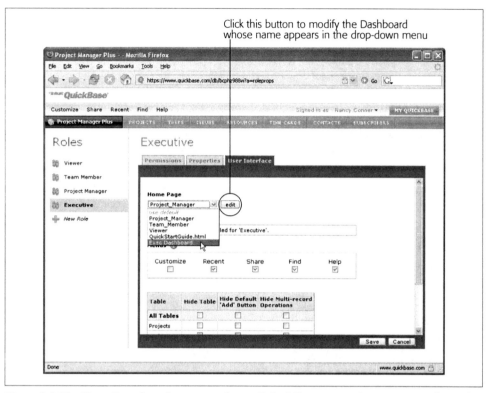

Click this button to modify the Dashboard
whose name appears in the drop-down menu

Figure 9-5. The Home Page drop-down menu shows all the different pages that you can use for a role's Dashboard—just choose the one you want. (As you can see here, you can also choose another page, such as a Quick Start Guide, as the first page users in a given role see when they open the application.) If you need to change a Dashboard (maybe you forgot to give it a descriptive name when you created it), then click the "edit" button. The Edit Dashboard page opens in a new browser window, so you don't have to leave the Roles page and then find your way back to its User Interface tab after you tinker with the Dashboard.

3. Click the Home Page drop-down menu and choose the Dashboard you want to associate with the current role.

   This menu shows the names of all Dashboards for this application. (See why it's important to give a new Dashboard a descriptive name when you create it?)

4. Click Save.

   QuickBase takes you back to the Customize Roles page, with the custom Dashboard's name to the right of the role you associated it with. From there, you can associate another Dashboard with another role if you want, or move on to something else.

Adjusting What Roles Can See and Do

By now, you've got a pretty good idea of the control and flexibility that roles offer you as an administrator. This section delves into the details of the things you can do with roles in your application.

Hiding tables or buttons

You may not want all tables in your application visible to all users. Along the same lines, you might not want people to be too quick with the Add New Record link. You can hide these elements from certain roles by following these steps:

1. Select Customize→Roles to open the Roles page. In the list of roles on that page, click the name of the role you want to work with.

   QuickBase shows you the specifics for that role.

2. Click the User Interface tab.

   The User Interface tab (shown in Figure 9-6) opens. When you're in a multi-table application, this tab shows all the tables in the application.

3. Find the table you want to hide and turn on its Hide Table checkbox.

   If you want to hide the Add New Record link that usually appears in the upper-right part of application pages, turn on the Hide Default "Add" Button checkbox.

4. When you're done, click Save.

   QuickBase saves your changes.

NOTE

Hiding a table or the Add New Record button is *not* the same thing as denying the ability to access records in that table or to add records—it just tells QuickBase not to display that table or that button. When you want to restrict a user's ability to access a table's records or to add records, do it by removing those permissions. ("Applying Field Restrictions" on page 309 tells you everything you need to know about setting permissions.)

Preventing multiple-record edits

If you don't want someone in a particular role to make big changes to your application, you can turn off their ability to import data ("Importing Data into Quick-Base" on page 102), use Grid Edit mode ("Grid Edit Reports" on page 52), or do a search and replace ("Searching for Data and Replacing It" on page 130). Start by navigating to the Roles page's User Interface tab (Customize→Roles→User Interface).

On the User Interface tab (shown in Figure 9-6), turn on the Hide Multi-record Operations checkbox, and then click Save. Now users in that role cannot make massive changes to your application in one fell swoop.

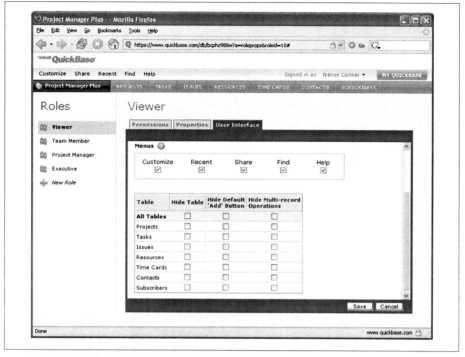

Figure 9-6. The Roles page's User Interface tab lets you customize what users in a given role can see. To hide a menu-bar button, turn off its checkbox in the Menus section. To hide a table or Add Record link, or to restrict a role's ability to edit multiple records, turn off the appropriate checkboxes in the table below the Menus section.

Hiding buttons on the menu bar

There are five buttons QuickBase can display on the menu bar that spans the top of an application's pages: Customize, Share, Recent, Find, and Help. You can hide any of these buttons (and their associated menus) from users in a particular role. Make your way to the User Interface tab of the Roles page (Customize→Roles→User Interface, shown in Figure 9-6) and then click the role you want. In the Menus section, turn off the checkbox of the menu-bar button you want to hide, and then click Save.

To restore a button to the menu bar (maybe users in that role need more help than you thought they did), simply come back to the Roles page's User Interface tab, turn on the appropriate checkbox, and then click Save.

Custom Access to Fields

Say you want to let users see most of the data in a table, but certain fields contain confidential information. You may have good reason to keep some of the fields in a table confidential—perhaps they contain information about salary or bonuses that you don't want everyone in the company to see. Yet you still need to let your team members work with other data in the table. Luckily, QuickBase gives you a way to let users see some fields but not others in the same table.

You can set permissions so that people have full access to some fields and limited or no access to others. You set permissions from the Permissions tab of the Roles page:

1. In the application that has the confidential info, from the menu bar, select Share→"Permissions (by role)", and then select the name of the role whose access you want to limit.

   The Roles page (shown back in Figure 9-2) opens to the Permissions tab.

2. In the Fields drop-down menu, select Custom Access.

   An "edit" link appears next to the menu.

3. Click "edit."

   A list of fields you can edit appears, as shown in Figure 9-7. Each field has a drop-down list to its right.

4. For each field you want to restrict, click its drop-down menu, and then select the level of access you want to assign: No Access, View, or View/Modify. When you're finished, click Save.

   Now, for any field you changed to No Access, users assigned to that role cannot see or work with the data in that field. Your secrets are safe.

Customizing Access. Assigning permissions to roles is an easy, straightforward way fine-tune who has access to your application and its data. Sometimes, though, you may find that an application calls for a little more flexibility than simply creating a role and giving everyone in that role an across-the-board permission to access the application's data. For example, say you've got an application that holds info from several different branch offices. You want each person who works in those branch offices to have access to data from his office—and his office only. It's a little tricky, but you can use table relationships to create a custom access rule that gives employees access to the info related to their branch, but not to data from other branches.

To make sure users have access to the data they need (and only to that data), the application that holds the need-to-know data must have two related tables:

- A master table named Branches that lists the branch offices
- A details table named Employees that lists all employees

This one-to-many relationship makes sense: one branch office has many employees, but each employee is based in only one branch office.

Make sure that each table has the information you need to set up the custom access rule. In the Employees table, each record needs a user field to hold each person's name. The table can also hold any other information you want it to include, such as job title, employee number, email address, and so on.

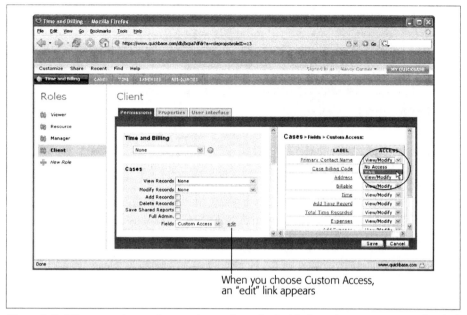

When you choose Custom Access,
an "edit" link appears

Figure 9-7. When you choose Custom Access from the Fields drop-down menu, an "edit" link appears. Clicking the link brings up the list of fields in the right-hand pane. When you click a particular field's drop-down list (circled), you can set access to that field for the role. When you want to limit access to these fields for more than one role, you have to go through the process for each role.

Here's where things start to get tricky. In the Employees table, add a field called something like Current User, and make it a formula-numeric field. Next, write a formula for that field: click Customize→Table, select the Employees table and then click the name of the field you just added (Current User, in this example). QuickBase opens the Properties tab for that field; scroll down to Formula Options and, in the Formula text box, type this formula:

If(User()=[Name], 1, 0)

Then click Save to add the formula to the field. This formula checks to see whether the current user matches a name in the Employees table; when QuickBase finds a match, it returns 1. Otherwise, it returns 0. This field, whether it holds 1 or 0, is key to creating your custom access rule.

Next, turn your attention to the master table (Branches, in this example). Because you're basing access to certain records on whether an employee works at a particular branch, you need a table that keeps track of all the different branches: one branch per record.

If you haven't done so already, create a relationship between the Branches table and the Employees table, with Branches as the master table and Employees as the details table. The two tables should contain the following fields:

- **Master Table:** Branches
  - —A Record ID# field that is the table's key field.
  - —A report link field named People that has *Branches: Record ID#* as its source field and *Employees: Branch ID* as its target field.
  - —A numeric (summary) field named something like *Current User Works Here*.
- **Details Table:** Employees
  - —A numeric (reference) field named Branch ID.
  - —A text (lookup) field named Branch Name that has *Branches: Branch Name* as its value field (which means that this table looks up the branch name in the Branches table and inserts it in this field).
  - —A numeric (lookup) field named something like *Branch ID: Current User Works Here* that has *Branches: Current User Works Here* as its value field.

Now you've set up a relationship that identifies the current user and determines the branch where she works. Your next step is to share that info with other tables in the application. For example, say you have a table called Accounts, which is related to the Branches table; Branches is the master table and Accounts is the details table (one branch has many accounts). Within that relationship, create a lookup field in the Accounts table that uses *Branches: Current User Works Here* as its value field. You can create a whole chain of relationships in this way—and each link in the chain can look up the current user's branch.

When the application's relationships are set up so that each relevant table has a lookup field whose value will be either 1 or 0—indicating whether the current user works for a particular branch—you're ready to write custom rules to determine access. Here's how:

1. In the application that holds the related tables, click Customize→Roles.

   QuickBase opens the Roles page you saw back in Figure 9-2.

2. Select the role that the access rules will apply to, such as Participant.

   Alternatively, you can create a new role, such as Branch Employee, and assign that role to all users.

   The Custom Permission page opens in a new window.

3. On the Permissions tab, select the Employees table: go to the View Records dropdown list and select Custom Rule, and then click the edit link.

   The Custom Permission page opens in a new window.

4. Write your custom rule: *Current user is 1*. Then click Accept Rule.

   QuickBase creates the rule for the Employees table. It means that users will be able to see only their own records in that table.

5. Repeat steps 2 and 3 for all the relevant tables in the application. In the example, you'd write the following custom rules:

In the Branches table: *Current User Works Here is 1.*

In the Accounts table: *Branch ID: Current User Works Here is 1.*

6. When you've written all the access rules you need, click Save.

Now, people who use the application can see only those accounts that belong to their branch office.

Restricting reports

Your application probably has a whole list of reports that let users see and understand the data in different ways. Application templates come with a number of predefined reports already built in. And, if you've been working with an application for a while, then you've probably created some reports of your own.

Of course, not every user has to see every single report. For example, in a Project Management application, you may have created one report specifically for the business analysts who are out there gathering requirements. But this report isn't anything that the developers need to see at this stage in the game—you'd rather they get this information once the specification's written up. You can set up roles so that the business analysts see this report on their Reports menu (or even on their Dashboard—see "Creating Different Dashboard Pages for Different Roles" on page 361), while it doesn't clutter up the developers' Reports menu.

NOTE

Hiding a report from a role doesn't prevent that role from getting at the information within that report. Users can find it in a different report (one they've got access to) or by doing a search. When you want to make certain information totally off limits, restrict the role's access to that info by using the Roles page's Permissions tab (see "Custom Access to Fields" on page 365).

To prevent a report from appearing on the Reports menu of users assigned to a particular role, follow these steps:

1. In the application where you want to hide the report, choose either Customize→Application→Roles or Share→Manage roles.

   The application's Roles tab opens.

2. In the menu on the left, click the Roles/Reports Matrix link.

   The Reports and Roles page opens. This page, shown in Figure 9-8, shows you all the reports that exist in your application, along with who has access to them. (In a multi-table application, it lists all the reports for each table.)

3. For any report you're interested in, turn on (or off) the checkbox under a given role. When you're done, click Save.

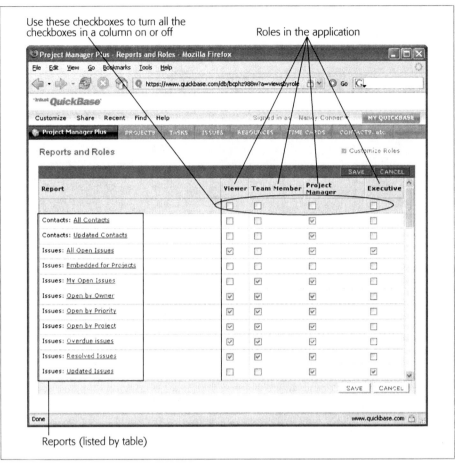

Use these checkboxes to turn all the checkboxes in a column on or off

Roles in the application

Reports (listed by table)

Figure 9-8. The Reports and Roles page gives you an overview of all the reports in an application and which roles can see those reports. Reports are listed in this format: <Table name>: <Report name>. Here, for example, the first three reports are All Contacts and Updated Contacts—both from the Contacts table—and All Open Issues from the Issues table. Roles appear as column headers. To adjust which reports a given role can see, turn the checkboxes in that role's column on or off. The checkboxes below the roles' names will turn all the checkboxes in that column on or off.

QuickBase confirms that it made the change and tells you how many reports it changed.

Restricting a user's ability to save reports

It's great to be able to create reports, with each report showing a different spin on your application's data. But if you've got dozens—or hundreds—of users all creating and saving reports, then the Reports menu will get impossibly long in, oh, about three days. So you can grant the ability to save reports to a privileged few, saving everyone the headache of having to search and search for that report they just *know* they saw two days ago.

Restricting someone's ability to save reports also takes away that user's ability to save changes to an existing report. In other words, if you aspire to be the application's Master of Reports, then this is a way to protect saved reports from would-be meddlers.

NOTE

Even if a user can't save reports, she can still create a personal report. That way, it doesn't clutter up everybody *else's* Reports list.

You can turn on or off the ability to save reports on the Permissions tab of the Roles page. (Click Customize→Roles, and then click the name of the role you want). Just turn off the Save Shared Reports checkbox (or turn it on if you want to restore permission to save reports), and then click Save.

Changing someone's role

A role doesn't have to be forever. When someone's job responsibilities change, you can change their QuickBase role in a matter of seconds. Just go to the application's Users page (Share→Manage users) and find the name of the user whose role you're changing. To the right of that name, in the Role column, is a drop-down list of roles. Select the role you want to assign, and then click Save Changes. Presto change-o—with a couple of clicks of the mouse, you've converted a Viewer to a Team Member (or whatever).

Copying a role

As you work with roles, you may find that you want to create roles that are similar but not *quite* the same—one role might see reports that the other doesn't, for example, or they might have similar permissions but different Dashboard pages. In those cases, thankfully, you don't have to build the new role from scratch. When you want to create a role that's a lot like an existing role, you can copy the existing role and then adjust it to fit.

You copy an existing role on the application's Roles tab. (To get there, select either Customize→Application→Roles, or Share→Manage roles.) On that page, the far-right column has a More button; click it, and then click "Copy this role". QuickBase adds to the list a new role named "Copy of...", which has the exact permissions of the role you copied. So if you copy the Viewer role, for example, then your new role's name is "Copy of Viewer." A fat black arrow points to the copy, so you can't miss it.

To edit the new role, click the aspect you want to edit:

- **Permissions.** QuickBase takes you to the Roles page for that role, with the Permissions tab already selected. Here you can fine-tune the role's permissions, as you did back in "Modify an existing role" on page 353.

- **Edit Home Page.** A new role may need a Dashboard of its very own. Click this link to edit the role's Dashboard.

- **Hide/Show Tables.** When you're on this application's Roles tab, this link offers a shortcut to a role's User Interface tab, where you can decide what tables users in a given role should—or shouldn't—see. (For the full scoop on hiding tables, see "Hiding tables or buttons" on page 364.)

- **More.** Clicking this button offers a plethora of choices. You can delete the copy you just made, copy it again, give it a new name, choose the reports you want to show or hide for this role ("Restricting reports" on page 369), or select an existing page as its Dashboard ("Creating Different Dashboard Pages for Different Roles" on page 361).

TIP

Don't forget to give the role you've copied a better name (nobody likes to be called a copycat). The place to do that is on the Properties tab of the Roles page (Customize→Roles→Properties). Or, if you happen to be on the application's Roles tab, just find the copied role and click More→Rename to land you in the same place. However you get there, you can change the copy's name by typing the new role's name in the Name box. Click Save when you're done.

Deleting a role

As projects move from phase to phase or business structures change, you may find that a role has become obsolete. If you don't want it hanging around anymore, you can delete a role from the application's Roles tab (you get there by choosing either Customize→Application→Roles, or Share→Manage roles). Locate the role you want to delete, and look to the far-right column for the More button. Click More, and then select "Delete this role". A prompt appears and warns you if you've got any users assigned to that role. Click "Yes, delete it," and that's that—the role has had its final curtain call.

NOTE

Deleting a role doesn't remove any users in that role from your application. It just changes their role to None. Those users still show up on your Users page, where you can reassign them to another group or remove them from the application.

Managing Groups

Imagine if you were limited to only one-on-one meetings, never getting a chance to have the whole team together in one place. You'd never get anything done! When you're dealing with a number of people, it's often a lot more efficient (not to mention easier) to interact as a group than to rely on one-to-one contact.

In your QuickBase applications, especially those you share with many people, you can save yourself a lot of time by putting your users into *groups*—a collection of users who have the same access, role, and permissions. Once you create a group you can manage all those users with a single stroke. For example, you might create a group of everyone involved in phase 1 of a project, another group for those involved in phase 2, and so on. After you create a group, you can add the group to applications, assign it a role, or even nest one group inside another. When you create a group, you're that group's manager. But you can transfer management ("Modifying an Application's Properties" on page 254) or create other group managers to share the responsibilities.

NOTE

The same people can belong to different groups, so you don't have to shuttle users between groups.

Creating a Group and Adding Members

If you're tired of managing your application's members individually and want to create a new group, it only takes a minute to do so:

1. On the application's menu bar, select Share→Manage users. When the Users page opens, click the Add Users tab. On the User Picker (which you saw back in Figure 8-8), click the Make a Selection drop-down menu, and then choose Select a Group.

   Available groups, if any, appear in the Groups box at left.

2. At the bottom of the list, click the last item: <Create a New Group>. When the Create a New Group button appears in the middle of User Picker, click it.

   The Create a New Group box appears, as shown in Figure 9-9. Your company's name (that is, the name on your billing account) already appears in a couple of places—the beginning of the group name and the billing account.

3. Give your new group a descriptive name like *northwest_sales_team*.

   You have some limits to how you can name your group; see the box in "What's in a Name?" on page 375 for an overview. Write a description of the group if you want. (If you're going to share group management with others, a description is a good way to make sure everyone understands who belongs in the group and how it's defined.)

4. If you have administrative privileges in more than one billing account, make sure the Account field displays the correct one. And, if you want account managers to be able to manage groups, then turn on the checkbox. When you're finished, click OK.

   QuickBase creates a new group, adds it to the User Picker's left-hand box, and shows you a confirmation prompt.

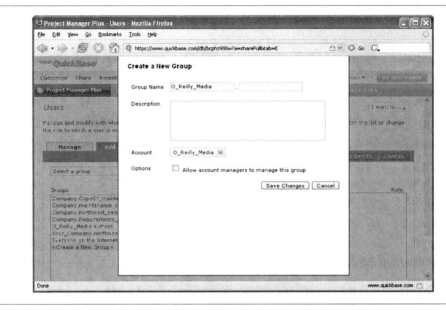

Figure 9-9. You create a new group right from the User Picker. When you choose "Select a group" from the User Picker's drop-down menu and then <Create a New Group> from the Groups box, you get a dialog box where you can name your new group, type up a description (if you like), assign it to a billing account (if you're involved in more than one), and allow billing account administrators to help manage your group. When you click Save Changes, QuickBase creates the group (with you as the only member) and adds it to User Picker's Groups box.

5. Click OK to make the prompt go away.

   You've created a new group. QuickBase has filled in some details about the group in the middle of the User Picker, including its name, the names of people in the group (as creator of the group, you're already in there), and a "manage this group" link.

TIP

When you create a new group, it isn't limited only to the application you created it in. The groups you create are available to any application in which you have administrative privileges, so it's super easy to create a new application and add users en masse. Just select a group you've already created and add its members to the new application.

What's in a Name?

QuickBase has some limitations on what you can name your groups. Here they are in a nutshell:

- Group names consist of two parts separated by a period. (Usually, the first part is the name of your billing account, although you can change this.)
- Each part of the group name has to begin with a letter.
- Each part of the name must be between 2 and 50 characters.
- Group names cannot contain any spaces.
- The only characters a group name can contain besides letters and numbers are hyphens and underscores.

So neither Gotham City.Super Heroes nor Superheroes@.Gotham*City would be a valid group name. The first is invalid because it contains spaces, the second because it contains invalid characters. But any of these would be okay:

- Gotham-City.Superheroes
- Gotham_City.Super_heroes
- GothamCity.A1Superheroes

TIP

If you're a billing account administrator ("Billing Account Administration" on page 25), you also have the option of creating a new group from your Manage Billing Account page. From My QuickBase, click "Manage your billing accounts." On the Manage Billing Account page, you can create a group from either the Summary tab or the Groups tab by clicking the left-hand Create a New Group link. Type in a name and description, click Save Changes, and you've got yourself a new group.

Being a group of one isn't a whole lot of fun. But when you first create a new group, you're the only member. To get the party started, you can add others to a new (or any) group starting from the User Picker. If you've just created a new group, you're already in User Picker with the new group in the Groups box. Otherwise, click Share→Manage users→Add Users. From the "Make a selection" drop-down menu, choose "Select a group," and then choose the name of the group you want to add users to. Then follow these steps:

1. In the User Picker's Groups box, click the "manage this group" link.

   The Manage Group page, shown in Figure 9-10, opens in a new browser window.

2. On the left-hand side is a list of actions you can perform from this page. Click "Add Users to this Group".

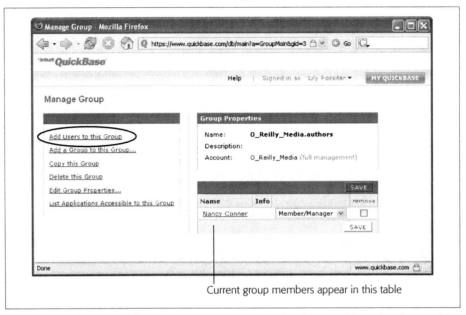

Current group members appear in this table

Figure 9-10. The Manage Group page is your starting point for everything related to working with groups. The Group Properties box gives basic info about this particular group; the table just below it lists current group members. The left-hand menu offers a plethora of options for managing your group. To add members, for example, click the "Add Users to this Group" link (circled).

The "Add Users to Group" page, shown in Figure 9-11, opens.

3. Type in the addresses or screen names of users you want to add to the group. Alternatively, click Import Users to paste in a whole bunch of users from a file (see "A Cast of Thousands" on page 289 for full instructions) or Add Multiple Users to open a new window with User Picker in it (for more about selecting multiple users with User Picker, see "Basic Sharing" on page 280). Click Save when you're finished.

QuickBase adds the users to your group. If QuickBase doesn't recognize an email address you've entered, then it prompts you for the person's first and last names and creates a provisional account. If it doesn't recognize a screen name, however, it tells you to try again (use the person's email address). You land back on the Manage Group page, with the new group members displayed.

FREQUENTLY ASKED QUESTION

Come to My QuickBase Party

Is there some way to give clients who aren't registered QuickBase users access to my application?

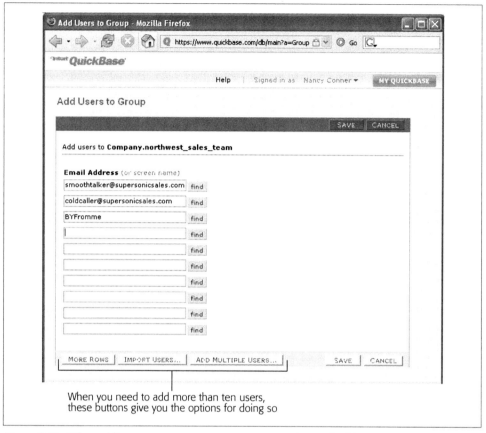

When you need to add more than ten users,
these buttons give you the options for doing so

Figure 9-11. When adding users to your group, you can type in email addresses or screen names one at a time (if you're creating a small group or adding a few users to an existing group). Click the More Rows button if you need more fields. To add lots and lots of members to a group, click either Import Users (to paste a list of users into a text box) or Add Multiple Users (to use the User Picker to add people to the group).

If you think about it, it would often come in handy to make a QuickBase application available to people who aren't part of your organization and who may not be registered with QuickBase. For example, it'd make your life a whole lot easier if customers could view the current product list as it's updated in QuickBase. Or you could use QuickBase to set up an online customer satisfaction survey, inviting your clients to give their two cents about your company's service. Similarly, you might have a questionnaire that you'd like potential clients to fill out. Or maybe you're setting up a conference and want to use QuickBase to organize the attendees list. Wouldn't it be great if people could register online, right in the application?

They can. In fact, you can do all this and more. One of the groups QuickBase recognizes is "Everyone on the Internet." This means just what it says: that anyone with Internet access also has access to your application. Use this group when you want large numbers of non-QuickBase folks to submit or view information in one of your applications—it's an economical way to use QuickBase with lots of users without having to register them individually.

When you create a new application, QuickBase automatically adds "Everyone on the Internet" as a member, with a role of "none." If you assign "Everyone" a role, that means that anyone, anywhere who has Internet access and a Web browser can peek at or work with your QuickBase application, even without a QuickBase account. So use this group with care and a good dash of common sense: When you assign "Everyone" a role in your application, make sure you restrict that role from seeing or manipulating sensitive data.

Designating Group Managers

Now that you've filled your group with people, you may start thinking, "Hmm ... I've got all these people in this group, but no one to help me manage it. How come I'm stuck with all the work?" (Of course, you may also be thinking, "I have absolute dominion over these poor fools! The power is mine—all mine!" If that's you, then skip to the next section.)

If you have no designs on world domination, you can have others help you manage your groups. For example, the team or project leader may know long before you do that Susan has left the company to pursue her dream of going pro as an alligator wrestler. Susan might be on her second tour of the 'gator-wrestling circuit before you think to remove her from the project management group. If her project leader had the ability to manage the group, though, he could take her out of the group as soon as she'd cleaned out her desk.

NOTE

The application's administrator can assign other users group management permissions. Group managers can add members to the group, delete them from the group, create additional managers, nest another group inside this one (see "Nested Groups" on page 379), and delete the group.

To share the group management load, follow these steps:

1. Start on your My QuickBase page. On the page's right side, click "Edit your user profile."

   The User Profile page appears. In the center of the page is a table called Groups I'm In.

2. Find the group you want to assign to a manager and click its name.

   The Manage Group page (Figure 9-10) opens.

3. Find the name of the person you want to help manage the group. To the right of the name is a drop-down menu. Click that to see these three options:

   Member. A member participates in the group and can do whatever the group's role allows. For example, in a group that has Viewer permissions, a member can view the application's data.

   Member/Manager. A member/manager both participates in the group and has the ability to manage it—adding or deleting other members, nesting another group inside this one, and so on.

   Manager Only. The user can manage the group but doesn't participate in its activities. You could choose this option for, say, an administrative assistant who'll manage the people in the group but whose job doesn't involve the group's actual work.

   Make your selection, and then click Save.

   QuickBase gives manager privileges to the person (or people) you selected.

If you're leaving the company to pursue your own 'gator-wrestling career (or just getting ready to retire), then you can give someone else management rights. After you're gone, the new manager can remove you from the group.

Nested Groups

As you create groups, you'll undoubtedly find that some groups have overlapping permissions. In fact, you may notice that one group is really a subset of another group. For example, you may have some applications that are accessible to everyone in your company (dealing with policies and procedures, for example, or a calendar application listing notices and events), other applications intended for a subset of employees (sales staff, for example), and still others intended for a smaller group within that subset (sales managers only). In a case like that, you can *nest* the smaller groups inside the larger ones.

Nested groups work just like Russian Matryoshka dolls—those little wooden dolls where you open up one to find another, smaller doll inside. You can then open that doll to find another, and then another. With nested groups, the larger group contains broad permissions, which any nested groups share, but the smaller, nested group has its own set of more specific permissions that apply to it alone. In other words, nesting lets you treat a whole group as just another user inside a different group.

And, when you need to make a change to a user within a nested group, you can do it once instead of multiple times. For example, say a sales manager retires. Without nesting, you'd have to remove the ex-manager from each group he belonged to, one at a time. With nested groups, you have to remove him only from the sales manager group, and the change automatically happens in any other groups in which the sales manager group is nested. So nesting groups can centralize group management, saving you a lot of work.

Before you start nesting groups, you must create all the groups you want to nest. Once that's done, here's what to do:

1. On your My QuickBase page, choose "Edit your user profile." Then, look for the name of the group you want to be the nest. (In other words, select the group you want to place another group *inside of*.) Click it to open the Manage Group page for that group.

TIP

Alternatively, if you're a billing account administrator, you can get to the Manage Group page from My QuickBase by clicking "Manage your billing account," and then clicking the Groups tab. Finally, click the name of the group you want to manage.

---

2. In the left-hand menu, click "Add a Group to this Group."

   The User Picker opens in a new window, with the groups you can add already in the Groups box.

3. Highlight the group you want to add, and then click the Add button. If you want to add more groups, then continue this process until you've added them all.

   You can nest groups within groups within groups. Say you nested the Company.sales_managers group inside the Company.sales_staff group. Now, if you nest the Company.sales_staff group inside another group (call it Company.the_whole_shebang), then you've got both groups nested inside the whole shebang.

4. When you're finished, click Done.

   QuickBase returns you to the Manage Group page. The group you nested now appears as a member of the group you nested it in.

Making Changes to Groups

As with all things QuickBase, groups offer you a lot of flexibility. You can assign them roles (thereby assigning that role to everyone in the group), copy or delete them, and so on. This section explains how to do the various things you can do with groups.

See who's in a group

You've just added the YourCompany.Sales_Staff group to the Sales Lead application, but Duane complains he can't get access. Isn't Duane in the Sales_Staff group? He should be.

To check the list of group members, start in My QuickBase and click "Edit your user profile." From your User Profile page, click the name of the group you want to check. The Manage Group page opens, with a list of all group members. (And if Duane isn't there, you can add him by clicking the "Add Users to this Group" link and following the steps in "Creating a Group and Adding Members" on page 373.)

See which applications the group can access

When you're managing lots of users, lots of applications, and lots of groups, it's not hard to lose track of which applications any given group belongs to—but it's easy to find out. Go to the Manage Group page (My QuickBase→"Edit your user profile," and then click the name of the group you want). On the left side of the Manage Group page, click the "List Applications Accessible to this Group" link. QuickBase shows you a page that lists all the applications the group is a member of.

Assign a group a role

Once you've created a group, you work with it as you would any individual user. So to assign a group a role, just follow the same steps you'd take to assign a role to any QuickBase user: Add the group to the application and assign a role in the User Picker ("Basic Sharing" on page 280 gives you all the details). Or, if you've already added the group to an application and want to change its role, then open the application and select Share→"Manage users," find the group in the table of that application's users, and then use the drop-down menu in the Role column to assign a new role.

Copy a group

Copying a group saves you time and steps. Instead of creating a new group from scratch, you start with an existing group and tweak it to create a new one that's similar, but not quite the same. Here's how:

1. On your My QuickBase page, click "Edit your user profile."

   The User Profile page opens.

2. In the Groups I'm In table, click the name of the group you want to copy.

The Manage Group page opens.

3. On the left side of the Manage Group page, click the Copy this Group link.

   QuickBase copies the group and takes you to your User Profile Page. The new group appears in the Groups I'm In table with a name that contains *CopyOf_*. So if the group you copied was called MyCompany.Sales-Staff, then the new group's name is MyCompany.CopyOf_Sales-Staff.

4. Click the copy.

   The copy's Manage Group page opens, where you can rename the group (a good first step), add or remove group members, assign manager privileges, and anything else you can do on the Manage Group page.

Delete a group

A project's finished. The team has disbanded, each person moving on to new challenges. But you've still got a group in your QuickBase account—a group that no longer exists in the real world. If you don't delete an obsolete group, it'll just clutter up your QuickBase account (and eventually leave you scratching your head about what that group was for).

Deleting a group is easy. Follow the first two steps above for copying a group. When you get to the Manage Group page, click the Delete this Group link at left. QuickBase tosses up a confirmation box (check to make sure you're deleting the right group). Click OK, and the group is gone.

Change a group's name or description

If you want to change an existing group's name or edit (or add) its description, you do so on the Manage Group page (on your My QuickBase page, click "Edit your user profile," and then select the group's name). Once you're on the Manage Group page, click Edit Group Properties. In the Edit Group Properties box that opens (it looks just like the box shown in Figure 9-9), type your changes, and then click Save Changes. QuickBase applies your changes and takes you back to the Manage Group page.

CHAPTER 10

Creating Relationships Between Tables

In the real world, relationships can be pretty complicated—just ask anyone who has an older sibling. In QuickBase, luckily, relationships actually make your life easier. After all, the tables in your applications have a lot to talk about—they live in the same neighborhood, they hold related information, they might even share a couple of fields. Table relationships get your tables talking—and make your work easier. This chapter explains everything you need to know about creating and using relationships between tables in a QuickBase application—or even between two tables in different applications.

How Table Relationships Work

In the world of QuickBase, a *relationship* is a link between two tables—a record in one table links up with one or more records in another table. For example, suppose you're using QuickBase to keep track of tasks in a project. So you create a Tasks table. For each task you add, you also list information about the person who's assigned the task: name, email, phone number, and so on. At first, this works out great. But later, as you assign multiple tasks to the same people, you get tired of having to add the same employee information to the Tasks table over and over again. Besides, your Tasks table is getting hard to read with all those extra fields thrown in. You'd rather have it focus on tasks, priority levels, due dates—things like that.

Wouldn't it make more sense to have a *separate* table that stores relevant data about your team and feed that info into the Tasks table somehow? What if you could click an Employee's name and bring up all the details you needed about that person? Well, that's exactly what relationships between tables let you do. By creating different tables and linking them, you keep relevant data together and each table focused on a particular kind of record. As a result, your application is better organized and easier to manage.

Relationships also minimize data-entry errors (not to mention repetitive-stress injuries), since you only have to enter each piece of information once. And because that information lives in only one place, mistakes are easier to correct when they do crop up. In fact, you can use relationships to avoid typing in data completely by creating a custom drop-down list of, say, existing employees. Anyone creating a new task chooses from the list to assign it, so no one can assign tasks to someone who's not in the Employees table. (That way, you won't get any smart alecks trying to give Hercules a thirteenth labor by assigning him to write the system spec for Project HYDRA.)

NOTE

In QuickBase, you can create a relationship between any two tables for which you have administrative privileges. Usually, you'll create relationships between two tables in the same application. But you can create cross-application relationships, as well —see "Creating a Relationship Across Applications" on page 389 for details.

The One-to-Many Relationship

The relationship that QuickBase creates between two tables is a *one-to-many relationship*: a record in one table links to one or more records in the other table. The "one" side of the relationship—the table holding single records that link to many records in the other table—is called the *master table*. The "many" side of the relationship—the table that holds many records linking back to a single record in the other table—is called the *details table*.

Here's an example to show how a one-to-many relationship works. Imagine you're using QuickBase to catalog all the novels in your vast library of rare books. You create two tables:

- **Novels.** Information about the books you own, such as title, author, edition, and year of publication.
- **Authors.** Biographical information about each author: date of birth (and death for deceased authors), nationality, and other facts.

You want to link these tables in a one-to-many relationship. First, you must figure out which table should be the master table and which should be the details table. The best way is to ask yourself the following questions:

- Does one novel have many authors?
- Does one author have many novels?

Because most novels are written by a lone author laboring away by candlelight in a garret somewhere, it's far more likely that one author will have written several novels than that one novel will have several authors. So it makes sense to make the Authors table (one author) the master table and the Novels table (many novels) the details table. Figure 10-1 shows how this works.

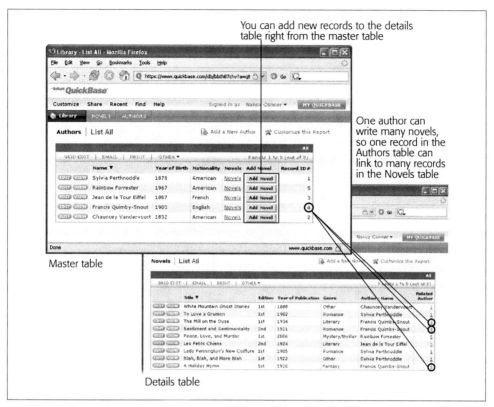

You can add new records to the details table right from the master table

One author can write many novels, so one record in the Authors table can link to many records in the Novels table

Master table

Details table

Figure 10-1. The master table (top) holds records that relate to one or more records in the details table (bottom). QuickBase uses the master table's key field (the Record ID #) to link to the details table's reference field (Related Author). Notice how the author's Record ID # appears in the Related Author column in the Novels table. Thanks to this relationship, you can view related detail records right from the master table (click the Novels link). The Add Novel button opens a form that lets you add another book linked to the same author.

Creating a Relationship

Once you've chosen a master table and a details table, you're ready to start a new relationship (er, in QuickBase, that is). To set up a relationship between two tables, here's what you do:

1. Open the application that contains the tables you want to relate. Choose Customize→Tables, and then click the Relationships tab.

    The Tables page opens to the Relationships tab (Figure 10-2).

2. Click the upper-right New Relationship button.

    The Create Relationship page (Step 1 of 3) opens. This page has two drop-down lists that let you select tables from your application.

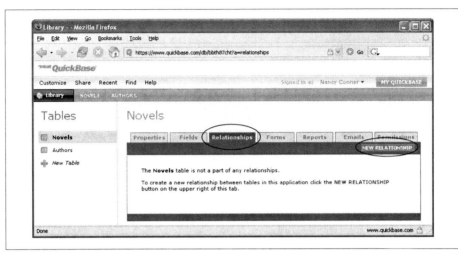

Figure 10-2. On the Tables page's Relationships tab (circled), you can see the relationships that exist (if any) in a multi-table application. In this example, the application doesn't yet have a relationship between its two tables. To create a new relationship, click the upper-right New Relationship button (also circled).

3. Use the drop-down lists to choose the two tables you want in your relationship, and then click Next.

   The Create Relationship page (Step 2 of 3) opens. As Figure 10-3 explains, this page helps you determine which table you want as the master table and which you want as the details table. (In the master table, one record can relate to many records in the details table.)

4. Turn on the radio button next to the diagram that best illustrates the master table–details table relationship you want to create. Click Next.

   The Create Relationship (Step 3 of 3) page opens, as shown in Figure 10-4. Most of the time, you won't need to make any changes here, so you can simply click Save. (You do have other options, though, as the box in "Linking Tables" on page 387 explains.)

5. Click Save.

   QuickBase opens a box that lets you choose fields that it will add to the forms in each table, as Figure 10-5 shows.

6. Turn on the checkboxes for fields you want on the named forms (the Linking Tables box explains your options), and then click OK.

   QuickBase creates the relationship and displays it on the Relationships tab of the Tables page.

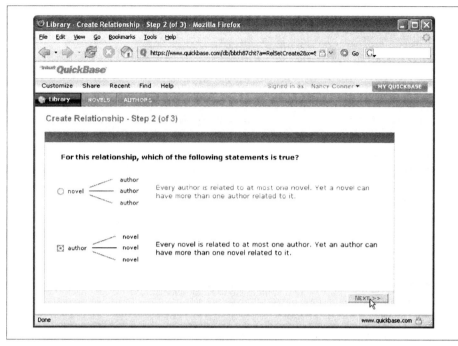

Figure 10-3. QuickBase uses diagrams to help you understand the master table–details table relationship. In a one-to-many relationship, the master table is the table in which one record can relate to many records in the other table (the details table). One author can write many novels, so the Authors table is the master table and the Novels table is the details table.

UP TO SPEED

Linking Tables

In the third step of creating a relationship (shown in Figure 10-4), QuickBase gives you some info and some choices about how it will relate your two tables to each other. Like a good marriage counselor, QuickBase has a knack for making relationships work, so most of the time, you can just go with the way QuickBase sets things up. But if you want to understand relationships better or tweak this particular relationship a bit, it helps to know what QuickBase is doing when it sets up a relationship.

On the left side of the Create Relationship page (Step 3 of 3), the master table list holds the following details, most of which are FYI only:

- **Key field.** As "The Key to Importing Data" on page 102 explains, this field is how QuickBase tells one record from another. The key field's contents must be unique to each record—in other words, the key field is a unique identifier for each record. Usually it's the Record ID field that QuickBase sets up automatically when you create a new table. In a relationship, QuickBase uses the master table's key field to track related records.

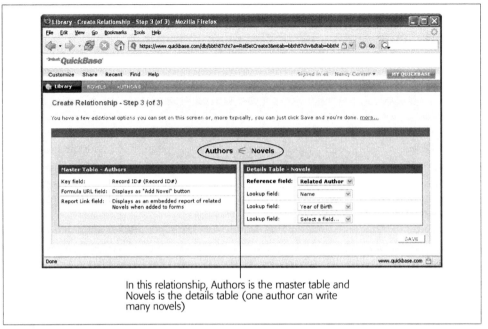

In this relationship, Authors is the master table and Novels is the details table (one author can write many novels)

Figure 10-4. Step 3 of creating a relationship shows a diagram of the relationship you're creating (circled) and gives you details about that relationship. On the left side, you see details about the master table: its key field, how users can add a detail record that relates to a master record, and how that detail record appears in the master table. Similarly, the details table list gives information—and some options—for linking the details table to the master table. The box "Linking Tables" on page 387 explains in detail how the fields in the master table and details table list work.

- **Formula URL field.** When you create a relationship, QuickBase automatically adds this field to your master table. It appears as a button in the master table that users can click to add a new record to the details table. For an example, look back at Figure 10-1; those Add Novel buttons in the master table are in a Formula URL field called Add Novel.

- **Report Link field.** When a user clicks the link in a Report Link field, a report opens displaying all the records from the details table that relate to this record in the master table. In Figure 10-1, for example, when you click any link in the master table's Novels column, you see a report showing all novels by that author.

- **Automatically add the Formula URL and the Report Link fields to the display form.** When you reach Step 3 of creating a relationship, this checkbox is already turned on for you. It's what adds the Add Novel button and the Novel link to the Authors table in Figure 10-1.

On the right side of the Create Relationship page is a list of options for the details table:

- **Reference field.** This field is the glue that holds your relationship together. It links a record in the details table to a particular reference in the master table and speeds

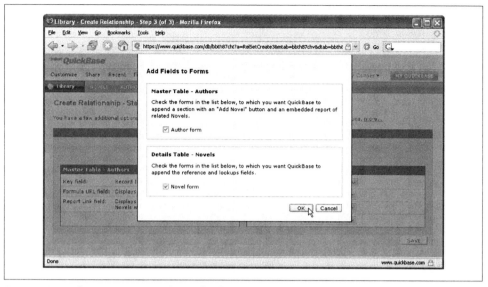

Figure 10-5. When you create a relationship between tables, QuickBase gives you the opportunity to add fields to the forms associated with the tables—making data entry a snap.

up data entry. For example, when you add a new record to the details table, like the title of a new novel you just bought, QuickBase pops up a list of existing author names that it gets from the master table. When you create a new relationship, QuickBase creates a new field to serve as the reference field. Usually, you can leave this field the way QuickBase sets it up. However, the "Reference field" drop-down list displays other fields from the master table that could serve as a reference field in case you want to choose for yourself.

- **Lookup fields.** These powerful little fields let you find display information from the master table in the details table. For example, you might want to include each author's nationality (information from the Authors table) in the Novels table, so you can sort your collection to easily find all novels by, say, American authors. In that case, choose Author—Nationality in one of the "Lookup field" drop-down menus. You can create your lookup fields when you create the relationship, or add them to a details table any time thereafter.

Creating a Relationship Across Applications

You don't have to live in the same house or work in the same office with people to have relationships with them. You can be friends or colleagues with people who live in a different neighborhood, state, or even country. In QuickBase, a *cross-application relationship* is much like a long-distance friendship—two tables living in different applications hook up and share their data.

Say you have a Products table in your Manage Inventory application and an Invoices table in your Sales application, and you want to be able to pull details from the Products table and display them in the Invoices table. Creating a relationship between two tables from different applications is essentially the same as creating a relationship within the same application—the main difference is that you've got to do a little prep work first.

NOTE

Cross-application relationships can happen only if both applications exist in the same billing account. You can't create a relationship, for example, between an application in your company's billing account and an application in a client's billing account.

Before you can link two tables in different applications, you need to open up communication between those applications. Here's how:

1. Open the application that holds the table that will become the master table in the relationship. Then choose Customize→Application.

   QuickBase opens the application's Settings tab. In the left-hand list is a link called Cross-Application Relationships.

2. Click the Cross-Application Relationships link.

   The Cross-Application Relationships section opens. If the application already has a relationship with another application, it shows up here.

3. In the Access Level section, click the Add Application button.

   The Select an Application box, shown in Figure 10-6, appears.

4. Turn on the radio button next to the application that holds the details table you want to link to. Click OK.

   QuickBase adds the application you chose to the Cross-Application Relationships section of the application's Settings tab.

5. Select the role you want users of the related application to have in this application.

   It's worth giving this issue a little thought before you click. When you grant a related application a role, you're granting that role to that application's users. So if you grant the other application too broad a role, you might be allowing its users to see confidential information that they shouldn't see. To tailor the access level, create a new role that specifies exactly what the related application's users can see in your application, and then assign that role to the related application.

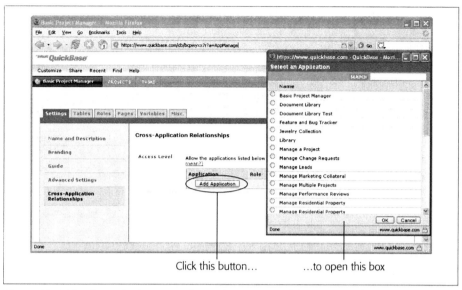

Click this button...   ...to open this box

Figure 10-6. The Cross-Application Relationships section of the Settings tab is where you select another application to link to this one. Click the Add Application button (circled) to bring up the Select an Application box, from which you choose the application that holds the table that will become the details table in the new relationship.

TIP

If you're just experimenting with creating relationships between tables in different applications, select "No access" here. This protects the data in this application from unauthorized peeking. Once you've got the relationship set up, you can change the role.

---

6. When you've assigned a role, click Save Changes.

    QuickBase paves the way for you to create a relationship between tables in these two applications.

To create the relationship, open the application containing the table that will become the details table, and then follow the steps in "Creating a Relationship" on page 385. There's a small difference in step 3, where you select the tables to link. In the left-hand drop-down list, scroll down to the bottom and choose <Select another table>. Quick-Base then asks you to choose the application and table you're linking to. When you've done that, follow the rest of the steps for creating a new relationship.

NOTE

Cross-application relationships must be created in the application that contains the details table.

When you create a cross-application relationship, each application's Tables page treats this relationship differently from same-table relationships. Usually, you'd look for relationships on the Relationships tab of the Tables page. For a cross-application relationship, however, the application that holds the details table shows the master table in red to show that it's an external table—located in a different application. In the master table's application, the relationship doesn't appear on the Tables page's Relationships tab. To see the relationship (and access its properties), you need to go to the application that holds the details table.

After you've created a relationship between two tables, you can manage that relationship in different ways—add a new field, delete an unused one, or delete the whole relationship. The next section tells you how.

TROUBLESHOOTING MOMENT

Looking for Your Lookup Field?

As explained in the box in "Linking Tables" on page 387, when QuickBase creates a relationship between two tables, it creates a reference field and (if you told it to) some lookup fields in the details table. These fields fill in the details table with records from the master table. So in the library cataloging example, the reference field lets you choose an author's name from a drop-down list when you add a new novel to the Novels table. Lookup fields automatically supply information about, say, each author's nationality to the Novels table.

After you've made the effort to create a relationship and select some lookup fields, it can be supremely frustrating when everything about your Novels table looks just the way it did before you linked it to the Authors table. Where are the fields you just added to the details table by creating a relationship?

QuickBase created those fields, but at first you might have to dig a little to find them. Open a report that should show the fields, such as List All, and then click the upper-right "Customize this report" link. In Report Builder's Columns To Display section, select the Custom Columns option. The section expands, showing you the fields the report displays. If there's nothing listed in the Your Columns box, click the "Set to default columns" button to see which columns normally appear there. Then from the Available Columns box, select a lookup field you want the report to show and click "Add to report." When you've got the report looking the way you want it, click Display to see how the report now looks or Save to make your changes permanent.

You can remove unwanted columns from a report in the same way. For example, you might find that the reference field, which usually lists the Record ID number of the related record in the master table, doesn't do much in a report besides clutter it up. Go to Report Builder, find the reference field in Your Columns, and then click Remove to take that column out of the table shown in that report.

Adding a Master Record from the Details Table

It's frustrating to be adding new records to a details table and find that the master table record you want to link to doesn't exist. For example, in the Manage Multiple Projects application, the Tasks table and the Projects table are related; Projects is the master table and Tasks is the details table (one project has many tasks). Imagine that you're adding new tasks to the Tasks table when you come across a task that belongs to the brand-new Simkins project, which is so new that no one's added it to the Projects table yet. When you look for Simkins in the multiple-choice list for the Customer Project field, it's not there.

But that doesn't mean you've wasted your time entering a task that can't link to any existing project. Instead, select <Add a new project>, way down at the bottom of the drop-down menu. This opens a box that lets you add a new record to the Projects table. When you've added the details of the Simkins project, click Save. QuickBase adds the new record to the Projects table and takes you back to where you where in the Tasks table. Now, though, Simkins appears in the Customer Projects field, so you can finish adding the new task.

Adding a Field to a Relationship

As you work with relationships, you'll find lots of opportunities to link your tables. After all, the whole point of a relationship is to make data from one table readily available in the other. This makes it easy for people using your application to work with both tables together—whether you're displaying information from one table as a field in the other, or providing links to make it easy to move back and forth between the tables. When you've got a good relationship going, adding a new field increases the number of ways in which tables share their information.

Here's how to add a new field to an existing relationship:

1. Open the application where the related tables live. (Or, if you're adding a field to a cross-application relationship, open the application that holds the details table.) Select Customize→Tables, and then click the Relationships tab.

   The Relationships tab of the Tables page opens.

   TIP

   For tables belonging to the same application, you can choose either the master table or the details table. For cross-application relationships, you have to go to the details table.

   ---

2. Find the relationship you want and click its Edit link.

   The Relationship Properties page, shown in Figure 10-7, opens. This page shows the master table's details at left and the details table's details at right. There are four kinds of fields you can add to a relationship: Report Link, URL (formula),

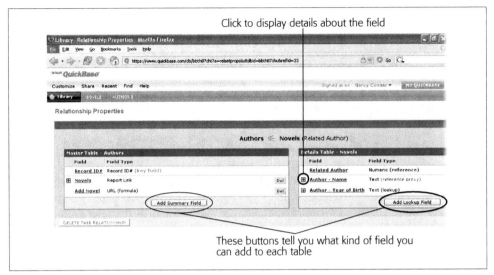

Click to display details about the field

These buttons tell you what kind of field you can add to each table

Figure 10-7. The Relationship Properties page shows you the specifics about how two tables in a relationship link up with each other. The left-hand box tells you about relevant fields in the master table; the right-hand box gives you the same info about the details table. Click the small plus sign (circled) to the left of a field to see detailed information about that field. From this page, you can add more fields to the relationship (see circled buttons), delete a field from the relationship (click its Del button), or delete the relationship itself (click the lower-left Delete This Relationship button).

Lookup, and Summary fields. (To learn about these fields in detail, skip over to "Working with Advanced Fields" on page 399.)

3. Click a button to choose a field type.

A page opens that lets you add a field. This page will vary depending on what kind of field you're adding.

4. Select the field you want to add, then click OK.

QuickBase returns you to the Relationship Properties page, where your new field has been added to the list. Click Done when you're finished tinkering with the fields.

Deleting a Field from a Relationship

If a relationship field doesn't prove very useful, you can delete it from the relationship. For example, in your Library Catalog application, maybe you don't really need to see authors' nationalities in the Novels table. Deleting a field from a relationship doesn't destroy the original field—just the link to it in the related table.

To delete a field from a relationship, open the application that contains the relationship and then surf your way over to the Relationship Properties page. Choose Customize→Tables, and then click the Relationships tab. Click the Edit link of the relationship

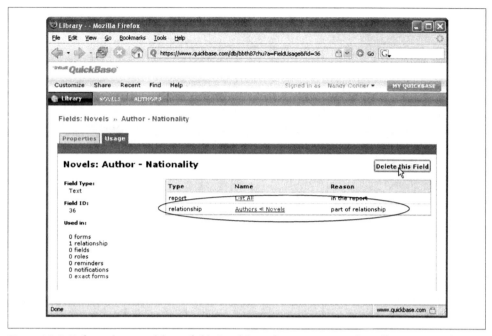

Figure 10-8. Before it lets you delete a field, QuickBase shows you a snapshot of how your application uses that field, listing the reports and relationships (circled) the field participates in.

you want to modify to get to the Relationship Properties page. As you can see in Figure 10-7, most fields have a Delete button (it's labeled Del) to their right. Click Del for the field you want to take out of the relationship. QuickBase opens a Usage page, which shows you how your application uses this field, as shown in Figure 10-8. If you're sure you want to delete the field, click Delete This Field, and then "Yes, delete the field" to confirm. QuickBase deletes the field from the relationship and returns you to the Relationship Properties page.

NOTE

You can't delete a key field or a reference field from a relationship, because these are the fields that define the relationship.

Deleting a relationship

In life—as everybody knows—breaking up can be hard to do. Not so in QuickBase. When the time comes to sever the ties between two tables, follow these easy steps (and remember, you'll always have Paris):

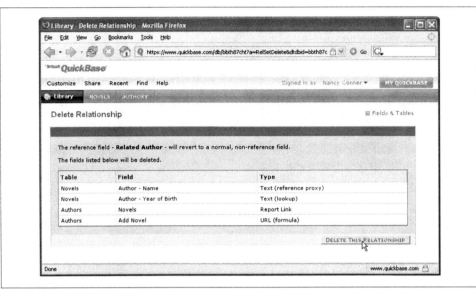

Figure 10-9. The Delete Relationship page shows you how deleting a relationship will affect each of the tables involved. Here, the Authors table will lose the Add Novel field and the Novels field. Similarly, the Novels table will lose its lookup fields (Author - Name and Author - Year of Birth). The Related Author field will switch from being a reference field to a regular numeric field; you can still enter an author's number there, but it won't link to the Authors table.

1. Open the application that contains the related tables. (If you're deleting a cross-application relationship, open the application that holds the details table). From the menu bar, select Customize→Tables, and then click the Relationships tab.

   The Tables page shows you the relationships that exist in the application.

2. Find the relationship you want to delete and click its Edit button.

   The Relationship Properties page (Figure 10-7) opens.

3. At the bottom left of the section displaying the details of the relationship, click Delete This Relationship.

   The Delete Relationship page opens. This page, shown in Figure 10-9, lists the fields that QuickBase deletes when you delete the relationship. (Typically, these are Report Link fields, lookup fields, and Formula URL fields.)

4. If your tables can live without those fields, click Delete This Relationship.

   A confirmation box pops up, giving you one last chance to change your mind.

5. Click OK.

   QuickBase breaks the relationship and deletes the fields it listed back on the Delete Relationship page.

Deleting Related Records

When you create a relationship between two tables, any change you make to a field in the master table also shows up in any relevant fields in the details table. In the Library Catalog application, for example, you may discover that a particular author was Welsh, not English. When you correct that author's nationality in the Authors table, the correction also appears in all related records in the Novels table. This kind of automatic change is the whole point of relating tables.

An exception, however, is when you delete a record from the master table. Deleting a record from this table does *not* delete related records in the details table. QuickBase errs on the side of caution here; you may not want those details table records deleted. It's not hard, though, to think of situations where it would be super-convenient to get rid of all "child" records from the details table when you delete a "parent" record from the master table. For example, imagine that a collector paid you a nice bundle of money to buy all the novels in your collection by a particular author. You want to update your Library Catalog application to reflect this change. It would be great if you could simply delete that author from the Authors table and have all related novels disappear. When you delete the author, though, that's not what happens. The author's novels remain in the Novels table—for those records, the Author Name and Author Nationality fields are simply blank. If you want to delete those novels, you have to hunt them down and delete them by hand.

There's gotta be an easier way—and there is. With a little bit of setup work, you can easily find and delete any details records left hanging around after you delete the relevant master record.

The key is to create a report that gathers together all the details-table records that have lost their relevant master-table record. In the Library Catalog example, you'd create a report that shows only those records that have no value in the Author Name field (in other words, the novels whose Author Name field is blank). To do this, open the application you want and select Customize→"Create a new"→Report. QuickBase asks you which table you want to create the report for; choose the details table (in the example, you'd select Novels).

Report Builder opens. You want to create a Table report (QuickBase has already preselected this option for you). In the Filtering section, turn on the "Show only novels that meet certain criteria" radio button. This expands the section to let you define your filtering criteria. You want to find records for which a particular field, taken from the master table, is blank. For the Library Catalog application, your filtering criterion would look like this:

Author Name is [blank]

Note that the last part of the filter is an empty text box, not the actual word *blank*.

Click Save. QuickBase asks you to name your report; call it something like Records To Delete. Choose the other settings for your report: whether it's personal or shared, which roles have access to the report, whether you want to add a description. (Read all about your options for creating reports in "Creating a Report from Scratch" on page 61.) When you're done, click OK to create your report.

Now, when someone deletes a record from the Authors table, the Records To Delete report shows you all records from the Novels table that are missing an author name. In other words, the report shows you all the "child" records from the details table that have no corresponding "parent" record in the master table.

When you open the Records To Delete report, you can delete all its records—that is, all novels with no data in the Author Name field—with just a few clicks:

1. Open the Records To Delete report. In the gray bar at the top of the table, click Other.

   A context menu appears.

2. From the context menu, choose "Other Operations on Records in this Report". (The menu option shows the name of whatever you call the records in this table; in the example, it would say *Novels* instead of *Records*.)

   QuickBase opens the "Other Operations on Records in this Report" window.

3. Click Delete to delete all the records listed in the report.

   Just to make sure, QuickBase tells you how many records you're about to delete and asks you to confirm that you really want to delete them.

4. Click Delete RECORDS? (Again, the word *RECORDS* is replaced by whatever kind of records you're deleting.)

   QuickBase deletes the records from the application.

5. Click Close Window.

   Now, your Records To Delete report is empty, until you delete another parent record.

Creating this type of report—one that finds details-table records whose parent master-table records have been deleted—offers you a couple of benefits:

- In a large application, it makes it a snap to find the records you need to delete. This is way easier than scrolling through a huge table, trying to spot them one by one.
- It also gives you a chance to scan all the Records To Delete records before you get rid of them *en masse*. This way, you can make sure that you don't delete a novel

whose Author Name record was inadvertently left blank, for example, and you have a chance to correct the problem in that record.

TIP

To make sure you know when there are details-table records that need deleting, create an automatic notification to email you whenever the Records To Delete report has new records added. Chapter 4 gives step-by-step instructions for subscribing to change notification emails.

Working with Advanced Fields

You know what it's like when two people embark on a brand-new relationship—they forget all their old, single friends and start hanging out with other couples. QuickBase tables aren't quite that fickle, but when two tables hook up in a relationship, they suddenly become open to a whole new set of fields. That's because these specialized fields only work with tables that are in relationships, where they play very helpful supporting roles. QuickBase has advanced fields that let you look up data from one table and display it in another, create a hyperlink between tables, summarize data from one table in another, and more.

Lookup Fields

Lookup fields come into play when you've created a relationship between two tables. A lookup field takes information from the master table and displays that info in the details table. In other words, the details table *looks up* the contents of a field in the master table and displays it. The cool thing about a lookup field is that when someone updates a record in the master table, that record gets updated in the details table, too —with no extra effort. For an example of lookup fields, see Figure 10-10.

To create a lookup field, you first have to create a relationship between two tables, as described at the beginning of this chapter. Without a relationship, the lookup field has nowhere to go to look up its information. When you've got two related tables and you want to create a lookup field in the details table, you do so from the Relationship Properties page:

1. Follow the steps for adding a new field to a relationship as described in "Adding a Field to a Relationship" on page 393. When you get to the Relationship Properties page, go to the Details Table section and click Add Lookup Field.

   The Create Lookup Fields page opens (Figure 10-11).

2. In the drop-down list, find the master table field that you want to display as a lookup field in the details table. Repeat if you want to create more than one lookup field.

3. When you're done selecting fields, click OK.

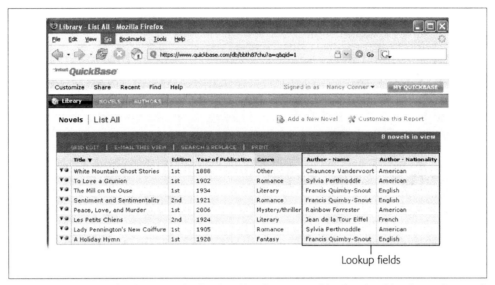

Lookup fields

Figure 10-10. Lookup fields exist in the details table of a master table–details table relationship. Each lookup field takes information from a field in the master table (here, Authors) and displays it in the details table (here, Novels). Notice that the lookup fields have the name of the master table in their column headings.

QuickBase creates your new lookup field.

NOTE

If you create a lookup field and don't see it when you display a report, you need to adjust the Custom Columns for that report. The box in "Looking for Your Lookup Field?" on page 392 tells you how.

Deleting a lookup field is the same as deleting any other field from a relationship. So if your details table starts looking a bit crowded and you want to delete a lookup field, follow the instructions in "Deleting a Field from a Relationship" on page 394. (When you delete a lookup field from a details table, you delete all the data that field holds—but only from the details table. The field still exists unharmed in the master table.)

TIP

You can use lookup fields and summary fields to create dynamic form rules. Rules change a form's appearance based on the contents of a particular field. For example, say you have a Performance Evaluation form that managers use to assess their employees' performance. You'd probably want sections specific to different departments, such as Sales, Marketing, Product Development, and so on. With dynamic form rules, QuickBase can look up a manager's department and automatically display only the sections relevant for that department.

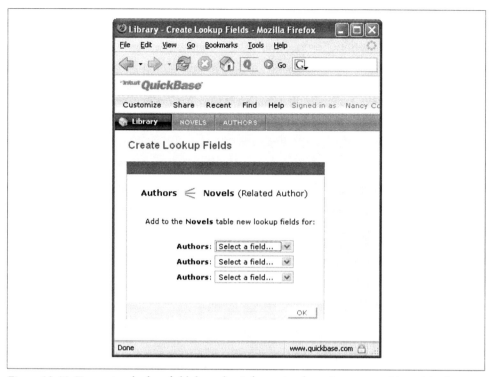

Figure 10-11. To create a lookup field that takes information from the master table and displays it in the details table, choose the master table field that you want to look up.

Snapshot Fields

A *snapshot field* is like a lookup field—but frozen in time. A lookup field looks up current data in a particular field from the master table and presents that current data in the details table. A snapshot field snaps a picture of some master table data at a particular moment in time, so when someone modifies the field in the master table, the details table's snapshot field keeps the original, unmodified value. You can do some cool things with snapshot fields: keep track of who was originally assigned a task, for example, if assignments tend to change frequently, or make sure that a customer who ordered a product at $129.99 pays that amount when the price jumps to $159.99 (or drops to $119.99).

To create a snapshot field, you need to follow these guidelines:

- You can only create a snapshot field in the details table of two related tables.
- You can create a snapshot field for any field type *except* the following: File Attachment, Formula, Numeric—Rating, Text—Multiple Choice, and Report Link.
- The field for which you create a snapshot must also be a lookup field.

- You cannot create snapshots of fields designated as required or unique ("Editing a field's properties" on page 299).

Keeping those rules in mind, here's how to set up a snapshot field:

1. Open the application that contains the details table with the lookup field for which you want to create a snapshot field. Open the Tables page (Customize→Tables) and make sure the Fields tab is selected. If necessary, select the details table from the left-hand list of tables. When all that's set, click the upper-right Create New Fields button.

   The Add Fields page opens.

2. Name your snapshot field and list its field type, which should be the same type as the associated lookup field.

   For example, if you want to create a snapshot field that captures the price of a product when a customer placed an order, you can call the field something like *Order Price* and designate its type as Numeric—Currency. This new field will hold the snapshot of a lookup field (say it's called *Price*).

3. When you're finished, click Add Fields.

   QuickBase creates the field and returns you to the Fields tab of the Tables page.

NOTE

QuickBase also shows you a confirmation box asking whether you'd like to add the new field to any custom forms. For now, click "Not right now."

---

4. On the Fields tab of the Tables page, click the name of the new field you just created.

   The Field Properties page opens.

5. Scroll down to Advanced Options near the bottom of the page and find the Snapshots drop-down list. From it, choose the name of the lookup field you want to freeze as a snapshot.

   The section expands, offering an "Initialize field for existing records" checkbox. Turn on this checkbox, and QuickBase updates all existing records with a snapshot of the master table record's current value. If you leave the checkbox turned off, the new snapshot field is blank for existing records.

6. Click Save.

   QuickBase takes you back to the Fields tab of the Tables page. There, Info column now identifies the field you just created (and edited) as a snapshot field.

Shared Multiple-Choice Fields

If you manage a number of tables and applications, then you've probably run across occasions when you wished you could take a multiple-choice field from *this* table and transfer it wholesale into *that* one. For example, suppose your organization uses five different priority levels for its projects' tasks and issues: *Who Cares?, Low, Medium, High,* and *Red Alert!*. Instead of creating a new multiple-choice field with these choices each time you create a new application, it'd sure save time to share that list among all applications that have a Priority field. And if a new boss arrives and tells you to change *Who Cares?* to *Very Low* and *Red Alert!* to *Urgent* (some people are no fun), you can make the changes once instead of hunting down all Priority fields in all your tables and applications. *Shared multiple-choice fields* let you do just that—create one multiple-choice field with a specific list of options and share it among different tables, even among different applications.

NOTE

Use shared-multiple choice fields only when several tables need access to the same list of choices. Shared-multiple choice fields are *not* for creating a drop-down list of records from another table—for that kind of list, create a relationship between the two tables and use the kind of record you want in the drop-down list as the reference field. Limit shared-multiple choice fields to times when you need the same list of stand-alone (not linked) choices in several different applications, such as a list of sales territories, business units, priority levels, status designations, and so on.

The first step in creating a shared multiple-choice field is to set up the list of choices to be shared (QuickBase calls this the *source multiple-choice list*):

1. Open the application that will hold the source list. Select a table to hold your list.

   Or you can create a whole new table ("Add a new table" on page 318) just to hold it.

2. In the table, find or create the field you want to hold your source list.

   This field must be either a numeric field or a text field (but *not* multiple choice). So if you want to create a source list for priority levels, for example, find or create a text field called Priority and add a record for each priority level you want: If you wanted three priority levels—say, Low, Medium, High—you'd add three records. If you wanted five priority levels, you'd add five records, and so on.

3. When you've finished adding records, click Save.

   To make sure you've added all the options you want, check your work by selecting Reports→List All to see the records you've just added to the table.

After you've created your source list, you can share it with other applications:

1. Open the application that holds the source list and then choose Customize→Tables.

   The Tables page opens. Make sure the Fields tab is selected.

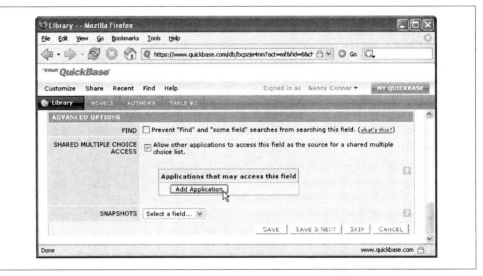

Figure 10-12. When you turn on the Shared Multiple Choice Access checkbox, the Field Properties page expands to let you select the applications you want to share the multiple-choice list with.

2. If you're in a multi-table application, select the table that holds the source list. Click the name of the field you want to make a shared multiple-choice field (in the example, you'd click Priority).

   QuickBase opens the Properties page for that field. Near the bottom of the page, in the Advanced Options section, is the a checkbox labeled "Allow other applications to access this field as the source for a shared multiple choice list."

3. Turn on the checkbox to allow shared access to the shared multiple-choice list.

   The section expands, as shown in Figure 10-12.

4. In the "Applications that may access this field" box, click Add Application.

   The Select an Application window opens, containing a list of all your QuickBase applications.

5. Turn on the radio button of an application you want to share your source list. Click OK.

   QuickBase adds the application to the "Applications that may access this field" list.

6. If you want to share the list with other applications, repeat steps 4 and 5 until you've selected all the applications you want. When you're finished, click Save.

   QuickBase saves your selections and returns you to the Fields tab of the Tables page.

You're halfway there. You've created a source list and selected some applications to share it with. Now you need to tell the applications with which you're sharing to go ahead and use the shared multiple-choice field. How you do that depends on whether or not the table you're sharing the field with already has the same field.

Sharing an existing multiple-choice field

Sticking with the Priority field example, say the table you're sharing with already has a Priority field, but it has a different set of options from your source list. To make an existing field display the same multiple-choice options as your source list, follow these steps:

1. Open an application with which you want to share the multiple-choice field and then choose Customize→Tables.

   The Tables page opens. If necessary, select the Fields tab.

2. In a multi-table application, click the name of the table you want. Find the name of the field (Priority, for example) and click it.

   The Properties page for that field opens.

3. Scroll down to the Text Options section and turn on the "Multiple-choice, shared" radio button.

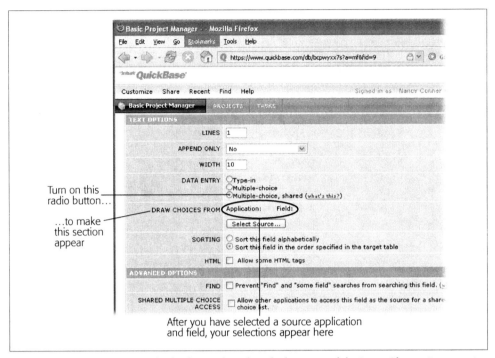

Figure 10-13. Turn on the "Multiple-choice, shared" radio button, and the Draw Choices From section appears. Click Select Source to choose the application that contains the multiple-choice list you want to use in this one. When you've selected an application and a field, QuickBase fills in those choices under Application and Field (circled). The field displays as a link; click it to see that field's properties.

The Draw Choices From section, shown in Figure 10-13, appears.

4. Click Select Source. When the Select an Application window opens, turn on the radio button of the application that holds your source list, and then click OK.

   The Select a Field window opens.

5. Find the name of the shared multiple-choice field you've created. (In a multi-table application, you have to pick the name of the table and the field.) Click OK.

   QuickBase lists your choice in the Draw Choices From section. What it shows under Field is a hyperlink. Click this link if you want to open that field's Field Properties page to make sure you've chosen the right field.

6. Click Save.

   QuickBase shares your source list of multiple-choice options with this application. Now, when you click Priority (or whatever field you chose to share), QuickBase offers the options you created in your source list.

Creating a new shared multiple-choice field

If you want to add a whole new field to a table, making the new field shared multiple choice, here's how to do it:

1. Open the application you want. If you're in a multi-table application, Click the table's name in the Table bar, and then choose Add a New Record. If you're in a single-table application, click the Add a New Record link. (Either way, the command says Add a New Task, Add a New Work Order, Add a New Lead, or whatever kind of record the table holds.)

   The Add Record form appears. (Again, the form displays the name of whatever kind of record you're adding.)

2. Decide where on the form you'd like the new field to appear. Right-click the field before it and choose "Add a field after this one" from the shortcut menu.

   The Add a Field to a Form page opens.

3. In the "Select a field" drop-down menu, scroll to the bottom and select <Create a New Field>.

   The Create a New Field box appears.

4. In the Create a New Field box, type a name for your field. Select Text—Multiple Choice as the Field Type, and then click Done.

   You can call the field whatever you want—it doesn't have to have the same name as the shared multiple-choice field. QuickBase returns you to the Add Record form, with your new field added.

5. Find the new field and right-click it. Then select "Edit the field properties for this field."

   The Field Properties page opens.

6. Go to step 3 of the previous section and continue from there.

   You've got a brand new field that displays the choices you created in your source list.

TIP

If you don't want to use the Add Record form to position your new field, you can take this shortcut: In the application you want, choose Customize→Tables, make sure the Fields tab is selected, and then click Create New Fields. From there, jump to step 4 of the above instructions.

One big advantage of creating a shared multiple-choice field: If you have to change its options, you can edit it once, automatically updating all the applications that share that field. To do so, display a report containing the table that holds your source list. Find the record that contains the choice you want to edit, click its Edit button, make your changes, and then click Save. As easy as that, you've updated the field across every application that has it.

Summary Fields

When you look at a table as a Summary report or display its data in a Chart report, QuickBase adds up your data to display a total—the total value of orders, the total number of tasks or work orders assigned, the total cost of purchase requisitions, and so on. Often, seeing this big picture is all the information you want. But sometimes you want to focus in on your data in different ways. For example, perhaps you want to total overdue tasks by team member or total sales by salesperson.

In QuickBase, you generate totals using a *summary field*. This specialized field takes information from the details table and displays it in the master table, usually calculated as a total. For example, a summary field could total the number of billable hours for each member of your maintenance staff.

Creating a summary field is easy:

1. In the application that holds the related tables, select Customize→Tables, and then click the Relationships tab. Find the relationship that has the data you want to summarize and click its Edit link.

   The Relationship Properties page opens.

2. At the bottom of the Master Table list (at left), click Add Summary Field.

   The Add a Summary Field page opens.

3. Use the radio buttons to tell QuickBase which field you want to summarize, and then click OK.

   As shown in Figure 10-14, QuickBase assumes that you want to create a summary field that shows the total number of details records related to each master record. In this example, QuickBase assumes you want to count the number of work orders (details table) linked to each property/unit (master table).

   If QuickBase guesses wrong, you can choose a field yourself. When you turn on the "A summary of a specific field" radio button, QuickBase shows you a drop-down menu that lets you choose what you want it to do with the values in the field you select: Total (add 'em up), Average (find the average value of a numeric field), Maximum (find the largest value or latest date, depending on the type of field), Minimum (find the smallest value or earliest date, depending on the type of field) and Standard Deviation (measure the distribution around a mean).

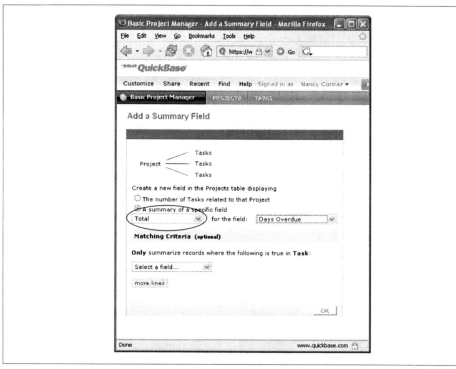

Figure 10-14. A summary field, which appears in a relationship's master table (here, Projects), adds up values from the details table (Tasks). When you specify the field you want QuickBase to summarize (here, Days Overdue), you have a choice of how QuickBase goes to work on that field: It can add up the records in that field (when you select the Total option [circled]), average them, find the highest or lowest value (or the latest or earliest date, if you're working with a date field), or calculate the standard deviation.

TIP

You can also set matching criteria to filter the data, directing QuickBase to summarize only certain records from the details table. For example, you might want to summarize only those work orders scheduled for the coming week. When you choose a criterion from the Matching Criteria section's drop-down list, other drop-down menus appear that let you set parameters. You can set several matching criteria; click the "more lines" button to choose other fields for QuickBase to match.

---

4. Click OK.

   A confirmation box appears, suggesting a name for your new summary field.

5. Rename the field if you want (you can usually go with QuickBase's suggestion), and then click OK.

   QuickBase creates your new summary field and returns you to the Relationship Properties page.

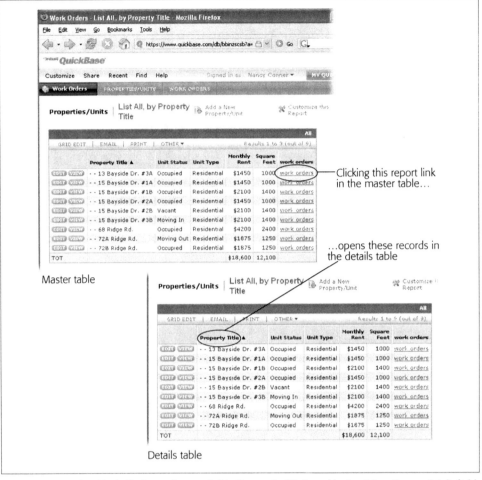

Master table

Details table

Figure 10-15. The Work Orders column of this Properties/Units table (top) is a Report Link field. When you click a link in that column, QuickBase shows you related records from the Work Orders table (bottom). So, for example, clicking the link for 13 Bayside Dr. #3A shows all work orders for that unit.

Report Link Fields

A *Report Link field* creates a hyperlink between records in one table and records in another, related table. It gives users an easy way to jump between two tables. No need to search for the other table, display it, locate the exact set of records you want, and then find your way back to the first table when you're done. Just click the Report Link to see the set of related records, and then hit your browser's Back button to return to the master table. Figure 10-15 gives you an idea of how a Report Link field works.

Create a Report Link field when creating a relationship

When you're creating a relationship between two tables, QuickBase automatically creates the Report Link fields that it thinks you might need and shows them to you on the Create Relationship—Step 3 of 3 page. (Glance back at Figure 10-4 for a peek at this page.) On this page, QuickBase lists any Report Link fields it's created in the new relationship and explains what a Report Link field does: "Displays as an embedded report of related records when added to forms." In plain English, that's telling you what you just saw in Figure 10-15: a Report Link field shows a link that you can click to zoom over to related records in the details table.

Create a Report Link field between existing tables

To create a Report Link between two tables in an existing relationship, follow these steps:

1. Add a new field ("Add a field" on page 219) to the table in which you want the Report Link to appear, selecting Report Link as the field type. Then, from that table's Fields tab (Customize→Tables, select Fields if necessary, and then click the table's name), click the name of the new field. (It has a fat black arrow pointing to it to help you find it.)

   The Field Properties page, shown in Figure 10-16, opens. Because you've set the field type as Report Link, the Field Properties page contains a Report Link Options section.

2. From the Source Field drop-down menu, select your table's *source field*—the field that QuickBase uses to match records with the other table.

   The source field is a field in the table you're working in now—that is, the table that will hold the new Report Link.

   Next, you'll select the *target field*, the field in the other table that holds the records QuickBase displays when a user clicks the Report Link.

3. Click the Select Target button. When the Select an Application page opens (in a new window), click the radio button of the application you want, and then click OK.

   The Select a Field window opens, listing all the fields in the application you chose.

4. Choose a field, and then click OK.

   QuickBase inserts the application and field you chose in the Field Properties page's Target Field section.

5. Set your options.

   Here are your choices:

   Open Target in New Window. It can be helpful to open the target in a new window, keeping the source table open in its window. This lets you refer to the report easily from the form. Report Links typically provide a reference, but when

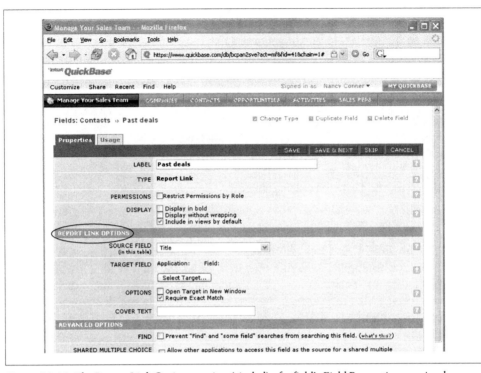

Figure 10-16. The Report Link Options section (circled) of a field's Field Properties page is where you select the source and target fields that will make up the link. You can choose to have the target of the Report Link open in a new window, or you can force QuickBase to display a link only if the source and target fields are an exact match. Type in some cover text if you want the hyperlink to say something specific, like Click here!

you click a Report Link, you don't necessarily want to navigate away from the form that you're currently using (and its data).

Require Exact Match. QuickBase usually requires source and target fields to match perfectly. You can loosen it up a bit by turning off this checkbox. With Require Exact Match turned off, Smith Enterprises and John T. Smith will match, because they're close but not exact.

Cover Text. If you want the hyperlink to say something different from what QuickBase puts in the box, type it here.

6. When you're all finished, click Save.

QuickBase creates your Report Link field.

Copying a Record and Its Related Details Records

After you've set up relationships between tables, there will likely by times when you want to copy some master records and all the details records associated with them. Say you have a project management application. Project management is complex: Each project is associated with many tasks, and each task has associated issues, resources, documents, and so on. So if you need to copy a task, you probably want to keep all of its associated details with it. The fancy name for this is *recursive copying*, which simply means that when you copy a parent record, you copy all its child records, too. Think of it as keeping the family together.

QuickBase has created a wizard that makes it super easy for you to do one-click recursive copying of master records. The wizard puts a "copy" link right in the table so that, when you work with a master table, you can easily copy any of its records *and* that record's children.

Before you begin, you need to have a couple of things in place so the wizard will work:

- The master table has to use Record ID# as its key field. (To see which field is your table' key field, select Customize→Tables and then choose the table you want from the left-hand menu. On the Fields tab, find the name of the field that has a little picture of a key next to it—that's the table's key field.) If the table uses a different key field, you can change it by following the instructions on "The Key to Importing Data" on page 102.

- If your application uses tokens for extra security, add this token to the application before you run the wizard: bqipbngdfsd6drc64a958wz4aua. (If your application doesn't require tokens, you don't have to worry about adding this token.) How do you know whether an application requires tokens? In the application, choose Customize→Application. On the Settings tab, select Advanced Settings and look in the Application Tokens section. If the Require Application Tokens checkbox is turned off, the application doesn't use tokens.

When you're ready to set up a master table to copy records, sign into QuickBase and point your Web browser to *http://tinyurl.com/parentchild*.

NOTE

If you try to start the wizard when you're not signed into QuickBase, you get an error message. When you click OK to close the error message, QuickBase opens its sign-in page. But when you sign in there, you go straight to your My QuickBase page, not to the wizard. So sign in first, and then start the wizard.

When QuickBase opens the Recursive Copy wizard, the first thing you see is a simple drop-down list. From the list, choose the application and table that holds the master records you want to be able to copy recursively. The items on the list are formatted like this: *Application name: Table name*. So if you're looking for the Issues table in the Manage Project application, you'd choose Manage Project: Issues.

When you've chosen the application and table you want, the Recursive Copy wizard expands to look like the page shown in Figure 10-17. This wizard creates a "copy" link and puts it in the table you chose, so use the following settings to specify how you want the link to work:

- **Where do you want the children records to come from?**
  - —**The record that the button is on.** This option puts a "copy" link on each record in the master table; when you click the link, QuickBase copies that record and its associated details records. In most cases, you'll probably choose this option.
  - —**Let me choose a record after I push the copy button.** If you choose this option, when someone clicks the "copy" link, QuickBase shows a drop-down list of master records in the table so that the user can select a record to copy.
  - —**Always the same currently existing record.** Choose this option if you've created a template that you want to copy. For example, say you have a Tasks template set up that shows the structure of a task and its related records without holding any actual data. If you've created any such templates and you turn on this radio button, a drop-down list appears when someone clicks the "copy" link so you can choose the template you want to copy. If you haven't created any templates for this table, ignore this radio button.
- **Where do you want the children records to end up?**
  - —**The record that the button is on.** This option copies the details records to the same master record from which they were copied.
  - —**Let me choose a record after I push the copy button.** If you choose this option, QuickBase shows a drop-down list of existing master records during the copying process. When you select a master record, QuickBase attaches copies of the details records to it.
  - —**A copy of the record that the button is on.** This is the most common option; it creates a copy of the master record and attaches all of the associated details records to it. If you chose "The record that the button is on" in answer to the first question, turn on this radio button to answer the second question. (With this setting selected, a drop-down list will appear when someone clicks the "copy" link in the table.) Choose the field you want to use to name the copied record. In the Issues table example, for instance, you'd pick Issue Name.
- **What do you want the browser window (where you clicked the copy button) to display after the copy process?**
  - —**Continue to display the page with the button.** Turn on this radio button if you *don't* want to see any changes onscreen after you copy a master record and its details records. With this setting selected, to see the copied records, you have

to refresh your Web browser, leave the page you're looking at and then come back to it, or switch to a report that includes the copied records (such as List All).

— **Refresh the page with the button on it.** Turn on this radio button to have QuickBase refresh the current page in your Web browser after you make a copy. Depending on the report you're looking at, you'll see the new, copied record.

— **The record that received the new children records.** Turn on this option if, after copying, you want to see a single record: either the newly created master record or the master you chose to receive copies of the child records (which you see depends on your earlier selections in the wizard).

• **Do you want to just copy the direct descendants of the parent record or do you want to copy all the children?**

— **Just the direct descendants.** To copy just two levels of records—the master record and the details records directly associated with it—turn on this radio button.

— **All the descendants (children of children... etc.).** Tables can have multiple relationships, so the details table in one relationship could be the master table in a different relationship. If you want your recursive copy to go deeper, turn on this radio button. When you do, QuickBase copies not just the details records of the master record you chose (that is, its children), but also any details records those children have—and so on, until there are no more details records to copy.

When you've made your choices in the Recursive Copy wizard, click "Create copy button". QuickBase adds a "copy" link to your master table and shows you a dialog box congratulating you on your hard work. Click OK and you're done.

TIP

Although QuickBase tells you it's created a copy *button* in your table, it's actually added a copy *link*. If you'd rather see a button than a link, select Customize→Tables and select the table you want. On the Fields tab, find the Copy field you created and click its name to open its Properties page. Find the Options section and turn on the checkbox labeled "Display as a button (vs. a link)" and then click Save. Now you see "copy" buttons instead of links in your table.

Now, you (or anyone who uses your application) can click a record's "copy" link in the master table and recursively copy that record and all its children.

TIP

If you don't want to let just anyone to copy the parent record and its children, customize access to that field so that only people in roles you approve can see the "copy" link or button.

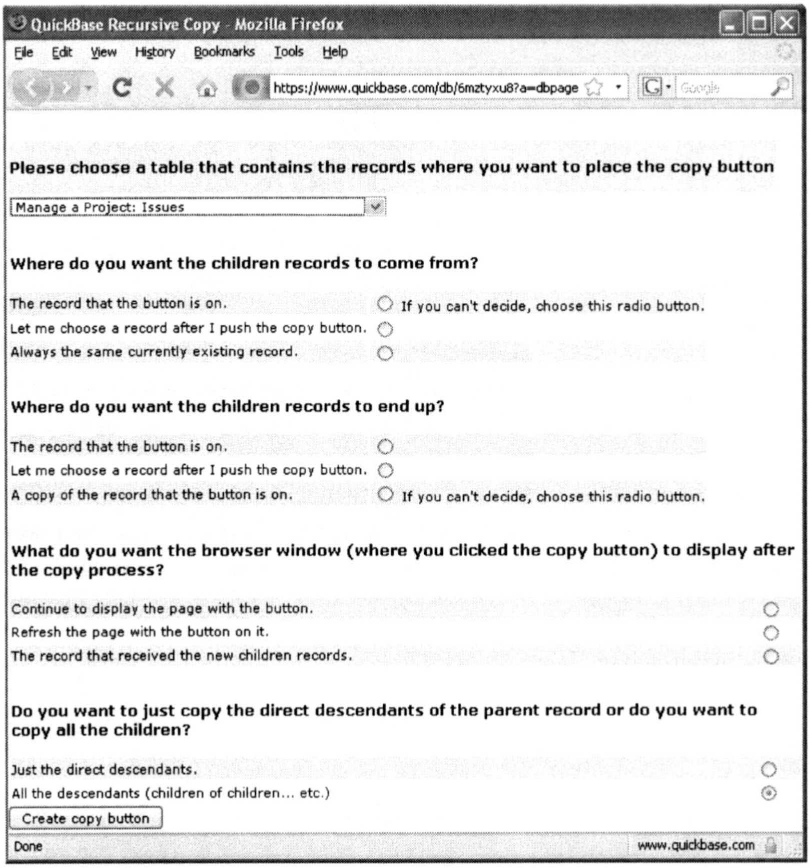

Figure 10-17. The Recursive Copy wizard asks you to choose which details records to copy, a destination for the copied records, what to show after copying, and whether to copy just the immediate child records or all their child records, too.

CHAPTER 11

Automating QuickBase with Formulas, Forms, and Dynamic Rules

You've learned the basics of creating and managing QuickBase applications. But with this chapter, you'll take your applications to the next level. And once you see how much complex applications can do—automate fields with formulas, build custom forms that suck in data from external Web sites, bring your forms to life with QuickBase's new dynamic rules—you'll never again be satisfied with a prebuilt application designed by someone else.

Writing Formulas

If the word *formula* conjures up images of a mad scientist cackling over bubbling potions in a secret laboratory, you've been watching too many old horror movies. QuickBase formulas can't turn Dr. Jekyll into Mr. Hyde, but they can do seemingly magical things to your data by performing powerful calculations. Once you add a formula to a field, QuickBase performs the calculation automatically as your data changes. For example, you might use a formula to figure out the average number of hours each employee worked last month, or to flag the names of people who haven't turned in a required form. You can write a formula to automatically fill in the name of someone's manager when that person is chosen in a user field. Formulas can calculate bonuses, fill in the total on invoices, determine sales figures by territory, and much, much more.

Once you get a handle on the different elements that go together in a formula, you can build a formula of your very own to do just about anything you want it to. This section breaks down formulas into their various parts, and then helps you put together your own formulas for use in your QuickBase applications.

The Parts of a Formula

Before you start writing formulas, it helps to understand the different parts that make up a typical formula. Once you understand these building blocks, you can put them together in various ways:

- **Field reference.** A *field reference* looks up the value inside a field and uses it in your formula. If you've created exact forms (Chapter 12) or customized email notifications ("Customizing Your QuickBase Emails" on page 172), you've used field references. In a formula, you create a field reference by enclosing the field label in square brackets, like this: *[Status]* or *[Assigned To]*. When QuickBase sees a field reference, it displays the contents of the named field or uses them in a calculation (depending on what your formula tells QuickBase to do).

- **Literal.** A literal-minded person is someone who believes exactly what you tell them (they're the people who call Animal Control when you say, "It's raining cats and dogs"). In formulas, a *literal* is similarly precise—it's a specified value that's exactly what you say it is. A literal can be numeric or text (enclose text literals in quotation marks). For example, QuickBase responds to the formula *"The total is"* *[subtotal]* + *10* by adding the numeric literal (10) to the contents of the subtotal field (say it's $23.52) and displaying that result along with the text literal, like this: *The total is $33.52.*

- **Operators.** *Operators* tell QuickBase how to act on the values it gets from field references and literals. Operators are usually symbols, such as + (add), - (subtract), * (multiply), / (divide), < (less than), > (greater than), and so on, but you can also use these operators: *not, and, or*. There are two types of operators:

  Unary operators. These go to work on a single value. For example, – in front of a number returns the negative value of that number (so –2 returns –2 and —2 returns 2).

  Binary operators. These act on two values, like when you add two numbers together (*2 + 4* returns 6) or multiply one number by another (*2 * 4* returns 8).

TIP

For a list of all unary and binary operators, with examples of how they work, check out the QuickBase Support Center. From My QuickBase's Applications list, click QuickBase Support Center→Formula Functions Reference (on the Table bar)→Operators—Unary (or Operators—Binary).

- **Function calls.** If field references and literals are the nouns of your formulas, function calls are the verbs—they make things happen with the values you've specified. A *function* is simply a procedure that returns a value, and a *function call* is what puts the function to work. A function call has two parts: the name of the function (what you want QuickBase to do) and, in parentheses, the function argument (the values you want the function to work on, as described next). Here's

---

an example: The *Average* function returns the average of several values, so the function call *Average (3, 18, 165)* returns 62. Similarly, the *Sum* function adds up values, so *Sum (3, 18, 165)* returns 186.

- **Function arguments.** *Arguments* are the values that go inside the parentheses of a function call. You can use field references or literals as arguments. For example, in the function call *Sum (15, [price])*, the arguments are *15* and *[price]*: *15* is a literal and *[price]* is a field reference. This function call adds the number 15 to whatever value is in the Price field, returning the total. The Max argument finds the highest value among several numbers, so *Max ([cost], 100)* returns either the value in the Cost field or the number 100, whichever is higher. *Max (100, 95, 364)* returns 364, which is the highest-value argument. Separate arguments with a comma, as shown in the examples.

TIP

For a comprehensive list of functions, start on your My QuickBase page. From its list of applications, click QuickBase Support Center→Formula Functions Reference→All Functions.

Understanding Data Types

Each kind of field has a particular kind of data—a *data type*—associated with it. Just as you can't add apples and oranges (orples? appanges?), you can't put some data types together in a formula. For example, you can't multiply someone's annual salary (a numeric data type) by their last name (a text data type). So to make your formulas work, you need to understand a little about data types.

When you write a formula, each field you put in the formula has a data type. So do the field in which you put your formula (see the box "Compatibility Check: Are You My (Field) Type?" on page 420) and the result your formula returns. When you think about formulas and calculations, you probably think about math. But formulas can perform calculations on a variety of information, not just numeric data. There are formulas for text, dates, times, durations, email addresses, and more (the box "Compatibility Check: Are You My (Field) Type?" on page 420 has the full rundown). For example, you might write a formula that displays a client's full name by pulling values from the First Name and Last Name fields. That formula would look like this: *[First Name] & " " & [Last Name]*. (The double quotes indicate a text literal that inserts a space between the two names.) Or you might want to write a formula that turns on a checkbox to identify employees above a certain salary threshold—$150,000, say. You'd use a Formula—Checkbox field type and write it like this: *[Salary] > 150000*.

Some formulas act on one kind of data type to produce a new type. For example, in a formula that returns a duration, QuickBase subtracts one date from another to find the length of time between them.

Treat your formula the same way you'd plan a party—make sure the types you invite are all compatible with each other. At a party, incompatible types lead to arguments and a serious drop in the fun factor. In a formula, incompatible types result in an "incorrect type" error message (and it's no fun when your formula doesn't work). For example, you wouldn't try to subtract a date from someone's first name—those types are incompatible. Knowing which data types can work together will save you a lot of frustration down the road—your formulas will give you the results you're looking for, and not just major headaches. (And if you meet this unfortunate fate, see "Troubleshooting Formulas" in "Troubleshooting Formulas" on page 436.)

UP TO SPEED

Compatibility Check: Are You My (Field) Type?

The first thing you do when you create a formula field is select its field type so QuickBase knows what kind of data the formula is supposed to produce. The key here is to ask yourself what kind of result your formula will return: If your result will be a number, choose Formula—Numeric. For a name or some other text, choose Formula—Text. If you want the formula to produce a true/false result that turns a checkbox on or off, choose Formula—Checkbox. If you want a result that lets you click a link to open a new email to someone, choose Formula—Email Address.

You get the idea. Here are the different formula field types QuickBase offers:

- **Formula—Text.** When your formula returns text or contains literals with letters and/or numbers, choose Formula—Text as the field type.

- **Formula—Numeric.** This type of field accepts only numeric results. So if you're doing math, you want a Formula—Numeric field. Numeric values can be whole numbers or decimals; they can be positive or negative.

- **Formula—Date.** Use this field type when your formula returns a date.

- **Formula—Time of Day.** When your formula returns the time of day, this is the field type you want. (If you're interested in timestamping changes to your data, see Table 11-1)

- **Formula—Duration.** This field type displays a length of time, such as the time between a task's scheduled start and projected finish. You can find a duration by subtracting one date or one timestamp from another. (Note that durations can be negative if you subtract a later date from an earlier one.)

- **Formula—Checkbox.** If the only possible results are true and false (or yes and no), use this field type. The results of this formula turn a checkbox on or off.

- **Formula—Phone Number.** Use this type of field to display a telephone number, bringing together area code and local number.
- **Formula—Email Address.** Your table probably stores names in one field and email addresses in another. This field type brings them together, displaying the result as a link that automatically opens an email for you to write and send.
- **Formula—URL.** This type of field tells QuickBase to create a Web address (URL, which stands for *uniform resource locator*) that takes a viewer to a specific Web page. A Formula—URL field lets you combine values from different fields to create URLs.
- **Formula—Work Date.** Unlike regular Date fields, this field type can use parts of days in date calculations. Work date fields are good for applications that have *predecessors*—where one thing needs to happen (Task A in a Manage Tasks application, for example) before another can take place (Task B). Say Leslie has to write the business requirements (Task A) before stakeholders can review the document (Task B), but as she's typing away, she realizes that she needs another day and a half to finish. When she adjusts the estimated finish time, a Formula—Work Date field pushes back the start of the document review by one-and-a-half days. (A regular Date field would ignore the half-day, pushing things back by just one day.)
- **Formula—Date/Time.** No big surprise here: This field type tells QuickBase to show a date and a time of day.

Creating a Formula Field

Once you get a handle on what goes into a formula, you can write formulas to automate calculations on your data. Although the specifics will vary depending on the formula you're writing, here are the basic steps:

1. Open the application that holds the table you want. In the menu bar, choose Customize→Tables.

   The Tables page opens, with the Fields tab already selected.

2. If you're in a multi-table application, click the name of the table you want from the left-hand list of tables. On the Fields tab, click Create New Fields.

   The Add Fields page, shown in Figure 11-1, opens.

3. Give your field a name and select a field type.

   You're creating a formula field, so when you click the "Select a field type" drop-down, scroll to the bottom of the list to select a field type that starts with the word *Formula*. When you've named the field and assigned it a type, click Add Fields.

   QuickBase returns you to the Fields tab of the Tables page and displays a confirmation box asking whether you want to add this field to any custom forms.

4. Unless you've already skipped ahead and read the custom forms section, click "Not right now."

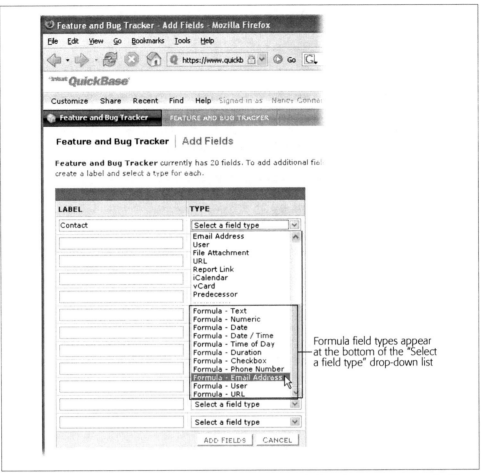

Figure 11-1. When creating a formula field, you add the new field in the same way you'd add any other field (see "Add a field" on page 219). Just be sure that you choose a field type beginning with the word Formula. (The formula fields are at the bottom of the list.) For a description of each field type, see the box in "Compatibility Check: Are You My (Field) Type?" on page 420.

The box disappears.

Now that you've created the field that will hold your formula, it's time to write the formula itself:

1. From the Fields tab of the application's Tables page, find the field you just created (QuickBase helps you out by marking the new field with a fat black arrow) and click its name.

   The Properties page for that field opens, as shown in Figure 11-2.

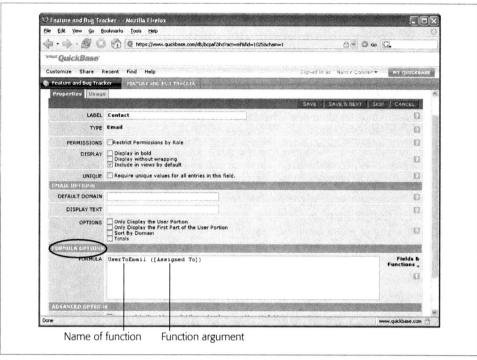

Name of function   Function argument

Figure 11-2. After you've created a formula field, open its Properties page to type in the actual formula for the field to use. The formula in this example will check the Assigned To user field and return the email address of the person in that field.

2. Find the Formula Options section and type your formula into the Formula text box. Modify any other settings you want for this field in the other sections of the Properties page. When you're finished, click Save.

   If you've messed up your data types, this is when QuickBase lets you know, presenting an error message at the top of the page. (If that happens, see "Troubleshooting Formulas" on page 436 for a little troubleshooting.) If it's all good, QuickBase applies your formula to the field and returns you to the Fields tab of the Tables page.

As you can see, the steps for creating a formula field are easy enough. The trick, of course, is writing a formula that gets QuickBase to do what you want it to. If your formulas are about as cooperative as a two-year-old at bedtime, check out the next few sections to get a handle on the basics of writing formulas, see a few examples, and get some troubleshooting tips.

Formula Writing Basics

If you're reading this book in English, left to right is a pretty natural flow of information for you. Of course, not all written languages work that way, including Hebrew, Arabic, and Chinese, to name a few. When QuickBase "reads" formulas, it has its own approach, too. It doesn't start at the left and work its way rightward until it reaches the end. Instead, it looks for the highest-precedence operator—the operator it works with first—and then follows an established order of precedence until it's evaluated the entire formula. Table 11-1 shows operator precedence in QuickBase.

Table 11-1. Operator Precedence

Precedence	Operator	What It Means
1 (Highest)	unary +	Returns a positive number or duration.
1	unary −	Returns the mathematical negative of a number or duration.
1	not	Returns the logical negation of a. (If a is true, it returns false; if a is false, it returns true.)
2	^	Raises a number to the nth power. For example, 4 ^ 2 returns 4^2, which is 16.
3	*	Multiplies (can be used with numbers or durations).
3	/	Divides (can be used with numbers or durations).
4	binary +	Adds (can be used with numbers, dates, times of day, timestamps, or durations).
4	binary −	Subtracts (can be used with numbers, dates, times of day, timestamps, or durations).
4	&	Concatenates text, meaning that it strings text values together. For example, *"Quick" & "Base"* returns QuickBase.
5	<	Less than (read left to right). Returns true or false. Can be used with numbers, text (alphabetical order), durations, dates, and timestamps. The data on either side of this operator must belong to the same type.
5	>	Greater than (read left to right). Returns true or false. Can be used with numbers, text (alphabetical order), durations, dates, and timestamps. The data on either side of this operator must belong to the same type.
5	<=	Less than or equal to (read left to right). Returns true or false. Can be used with numbers, text (alphabetical order), durations, dates, and timestamps. The data on either side of this operator must belong to the same type.
5	>=	Greater than or equal to (read left to right). Returns true or false. Can be used with numbers, text (alphabetical order), durations, dates, and timestamps. The data on either side of this operator must belong to the same type.
6	=	Equals. Returns true or false. The data on either side of this operator must belong to the same type.

Precedence	Operator	What It Means
6	<>	Does not equal. Returns true or false. The data on either side of this operator must belong to the same type.
7	and	Both. Returns true if both *a* and *b* are true; otherwise returns false.
8 (Lowest)	or	Either. Returns true if either *a* or *b* is true; otherwise returns false.

If you wrote this formula: 5 + 6 * 2, reading from left to right, you'd expect the answer to be 22, because 5 + 6 = 11, and 11 * 2 = 22. But when you look at Table 11-1, you can see that multiplication has a higher precedence than addition. In other words, QuickBase looks for the * operator before it looks for the + operator, doing multiplication first, and then going back through and adding. For your formula of 5 + 6 * 2, QuickBase would do the multiplication first (6 * 2 = 12), and then add (5 + 12 = 17), giving a result of 17.

Humans, however, don't think like computer programs. You'd find it unbearably tedious to make several passes through your formula, looking for a different level of operator precedence each time. Good thing you don't have to. You can use parentheses (just like in ninth-grade algebra class) to group certain parts of your formula together. If you wrote the previous formula like this: (5 + 6) * 2, QuickBase still looks for the * operator first, but it multiplies 2 by what's inside the parentheses, which adds up to 11, giving the answer 22.

So parentheses serve two functions in QuickBase formulas: they group items together and they identify function arguments. You can put sets of parentheses inside other sets of parentheses—that's called *nesting*. Just be aware that QuickBase starts from the deepest-nested set of parentheses and works outward from there. And if you type an opening parenthesis, don't forget to type the closing one, or QuickBase gets confused.

TIP

To make your formulas easier for you to read—for example, to keep track of all those parentheses—you can insert line breaks and extra spaces when you type formulas into the box on the field's Properties page (which you saw back in Figure 11-2). QuickBase ignores the extra breaks and line spaces, but that white space can make things a lot easier on human eyes.

Example 1: Calculate a Minimum Payment

Your company requires its customers to pay at least $15 per month on their bills; if the balance is less than $15, the customer pays the whole amount. You could go through all the records yourself and compare the current balance against the $15 minimum payment: Customer A owes $134.95, so the invoice requires a minimum payment of $15. Customer B owes just $12.32, so *that* amount is the minimum payment. But doing those comparisons is not how you want to use your time, so you can write a formula to pass the job over to QuickBase.

You want your formula to tell QuickBase to check the amount in the Balance Due field and compare it to 15, returning whichever amount is smaller. You're working with numbers, so when you create the new field (call it Minimum Payment), choose Formula —Numeric as the field type. QuickBase now knows that the new field uses a formula, works with numbers, and shows the result as a numeric value.

Next, write your formula. To find the lesser of two values (or the least in a series of values), use the *Min* function. The formula looks like this:

Min([Balance Due], 15.00)

To fill in the Minimum Payment field, QuickBase looks at the contents of the Balance Due field for each record and compares that amount to 15.00, and then displays whichever is smaller. In other words, it does the same thing you used to do by hand, except now you have time for a second cup of coffee while QuickBase does the work.

TIP

The *Min* function isn't restricted to numeric values. It can work with two or more arguments (the values inside the parentheses), as long as the arguments all belong to the same data type. If you use Min with text arguments, for example, it returns the text that comes first alphabetically. If you use it with dates, it returns the earliest date.

Example 2: Keep a Countdown to a Project's Launch Date

When you want to keep your team aware that the clock is ticking, you can create a field that shows how much time remains between now and the start date of a project or task. To do so, you want to tell QuickBase to calculate a duration and display it as a number —the number of days left. So when you create your formula field (call it something like Days to Launch), assign it the Formula—Numeric field type.

In the Days to Launch field, use the *ToDays* function, which takes a duration and converts it into a number of days. Here's the formula:

ToDays([Start Date] - Today())

This formula tells QuickBase to look at the date inside the Start Date field and subtract today's date from it, returning the difference as the number of days between now and when the project or task will start. Notice that Today has an empty set of parentheses after it. That's because *Today* is a function, and a function must always have a pair of parentheses after it, even if they're empty. The *Today* function—which simply calls today's date—doesn't need any arguments, and so its parentheses are empty. This formula is a nested formula: It has one function (*Today*) inside another (*ToDays*). QuickBase starts from the inside and works outward, calculating today's date before calculating the number of days left before the launch.

If you *really* want your team aware of how fast that clock is ticking, you can adapt this formula to show how many hours, minutes, and seconds—even milliseconds!—are left before the launch. The function names (as you've probably guessed) are *ToHours, ToMinutes, ToSeconds,* and *ToMSeconds.*

Example 3: List a Name and Mailing Address in Standard Address Format

If you want to pull information out of a table and display it in the standard format you'd see on an envelope or at the top of a letter, use the *List* function. This function concatenates (strings together) its arguments, starting with the *second* argument. The first argument is what tells QuickBase how you want to separate the other arguments from each other. As a simple example, say you want to display client names with the last name appearing first, like this: *Fothergill, Algernon.*

Here's the formula that returns that result (assuming, of course, that you have a client named Algernon Fothergill):

List(",", [Last Name], [First Name])

Look at the arguments in that function call: The first is a literal—a comma inside quotation marks—which tells QuickBase to insert a comma between items on the list. The second and third arguments are field references, blanks for QuickBase to fill in with the contents of the fields named.

When you use the *List* function, you're working with text. (Even if some numbers appear in, say, a mailing address, QuickBase treats them as text.) So when you create your Address Label field, make it a Formula—Text field. Then, write the formula like this:

List("\n", [Name], [Address Line 1], List(", ", [City], [State], [Zip]))

The first argument, *\n*, means "move to the next line down," so QuickBase displays each item in this list on its own line. The next two arguments are field references, each displaying its contents on a separate line. The third argument is another function call, this time telling QuickBase to list the contents of the City, State, and Zip fields all on one line, separated by commas. Using this formula displays the data for a particular record like this:

> Algernon Fothergill
> 1515 Springside Lane
> Chicago, IL, 60609

NOTE

If one of the fields in a formula using the *List* function is blank, QuickBase skips over that field.

Using Special Functions in Formulas

Now that you've got down the basics of formulas, you can use some special functions to make your data jump through even more hoops.

The If Function

Lots of times, events can move forward only if something is true: If your lottery numbers came in last night, you can quit your job and book that 'round-the-world cruise. If you forgot to buy a lottery ticket, you can get up with the alarm and join the commuters in seven-thirty-gridlock land. Notice how two very different paths depend on that little word *if*: If you win the lottery, you're off on the next luxury liner; if you don't win the lottery, you're on your way to work.

If also plays a big role when you're working with data. Say you want to flag purchase requisitions only *if* they're above $100. Or maybe you want to show the total on an invoice *if* the order status is Complete. Or perhaps you want to calculate a bonus for salespeople *if* their total sales for the month exceed $250,000. In each case, QuickBase performs a calculation on a record only if that record meets a certain condition.

The *If* function looks to see whether something is true or false, and then returns one value if true or a different value if false. For example, if you want to flag purchase requisitions over $100, create a Formula—Checkbox field (call it Needs Approval) and give it this formula:

If([Estimated Cost] > 100, true, false)

In this example, QuickBase turns on the Needs Approval checkbox if the amount in the Estimated Cost field exceeds $100.00. If the amount in Estimate Cost is $99.99 or less, QuickBase leaves the checkbox turned off. Note that the field that holds this formula must be a Formula—Checkbox field.

Instead of using a simple checkbox, you could make Needs Approval a Formula—User field and do this:

If([Estimated Cost] > 100, [Requested By], null)

This formula tells QuickBase to return the name of the user who made the request if it's over $100. If the request is less than that, QuickBase leaves the field blank. (For more on null values, jump to "Null Values" on page 430.)

To have QuickBase total an invoice only if the order is marked Complete, create a Formula—Numeric field called Total and use this formula:

If([Order Complete] = true, [Subtotal] + [Tax], null)

This formula tells QuickBase to check and see whether the Order Complete checkbox is turned on. If it is, QuickBase adds the contents of the Subtotal and Tax fields and displays the result in the Total field. If the Order Complete checkbox is turned off, QuickBase leaves the Total field blank.

To calculate a 2 percent bonus on sales over $250,000, create a field called Bonus, defining it as a Formula—Numeric field. Then use this formula:

*If([Total Sales] >= 250000, [Total Sales] * .02, 0)*

When QuickBase runs this formula, it calculates 2 percent of any amount that's $250,000 or more and shows the result in the bonus column. If the amount in the Total Sales field is less than $250K, QuickBase displays a zero in the Bonus column.

The Case() Function

The *If* function is great in either/or situations, when you want to test whether one field does or does not meet a certain criterion before QuickBase performs a calculation. But sometimes you want to display several possible results, depending on a series of tests. For example, you might want to sort major cities into sales territories. You could string together a whole bunch of *If* functions, but you don't have to get that complicated. Instead, you can use the *Case* function.

To show what sales territory a major city belongs to, you could create a Formula—Text field called Territory and write a formula that looks like this:

Case([City], "Boston", "Northeast", "Atlanta", "Southeast", "Chicago", "Midwest", "Seattle", "Northwest")

This formula tells QuickBase to check the contents of the City field: If QuickBase finds Boston, it displays Northeast in the Territory field; if it finds Atlanta, it displays Southeast—and so on.

Your formula might be a little easier to read if you break it up a little, putting the city names and associated territories on separate lines. You can add extra spaces and even Returns to a formula—QuickBase ignores them when it evaluates the formula. So the Territory formula could just as easily look like this:

Case([City], "Boston", "Northeast",

"Atlanta", "Southeast",

"Chicago", "Midwest",

"Seattle", "Northwest")

A little easier to follow, no? You can use hit Return to make your formulas more readable, as long as you don't forget to put in the commas and parentheses that QuickBase needs to understand the formula.

Null Values

Sometimes, a field is empty, blank—this could be because no one's entered a value for that field, or it could be a formula field that returned no result. A blank field's value is called *null*. A null value is not the same as zero. Zero is a number with the numeric value zero; a null field is just plain empty—QuickBase sees it as undefined.

NOTE

Text fields can never be null. If a text field is empty, QuickBase sees that field as having zero characters. (In geekspeak, that's known as the *empty string* value.) Similarly, *Boolean* (true/false) fields are never null. In a Boolean field, if a value isn't true, it's false. If a checkbox isn't turned on, it's off. There's no room for null.

Here's a quick example to give you an idea of how a null field works. Earlier, you saw this *If* formula, which tells QuickBase to calculate an invoice total only if the order is marked Complete:

If([Order Complete] = true, [Subtotal] + [Tax], null)

If an order is complete, you know what the total is: the subtotal plus any tax. If an order is incomplete, however, you don't yet know what the total is, because you don't know whether the customer will add more items to the order. In that case, you don't have all the information yet. Since the total is still undefined, a null value makes sense.

There are also functions that make specific use of null values. (To see a complete list, start with the Applications list on your My QuickBase page: click QuickBase Support Center→Formula Functions Reference→All Functions, and then scroll down the page to the Null Handling section.) The *IsNull* function works with any data type (except text or Boolean) and returns true if the field referred to in the argument is null; it returns false if there's any value besides null in the field. You might use *IsNull* like this:

IsNull([Assigned To])

This formula returns true if the Assigned To field (a user field) is blank (undefined); if the field holds a user, then the formula returns false.

Remember that null is not the same as zero—you can't multiply by a null value or calculate an average with it. But sometimes you might want to treat null as a zero. For example, maybe at the end of the year you want to figure out the average quarterly bonus that each person on your sales team has earned. If there's no value in a Bonus field, it means the sales rep didn't get a bonus. But you still want to include that field in the average calculation—as a zero bonus.

You could use a formula like this:

Average(Nz([Winter Bonus]), Nz([Spring Bonus]), Nz([Summer Bonus]), Nz([Fall Bonus]))

With this formula, if QuickBase finds any null values in your reference fields, it treats them as zeros, including them in the average.

NOTE

The Properties page for numeric fields, under Advanced Options, has a checkbox labeled "Treat blank as zero in calculations." When you create a new numeric field, QuickBase turns on this checkbox by default. So you may never actually have to use the *Nz* function to get QuickBase to look at nulls as zero in numeric fields.

The Fields & Functions Menu

As you saw in the previous sections, writing formulas basically involves combining functions and field references. QuickBase can be awfully picky about the formulas you write. It's not very good, for example, at guessing what you mean if you make a typo or you call a field *Requested* when the field's actual label is *Requested By*. Fortunately, QuickBase is willing to help you out with getting field names and functions right.

When you're writing a formula on a field's Properties page, as soon as you click inside the Formula box, a drop-down menu appears to its right (jump back to Figure 11-2 to see what this looks like). That's the Fields & Functions menu, which Figure 11-3 shows in all its glory. This menu lists all the fields in your table. When you want to insert a field into your formula, open the Fields & Functions menu, find the field you want, and then click its name. QuickBase slots the field into your formula, complete with brackets.

But that's not all the Fields & Functions menu does. It can also look up functions for you—taking a lot of the trial-and-error out of getting the syntax right. Finding and inserting a function into your formula takes just a few, quick steps:

1. On the field's Properties page (Customize→Tables, and then click the name of the field you want), click inside the Formula box.

   QuickBase shows the Fields & Functions drop-down to the right of the box. (You can see it back in Figure 11-2.)

2. Point your cursor at the words Fields & Functions to see the menu. Choose "Select a Function...."

   QuickBase opens the QuickBase Formula Functions box (Figure 11-4). This box presents a couple of lists: The top drop-down list lets you select either All Functions

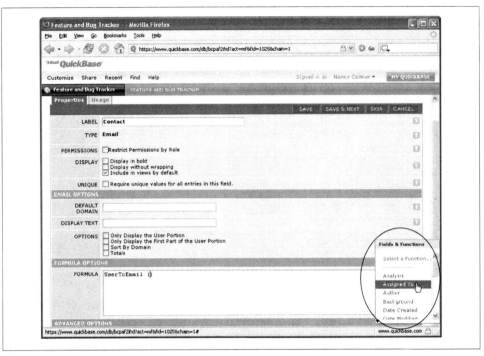

Figure 11-3. The Fields & Functions menu (circled) lists every field in your table. Select a field from the menu and QuickBase inserts that field where your cursor is in the Formula text box. It even throws a pair of brackets around the field name for you.

or a specialized set of functions (such as Dates Functions or Null Handling Functions). The bottom list shows you functions related to whatever category you choose in the top list.

3. Make your selections in each drop-down. For example, if you're writing a formula to create a timestamp, you'd choose Timestamp Functions from the top drop-down and Now from the bottom.

   When you choose a function from the bottom list, QuickBase shows the function itself and helpfully gives you both a description of what the function does and an example of how you might use it.

4. When you've selected the function you want, click Insert.

   QuickBase inserts the function into the Formula box.

   To make sure you get the syntax right, the function includes placeholders for arguments where necessary. This helps you get the required data types right. For example, when you select Begins from the drop-down, QuickBase inserts this: *Begins (Text u, Text v)* to remind you that this function takes text data types as its argument.

5. Replace the placeholders with actual values.

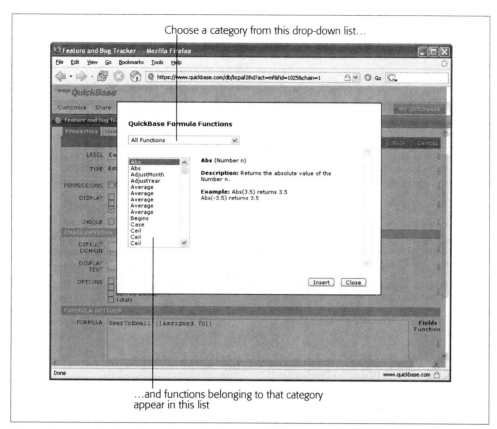

Choose a category from this drop-down list…

…and functions belonging to that category
appear in this list

Figure 11-4. In the QuickBase Formula Functions box, use the top drop-down menu to select a category (such as Numbers Functions, Text Functions, Durations Functions, and so on). The bottom list changes to show functions related to whatever category you select. When you choose a function, look to the right of the list: QuickBase shows the function itself, defines what it does, and offers an example of how you might use it.

In the example, you'd change *Begins (Text u, Text v)* to something like this: *Begins ([Last Name], "a")*. This would find all the records where the text in the Last Name field begins with the letter *a*.

Using Variables in Formulas

When you're typing out a formula, particularly one that's long and complex, you probably wish you got paid by the keystroke—or that there were some way to avoid typing the same thing over and over (and over and over) again. Wouldn't it be nice, for example, if there were a faster, easier way to insert someone's name into a formula than always typing *[First Name] & " " & [Last Name]*?

Since most of us don't get paid by the keystroke, the ability to use variables in QuickBase formulas is a very good thing. A *variable* is some text that substitutes for a longer segment of code. So it's best to use a variable for some piece of a formula that repeats several times within that formula. For example, you might want to write a formula that automatically applies a 15 percent discount to customer purchases over $250. The formula calculates the total by multiplying the contents of the Price field by the contents of the Quantity field. So instead of writing a formula that looks like this:

if ([Price] * [Quantity] > 250, [Price] * [Quantity] * 0.85, [Price] * [Quantity])

You can create a variable, perhaps called *total*, to replace each occurrence of *[Price]* * *[Quantity]* in the formula. Doing so will save you some typing and reduce the chance of typos in your formula.

After you've defined a variable, you can use it over and over again wherever you need it in your formula. (You can't, however, use a variable defined for one formula in a different formula—when you want to use a variable in a formula for another field, you have to define it for that field. But isn't that why they invented Copy and Paste?)

Using variables requires two basic steps:

1. Define the variable.

   Before you can use a variable, you've got to tell QuickBase what the variable stands for. You do that at the top of your formula. Here's how you'd define a variable to insert people's full names:

   var Text fullname = [first name] & " " & [last name];

   The first part of the variable, *var*, indicates that what follows defines the variable. The next part, *Text*, defines the data type (here, the data type is Text, but in another situation you might use Number or any other data type). Next comes the name you've given your variable: in the example, that's *fullname*. The equals sign tells QuickBase that what follows is the contents of the variable—in other words, what the variable replaces in the formula. In this example, the variable's content is *[first name] & " " & [last name]*. Now you've defined the variable, but you're not quite done. See the semicolon at the end? That's important. It tells QuickBase that this variable definition is separate from the formula itself—so don't forget it or Quick-Base will get confused.

   NOTE

   Variable names can only contain letters. That means no numbers, spaces, hyphens, dashes or any other fancy characters—just letters.

   ---

2. Type your formula.

   Now that you've told QuickBase what your variable is and what it stands for, you can create a formula that saves you some typing (and possible mistakes) by using the variable in your formula. To indicate that something in the formula is a variable, stick a dollar sign ($) in front of it.

Suppose you're creating a formula that will insert customers' names after their title. It would look something like this:

var Text fullname = [first name] & " " & [last name];

Case([title], "Dr.", [title] & " " & $fullname,

"Mr.", [title] & " " & $fullname,

"Mrs.", [title] & " " & $fullname,

"Ms.", [title] & " " & $fullname,

"Rev.", [title] & " " & $fullname,

$fullname)

When QuickBase reads this formula, first it checks out how you've defined the variable. Now it knows that every time it comes across *$fullname*, it's the same as if you'd typed *[first name] & " " & [last name]*. This formula then goes on to tell QuickBase to look in the title field; if the title field contains Dr., then QuickBase displays Dr., followed by a space, followed by the contents of the first name field, then another space, and then the contents of the last name field. And so on down the list, whether the title field contains Mr., Mrs., Ms., or Rev. In any case, you've just saved your fingers a whole lot of keyboard tapping. Nice.

NOTE

If the title field is empty or holds something else, QuickBase displays the full name without any title.

Using Formulas to Design Reports

One cool thing you can do with a formula is create a custom column that shows up in one particular report but isn't really part of the application as a whole. When you have the report open, the column looks and acts just like any other field—but it's available only in that report. For example, perhaps you don't have administrative privileges in a particular application, so you can't add a field, but you want a custom column for your own use. Or perhaps you simply don't want to clutter up your application and confuse other users with yet another field. Or you may need a formula to create the exact report you want—comparing the contents of two other columns.

Here's how to use a formula to add a custom column to a report:

1. Open the report you want to customize and click the upper-right Customize this Report link. (Or, if you're creating a brand-new report from scratch, open the application and select Customize→Create a new→Report from the menu bar. In a multi-table application, select a table, and then click Create a New Report.)

Report Builder opens. (Chapter 2 tells you all about using Report Builder.)

2. In Report Builder's Additional Options section (down at the bottom), make sure that "Custom options" is turned on, and then turn on the "Define a custom formula column for this report" checkbox.

   The Additional Options section expands, as shown in Figure 11-5.

3. Choose a field type from the drop-down menu, give your custom column a name in the Label box, and type your formula into the Formula box. (When you click inside the Formula box, the Fields & Functions menu appears to its right—see "The Fields & Functions Menu" on page 431.) To see how the column looks, click Display.

   If your custom column fits the bill, click Save. (You can also click Save or Save & Display right in Report Builder.)

   QuickBase saves the custom column in this report only.

If you have any experience with formulas, as described in the first part of this chapter, then you know how to create just about any kind of custom formula column. Any kind of formula field you might create for an application can be applied to a column within one particular report. If you want to compare values in two fields, for example, flagging those reps whose sales slid last quarter, you could make your custom column a Checkbox field and write a formula like this:

If(Nz([Q1 Sales]) > Nz([Q2 Sales]), true, false)

QuickBase turns on the checkbox for any sales rep whose second quarter sales are less than their first quarter sales.

TIP

Use the formula field to filter records. In Report Builder's Filtering section, set a condition like *show records where custom column is Yes.*

Troubleshooting Formulas

You've created a formula field, and everything's going great. You added a new field, gave it a field type, and typed in the formula on its Properties page. But when you click the Save button, QuickBase returns an error message. Don't feel bad—this happens to everyone. Testing, retesting, and working out all the bugs are what formula development is all about.

When you write a formula, QuickBase checks for errors in three major areas:

- **Syntax.** Just as your English teacher used to make sure you dotted all your *i*'s and crossed all your *t*'s, QuickBase checks your formulas for faulty punctuation or, to use the fancy term, *syntax errors.* QuickBase looks to see whether you've closed all your parentheses and inserted all your commas. If you've left out a square

---

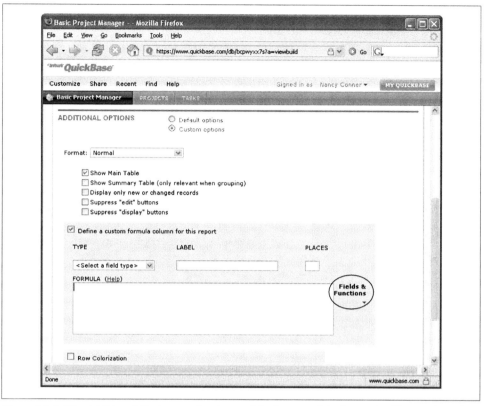

Figure 11-5. The Additional Options section (toward the bottom of the Report Builder page) is where you name, define, and create a formula for a custom column that appears only in this report. (The field types that appear in the Type drop-down list don't say Formula in front of their names, but they're all formula field types.) If you want help writing your formula, choose field names or function types from the Fields & Functions menu (circled), which appears when you click inside the Formula box.

bracket or a quotation mark somewhere, QuickBase tells you you've made a syntax error.

- **Validation.** You can write a sentence that's perfectly punctuated, but if it doesn't make sense, your English teacher would pull out the red pen. Same thing with QuickBase. If your formula's syntax checks out OK, QuickBase next checks to see if the formula makes sense. Some of the validation issues QuickBase looks for are whether field references refer to actual fields in the table (your field references must match field labels *exactly*), whether the data types match up, whether those data types work with the operators ("The Parts of a Formula" on page 418) you've chosen, and so on. If QuickBase doesn't understand the formula (even though it made perfect sense to you), you get a validation error.

- **Evaluation.** *Evaluation* is another word for running a formula. Even if your formula passes its initial tests, QuickBase runs it to make sure it actually works. That way, you won't run the formula later on and discover that your formula field comes up blank. If you get an evaluation error, it means that even though the formula itself is put together OK, some problem is preventing it from running properly. As with syntax and validation errors, QuickBase reports what it found, so you can figure out the problem.

If QuickBase finds a problem in one of those three main areas, it lets you know by displaying a big yellow error message. Here are some steps you can take to iron things out:

- **Syntax errors.** If there's a problem with the grammar of your formula, QuickBase tells you there's a syntax error and shows you where the formula went wrong, underlining the part of the formula it didn't understand. Look for missing or extra commas, quotation marks, parentheses, and square brackets. Be aware that, unlike your English teacher (whose grammar was so perfect she actually knew the difference between *who* and *whom*), QuickBase isn't always right in its analysis of syntax errors. For example, if QuickBase sees this formula—*FirstDayOfPeriod(date, Weeks(2), Date2007,1,1))*—it may insist that you've included an extra parenthesis at the end. The problem with this formula, however, is not an extra parenthesis: The formula is missing an opening parenthesis between the function Date and its arguments 2007,1,1. The formula should look like this: *FirstDayOfPeriod(date, Weeks(2), Date(2007,1,1))*. Syntax errors can be tricky to catch, so you might have to try several times before you get all those commas and parentheses right. It's just par for the course.

- **Validation errors.** The most common kind of error that keeps your formula from flying is when its data types can't work together. QuickBase calls this an *incorrect type* error. In this type of error, QuickBase shows you an error message like this: "The types of the arguments supplied do not meet the requirements of the operator," and then lists the data type or types causing the problem. Take a look at the data types in your formula, and ask yourself the following questions: Are you trying to force incompatible data types to work together? Are you trying to use data types as arguments that can't produce the data type in your formula field? Are you trying to use the wrong data type with a particular operator or vice versa (for example, are you trying to use the + operator with text, when you should be using & instead)?

  Sometimes, though, you need different data types to work together. For instance, you might want to take a duration and display it as the number of days, like the example in "Example 2: Keep a Countdown to a Project's Launch Date" on page 426. But QuickBase treats duration (a measurement of time) differently from plain-vanilla numbers. Because it's sometimes useful to make different data types work together, QuickBase offers special functions that let you convert one data type to another, so you can use them in the same formula. These *type conversion* functions always start with To: *ToNumber, ToText, ToDate*, and so on. (You can see a whole list of type conversion functions in the QuickBase Support Center. From My QuickBase, select QuickBase Support Center→Formula Functions Reference→All Functions, and then look for the Type Conversion section of the table.)

Other validation errors might spring up because you've misspelled a field name or you're trying to refer to a field that doesn't exist.

- **Evaluation errors.** QuickBase evaluates (or runs) a formula whenever you display a record that uses the formula or sort a table on a formula field. So evaluation errors can pop up at any time—not just when you first create a new formula field. The major causes of evaluation errors are when someone deletes a field that the formula needs, when your formula relies on another formula field and *that* field has a problem, or when a field your formula relies on holds weird values (for example, if your formula divides the contents of the Total Hours field by the contents of the Billable Hours field and Billable Hours has some zeros in it, QuickBase runs into a problem because it can't divide by zero).

Customizing Forms

Computerized or paper, simple or complex, forms are everywhere. They're the basic mode of interaction between people and information. On a given day, you might fill out a form to apply for admission to a school, to buy a lottery ticket, or to make a restaurant reservation online. *Forms* are also how QuickBase lets users interact with a single record. Some forms are interactive, others are view-only. When you create a new table ("Add a new table" on page 318), QuickBase automatically creates three forms:

- **Add.** This interactive form consists of blank fields for the user to fill out when creating a new record.
- **Edit.** An Edit form looks just like an Add form, but because it's for an existing record it already has some fields filled in.
- **Display.** When users click the View button to take a closer look at an existing record, they see this form. You can't edit a Display form, but you can click its Edit button to open an Edit form.

These built-in forms are plenty to get you started with your QuickBase application, but you don't have to work with an application too long before you start thinking about ways that you might improve your form. QuickBase makes it easy to modify an existing form by adding new fields ("Add a field" on page 219), deleting fields you don't need ("Delete a field" on page 225), changing a field's type ("Modify a field" on page 223), rearranging fields ("Reordering fields in the default report" on page 297), and so on. But why settle? QuickBase lets you tailor data entry to job role, situation, or whatever you want. For example, you can let different roles edit different fields—so employees can change their address and phone number in their HR record but not their salary or benefits. Or you can create a form where, when a maintenance worker changes a work order's status to Delayed, a required Explanation field automatically appears.

You can create as many custom forms as you need for any application you manage. Custom forms may not eliminate human error from data entry, but they let you minimize it with well-designed forms that guide users through the process of entering or editing data. (For some ideas, see the box "What Custom Forms Can Do" on page 440.)

GEM IN THE ROUGH

What Custom Forms Can Do

If you've ever been frustrated because someone messed up your data by editing a field they weren't supposed to touch or left an important field blank, custom forms just might save your sanity—or at least your business. Here's what you can do with custom forms:

- **Create different forms for different roles.** Tailoring forms to roles is one of the handiest things you can do with custom forms. Data entry clerk, sales rep, manager, Big Boss, marketer, project leader, maintenance worker, whatever—everybody sees only the fields that they need to get their job done.

- **Display only certain fields in a form.** Even if you need a whole bunch of fields, not everyone needs to see them all. You can show different fields to people in different roles, controlling access to the data.

- **Set fields' order.** You can minimize mistakes by arranging fields in a way that makes sense when entering data.

- **Require fields.** One of the cool things about required fields on custom forms is that you can require a field on some forms but not on others. For example, you might require field techs to list their supervisor when requesting inventory, but a request coming from a supervisor doesn't need that field.

- **Embed reports.** When someone on your team looks at a task, you can make the form display related tasks (maybe all those other tasks that must be done before this one can begin), tasks assigned to that user, or all open tasks. So instead of looking at just one record through a magnifying glass, users can see a report holding related records, based on criteria you choose.

- **Design your form.** Use HTML tags, section headings, horizontal lines, and explanatory text to make a custom form clear and easy to use.

- **Set dynamic rules.** A *dynamic form* is a specialized kind of custom form that give you even more flexibility to design just the form you want. For example, if someone selects a rating of Poor from a multiple choice list, you can set a dynamic rule that requires that person to fill out the Comments box before submitting the form. Or if someone turns on the Reviewed checkbox, you can create a rule that automatically populates the Date Reviewed field with the current date. (To learn more about dynamic forms, check out "Dynamic Forms" on page 448.)

- **Use live dynamic formula and lookup fields.** One cool feature of QuickBase that other databases can't match is the ability of formula fields to do calculations as a user enters values in the reference fields. Normally, reference field values have to be entered and saved before the formula can do its work. With QuickBase, such

---

calculations happen live. For example, if you have a formula that calculates an invoice's total based on the values in the Subtotal and Tax fields, QuickBase shows the total as soon as a user has entered values into Subtotal and Tax and tabbed or clicked away from those fields, making errors easier to spot and correct.

Creating a Custom Form

Now that you know what custom forms can do, you're probably champing at the bit to create one. So here are the steps to follow:

1. In the application for which you want to create a form, go to the menu bar and select Customize→Create a new→Form. (If you're in a multi-table application, select a table.) Or, if you prefer to take the scenic route, choose Customize→Tables (if necessary, select the table you want), click the Forms tab, and then click "Create a New Form".

   QuickBase asks you to name the form you're creating.

2. Type a name in the text box. For example, the form's name might show its associated role, like Sales Rep Form or Field Tech Form. If you're not feeling creative, you can go with the default name, Untitled Form (you can change the name later). Click OK.

   QuickBase opens a form editor, with the Elements tab selected. This editor is where you select and configure the fields for your new form.

3. Select from the offerings on the form editor's Elements tab, shown in Figure 11-6.

TIP
Don't confuse the field's Properties button with the form's Properties tab.

---

4. Select and configure the different fields that will appear on your custom form. When you select a field in the left-hand pane, configuration options appear in the right-hand pane. Here's what you can do with a field in a custom form (your actual choices depend on the type of field you select):

   - **Select and reorder fields.** When you click a field and highlight it, you can use the buttons below the left pane to move that field up or down the list or to remove it from the form. You can also move fields by using the drop-down lists where field names appear: Click and choose a different field to move up to the current spot.

   - **Use Alternate Label Text.** To give the field a different name in this custom form only, turn on this checkbox and type in the new name in the text box that appears.

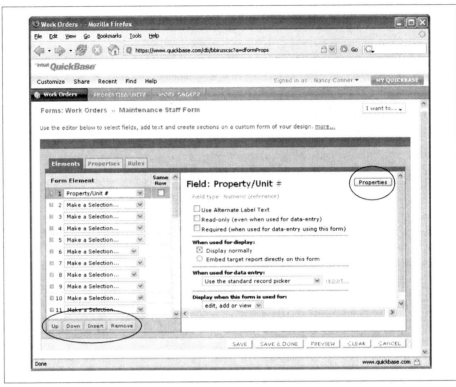

Figure 11-6. When you select and highlight a field in the left pane, you can move it up or down, remove it from your custom form, or insert a different field before it (using the circled buttons at bottom left). The selected field appears in the right pane, where you can tweak the field to make it read-only, required for data entry, and so on (your options in this pane depend on the actual field you've selected). To see or edit a field's properties, click the Properties button (also circled).

- **Read-only.** When you turn on this checkbox, users working with this form can only view this field, not delete or modify it (even when they're using the form to edit a record).

- **Required.** If users must put something in this field before saving the form, turn on this checkbox.

- **When used for display.** This section determines how the form looks when a user clicks the Display button to see a particular record. You have two choices here: display the form as usual (like in the built-in Display form) or embed a report right inside the form. If you want to embed a report, turn on the appropriate radio button and select the report you want from the drop-down menu.

When you embed a report from another table, that table and the table holding the custom form must have a relationship.

- **When used for data entry.** In this section, you can specify the report on which you want the Record Picker based, which limits the records users can select.
- **Display when this form is used for.** Your choices here are edit, add, view, or any combination of those operations.

When you're done working with the form's elements, click the Properties tab.

This tab lists your custom form's properties, as shown in Figure 11-7. If you want to change the form's name, this is where you do it.

5. Turn on or off the Properties checkboxes as you wish. Use the drop-down to tell QuickBase how the form should act when new fields are added to its table: do nothing, ask whether to add the fields to this form, or automatically add any new fields to the bottom of this form.

   If you want to create dynamic rules, click the Rules tab and take a look at "Dynamic Forms" on page 448.

6. Click Save or (if you're finished creating custom forms for now) Save & Done.

   QuickBase creates your custom form.

Working with Embedded Reports

When you have two related tables, such as Customers and Orders, it can be super helpful to see approrpriate records from the details table when you're looking at a form in the master table. (In a relationship, the master table and details table have a one-to-many relationship; for example, one customer can have many orders. In that example, Customers is the master table and Orders is the details table.) When you're looking at the form for a particular customer, it'd be nice to see that customer's orders at a glance. And that's just what *embedding* a report lets you do. When you embed a report inside a form, opening the form shows you related records from the details table.

But it gets even better. Once you've embedded a report in a form, you can edit that report's records without leaving the master form. (A *master form* is simply a form in the master table.) What that means is that you can make and save changes to the details table without navigating all the way over to that table, then finding your way back to the master form. Quick, convenient, and oh so easy. This section shows you how to get those detail records into a master form, and how to edit them once they're there.

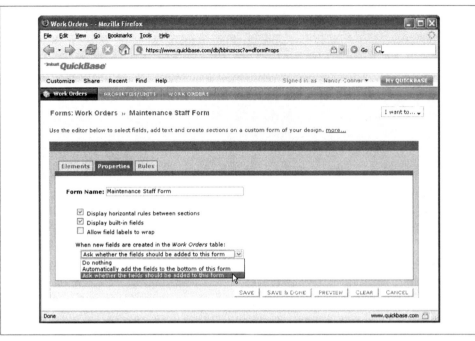

Figure 11-7. Form Builder's Properties tab lets you set the properties of your custom form: You can display horizontal rules between sections to visually organize a long form. You can display or hide the built-in fields usually found at the bottom of forms. (These fields show when a record was created, its owner, and who last modified it and when.) You can use automatic text wrapping to make long field names look neater. And finally, you can tell QuickBase what this form should do when someone adds a new field to its table.

Embed a report within a form

NOTE

Not sure which is the master table and which is the details table? Select Customize→Tables, then click the Relationship tab, which shows you all the relationships in which a table is involved. The master table is on the left; the details table is on the right.

Embedded reports are possible only in the context of a relationship between two tables. So first, make sure that the tables you're working with are related. (If not, it's a snap to create a relationship.) Next, determine which is the master table and which is the details table. This is important, because you can embed reports inside a master form only. Figure 11-8 shows a report embedded in a form.

Once you know which table is the master table, you can embed a report from the details table in a master form. Just follow these steps:

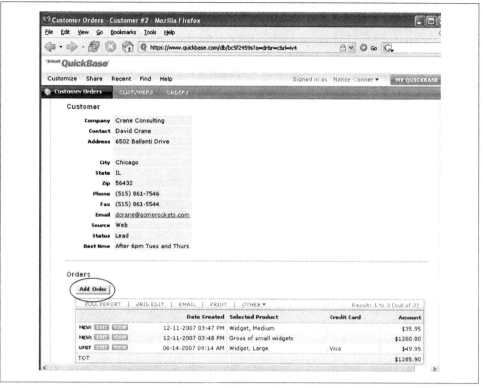

Figure 11-8. In this application, Customers is the master table and Orders is the details table. Here, QuickBase displays a form from the Customers table. At the top of the form, you see the usual customer data: name, address, email, and so on. At the bottom of the form is the embedded report. This one shows all the records from the Orders table that link up to this customer. You can view the customer's past or open orders. Clicking Add Order (circled) opens a new window with an Add Record form for the details table.

1. In the master table, display the form in which you want to embed a report. To do this, open a report that shows the master table's records, then click the View or V button (which one you see depends on how you've set your user preferences) to the left of a record. For example, for the Customers table, you could display List All, choose any record in the table, and click its left-hand View or V button.

   QuickBase displays a form for the master table.

2. In the upper-right part of the form, click the "Customize this Form" link. From the menu that pops up, select "Edit the layout of this form in the Form Builder."

   Form Builder, shown back in Figure 11-6, opens.

3. In the left-hand list of Form Elements, find the Report Link field. In the master table, the contents of this field display as a link. When someone clicks the link, QuickBase opens a report that shows relevant records from the details table. Usu-

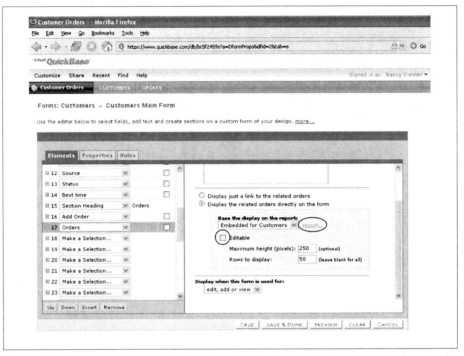

Figure 11-9. When you turn on the "Display the related records directly on the form" radio button, a new section appears in Form Builder, giving you options for setting up your embedded report. You can choose a report from the drop-down list (although normally you'll want QuickBase's default suggestion here). To tweak a report in Report Builder before you embed it, click the "report" link (circled). Turn on the Editable checkbox (also circled) to give users the power to work with records from the details table at the same time they're working in the master table's form. You can limit the size of the embedded report and define the kinds of forms (edit, add, view, or a combination of these) that display the report.

ally, the Report Link field is named after the details table, so in the example, it's named Orders. When you've found the Report Link field, click the little blue arrow to its left.

QuickBase shows information related to this field in Form Builder's right pane, as shown in Figure 11-9.

4. In the right-hand pane, turn on the "Display the related records directly on the form" radio button. (In the example, the records being displayed are orders). Turning on this radio button tells QuickBase that you want to embed a report that shows the related records. If you turn on the other radio button instead ("Display just a link to the related orders"), QuickBase does just that—the form displays a link to the related records, not a report that shows the records themselves.

The section expands to give you some options:

Base the display on the report. Use this dropdown list to select the report you want to embed.

Editable. Turn on this checkbox if you want users to be able to edit the embedded report from this form. That means that the report will appear as a Grid Edit report when the form is in add or edit mode. (For more about editing embedded reports, see the next section.)

NOTE

You might find that a report has already been embedded in a master table's forms. For example, many prebuilt applications are set up this way. When you make an existing embedded report editable, make sure you remove any formula—URL fields for adding detail records that might be hanging around. This kind of field, which appears as a button or a hyperlink, lets users add new records to the details table from a master form. Because you're making the embedded report editable, giving users even more flexibility, you don't need that formula—URL field any more (and it might be confusing). Read about deleting fields here.

Maximum height (pixels). This setting, which is optional, lets you limit the height of the displayed report. (After all, you don't want the report to get so big you can't see what's on the master table's form!)

Rows to display. This is another way to keep an embedded report from sprawling. Use it to set the maximum number of rows that appear in your embedded report. Say you set the max to 10 rows, but a particular customer has placed 82 orders. In that case, QuickBase divides the report into several pages, each with a maximum of 10 rows. Users can navigate through the pages to find a particular record. All the records are there; they just don't display at the same time. (If you don't want to limit maximum number of rows in this way, simply leave this box blank.)

5. Make your selections. Then, if you want your embedded report to appear only in a particular mode, take a look at the "Display when this form is used for" dropdown menu. You can have the form show up in the mode of your choice—edit, add, view—or any combination of those. When your choices are all set, you can preview how the form will look by clicking the Preview button.

   A new window opens, showing your the form with its embedded report.

6. When you're all set, click Save & Done.

   QuickBase embeds the report in your form and takes you back to the form you were customizing.

Edit an embedded report

Viewing an embedded report is only half the fun. If you turned on the Editable checkbox when you embedded a report in a form, people who use your application can add or edit records in the details table without leaving the master form, which can be a great timesaver. For example, imagine you're setting next year's sales targets for your sales reps—wouldn't it be convenient to add new opportunities at the same time, then save everything with just one click? Or if you're defining a new task for a project, you can add related issues for the new task, with no need to navigate between forms.

An editable embedded report looks like a Grid Edit report, as Figure 11-10 shows. And you work with it in just the same way—a lot like editing an Excel spreadsheet. Click a cell in the report to select it (a thick black outline surrounds the cell); double-click to edit the cell's contents (the outline becomes red).

NOTE

You must be looking at a form in add or edit mode (not just view) to edit its embedded report.

You can probably think of all kinds of situations where the ability to edit embedded reports will make life easier for your team. But there are a few times where editable reports aren't so helpful. This is simply due to the nature of Grid Edit reports: They don't show totals or subtotals. So if you want the embedded report to show averages or totals, you *don't* want to turn on the Editable checkbox.

Similarly, Grid Edit reports don't show running changes to formula fields as users change the data in the fields the formula requires. If users need to be able to see those running changes as they work, an editable embedded report isn't going to help them much—they'll have to keep clicking Save to see how the formula fields have changed. And if the details table is a document library that stores attached files, there's not much point in creating an editable embedded report, because you can't upload documents in Grid Edit mode. Finally, form rules don't work in Grid Edit mode, so if you've set up such rules for the details table, don't use editable embedded reports. Bottom line: if you wouldn't use a Grid Edit report for working with the data in your details table, don't make embedded reports from that table editable.

Dynamic Forms

Custom forms are great, but adding *dynamic rules* to your custom form is a lot like putting a cape and a spandex jumpsuit on a mild-mannered average Joe—it elevates your form to superhero status. Dynamic rules let your form change with the situation: If a purchase order's status changes from Pending to Approved, for example, QuickBase can automatically put today's date in the Date Approved field. Or if a task's status changes from Planned to Started, QuickBase can note the start date and adjust the projected completion date. If, on the other hand, a task's status goes from Planned to At Risk, QuickBase can show and require a Comments text box where the user must type in the risks involved. How cool is that?

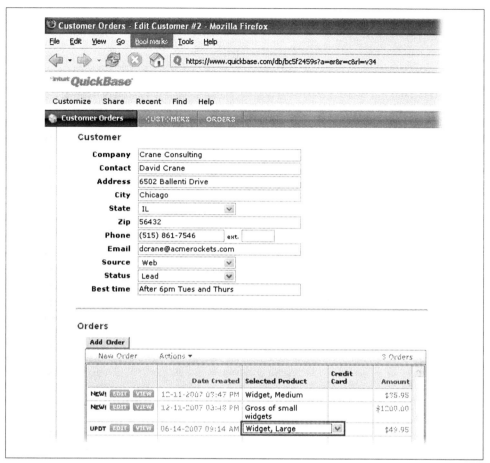

Figure 11-10. When you make an embedded report editable, you can easily add or edit a details table's records from a master table's form. Click any cell to select it; double-click to work with its contents. If the contents of a particular cell are a multiple-choice field (as in this example), double-clicking that cell displays a drop-down that holds the multiple-choice selections. Note that you can't edit some cells; if a cell holds a built-in field (such as Date Created) or a formula field (such as Amount), trying to edit it will get you an error message.

You can write dynamic rules for a custom form when you first create the form; if you're doing that, these instructions jump in at step 4 of creating a custom form ("Creating a Custom Form" on page 441). You can also add dynamic rules to an existing form. To do that, find the form you want on the Tables page (Customize→Tables, select the table if necessary, and then click the Forms tab), and then click its Rules button. This takes you straight to the form editor's Rules tab (Figure 11-11).

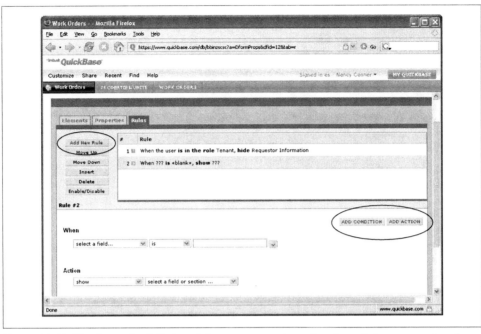

Figure 11-11. The form editor's Rules tab lets you create dynamic rules to bring your custom forms to life. To get started, click the Add New Rule button (circled). QuickBase puts Rule #1 into the Rule box. (As you create more rules, QuickBase numbers them automatically.) Building a rule is like constructing a sentence: "When these conditions are in place, this is what happens." You can make your sentence more complex by clicking the Add Condition or Add Action button (also circled).

NOTE

If a table has only one form, you won't see a Rules button on the Tables page's Forms tab. Instead, the Forms tab has a link that says, "Edit the Rules for the form". Clicking that link takes you to the form editor's Rules tab.

On Form Builder's Rules tab, click the Add New Rule button. When you do, QuickBase automatically starts writing out the rule for you in the Rules box. As you make selections from the following areas, QuickBase revises the sentence in the Rules box to reflect your choices:

Set the condition

A rule's *condition* defines its trigger—the circumstances under which you want Quick-Base to take some action. There are three parts to the condition, represented by the three drop-down lists under the word When:

- **A form element.** Possible elements include the record itself, the user looking at the record, a field inside the table, or a combination of elements.

- **An operator.** Your choices in the second drop-down list depend on what you chose for the first, but this list holds different operators, such as *is, is not, is greater than, is less than,* and *is equal to.* So if you pick *The user* in the first list, the second drop-down list offers *is in the role* and *is not in the role* (you'll pick the role in the third list). If you choose *The record* in the first list, the second offers *is opened* and *is saved.* If you choose a numeric field, like Subtotal or Billable Hours, you can choose among these operators: *is, is not, <, < or =, >,* and *> or =.* (For more info on operators, jump back to "Formula Writing Basics" on page 424.)
- **Set criterion.** QuickBase knows what it's looking for in a condition and what the operator is, but it needs one more piece of information before the trigger is complete. If you've selected, for example, *The user* and *is in the role* in the first two drop-downs, you need to tell QuickBase what role you mean. Or if you've selected *Estimated Cost* and *> or =,* QuickBase needs to know the threshold amount. The third drop-down list completes the condition that makes QuickBase take a specific action. You'll define that action in the next section.

Much of the time, you'll have several conditions come together to trigger an action. For example, you may want to specify that the user is in the role of Maintenance Person *and* the contents of the Assigned To field match the current user before you put a rule into effect—which could indicate Millie the plumber looking at her own assigned work orders. Or you might want any of several different conditions to trigger the same action. In either case, you can choose Multiple Conditions from the leftmost When drop-down list or click the Add Condition button. Either action adds more lines to the When section. You specify whether all the conditions must come together to activate the rule or whether any *one* of the conditions in the list can cause QuickBase to act.

Specify the action

You've set up the trigger, the condition that needs to be in place for the rule to take effect. Now it's time for a little action. This section tells QuickBase what to do when it encounters the trigger you defined in the When section. The actions you can choose from depend on the choices you've already made, but these are typical actions you can set up with a rule:

- Change a field's value.
- Show a particular field or section.
- Hide a field or section.
- Require a field (or remove its required status).
- Make a field read only.
- Allow the user to edit a field.
- Display a message.
- Change the value to one you specify.

You can make more than one action happen in response to a condition or set of conditions. Click the Add Action button to add more lines to the Action section.

As you work on rules, you might want to make some changes, like maybe you realized that you hid a field that's also required (meaning users can't save the form because they can't see the field that they have to assign a value before they can save!). If you want to remove a condition or an action without clearing the whole form and starting over, click the leftmost drop-down menu of the rule or condition you want to get rid of, and then select <remove this condition> or <remove this action>. After you've set up all the rules you want to apply to this form, click Save or Save & Done. (You can also click Preview to take a peek at how these rules will affect the form.)

TROUBLESHOOTING MOMENT

Playing by the Rules

Using rules to make your forms dynamic saves a lot of time, adjusts a form to its context, and nips human error in the bud. But until you've worked with them for a while, rules can sometimes be a little confusing. Read on to find out some potential trouble spots (and their fixes) when you're working with rules:

- Rules run in a user's browser. This means that, even though the rule may be changing fields' values as a user works in the form, those values aren't yet part of QuickBase—and they won't be until the user clicks Save. Assuming that QuickBase "knows" something because a dynamic form filled in a field can lead to confusion. For example, say you have a rule that automatically populates the Date Reviewed field when a user turns on the Reviewed checkbox. When the date shows up in Date Reviewed, it looks like QuickBase has that info—but if the reviewer gets distracted and doesn't click Save, QuickBase never stores the date (or the fact that the review took place).

- If you set up several rules for one form, they run in the order they appear in the Rules box of Form Builder's Rules tab. In fact, QuickBase runs a list of rules numerous times, because a rule that appears late on the list can generate a condition that affects a rule earlier in the list. If you want to streamline your rules, you can change the order in which they run: Find your way to the Rules tab. Next to the number of each rule is an icon of a right-pointing arrow. Click it, and then click the left-hand Move Up or Move Down button to change the order.

- Sometimes, you might have a rule that no longer applies at the moment, but that you might need again later on. For example, when it's time for the annual per-

---

formance review, you might want personnel records to display an editable Annual Review text box to users in the Manager role. The rest of the year, you want that text box to be read only, no matter what the user's role. So you've created a rule that makes the Annual Review field editable by Managers. But when the review period is over, what do you do—delete the rule? If you need to suspend a rule for a while, you don't have to delete and then re-create it. Just click the rule's arrow icon to select the rule you want, and then click the left-hand Enable/Disable button. So in the example, you could create a rule for Managers and enable it for one month of the year, and then suspend it for the other eleven. (Of course, if you do want to delete an obsolete rule, you can select it and click the Delete button.)

Using Form Rules to Create Nested Multiple-Choice Lists

Nesting helps you keep forms uncluttered and accurate by showing a field only *after* a user has made a choice from a drop-down list. When you select from a multiple-choice field, a new field appears, showing options related to your selection. You can nest a field inside a field inside a field in this way.

Here's an example of how nesting works: An application that tracks inventory for a used car dealer might have a multiple-choice field that lists makes of cars: Audi, Chevrolet, Ford, and so on. When someone chooses a make—Toyota, say—another field displays all the relevant models: Avalon, Camry, Corolla, and all the other options. If a user chooses a different make—like Honda—the form displays Honda models instead (Avalon, Civic, Element, and so on). This kind of nesting helps keep the data accurate: people can't select Ford Camrys or Toyota Civics by mistake. It also keeps the form nice and clean by hiding irrelevant multiple-choice fields: you don't need to see Chevy or Honda models if you've chosen Ford as the make.

Once you understand how to create the rules that govern dynamic forms, creating nested forms is easy. They take a bit of setting up, but the fine-tuning they offer is worth the effort.

Before you start adding fields to your application, take a few minutes to map out your needs. How can you organize the fields and subfields to make the most sense to your users? In the car dealer's inventory application, for example, you might start off with Make as the main field, then have Models as subfields, and then Editions as a subfield of relevant models. Or you might start off with Vehicle Type (car, truck, SUV, and so on), then list relevant body types (convertible, hatchback, station wagon) as a subfield of Vehicle Type.

Once you've decided on a structure for your fields and their subfields, it's time to get busy nesting them. First, open the application you want to add fields to. From the menu bar, select Customize→Tables. (If you're in a multi-table application, choose the appropriate table from the left-hand list.) Click the Fields tab (if it's not already selected), and then click the upper-right Create New Fields button. This opens the Add Fields page. Add as many fields as you'll need, choosing Text-Multiple Choice as the field type for each. (You can also add fields later, if necessary.)

TIP

Make the names of your subfields specific. In the car dealer example, for instance, the Make field will have several choices: Ford, Chevrolet, Honda, and so on. Each make gets its own specific subfield, so the subfield names should reflect that: call them Ford Model, Chevy Model, Honda Model—you get the idea. This naming system will make your life a whole lot easier when you create the rules that tell QuickBase when to display each subfield.

After you've clicked Add Fields to get the new fields into your application, QuickBase takes you through each field, asking for the choices that will appear on that field's drop-down list. You can provide the choices now, or you can do it later by editing the field.

When you've created your fields and subfields, the next step is to tell QuickBase when to display what—that's how you nest the fields inside each other. To do this, write a series of rules to make the form dynamic, showing a subfield only when someone chooses its corresponding selection from the main list.

To write rules, select Customize→Tables. If necessary, select the table you want. Click the Forms tab, then click "Edit the Rules for the form" to get to the page shown in Figure 11-8. This is where you write your rules, selecting the conditions under which QuickBase displays a particular submenu on the form. Here's how that might look in the car example:

When Make is Audi, show Audi Model.
When Make is Chevrolet, show Chevy Model.
When Make is Ford, show Ford Model.

And so on, as Figure 11-12 shows.

You can also nest yet another multiple-choice subfield inside a subfield. For example, if someone selects Toyota from the Make drop-down list, then Corolla from the Toyota Model drop-down list, you might want to have a Corolla Edition list appear that offers choices representing the different special editions of that model: CE, DX, LE, or none. To do this, you'd first create this rule:

When Make is Toyota, show Toyota Model.

Then follow it with this rule:

When Toyota Model is Corolla, show Corolla Edition.

You need to create these as two separate rules, rather than two conditions within one rule, because you're setting up two separate actions: You're telling QuickBase, "When someone chooses Toyota in the Make field, then you can display the Toyota Model

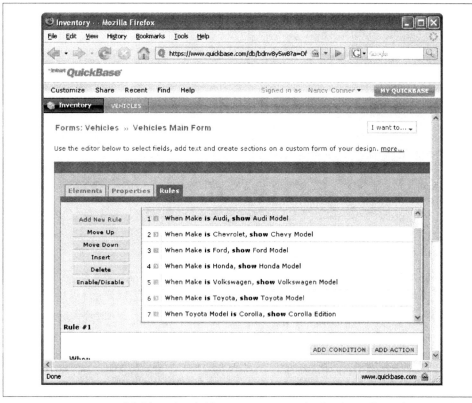

Figure 11-12. To nest subfields within fields, create a series of rules that tell QuickBase to show a particular subfield only when a person chooses the relevant item from the main field's multiple-choice list.

field—don't display any Model field at all before you have the Make info. Then, once you know the Model is Corolla, go ahead and display the Corolla Edition field."

After each rule you write, click Save. When you've written rules for all your subfields, click Save & Done. That's it!

TIP

After you've created some nested subfields, you can create different reports that focus on the info you want to see. In the example, you might create a separate report for each make of car, while hiding subfields from List All.

Letting Users Select a Form to Add a Record

A single table can hold tons of information. And when you have different groups of people using the same table, they're likely using the table for different reasons. For example, imagine that an appliance company's Marketing department is running cus-

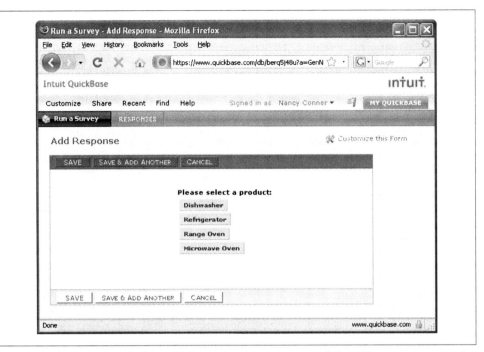

Figure 11-13. An example of a form dashboard: When a customer clicks Add a New Response, this form appears. The customer then clicks a product button to open the right form for that product.

tomer-satisfaction surveys for various product lines; each survey is different, since the questions about refrigerators, dishwashers, and microwaves don't have much overlap. Or say a property management company collects maintenance requests from both tenants and staff but requires different info from each, asking tenants for preferred time windows for repairs and maintenance staff for priority levels and estimated completion times.

In cases like those (and you can probably think of a whole lot more), it would be handy to have a dashboard that lets users choose the right form to add new data to the table. That way, when someone clicks Add a Record, QuickBase displays a page with buttons linked to custom forms designed for specific groups of users or kinds of record. So, for example, someone who wants to fill out a customer-satisfaction survey to let Marketing know how much they love their new fridge would see buttons labeled Refrigerator, Dishwasher, Range Oven, and so on, as shown in Figure 11-13. The happy customer could then click Refrigerator to open the form for that product.

Creating a form dashboard takes a little setting up, but it's worth the effort because you can fine-tune your forms to get the best data in a given context. For example, you may have a field that's required for some users but optional for others. Or perhaps you want managers, but not their employees, to be able to add options to a multiple-choice list. Or there might be a field that's read-only in some contexts but editable in others. A form dashboard makes it easy for you to get the right information in the right context.

Before you set up your form dashboard, make sure that your table has all the fields it'll need for the different forms, including the form that will serve as a dashboard. So if you need to add fields to the table, do that now. (Choose Customize→Tables, select the table if you're in a multi-table application, and then click Create New Fields.) You also need a new field to make your form dashboard work, and this is a good time to set that up; on the Add Fields page, type *Prevent Save* in the Label box and select Checkbox from the Type drop-down menu. (This field will ensure that users *must* select a form from the dashboard to add a new record.) Then click Add Fields to add the new field to your table.

Next, create the custom forms you want to appear on the dashboard. (In the application, select Customize→Create a new→Form; if it's a multi-table application, select the table you want.) Give each custom form an appropriate name. For example, Marketing's Survey Responses table might have forms named Response: Dishwashers, Response: Refrigerators, and so on. The Maintenance Requests table for the property-management application might have custom forms called Request: Tenant and Request: Staff. Set up each form with the appropriate fields.

To perform the next step, you need two pieces of information:

- **The table's database identifier (dbid).** A table's dbid is part of the address that appears in your Web browser's address bar when you work with that table, whether you're adding or editing a new record, viewing a report, changing field properties —whatever. To figure out a table's dbid, open any page related to the table and then look at the address bar at the top of your Web browser. In that Web address, the dbid is the string of letters and numbers between */db/* and the question mark (*?*). So if your address bar reads *https://www.quickbase.com/db/berq5j49u?a=nwr*, that table's database identifier is *berq5j49u*.

- **The form identifier (dfid) for each form you want to be able to open from the form dashboard.** To find the dfid, select Customize→Tables. (If you're in a multi-table application, select the table you want.) Click the Forms tab, and then find the form whose dfid you want and click its Layout button. Look at the Web address in your browser's address bar. In that address, you'll see *dfid=* followed by a two-digit number, which is the form identifier. So for this Web address, *https://www.quickbase.com/db/berq5j49u?a=DformProps&dfid=12&tab=e*, the form identifier is 12.

Make sure you've got the name and the corresponding dfid of each form you want to make available from the form dashboard—write them down or copy and paste them into a list. You'll need this info to create the buttons that users will click to choose a custom form.

Next, create a brand-new custom form that will serve as the dashboard. (Name it something like, well, *Dashboard*.) This form has just two elements:

- The Prevent Save checkbox you created earlier. For this element, turn on the Read-only and Required checkboxes. (You can see these checkboxes on the right-hand side of Figure 11-6.)

TIP

If you don't want the words *Prevent Save* to appear on your form dashboard, turn on the Use Alternate Label Text checkbox. A box opens for you to type in some text; just leave it blank.

- A text element that contains the following HTML code (replace the bolded sections with info appropraite to your table and your forms—details in a moment):

```
<TABLE>
<TR><TH align="center"><B>Please Select a Form</B></TH>
<TR>
<TD><A class="stdButton" HREF="https://www.quickbase.com/db/yourdbid?a=Gen
NewRecord&dfid=XX"><B>Name of form</B></a></TD>
<TR>
<TD><A class="stdButton" HREF="https://www.quickbase.com/db/yourdbid?a=Gen
NewRecord&dfid=XX"><B>Name of form</B></a></TD>
<TR>
</TABLE>
```

After you've put that HTML in the text box, turn on the HTML (Limited) checkbox so QuickBase knows that the text you've inserted is HTML and not just plain old text. From the "Display when this form is used for" drop-down list, select "add".

This HTML tells Web browsers to display a heading (in the example, the heading says *Please Select a Form*) and two buttons. Each button links to a form and displays the name of that form. To make the HTML work, you need customize it by making the following replacements in the code:

- Replace *yourdbid* with the table's actual database identifier.
- Replace *XX* with a form identifier.
- Replace *Name of form* with the name of the form that has that form identifier. This name appears on the button.

TIP

You can create as many buttons as you need by adding more lines like the ones between the <TD> and </TD> tags. For each line you add, insert the database identifier, form identifier, and name specific to your forms. The <TR> tells Web browsers to create a new table row, putting the button defined after the <TR> tag on a new line.

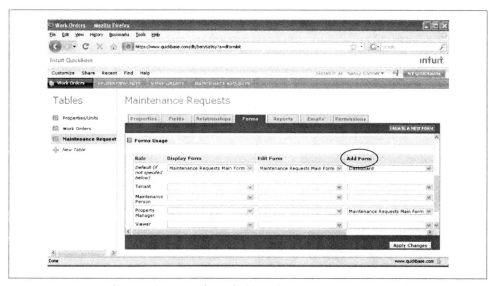

Figure 11-14. To make sure that your form dashboard appears when someone clicks Add a New Record, select Dashboard (or whatever you've named the custom form that serves as a dashboard) in the Add Form column (circled). You can make your dashboard the default for everyone or for just the roles you choose.

You're almost done! Now you just need to make sure that your application's users will see the dashboard when they go to add a new record to this table. Select Customize→Tables (select the table if necessary), and then click the Forms tab. In the Forms Usage section's Add Form column, shown in Figure 11-14, select Dashboard from the drop-down for the appropriate users. You can make this the form that always appears whenever anyone adds a new record, or you can make it the default form for specific roles. Click Apply Changes when you're finished.

Collecting Data via Web Page Forms

Before there was the Web, gathering information from your customers was about as efficient as sending smoke signals. You either transcribed people's names, addresses, favorite colors, and so on over the phone, or you somehow convinced them to fill out and mail in a form (and crossed your fingers that what they wrote was legible). Enter the Web page form, that handy online receptacle that's perfect for capturing reams of neatly organized data. Problem is, you're a QuickBase maven, which means to score big efficiency points, you probably want to create a Web form that automatically funnels info directly *into* QuickBase. You're in luck! And here's the best part: Once you set up a Web-form-to-QuickBase pipeline, your customers don't need QuickBase accounts. In fact, they don't even need to know you use QuickBase—all the magic data collection happens behind the scenes.

Figure 11-15. QuickBase helps you create custom Web-based forms that let people visit your Web site and add data directly to your QuickBase application—they don't even need QuickBase accounts.

NOTE

For this setup to work, of course, you need a Web site. But those are getting easier than ever to create. Both Google and Yahoo, for example, offer simple page-creation tools; for advice on building a more complex site, check out *Creating Web Sites: The Missing Manual (http://www.oreilly.com/catalog/creatingwstmm/).*

QuickBase-friendly Web forms are easy to create using QuickBase's handy Form Creation wizard. You simply tell the wizard which fields you want to appear on your custom form, and QuickBase generates all the necessary HTML code, which you then paste into your site. Even if you've never written a lick of HTML before, don't worry—this section walks you through every step. In no time at all, you'll know how to create spiffy Web-based forms like the one shown in Figure 11-15.

First Things First: Setting up Your Application

Before creating a Web page form, you first need to tweak a few things in the QuickBase application that you want to act as the receptacle. First, you'll set up and assign a role that gives anyone on the Internet—whether or not they have a QuickBase account—

limited, input-only access to your application. Then you'll make sure your application's table's fields are set up to collect exactly the info you want.

Creating a role

In QuickBase, a *role* determines the level of access someone has to your application. As an application manager, you can create and assign roles to make sure that people use your application as you intend. When you put a form on your Web site that lets anyone send information to your QuickBase application, you want to be sure of two things:

- **Anyone can add a record to the appropriate table.** This means you can collect data, such as names and addresses for a mailing list, from anyone who visits your Web site.
- ***Not* just anyone can see, modify, or delete the information the application holds.** Confidential info remains confidential, and there's no unauthorized messing around with you QuickBase application.

To make sure both these conditions are true, you need to create a role just for Web site visitors. Here's how:

1. Open the application you want them to have access to, and then click either Customize→Create a new→Role, or Customize→Application→Roles→Create a new Role.

   QuickBase asks you to name the role you're creating.

2. Give your new role a name like Customer or Subscriber or Tenant—whatever describes the kind of person who'll fill out your form—and then click OK.

   QuickBase takes you to the Roles page for your new role, shown in Figure 11-16, which is where you specify what people in this role can and cannot do.

3. On the Permissions tab of the Role page, turn on the Add Records checkbox.

   This lets them send you information (but *not* mess with the data already in your application). Be sure that this is the only permission this role has—no viewing or adding records or otherwise messing around with the application.

4. Click Save to create the role.

TIP

When you're working in a multi-table application, the Permissions tab of the Create a New Role page shows a separate set of permissions for each table in that application. Make sure that you grant Add Records permission *only* for the specific table you want the records added to.

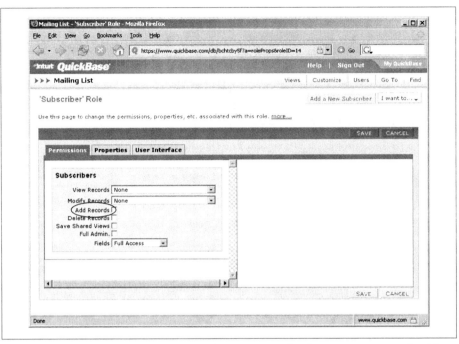

Figure 11-16. Before visitors to your Web site can send information to your QuickBase application, you need to create a role for them and turn on the Add Records checkbox (circled) —that's the green light that lets them add records to your application.

Assigning users to the new role you just created

You've created a new role, but so far it's like a new car with no one to drive it. You need to assign a user to the role so that users can take it out for a spin. In this case, the user will be a group: anyone with Internet access. That way, everyone who visits your Web site and fills out your form can add a record to your application.

To assign users to a role:

1. Go to the appropriate application and select Share→"Manage users" to get to the Users page.

2. On the Users page, click the Add Users tab, which takes you to the page shown in Figure 11-17.

3. From the drop-down menu just below the Add Users tab, choose "Select a group".

   When you do that, you'll see any groups you've created listed in the left-hand box along with some groups that come with QuickBase, like "Everyone on the Internet".

4. Select "Everyone on the Internet" by clicking it, and then click the Add button to add it to the box on the right.

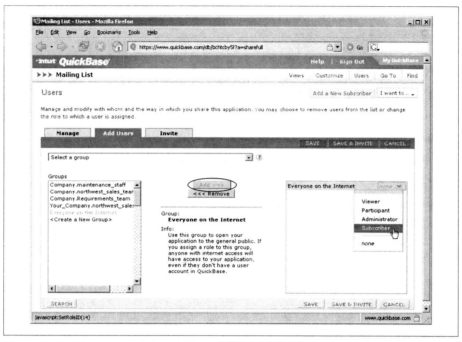

Figure 11-17. The purpose of the Add Users tab is to let QuickBase know who can access your application. In this example, you want anyone and everyone who visits your Web site to subscribe to your newsletter, so you add the group "Everyone on the Internet" to the role you've created.

5. When "Everyone on the Internet" shows up in the right-hand box, a drop-down list appears next to it. This list shows the role assigned to the group; initially it says, "none". Click the arrow next to "none" and, from the list that appears, select the new role you created (Customer or Subscriber or whatever you named it).

6. QuickBase asks whether you're sure you want to grant everyone on the Internet this role. Click OK, and then click Save to assign the role.

Now, anyone who visits your Web site can add records to your application.

Checking your application's table

If you're throwing a dinner party, you don't want your guests to arrive before the table is set. Likewise, you want your QuickBase table all set before everyone on the Internet starts adding records to it. So it's a good idea to look over your table before creating your Web page form. Ask yourself these questions: Do the fields in the table match the fields in your form? Are there any fields you want to *require* users to fill out, such as name and email address? Do you need to change the order of the fields? (When you run the Form Creation wizard—as described in the next section—you can choose the fields you want to appear on the Web form, but you can't reorder them at that point.)

And if you're including a phone number field, you need to handle it a little differently than other fields (see the box in "Sorry, Wrong Number" on page 464).

To add fields or change a field's properties ("Adding and Modifying Fields" on page 293), go to the Fields tab of the Tables page (Customize→Tables) and make the adjustments you want. For example, if you notice there's no field where subscribers can enter their email address (a must if you're collecting names for an email newsletter), you can use the Fields tab of the Tables page to add an email field. Or if you want to make certain fields required (like that email address field), the Fields tab is also the place to go.

WORKAROUND WORKSHOP

Sorry, Wrong Number

Phone numbers present a bit of a challenge for QuickBase. People write phone numbers lots of different ways: Some use parentheses to mark off area codes while others use hyphens; some include extension numbers; and some tack on international calling codes. Because of all this variation, it's hard for QuickBase to *format* phone numbers. QuickBase has special fields specifically for phone numbers, but they're only designed to handle 10-digit numbers that have parentheses around the first three digits. If someone enters a phone number in some other format, QuickBase can get confused—it might cut off part of an international number, for example. Text fields, on the other hand, will accept whatever folks type in without changing the data or cutting anything off.

So if you want your custom form to have a phone number field that can handle all this variation, make it easy on QuickBase (and yourself) and change the phone number field to a text field *before* you create your form. Here's how:

1. Open the application that folks will add records to.
2. Select Customize→Tables. (When the page opens, the Fields tab is already selected.)
3. On the Fields tab, find the phone number field and click its name to edit it.
4. Click the Change Type link. On the Change Field Type page, use the drop-down menu to change the field's type from "phone number" to "text".
5. Click Convert Data to confirm this change.

Now QuickBase can handle any phone number your Web site visitors throw at it.

The Form Creation Wizard

Now that your application is properly set up, you're ready to create the form for your Web page. You can muck around with HTML and Web developer tools if that's how you get your kicks, but the fastest, simplest, most foolproof way to create a Web form is to use QuickBase's Form Creation wizard. The Form Creation wizard helps create all the HTML you need; all you have to do is copy the code and then add it to your Web page.

To get to the Form Creation wizard, fire up your Web browser (either Internet Explorer or Firefox) and go to: *http://tinyurl.com/2hwdqw*. In just four easy steps, the wizard generates HTML that lets you put a QuickBase form on your Web site:

1. Choose a database.

   When you start the Form Creation wizard, you see a drop-down list of all your QuickBase applications and tables, alphabetized by application name. Select the application and table you want, and then click Next. The wizard shows you a list of all the fields that are in the table you've chosen.

2. Select the fields you want to display on your Web page.

   To select multiple fields, hold down either the Shift key (to select fields listed next to each other) or the Ctrl key (to select fields scattered around the list) as you click your mouse button. Once you've selected the right fields, click Next.

   A new page opens. Here, the wizard asks you to type the URL of the Web page you want visitors to see after they've filled out your form.

3. Type in the address of the page you want to use as a confirmation page.

   This can be a special confirmation page that says "Thanks for filling out our form!" or your site's home page. (Because the URL needs to start with *http://*, the wizard has already filled that part in.) After you've typed in the URL, click Make My Custom Form.

   Faster than the world's most lightning-fingered HTML expert, the wizard generates the HTML that lets you put your custom QuickBase form on your site. Figure 11-18 shows what the wizard-generated code looks like.

4. Copy the HTML for your form.

   An example below the text box shows you what the form will look like—take a quick glance to make sure it looks okay. If it does, click inside the text box, press Ctrl+A to select all the text in the box, and then press Ctrl+C to copy it to the Clipboard. (If you want to make changes, such as reordering the fields, you'll need to make those changes in your QuickBase application, and then run the wizard again.)

   Now you've got all the code you need. Paste the HTML from your Clipboard into your Web page's HTML editor (Ctrl+V), and then publish the form on your site.

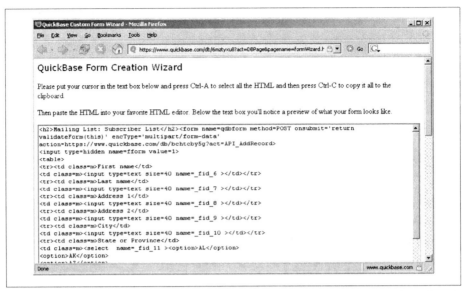

Figure 11-18. Here's a glimpse of the HTML that QuickBase generates to create a form. (Aren't you glad you didn't have to type all that out?) Below the text box (but not shown in this figure) is a preview of the Web form itself.

<hr/>

NOTE

After you've copied the Form Creation wizard's HTML, *don't* click the Save button at the bottom of the page. This button isn't part of the wizard (who's hung up his magic wand and gone home); it's part of your new custom form. So if you click Save, you'll add a blank record to your application. If you want to take the new form for a test drive, you can fill in the fields and click Save, and then check out the new record you've just added to your table.

<hr/>

Now, when someone fills out the form and clicks Save, the new record automatically appears in your QuickBase application. (If you have the table open when a new record arrives, then you'll need to refresh your screen to see the new record.)

<hr/>

NOTE

The HTML that QuickBase generates corresponds to how your table's fields are set up *right now*. If you want to change the form you've put on your Web page—make some fields required or change their order, for example—you need to make the changes in your QuickBase application, run the wizard again, and then copy and paste the new HTML into your HTML editor and republish the page.

<hr/>

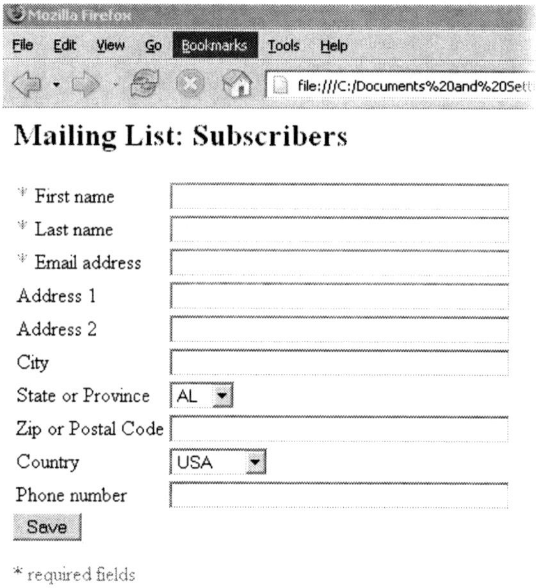

Figure 11-19. The HTML that QuickBase generates gives your form a header written in classic database-ese: "Mailing List: Subscribers". Fortunately, you can change this header and make it say anything you want.

Customizing Your Form

The Form Creation wizard is good, but it's not a mind-reader. For example, the wizard automatically gives your custom form a header that matches its name in your QuickBase application, without asking whether you want a different header on your Web site. Fortunately, it's easy to change the form's header and even add a little explanatory text. All you need to do is tweak the HTML slightly, which is easy—the steps below show you exactly what to do.

Say you've created an application called Mailing List to hold information about your company's newsletter. Your Web form lets visitors to your site sign up for your news-letter by submitting their names and addresses. When QuickBase creates your Web form, the form's header matches the name of your table: "Mailing List: Subscribers" (see Figure 11-19). Not too welcoming, is it?

You can change what this header says and even add a line of instructions about how to fill out the form. Here's how:

1. Open your HTML editor and paste in the wizard-generated HTML that you've saved to your computer's Clipboard.

    The header appears right at the beginning of the HTML, surrounded by header tags. The section you want looks like this:

```
<h2>Mailing List: Subscribers</h2>
```

2. Delete the text between the <h2> and </h2> tags and replace it with the text you want, so it looks something like this:

```
<h2>Subscribe to Our Newsletter!</h2>
```

Now, Web browsers will display your new header.

If you want to add a line of text below the header but above your form, insert the text between the </h2> tag and the <form name> tag that immediately follows it. Use <p> tags, like this:

```
<p>Fill out this form to receive our very next newsletter:</p>
```

Now, when you publish this HTML on your Web site, it will display your new header and text. Your form will look just like the one in Figure 11-13.

TIP

To see what your form will look like before you publish it on your Web site, paste the HTML into a text editor such as Notepad. When you've made any changes you want, save the file in text format by selecting File→Save As. The Save As dialog box appears. Give your file a name that ends with *.html*, and in the "Save as type" drop-down menu, select Text Document. Save the file and confirm that you want to save it in Text Only format.

Next, in your Web browser, select File→Open (if you're using Internet Explorer) or File→Open File (if you're using Firefox). Find the file you just saved and open it. Your browser shows you the file as it will display on a Web page. If you want to make changes, go back to your text editor, make the changes, save the file, and click your browser's reload button.

The QuickBase API

If the first thing that comes to mind when you hear API is Air Pollution Index or the American Petroleum Institute, you can probably skip this section. But if you know that API stands for *application program interface*—which offers the building blocks that let a programmer create a program to communicate and work with QuickBase—then read on. The folks at Intuit have made it easy for you to write your own programs to work with QuickBase by creating the QuickBase API.

An API is a set of routines, calling conventions, and tools that let one program use features provided by another. If you're a developer (or just someone who knows a thing or two about programming), you can use an API to build programs that are consistent with a particular operating environment—in this case, QuickBase. The QuickBase API offers a reliable, stable interface that lets you write programs to access your QuickBase tables.

What Can the QuickBase API Do?

The QuickBase API lets you write programs for these tasks:

- Add, modify, or delete records.
- Change an application's permissions.
- Add or delete fields.
- Change a field's properties.
- Find database IDs by database name.
- Copy a database.
- Retrieve records one at time.
- Find records by executing queries.
- Retrieve and modify the schema of an application.
- Build your own Web applications on QuickBase, such as a generic data entry form for your own Web site.
- Automate back-end processes, like nightly updates of your data.

The QuickBase API works with any environment that supports HTTP POSTs and GETs (methods used to send data from a Web page). That includes, but isn't limited to Perl, Java, Visual Basic, C, C++, Python, Cold Fusion.

TIP

If you're not a programming whiz and you think the QuickBase API can do some cool things for your applications, talk to someone in your company's IT department. By bringing them onboard, you can automate your applications in the ways listed above.

Online API Resources

To get started using the QuickBase API, check out QuickBase's extensive documentation: From your My QuickBase page, look in your list of Applications and click QuickBase Support Center→KnowledgeBase→QuickBase HTTP API Documentation. This gets you to the page shown in Figure 11-20. In the table's Files column, click the *QuickBaseAPI.htm* link. You're whisked right over to the QuickBase HTTP API Reference, a frequently updated document that tells you everything you could ever want to know about working with the QuickBase API.

Community Forum

When you've got a sticky API question, often the best and quickest way to get a good answer is to ask other programmers. QuickBase offers a user-to-user forum where you

Figure 11-20. QuickBase's Support Center is your link to information on the QuickBase API. In the QuickBase HTTP API Documentation table, click the QuickBaseAPI.htm link (circled) to find the API reference document. This table also contains answers to some frequently asked questions about the QuickBase API.

can search existing posts or submit your own question. (And QuickBase staff often monitor the forum, so you might get your answer directly from the horse's mouth.)

Even better, the QuickBase Community Forum is a place to discuss all things QuickBase, so if you've got any question at all about working with QuickBase, it's the place to go for fast answers from people who've been in the same boat.

To get to QuickBase's Community Forum, start on your My QuickBase page and, in the Applications list, click QuickBase Community Forum. This opens the Community Forum's Dashboard, shown in Figure 11-21.

From the Community Forum Dashboard, you can search for a specific topic (click Find) or browse existing topics and their replies, called *threads*. To post a topic of your own, click the upper-right Add a New Message button. The Add Message page opens; type in your subject line and message (you can even attach a file if you want), and then click Save, just as you'd do when adding any other new record. QuickBase posts your message where other QuickBase users can see it and respond. If you want to see the message you just posted, click Reports→Threads (today) or Reports→List All.

TIP

The QuickBase Community Forum is an application with a bunch of different reports, just like any other QuickBase application. To keep up with what's going on in the Forum, you can subscribe to one of its reports.

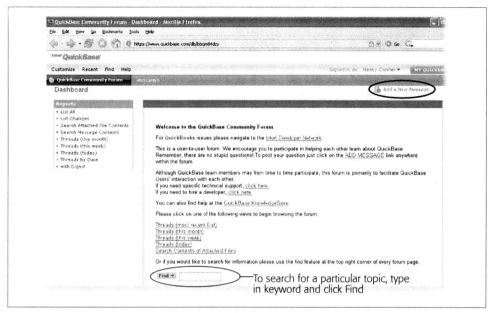

To search for a particular topic, type in keyword and click Find

Figure 11-21. The Community Forum's Dashboard gets you oriented before you jump in on a discussion. If you're searching for a particular topic, use the Find box (circled), or click Find on the menu bar on any page. To ask a question or start a new topic, click the Add a New Message link (also circled). The left-hand Reports menu lets you choose which threads you'd like to view: today's, the past week's, the past month's, the whole shebang, and so on.

When you see a topic that interests you, click its Display button to read it. Each message has a Reply link; click that link to open an Add Message form that puts your reply under the post you were reading.

Play Nicely!

Like every online forum (the ones that are worth reading, anyway), the QuickBase Community Forum has a few rules about posting. These rules are just good common sense, but before you put up your first post, it's worth taking a minute to review them:

- **Post thoughtfully.** Think about what you're saying before you put your words out there for all the world to see. The Forum isn't just for questions; it's also for observations, tips, insights, and opinions—as long as they're related to QuickBase.

- **No ads, no spam, no nastiness.** The Forum is a place for QuickBase users to share their thoughts about QuickBase. It's not a place to advertise your services, post cutesy chain letters, attack others, or use the kind of language that would make Aunt Ethel threaten to wash your mouth out with soap.

- **Stay on the right side of the law.** Using the Forum means you agree that Quick-Base isn't responsible for any third-party information you get there. So if someone in the Forum gives you advice that causes your computer to burst into flames, you can't sue QuickBase over the charred remains. In your own posts, don't use the Forum for commercial purposes, plagiarize, break obscenity laws, or otherwise behave badly. (You also agree to let QuickBase republish anything you post in the Forum—but they won't use your posts for advertising without your permission.)

- **Help keep the Forum clean.** If you see a post that violates QuickBase's guidelines, you can report it. Here's how: Open the offending post and copy its URL (from your browser's address bar). Then click QuickBase Community Forum (it's in the upper-left part of the screen, under the menu bar) to get to the Forum's Dashboard. Once you're there, scroll down to the bottom of the QuickBase Community Forum Dashboard and click the "Send the location (URL) of any offending messages here" link. On the page that opens, scroll down to the Send Us Feedback link. Click it to send QuickBase staff an email with the URL of the rule-breaking post.

CHAPTER 12

Exact Forms: Creating Sophisticated Documents

QuickBase gives you some terrific ways to put your information to work. For example, you can display data in a bunch of different ways using reports, share information by email, print charts ("Chart Reports" on page 56), and export QuickBase data into other programs ("Exporting Data" on page 137). And even though QuickBase is an online database, there's an easy way to get your data into routine business documents, like invoices and letters. By customizing a special template called an *exact form*, you can insert QuickBase data into a Microsoft Word document. Then, just like any document, you can format, print, and send it out into the world.

Exact forms let you insert your QuickBase data into the appropriate places in a letter, report, or invoice. If you've ever used Word's mail merge tool to grab names and addresses from one source and place them in just the right spot in letters or on envelopes, you'll feel right at home with exact forms. And while you can use QuickBase to do a mail merge, you can use exact forms to do a whole lot more. Consider the possibilities:

- Monthly invoices that automatically generate not just the total amount owed, but a list of current orders.
- Personalized sales or fundraising letters.
- Reports to shareholders or customers, presenting up-to-the-minute data.
- Progress reports that show the current status of a project's open tasks, sorted and grouped by team member and priority, to distribute at weekly meetings.

Whatever information your QuickBase application holds, you can get that information into a Word document of your own design. You can even tell QuickBase to insert your company logo or other stored image.

To create exact forms, here's what you need (beside QuickBase, of course):

- Microsoft Word 2000, 2002 (which is part of Office XP), or 2003. At this writing, these are the only versions that work with exact forms.

- Microsoft Internet Explorer 6.0 (or higher) for Windows or Mozilla Firefox Web browser.
- Administrator-level permission in QuickBase. In other words, if you can create an application, you can create an exact form.

NOTE

Currently, exact forms do not work with Word 2007.

Once you've got the right software and the right permission level, here's the basic outline for creating exact forms:

- Download the exact forms template from QuickBase and then open it on your computer.
- Design your form in Word, saving the template to QuickBase when you're done.
- Go to your QuickBase application and print the exact form–generated documents.

This chapter shows you, step by step, how to get the most from this powerful QuickBase feature.

Downloading and Opening the Template

Because you create and edit exact forms in Microsoft Word, the first thing you need is QuickBase's Exact Forms template, which lets you create a Word document and use field codes ("Using Field Codes to Place Information" on page 478) and formulas ("Writing Formulas" on page 417) that tell QuickBase what data to insert into your text. A Word *template* is a predesigned page you can use to generate new documents —in this case, a form. The QuickBase exact forms template also contains bits of code called *macros* (see the box in "What's a Macro?" on page 476) that let QuickBase understand and use the codes and formulas in your form.

You only have to download QuickBase's exact forms template once. After you've got it on your computer, just double-click it whenever you want to create a new exact form or edit an existing one.

Downloading the Exact Forms Template

You create exact forms using a special Word template that allows you to get that QuickBase data into a Word document. You can find the template from within any application:

1. From the menu bar, choose Help→Application Site Map.

QuickBase opens the Site Map, showing everything you can do in an application. Smack in the middle of the page is a section called Forms; in that section is an Exact Forms link.

2. Click the Exact Forms link.

   The Exact Forms page opens, showing you some general information about exact forms. Look for the *QuickBase Exact Forms.dot* link that lets you download the template. As shown in (Figure 12-1), the link appears in large letters in the middle of the page.

3. Right-click the *QuickBase Exact Forms.dot* link. From the shortcut menu that appears, select Save Target As (in Internet Explorer) or Save Link Target As (in Firefox).

   A window opens, asking where you want to save the file.

4. Keeping the same name (*QuickBase Exact Forms.dot*), specify a location to save the template (the desktop is a good place, making it easy to find and open the template later).

   Your computer downloads the file and saves it where you indicated. You're ready to use the template to create an exact form.

Open the Template

After you've downloaded the template, look for it wherever you told your computer to save it. For example, if you downloaded the template to your desktop, look on the desktop for *QuickBase Exact Forms.dot*. Double-click the template to open it. When you open the template, Word launches (if it's not already open). Depending on Word's security settings, you may see a message box asking whether it's okay for Word to run the macros in the template. (See the box in "What's a Macro?" on page 476 for the scoop on macros).

TIP

To view or change Word's security settings for macros, choose Tools→Options (in Word). Click the Security tab, and then click the Macro Security button. Possible settings are Low, Medium, High, and Very High. In general, the High setting offers both good security and a measure of control over which macros Word disables.

The template itself, shown in Figure 12-2, contains some advice for getting started and links to sample forms you can use for a little inspiration in designing your own. Before you start designing an exact form, don't forget to delete this introductory text.

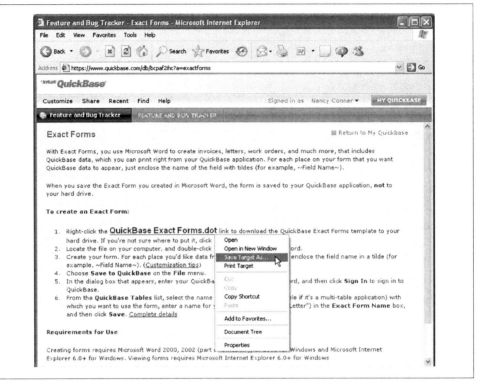

Figure 12-1. Right-click the QuickBase Exact Forms.dot link, and you can choose Save Target As to download the template and store it on your computer.

UP TO SPEED

What's a Macro?

The first time you open the QuickBase exact forms template, Word may show a message warning you that the document you're opening has macros in it and asking whether you want to disable those macros. The warning can look dire, making you wonder whether you want those things—whatever they are—in your template.

A *macro* is like a mini-program. It contains a series of commands that automate frequently performed computer tasks. For example, macros are what make Word's keyboard shortcuts possible. When you type Ctrl+B to turn on bold formatting, you're actually using a macro. Not only does Word use macros behind the scenes, but anybody with a small amount of computer savvy can create macros and save them in documents or templates. Unfortunately, it's that convenience that also makes macros potentially dangerous. Some of the oldest viruses around use Microsoft's macro programming language to do their dirty deeds, and use Word documents to infect one computer after another. When you open a document containing a macro virus, the macro can disable Word commands, insert unwanted text, or even destroy data on a network. That doesn't mean you have to always click Disable Macros when you get that message box,

---

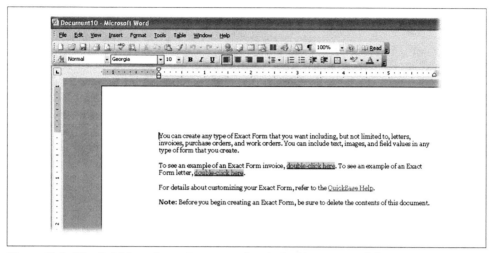

Figure 12-2. The QuickBase Exact Forms template looks like any Word document. Rather than starting you off with a blank page, however, the template offers both text and links to some examples: a sample invoice and a sample letter that you can adapt or use as a starting point to create your own form. Also handy is the link to QuickBase's Help pages. Ctrl-click the link to open a browser window with advice on customizing exact forms.

but you do want to be careful. If you don't know who sent you a document or why it contains macros, then don't let Word run the macros, and delete the document immediately.

QuickBase macros, of course, aren't viruses. The QuickBase template relies on macros to get data from your QuickBase application into your Word documents. Without the macros, you can't create exact forms. If Word asks you whether you want to disable the macros in the template, turn on the checkbox that says you trust Intuit, and then click Enable Macros. Then you can use the template to insert QuickBase data into Word documents.

NOTE

If you have another Word document open when you're working with the exact forms template, you might find that the options in the other document's File menu change to list the template's options (for example, Open becomes Open from QuickBase and Save becomes Save to QuickBase). Things go back to normal after you close the exact forms template. But if Word asks whether you want to save the changes to the template for your non-QuickBase document, select No. You don't want to overwrite your standard template for most Word documents (that template goes by the name of *normal.dot*).

Designing Exact Forms

There's an art to designing an exact form. You've got to become adept at field codes and a few other formulas, but the huge benefit of slipping current QuickBase data into your documents is worth the learning curve. Plus, the folks at Intuit have made it easy to get started. As shown in Figure 12-2, the QuickBase Exact Forms template already has some content to get you started. If you want to compose a letter or send out invoices, you're in luck—the template has links to examples of these documents. Just double-click the appropriate link to open another Word document that contains the sample form. A tweak or two of the invoice, perhaps, and you're ready to save your own exact form.

Using Field Codes to Place Information

Even if you're designing your exact form from scratch, it's easy to get started. The main thing to understand is *field codes*, which tell QuickBase which fields to use in your document. Whenever you want to insert data from a QuickBase record, type the field name surrounded by tildes (~), like this:

~First Name~ ~Last Name~

When QuickBase sees those field codes in your exact form, it looks in the field you've named and replaces the code with the actual field contents. So, when QuickBase looks at the record for Guy W. Sinclair, for example, where you've typed *~First Name~* into the exact form, QuickBase inserts *Guy*, and where you've typed *~Last Name~*, Quick-Base inserts *Sinclair*. And so on through all the records.

WARNING

Pay careful attention to the capitalization and spelling of your application's field names. For field codes to work, the field name within the code must match the field's name *exactly*. For example, if you use *~lastname~* as a field code in your form but the field's actual label in the application is *Last Name*, QuickBase won't insert the contents of the Last Name field into your document.

Use field codes as placeholders for the data you want QuickBase to insert. Here's an example of field codes in a letter. If you type this:

~First Name~ ~Last Name~

~Company Name~

~Address~

~City~, ~State~ ~Zip~

Dear ~First Name~,

Thank you for your order, ~PO Number~...

QuickBase inserts the contents of those fields, making the result look something like this;

Boris Karloff

Spare Parts, Inc.

123 Cemetery Lane

Frankenstein, MO 65016

Dear Boris,

Thank you for your order, QT-7462...

Inserting a Date Using Formulas

If you want to add a date to your exact form, you use a formula instead of a field code. The formula's code tells Word what date to display, and also specifies the date's format. For example:

- To display today's date in this format—November 23, 2007—use this formula: *~=date = new Date();qdb.format(date.getTime(), "date friendly")~*

- To display today's date in this format—11/23/2007—use this formula: *~=date = new Date();qdb.format(date.getTime(), "date")~*

Of course, you don't always want today's date when you're printing out a batch of letters or invoices; the letters might not go into the mail until tomorrow or the next day. To prevent your exact forms from looking like old news before they even leave the office, use these formulas:

- To display tomorrow's date in this format—November 30, 2007—use this formula: *~=date = new Date();qdb.format(date.getTime()+(24*3600000), "date friendly")~*

- To display tomorrow's date in this format—11/30/2007—use this formula: *~=date = new Date();qdb.format(date.getTime()+(24*3600000), "date")~*

- To display the day after tomorrow's date in this format—December 1, 2007—use this formula: *~=date = new Date();qdb.format(date.getTime()+(24*2*3600000), "date friendly")~*

- To display the day after tomorrow's date in this format—12/1/2007—use this formula: *~=date = new Date();qdb.format(date.getTime()+(24*2*3600000), "date")~*

Adding an Image Stored in QuickBase

There are two ways you can add an image to your exact form. The method you use depends on whether you want to insert an image that's attached to a record or whether you want to add a particular image (like your corporate logo) to each document that you print out.

Inserting images from QuickBase records

If you have an image attached to each record in an application—a product photo, for example—you can include those images in an exact form. To add the image, just place the field's name between tildes to create a field code. For example, if your image field is called ProdPic, type *~ProdPic~* in your exact form where you want to place the image.

Adding the same image to every document

Putting an image—your organization's logo, for example—on every document you print is a neat trick, but it takes a little setting up. Before you can put an image on the documents generated by an exact form, you first have to store the image somewhere in QuickBase, so QuickBase can find it when printing out your documents. In addition, you must store the image in an application that's accessible to "Everyone on the Internet." (As "Come to My QuickBase Party" on page 376 explains, when you create an application, one of the groups included in the new application is Everyone on the Internet.) Often, you'll grant this role a permission level of No Access. But for your exact forms to print a logo on your documents, you need to make sure the application where you store the image is accessible to Everyone on the Internet.

Don't worry, you don't have to grant Everyone on the Internet full access to your application. Viewer-level permission works just fine. If your application already gives access to Everyone on the Internet—or if you don't mind giving the Everyone on the Internet role some level of access—simply create a new field in the application to store the image. Assign your new field the field type File Attachment. Then add a new record ("Add or Modify a Record" on page 40) to the application, using the new File Attachment field to hold the image file.

Once you've stored the image on QuickBase, you can add an image link to your exact form. Here's how:

1. Make sure that your logo is stored in QuickBase, in an application accessible to Everyone on the Internet. Open the record that holds the image, and then click the file name (it might be something like *logo.gif* or *image.png*) to display it.

   A new browser window opens, showing the record.

2. Right-click the image.

   A context menu pops up.

3. Select Copy Shortcut (in Internet Explorer) or Copy Image Location (in Mozilla Firefox).

   You computer copies the image location onto the Clipboard.

4. In Word, open the exact form in which you want to place the logo. Position the insertion point where you want the logo to appear, and then select Insert→Picture→From File.

   The Insert Picture dialog box opens. At the bottom of the dialog box is a box called "File name."

5. Click in the "File name" box, and then paste your image's QuickBase location.

   Word gives you three different ways to paste your image: press Ctrl+V; click the Standard toolbar's Paste button, which looks like a miniature clipboard; or select Edit→Paste. Pick your favorite. Next, look at the Insert Picture dialog box's Insert button—it's not just a button, it also has a little, downward-pointing arrow.

6. Click the Insert button's arrow. From the shortcut menu that appears, select Link to File.

   Word inserts your image and creates a link in the document.

TROUBLESHOOTING MOMENT

The Link Won't Link!

When you try to insert a link to an image into your exact form, you may see a Convert File dialog box or an error telling you that Word can't import the file. Although these error messages look final, it doesn't mean you have to draw the company logo freehand on your documents—it just means that Word can't find the file you told it to find.

This error usually occurs because Word can't access the file in your QuickBase application, which means you need to step in to help. If you see a Convert File dialog box when you try to insert an image into your exact form, go back to the application that stores the file and check its access permissions. (To do so, select Share→"Manage users." Then find Everyone on the Internet in the table that lists the application's users.) Everyone on the Internet must have a role other than None. Viewer works well as a role, because you don't want everyone with Internet access to be able to modify your application. (If you're storing the image in an application that you want to keep off-limits for Everyone on the Internet, see the Tip in "Adding the same image to every document" on page 480 for an alternative.)

Once you've set the permissions for Everyone on the Internet to grant some level of access higher than None, follow the steps in "Adding the same image to every document" on page 480 again. With the right access level, Word can insert the image into the form.

Inserting a Table of Detail Records

You can send out an invoice that simply shows the total amount your customer owes, but if you do, you're likely to field some phone calls asking for the details—like a list of the products you're invoicing. The smarter approach is to include those details right on the invoice. You can have your exact form find those details and embed them in your invoice using QuickBase's Report Link field. In a nutshell, when you create a relationship that links two tables, you designate one table as the master table and the other as a details table. One record in the master table (Invoices, for example) links to many records in the details table (Orders, for example). The Report Link field is a field that appears in the master table as a hyperlink. When you click the link, QuickBase shows related records from the details table. Say you're looking at the Invoices table and you want to get a quick peek at all the orders for a particular customer. The Orders field is a Report Link field that shows a hyperlink. You click the link, and QuickBase displays all orders for that customer. Report Link fields are a great way to let users zip from one table to related information in another. (Read all about Report Link fields in "Report Link Fields" on page 410.)

You can put Report Link fields to work in your exact forms. First, find the name of the Report Link field: For example, check out the list of field names that appear on the Fields tab when you select Customize→Tables, and look in the Type column for Report Link. Once you know the name of the Report Link field that links to the records you want, treat it like any other field code by inserting it in your exact form between tildes. So if you want your invoice to list individual orders and the name of the Report Link field is Orders, type ~Orders~ where you want the list to appear. When your exact form generates this month's invoices, each invoice lists that customer's individual orders related to that specific invoice. Figure 12-3 shows an example of Report Link fields at work.

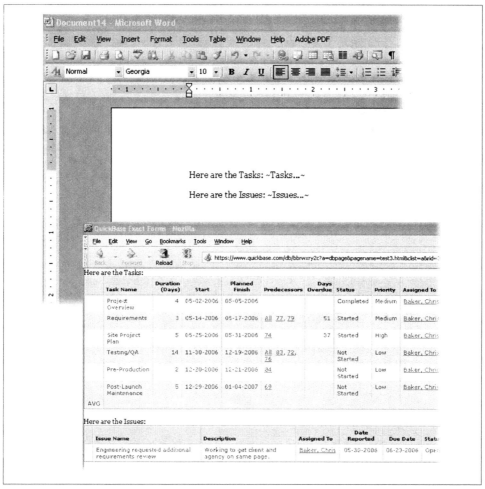

Figure 12-3. Inserting a Report Links field into an exact form is a lot like clicking a link inside a QuickBase table—QuickBase finds and displays the records related to the link. Notice how the ~Tasks...~ and the ~Issues...~ (top) are replaced by the actual data from the QuickBase table (bottom).

Choosing Which Columns Appear in an Embedded Table

When you insert a table into the documents generated by an exact form, you can use formulas to specify which columns appear in the embedded table and how to sort and group its records. In essence, these *formulas* tell QuickBase to perform some sort of calculation on your table. Chapter 11 gives you the lowdown on working with formulas, but here's how to use them to format tables that you embed in your exact form–generated documents.

To format embedded tables, you need to add database and field identifiers to your formulas:

- **Database identifier.** QuickBase uses this unique string of text to identify a particular database. To find the database identifier (dbid), open the report you want and look at the Web address in your browser's address bar. Between the first part of the Web address *(https://www.quickbase.com/db/)* and the question mark *(?)* is a string of letters or letters and numbers. This text string is the table's database identifier. So in this Web address: *https://www.quickbase.com/db/bbrwxryz9? a=q&qid=1,* the database identifier is *bbrwxryz9.*

- **Field identifier.** As its name suggests, a field identifier (fid) is how QuickBase tells one field in a table apart from all the others. You can find a field identifier for a particular table by selecting Customize→Tables. Make sure the Fields tab is selected and, if necessary, choose a table from the left-hand list. Find the field you want, and follow its row to the right, to the Field ID column, which shows the number that's the fid for each field. When you've got the number, you've got that field's fid.

TIP

If you don't see a Field ID column on the Fields tab of the Tables page, click the lower-right button labeled Show Field IDs. QuickBase adds the Field ID column to the list of fields.

If you don't tell QuickBase which columns you want to display in an embedded table, QuickBase uses the default order (Figure 2-16) for those columns. If, however, you want the embedded table to display only certain columns or to display columns in a particular order, you can tell QuickBase to do that by putting your own values into this formula:

```
~=qdb.GetURL("targetdbid",
        "API_GenResultsTable^query={'10'.EX.'"+ field["Source
        Field"]+"'}^clist=18.17.21.22.24^options=nvw.ned.phd.nfg.sortorder-A^slist=3");~
```

To get this formula to work, you have to make some substitutions with actual information from the application for which you're creating the exact form:

- Replace *targetdbid* (the target database identifier) with the database ID of the details table that will produce the embedded table in your document.

- Replace the number *10* with the field identifier of the target field in the details table. (Usually, this is a reference field. To find a table's reference fields, select Customize→Tables, make sure the Fields tab and the table you want are selected, and then look in the Info column.)

- Replace the words *Source Field* with the actual name of the master table's source field, usually the key field.

- Replace the string of numbers *18.17.21.22.24* with a list of field identifiers that match the columns you want to display. Start with the fid of the column that you want to appear at the far left of your table, and separate fids with periods. In this case, the field whose fid is 18 would be the leftmost column, followed by the field whose fid is 17, and then 21, and so on.

- Replace the number 3 with the fid of the field you want to use for sorting ("Table Reports" on page 70).

Besides choosing only certain columns and putting them in a certain order, you can also tell QuickBase to display just certain records. This comes in handy when you're printing out invoices, for example, and you want the embedded table to show only those orders whose status is unpaid. The formula looks a lot like the previous formula for displaying certain columns, with a new section added:

```
~=qdb.GetURL("targetdbid",
        "API_GenResultsTable^query={'10'.EX.'"+ field["Source
        Field"]+"'}AND{'15'.EX.'criterion'}^clist=18.17.21.22.24^options=
        nvw.ned.phd.nfg.sortorder-A^slist=3");~
```

In this formula, the same substitutions you made for selecting certain fields apply. In the new section—*AND{'15'.EX.'criterion'}*—make these substitutions, as well:

- For the number *15*, substitute the field identifier from the details table that Quick-Base will use to select a group of records from that table. For example, if you want to print only those records marked Unpaid in the Status field, use the fid of the Status field.

- For the word *criterion*, substitute the actual criterion you want QuickBase to use in selecting certain records. In the example, you'd use the word *Unpaid*.

By selecting and printing only pertinent records in an embedded table, you can avoid confusing your customers ("Why does the invoice show this order I paid for last month?") and maybe even spare a few trees.

There's another neat trick you can do when embedding tables in exact form–produced documents. Normally, an embedded table doesn't group the records it displays into subtotals. If you want the table to show subtotals, use this basic formula:

```
~=qdb.GetURL("targetdbid",
        "API_GenResultsTable^query={'10'.EX.'"+ field["Source
        Field"]+"'}^options=
        nvw.ned.phd.nfg.sortorder-A.groupby-V^slist=3");~
```

To make this formula your own, make the same substitutions you made earlier for *targetdbid*, the number *10*, and the phrase *Source Field*. For the number *3*, substitute the fid of the field in the details table that you want QuickBase to group for subtotaling.

Saving Your Exact Form

After you've created and customized your form, you're ready to generate documents. Well, almost ready: First you have to save the form. Because your exact form draws information from your QuickBase tables to create documents, you save the form in

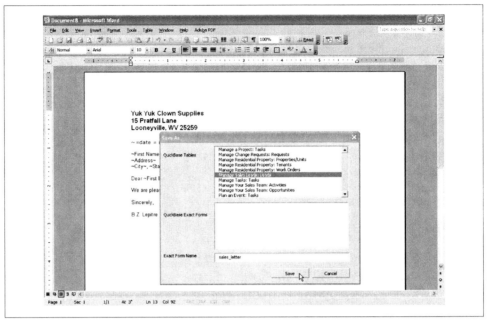

Figure 12-4. When you save an exact form to QuickBase, QuickBase displays all the tables in your applications. Select the table you want the form to pull its data from. Be sure to give your form a descriptive name so you can find it later.

QuickBase—not on your computer's hard drive. So when you've created and customized your exact form, follow these steps to save it:

1. From within Word, select File→Save to QuickBase.

   A dialog box opens, asking you to sign in to QuickBase.

2. Type your QuickBase user name (if it's not already filled in) and password, and then click Sign In.

   The Save As dialog box (Figure 12-4) opens, listing all the tables in your QuickBase applications.

3. Select the table that your exact form will get its data from.

   If there are any exact forms currently associated with that table, they appear in the QuickBase Exact Forms box. If you're updating an existing form, click that form's name to put it in the Exact Form Name box.

4. Type the name of your new form in the Exact Form Name box, and then click Save.

   QuickBase saves your form and displays a confirmation box.

5. Click OK.

   Now you can open the application in QuickBase and print out documents from your exact form (the next section tells you how).

Query identifier

Click any link in this column
to print the exact form related
to a particular record

Figure 12-5. To save your exact form, QuickBase creates a new field for each record, displaying this field in the Print <Exact Form Name> column of the table where you saved the form. To see how the form will look with the details from a record filled in, click any link in that column. The query identifier (qid, circled) helps you print out exact-form documents for all records in the table—see "Downloading and Opening the Template" on page 474.

QuickBase saves your form as a set of HTML pages—one page for each record in the table. To store those pages, QuickBase creates a new field in the table where you save the form. In Figure 12-5, the new field is the far-right column labeled "Print sales_letter." (This column header reflects the name you give your exact form when you save it. So if you name the form Invoice, for example, the column says Print Invoice). Each row in the Print column holds a link that opens the document your exact form generates: the finished sales letter or invoice (or whatever) for that record. Click any link to open a new browser window that shows the document for that record. When you print your documents, as described in the next section, you're actually printing these HTML pages.

Printing Your Documents from an Exact Form

Now that you've done the work of creating, customizing, perfecting, and saving your exact form, you don't want it just to sit in QuickBase, never seeing the light of day. The whole point of creating an exact form is to make it easy to get the details of a QuickBase

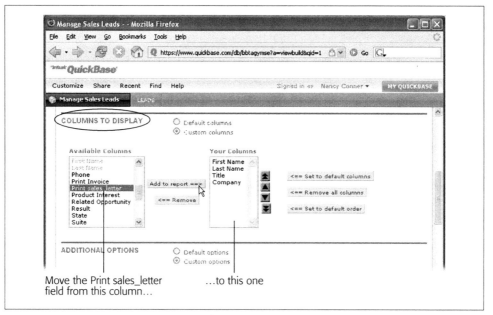

Move the Print sales_letter
field from this column...

...to this one

Figure 12-6. When you can't find your exact form in a table where it should be, check in Report Builder's Columns To Display section (circled) to see whether the report is set up to display the field that holds the exact form. If it's not, move the exact form (Print sales_letter in this example) from the Available Columns box to the Add Columns box, and then save or display the report.

application into printed documents. Printing an exact form is about as easy as clicking a link:

1. In the application that holds the exact form, open a report where you can see the Print <Your Exact Form Name> field. Find the record you want to print, and thenclick the link in the Print <Your Exact Form Name> column.

   A new browser window opens, displaying the document.

2. Check to make sure the document looks the way you want it to. (If it doesn't, go back and make adjustments to your exact form, and then save the changes.) Click File→Print.

   The Print dialog box opens.

3. Check the print settings and click OK.

   Your printer spews out a hard copy of the document, with the QuickBase data inserted.

Printing out one document generated by an exact form is all well and good, but you're more likely to need to print whole batches of letters, invoices, work orders, purchase orders, and so on.

To print exact-form documents for all the records in a table, start by finding the query identifier for the report that contains the records you want to print. A *query identifier* (also known as a *qid*) is how QuickBase distinguishes one particular report from all the others. The qid is easy to find. Open the report you want (such as a Customers table holding the exact form), and then look at the Web address in your browser's address bar. The very last number of the Web address is that report's qid (Figure 12-5). It appears at the end of a text string that looks like this: *&qid=*. Immediately after the equals sign is a number (which can be more than one digit) that represents the query identifier. When you've found the qid, either memorize the number, write it down, or select and copy it.

After you know the qid for the report that holds the records you want to print, click the "print <Your Exact Form Name>" link for any record. A new browser window opens, just as in step 1 of printing individual records. To make QuickBase print all the records in your chosen report instead of just that one, you'll make some changes to the Web address that appears in the address bar of this window. At the end of the Web address is the text string *&rid=* followed by some number, as shown in Figure 12-7. Change this text string to point to your report's query identifier. So, for example, if your qid number is 15, change *rid* to *qid* and change the number after the equals sign to *15*. In other words, you're changing the letters *rid* to *qid* and making sure the number at the end is the query identifier of the report you want.

After you've adjusted the Web address, click Enter. QuickBase displays all the records of your report in one document. When you print the document ("Print a Report" on page 68), you get all the records, one per page.

Editing an Exact Form

Some exact forms you can use over and over again, just as they are. Once you've created an exact form to print out invoices, for example, you can use that same form at intervals to generate invoices for the current records in the Invoices table.

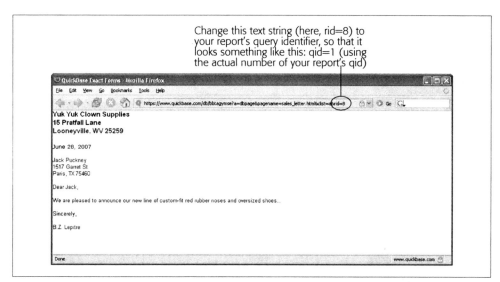

Figure 12-7. *You don't have to print out your exact form documents one by one. By changing the end of the Web address, you can print all records in a particular report in one big batch. You'll save yourself tons of time and not wear out your mouse with zillions of unnecessary clicks.*

Other exact forms, though, you'll want to change over time. For example, a quarterly fundraising letter for a nonprofit will probably say something a little different each time you send it out. After all, you'll want to keep potential donors informed of recent developments, new initiatives, and why you need more money on top of what they already sent last quarter. For a case like this, you don't have to create a whole new exact form for each new version of the fundraising letter—you can edit an existing form, fleshing out your new letter on the bones of the old.

When you want to modify an exact form you created previously, here's what you do:

1. Open the exact forms template (*QuickBase Exact Forms.dot*) by double-clicking it.

   If you don't already have Word open on your computer, the template starts it up. The template opens in Word.

2. From within Word, choose File→Open from QuickBase.

   A QuickBase sign-in box appears.

3. Type in your sign-in information and click Sign In.

   The Open box appears, looking very much like the Save As box shown back in Figure 12-4.

4. In the Open box's QuickBase Tables list, find and select the table that has the exact form you want to modify.

   When you select a table that has exact forms associated with it, the names of the forms appear in the QuickBase Exact Forms section.

5. Choose the exact form you want to change, and then click Open.

Word opens the form, ready for you to edit.

Now you can make whatever changes you want—rearrange fields, add new text, alter the date from tomorrow to next Tuesday, and so on. ("Downloading and Opening the Template" on page 474 describes your various options for customizing an exact form.)

When your new and improved form is all set, save it to QuickBase ("Saving Your Exact Form" on page 485). If you're editing an existing form, then you've got two options for how you save it:

- If you want to overwrite the previous version of the form, choose File→Save to QuickBase. QuickBase updates the existing exact form and displays a confirmation prompt to tell you it's saved your changes.

- If you want to preserve the previous version of the form and save this one with a different name, choose File→Save to QuickBase As. The Save As dialog box (shown in Figure 12-4) appears. Select the table where you want to save the form, give the form a descriptive name in the Exact Form Name text box (something like Fundraising Letter Spring 08 works well), and then click Save. QuickBase confirms that it's saved the form. Now you can go to the application and print out your documents ("Printing Your Documents from an Exact Form" on page 488).

Deleting an Exact Form

They say all good things must come to an end, so there may well come a time when you no longer need an exact form you created. Just as you open, save, and print exact forms from your QuickBase application, you also delete them from there.

You can delete an exact form in a flash:

1. Open the application that holds the form and select Customize→Application, and then click the Pages tab.

   The application's Pages tab, shown in Figure 12-8, opens. Here you see all the different pages associated with your QuickBase application.

2. Find the exact form you want to delete. Its name ends with .html and its type, of course, is Exact Form. Click the far right Delete button.

   QuickBase asks whether you're sure you want to delete the form. (Be extra certain, because once you've deleted it, you can't get it back.)

3. Click "Yes, delete it."

   Poof! Your exact form disappears.

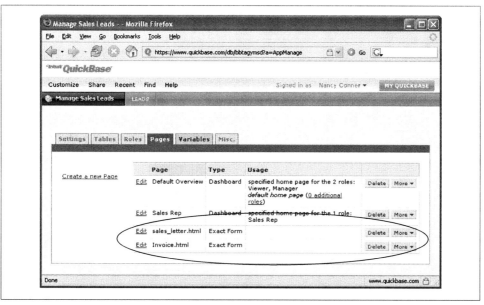

Figure 12-8. To delete an exact form from QuickBase, navigate to the application's Pages tab, find the exact form in the list of pages (two examples are circled), click Delete, and then confirm. It's that simple.

NOTE

In Figure 12-8, you may have noticed that there's an Edit link to the left of each exact form. If you click it, though, you'd better be fluent in HTML (hypertext markup language). When you click Edit, QuickBase opens a text editor that displays your exact form—along with all the code QuickBase uses to display it. If you don't know HTML, you're likely to mess up your form by trying to edit it here. Bottom line: The best, easiest, most foolproof way to edit an exact form is to follow the steps listed in "Editing an Exact Form" on page 490 .

CHAPTER 13

Switching from Microsoft Access to QuickBase

As your company changes, so do its database needs. What worked a few years ago may no longer be serving your organization. You need a solution that works equally well for workgroups, departments, branches, and the entire enterprise—plus folks outside your company like partners, vendors, and customers. And because you know that change happens fast and can be unpredictable, you want something that will still be working five years down the road.

QuickBase can meet these challenges and more. But your employees are used to working with Microsoft Access, and you want to be sure that their learning curve won't be too steep when you switch. This chapter can help put your mind at ease by showing you how to move from Access to QuickBase: what's similar, what's different, and how common tasks and terminology compare.

Why Make the Switch?

The reasons to switch to QuickBase are the same ones that make so many organizations choose QuickBase in the first place. QuickBase is powerful, flexible, and easy to use. If you're used to the old-style model of software that's installed on site, the software-as-a-service (SaaS) model that QuickBase uses offers some additional perks. When software is a service you subscribe to, you don't have to buy licenses. With QuickBase, your monthly cost is based on the number of people in your organization who use the service. Technical issues such as installation, upgrades, and bug fixes become a thing of the past. And with all your data in one place, you can be sure that everyone always has the most up-to-the-minute information. Read on to see why switching to QuickBase is a good idea.

Ease of Use

Unlike some programs, where you practically need an advanced degree in computer programming to get past the welcome screen, QuickBase is simple to learn and a cinch to use. Within seconds of opening your account, you can create a new application by using one of QuickBase's prebuilt templates (Chapter 6) or based on your own data and design (Chapter 7). And because QuickBase is so flexible, you can customize your applications in ways that makes sense to you—there's no need to create elaborate workarounds or beg IT to tweak things for you.

TIP

Though QuickBase is easy to use, you may come up with questions from time to time. Fortunately, getting answers is easy, too. You've already found this book (smart you!). Other resources include the QuickBase Help files, KnowledgeBase, Community Forums, Video Tutorials, and more. To use these resources, click Help in the gray menu bar at the top of any QuickBase page.

Sharing Data

What's the point of collecting, organizing, and storing data if you're going to keep it all to yourself? Unless you're cataloguing the contents of your sock drawer, databases are meant to be shared, giving folks access to essential information. Besides, why keep all the work—er, *fun*—to yourself when others can pitch in?

When you use Access, you can share your database only with other people who use Access. For example, you could put your database on the network server at work, making it accessible to folks with Access on their computers. But what if you want to share with someone who doesn't use Access, or with people who don't use your organization's internal network? That's when things get tricky.

With QuickBase, there's no expensive software to install and no server for you to maintain. Anyone with a Web browser and Internet access (and your permission) can share your database, letting you share information with consultants or freelancers without having to take a poll about who has what software. QuickBase also lets you share databases with your branch offices, whether they're in Bangor or Bangkok. And if you want to collect info from visitors to your Web site—like product orders or addresses for a mailing list—you can do that, too.

Keeping Your Data Secure

If you're new to SaaS (or even if you're not), you probably have questions about security. It can be a little nerve-racking to transmit your organization's sensitive data via the Internet and store it in someone else's data centers. Intuit understands, and that's why they've taken steps to make sure that your data is extra secure when you use QuickBase:

- **Safe travels.** As your data crosses the Internet, it's secure. QuickBase uses the Secure Socket Layers (SSL) protocol, which means that your information is encrypted as it travels through the World Wide Web, keeping it safe from anyone who might want to take a peek.

- **Safe storage.** The data centers where QuickBase stores your information use state-of-the-art security such as:

   —The most advanced firewall available.

   —Encryption of your stored data.

   —Daily backups of all data.

   —Rigorously tested software and hardware that detect and stop intrusion attempts.

   —Uninterruptible power supplies and multiple backup generators in case the power goes out.

   —Round-the-clock, on-site security that never takes a day off.

- **Safe access.** To use QuickBase, you (and everyone else) has to register. Nobody gets access to your information unless you explicitly allow it—and that includes QuickBase staff. In fact, as Chapter 9 explains, you can set permissions that give you fine-grained control over who can see, add to, edit, or delete your data. You can even limit access to specific information within your database by setting field-level permissions (see "Applying Field Restrictions" on page 309 to learn how).

- **A trusted name.** If you're among the millions of people who've done their taxes using Intuit's TurboTax on the Web, you'll be pleased to know that QuickBase uses the very same data center for QuickBase.

TIP

If you want, you can also back up your QuickBase data and store it offline. Simply export the data (see "Exporting Data" on page 137) and save it wherever you like.

Additionally, the QuickBase Enterprise Edition (see "Using QuickBase Enterprise Edition" on page 332) enhances security by letting you create centralized password and security policies, use IP address filtering, and employ LDAP authentication to integrate QuickBase with your existing corporate password systems and directory servers.

Ending Maintenance Headaches

When you subscribe to QuickBase, Intuit takes care of the software and its maintenance for you. That means you don't have to worry about incompatible hardware, installation hiccups, permissions and licenses, upgrades, security patches, bug fixes, or performance problems. That's a lot of burdens lifted from your shoulders.

In addition, because QuickBase is easy to learn and use, it can save you time and money on training. (If your users can set up an Excel spreadsheet, they can create a database in QuickBase.) And you can customize your applications (that is, your databases) however you like—without having to explain to IT exactly what you want.

When You're Ready to Learn More

Want to get to know QuickBase better before you take the plunge? You've got a couple of options:

- **Try it free.** Take a few spins around the QuickBase block with a 30-day free trial. During the trial period, you can create applications by choosing from QuickBase's ready-made templates, then customize your applications and share them with up to 10 people. To get started, go to *http://quickbase.intuit.com* and click the Get Your Free Trial button. Then follow the registration process outlined in "Creating an Account" on page 2.
- **Learn about QuickBase online.** Taking a Webinar—an interactive online seminar—can give you a good introduction to QuickBase and answer questions you have about it. Intuit conducts free Webinars every weekday on topics such as how to use QuickBase for project management; how to track, share and manage your data online; general introductory sessions to QuickBase; and new customer orientations. To see a list of current Webinar offerings and sign up for one (or more), go to *http://quickbase.intuit.com/webinars*.

Getting Started

In QuickBase, a database is called an *application*. As in Access, an application stores information in one or more *tables*. Within a table, pieces of specific information get stored in *fields*.

Here's an example: Say you want to create a Human Resources database. You'd probably start off with a table called Employees that you'll use to collect info about the people who work for your organization. That table would be made up of fields that hold specific pieces of information about each employee: Last Name, First Name, Job Title, and so on. Taken together, the fields that hold information about a single individual make up a *record*—in this case, a complete picture of that employee.

QuickBase calls a database made up of just one table a *single-table application*. As your database grows, you may add more tables (like ones for benefits, departments, and so on), creating a *multi-table application*.

In Access, how you create a new database depends on the version of Access you're using. One of these methods should be familiar:

- In Access 2003, click File→New to open the File New Database dialog box. In the box, tell Access where to save the file, what to name the database, and what type of file to save as, and then click Create.
- On Access 2007's Getting Started page, click the Blank Database icon. On the screen that opens, name your database and then click Create.

In QuickBase, after you've signed in, you land on your My QuickBase page. (To see what this page looks like, flip back to Figure 1-4.) Click the Create a New Application button to open the Create a New QuickBase application page, where you can add an application by doing one of the following:

- **Use one of QuickBase's prebuilt applications as a template.** You can choose from templates designed for tasks like project management, sales management, and customer service, and then customize them to fit your needs. Chapter 6 has details.

TIP

One advantage of using a prebuilt application is that you can look at the application's sample data to get a feel for how things work, and then delete that data and replace it with the real info.

- **Start from scratch.** If you choose this route, you have several options:
  — Import your data from an existing database, like Microsoft Access or FileMaker (see "Creating an Application by Importing Data" on page 245).
  — Import your data from a project-management program like Microsoft Project (see "Importing from Microsoft Project" on page 249) or Salesforce.com.
  — Enter data manually into a new application like a spreadsheet, using columns and rows (see "Creating a Single-Table Application: Spreadsheet Style" on page 231).
  — Design the application database-style, setting up its tables, fields, and relationships (see "Creating a Multi-Table Application: Database Style" on page 240).
- **Use Intuit's Access Import Service** to get your data into QuickBase (more on this below).

Intuit's Access Import Service helps move your data over from Access. You can find out more about it during your 30-day trial by contacting your QuickBase coach, the person Intuit assigns to help you out with any questions you have during your trial period.

For even more templates, take a look at QuickBase's Application Library, shown in Figure 13-1, which contains more than 200 sample applications developed by Quick-Base users to meet a wide range of database needs, from finance to customer support to product management. You'll even find applications to track things like whose turn it is to drive in the carpool and what bottles are in your wine cellar. To get to the

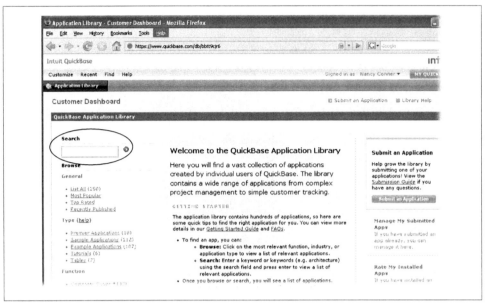

Figure 13-1. To search QuickBase's Application Library for an application you want to use as a template, type a keyword or phrase such as "sales" or "human resources" into the left-hand Search box (circled). Alternatively, you can browse the categories listed beneath the Search box.

Application Library, start on your My QuickBase page. Click "Create a New Application" and, on the page that opens, click "Visit the QuickBase Application Library".

Working with Tables

The heart and soul of any database are the tables that hold its information; this is true of both Access and QuickBase. As you create and work with tables, however, you'll see that QuickBase does things a little differently than what you may be used to with Access. This section gets you up to speed with using QuickBase tables.

Creating a Table

As you work with an application, you may need to add a new table. For example, say you've been collecting classical music recordings on vinyl for years, and you have a table where you catalog all your LPs. Recently, you've decided to join the digital age and collect CDs as well, but you want to keep the two collections separate in your database. In that case, you'll want to add a new table devoted to CDs.

As someone who works with Access, you're used to creating a new table in one of these views:

- **Datasheet view.** This view lets you shape the table by adding records for a build-as-you-go approach.
- **Design view.** In this view, you define the table—field names, data types, and so on—before you create the table. (You can't add data while in Design view.)

Most database power users prefer the second approach: design your table first and then, after it has a good structure, start entering data. QuickBase takes this approach, too.

In QuickBase, all you need to create a new table is a name for it and an idea of the kinds of records it will hold. For example, in your Music Collection application you'd probably name both your new table and its records *CDs* . Once you've decided that, open the application that will contain the new table and do one of the following:

- Click Customize→"Create a new"→Table.
- Click Customize→Application→Tables→"Create a new Table".
- Click Customize→Tables→New Table.

QuickBase asks what you want to call the new table's records (for the exact steps, see "Add a table" on page 226). Once you give it that info, QuickBase creates the table and takes you to the new table's Properties tab. QuickBase gives the table the same name that you chose for the records; if you want to change the table's name, you can do that on this tab. Then, click the Fields tab (see Figure 8-15) and click Create New Fields to open the Add Fields page (Figure 6-11). This is where you design the table: label each field and select its type, such as Text, Numeric, Date, and so on ("Assigning field types" on page 235 explains QuickBase's field types). Then click Add Fields and your new table is ready for you to start entering data.

Working with Table Fields

In any database, fields hold individual pieces of information that, taken together, make up a complete record. Picture a table: Each column represents one field. In a database that tracks customers, for example, you'd have columns for names, street address, phone numbers, and so on.

In QuickBase, as in other database programs, you enter data into a table's fields using a *form*. Each field in the form accepts a particular kind of info, known as a *data type* or a *field type*. When you design a database's tables, you designate the kind of information each field in each table will hold.

Some field types have different names in Access and QuickBase. For example, a field that holds big chunks of text is called a Memo field in Access; the QuickBase equivalent is called a Text—Multi-line field. Similarly, a Yes/No field in Access is called a Checkbox field in QuickBase. For a complete list of QuickBase field types, head over to "Assigning field types" on page 235.

Editing a Field in a QuickBase Table

To edit a field in QuickBase, click Customize→Tables. On the left side of the page, click the name of the table you want to edit (if it's not already highlighted), and then click the Fields tab. Find the field you want to edit and click its name to open that field's Properties page. "Modifying Fields" on page 297 gives you the lowdown on editing field properties.

TIP

When you're working with a form and want to edit a field, use this shortcut: Right-click the field and, from the context menu that appears, choose "Edit the properties for this field."

Writing Formulas

As database gurus know, formulas save time, reduce work, and improve efficiency. Back in math class, you used formulas to perform calculations of various kinds, like finding the area of a triangle. Database formulas also perform calculations. When you put a formula into a field, the database automatically calculates whatever you told it to. For example, a formula can total items on an invoice and calculate sales tax. Or it can figure out average sales for a particular product, salesperson, or region. It can even calculate the number of days a task is overdue. And that's just for starters.

In Access, you probably use Expression Builder to write and edit formulas. (Expression Builder is a tool that helps you write formulas, even when you can't keep track of all the function names, arguments, and so on that can go into the formula.) QuickBase gives you a head start on writing formulas with its specialized formula fields (see "Writing Formulas" on page 417). Each kind of QuickBase formula field works with a particular kind of data. For example, if your formula will return a number, such as the total on an invoice, you'd choose the Formula—Numeric field type. If you're writing a formula that will calculate a length of time, such as the duration of a marketing campaign, you'd choose Formula—Duration.

NOTE

QuickBase has nearly a dozen different kinds of formula fields. For a complete list, along with the kind of data each field type returns, see "Compatibility Check: Are You My (Field) Type?" on page 420.

Once you know the kind of data your formula will return, you can create a formula field that holds your formula and its result. In QuickBase, writing a formula involves two steps, as "Creating a Formula Field" on page 421 explains:

1. Create a formula field.
2. Write the formula on that new field's Properties page.

QuickBase doesn't leave you to struggle through formula writing on your own. On the formula field's Properties page, click Fields & Functions (to the right of the Formula box) to open the Fields & Functions menu. (To see this menu, flip back to Figure 11-3.) As its name suggests, this menu helps you with two aspects of formula writing:

- **Fields.** If your formula draws information from a particular field, getting that field's name even slightly wrong can throw the whole formula out of whack. So making a typo or misremembering a field's name (*Manager* instead of *Supervisor*, for example) can be fatal to your formula. The Fields & Functions menu lists all the fields in your application so you simply click the one you want and QuickBase inserts it into your formula.

- **Functions.** *Functions*, which perform calculations, let you supercharge your formulas. QuickBase recognizes a gazillion different functions (which is good), but it can be hard to remember them all (which isn't so good). Not to worry: When you click the Fields & Functions menu's "Select a Function" option, you see a dialog box that lists all the QuickBase functions. (You can get a look at this dialog box in Figure 11-4.) In the box, choose a category, such as Numbers Functions, Text Functions, or Timestamps Functions. When you do, QuickBase shows you the functions in that category, along with an explanation of what each function does and an example of how you might use it. All you have to do is select a function and then click Insert to put the function in your formula.

TIP

"The Fields & Functions Menu" on page 431 gives you step-by-step instructions for using the Fields & Functions menu.

Relating Tables

When you've got several tables in your database (QuickBase calls that a multi-table application), you can create relationships between those tables. When two tables are *related*, there's a link between their records. For example, in a Human Resources database, you might create a relationship between an Employees table and a Departments table so that updates to the Departments table (such as a new department manager) automatically update related records in the Employees table.

As Chapter 10 explains, QuickBase tables relate on a one-to-many basis. In the Human Resources example, for instance, one Department has many Employees. The "one" side of the relationship is called the *master table*, and the "many" side is called the *details table*. This means that many records in the details table can relate to a single record in the master table. In other words, several employees are linked to a single department. Figure 13-2 shows how QuickBase illustrates a one-to-many relationship.

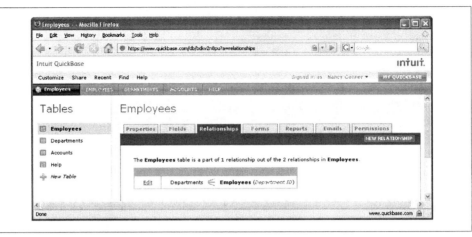

Figure 13-2. A one-to-many relationship: One department has many employees, which you can tell from the little crow's foot icon (the "toes" point toward the details table).

When you create a relationship between two tables, QuickBase walks you through the process with the easy-to-use Create Relationship wizard (see "Creating a Relationship" on page 385). In a nutshell, there are three steps to creating a relationship between tables:

1. Choose the tables you want to link.
2. Decide which is the master table and which is the details table.
3. Check the details. QuickBase analyzes your tables and automatically sets up relationships between fields, including a reference field and one or more lookup fields (see "Linking Tables" on page 387). You can adjust these fields if you like, but QuickBase's analysis is so good that most of the time you'll just want to OK them.

Working with Forms

In both Access and QuickBase, you put information into a table in your database using a form that collects data field by field. In Access, you set up and edit a form in Design view and enter data into the form in Datasheet view. QuickBase does things a little differently, but in an intuitive way that's easy to master. This section gives a quick overview of working with forms in QuickBase and tells you where to learn more.

Adding a New Record

Adding a record to a table in your QuickBase application is a snap. Simply open the application you want and, in the blue bar at the top of the page, click the name of the relevant table and then select "Add a New Record." (The actual menu item will specify the kind of record you're adding. For example, in a time-tracking application, it will say "Add a New Timecard," in the Employees table, it will say "Add a New Employee," and so on.) This opens a blank form, similar to the one shown in Figure 13-3. Enter your information and then click Save or Save & Add Another to add the record to the table.

TIP

In a single-table application, you don't have to choose a table; simply click the upper-right "Add a New Record" link.

Editing an Existing Record

When you need to make changes to a record, open the relevant application. In a multi-table application, head to the blue bar at the top of the page and click the name of the table you want, then select List All. If you're working a single-table application, open the application and click List All in the left-hand Reports menu. Then find the record you want and click the Edit button to its left.

TIP

You can use the Find box to zero in on the precise record you want. Open the appropriate application and then go to the gray menu bar and click Find. In the box that opens, type in some part of the record: a last name, a Zip code—whatever you can recall. In a multi-table application, choose the table you want from the dropdown list (or simply search all the application's tables). Click Find to see a list of records that match what you searched for. To learn more about searching an application's records, see "Find an Existing Record" on page 42.

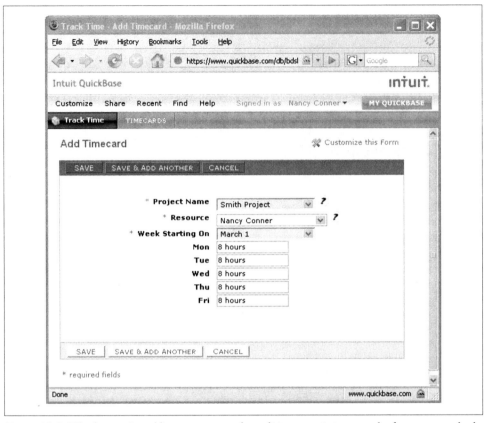

Figure 13-3. Whether you're adding a new record or editing an existing one, the form you use looks something like this.

Editing a Form

As you go merrily along adding or editing records, you may realize that the form you're working with needs some tweaking. Maybe your workflow would be smoother if the fields were reorganized. Or maybe someone's error has assigned the wrong data type to a field. Not to worry; you can make the fix easily. In QuickBase, there are two ways to edit a form:

- **From the form itself.** Use this method if you want to add a new field, remove an existing field from the form (while keeping the field and its data in the application), or edit the field's properties (such as its name, type, and so on). Right-click a field (Control-click on a Mac) and, from the context menu that pops up, choose the option you want. For specific instructions about making changes to a form's fields, see "Customizing Fields and Tables" on page 219.

- **Using Form Builder.** Form Builder ("Customizing Forms" on page 439) makes it easy to edit your form—whether you're making a small tweak or completely redesigning it. To use Form Builder, open the form you want to modify. (Just click the upper-right "Add a New Record" link or, for a multi-table application, go to the blue bar and click the table's name and then choose "Add a New Record". In either case, the word *Record* is replaced by the kind of records the table holds—Employees, Products, Work Orders, and so on.) This opens the Add Record form. In the form's upper-right corner, click the "Customize this Form" link and select either "Edit the layout of this form in the Form Builder" or "Edit the rules of this form in the Form Builder". QuickBase opens (you guessed it) Form Builder (Figure 11-6), which has three tabs, each of which lets you customize a particular aspect of a form:

— **Elements.** Use this tab to organize the form's fields by moving them up or down, or to tell QuickBase to display two fields in the same row. You can also tell QuickBase whether a particular field is required, read-only, or displayed only under certain conditions (edit, add, view, or a combination of these). You can also add text or a section header to the form.

— **Properties.** This tab lets you give the form a name and tell QuickBase whether to wrap text or to show horizontal lines between the form's sections.

— **Rules.** In QuickBase, you can create dynamic rules for your forms ("Dynamic Forms" on page 448). These rules are called *dynamic* because they change the data in a table according to the current situation. For example, you can write a dynamic rule in a project management application so that when someone marks a task as completed, QuickBase automatically enters today's date in the Date Completed field. Or when the user is in the role of Manager, the Assigned To field becomes editable (while people in other roles can only read the field, not edit it). The Rules tab is where you set up such rules.

NOTE

In Access, you use the subform control to display a form inside a form, showing linked records. To do this in QuickBase, use embedded reports ("Working with Embedded Reports" on page 443).

Finding and Displaying Data

In any database, setting up tables and filling them with data is only the beginning. Say you've got a table that holds all of last quarter's sales data. So far, so good. But suppose you want to know which product sold best in each territory or who were the quarter's top three salespeople. To pull that info out and share it with others, you need to be able to query the database for the information you want and then arrange the results in an easy-to-understand format. That's where QuickBase reports come in handy.

One of the main differences between Access and QuickBase is what each program means by the term *report*. In Access, a report is paper-based; it's a hard-copy representation of your data with a layout that you can customize. In QuickBase, a report is an extremely flexible way to view an application's data onscreen, based on criteria you specify. QuickBase reports are easy to share with others who use the application. For example, as the application's administrator, you can put a specific report on the Dashboards of users in a certain role, such as "My Open Leads" for salespeople ("Creating Different Dashboard Pages for Different Roles" on page 361).

Chapter 2 tells you all about QuickBase reports, including the different kinds of reports you can create (bar charts, timelines, tables, and more). This section contains a brief introduction to reports for people coming to QuickBase from Access.

TIP

Although QuickBase reports aren't primarily paper-based, you can create a report and then print it out. "Print a Report" on page 68 gives you step-by-step instructions for how to do that.

Querying a Table

Database applications are all about storing and organizing data. But if you can't find specific records within that ocean of information, there's not much point. Both Access and QuickBase let you query tables to find specific records, but each program has its own terminology and approach to querying. If you're used to the way Access lets you hunt for information, this section shows you how to do the same things in QuickBase.

With QuickBase, you don't need to know SQL (that's short for *Structured Query Language*, in case you've ever wondered) to write a query. When you query an application, QuickBase takes care of all the fancy programming-language stuff behind the scenes, thanks to its Report Builder (shown in Figure 2-11). Report Builder makes it easy to comb through all the information in your application to find exactly what you're looking for.

If you currently use SQL to write queries, you're used to thinking in terms of these elements:

- **SELECT.** What are you trying to retrieve?
- **FROM.** In which table is the data located?
- **WHERE.** What criteria are you using?
- **ORDER BY.** How do you want the data displayed?

In QuickBase, the criteria you specify when building a report answers all those questions—but you don't need to know SQL to put a query together. Here's how you specify those questions in QuickBase:

- **In which table is the data located?** Before you even open Report Builder, you select the table whose data you're querying.

- **What criteria are you using?** Use Report Builder's Filtering section to specify which data to find and display.

- **How do you want the data displayed?** Report Builder has a Sorting/Grouping section that lets you customize how your report presents the data.

- **What are you trying to retrieve?** Use Report Builder's "Columns to Display" section to answer this question.

Instead of dragging and dropping the elements of your query (or wrestling with SQL syntax), you use Report Builder's radio buttons, drop-down lists, and checkboxes to select, format, and organize your report.

Access also has specialized queries, called *action queries*, that not only find data but act on it. Here's a list of common action queries and their QuickBase equivalents:

- **Update query.** For this kind of query, Access searches for certain records and makes changes to them. To do the same thing in QuickBase, see "Searching for Data and Replacing It" on page 130.

- **Delete query.** This kind of query sends Access on a search-and-destroy mission; you specify some criteria, and then Access finds and deletes records that match those criteria. In QuickBase, you can accomplish this by creating a report using the criteria you want to match and then deleting its records. See "Delete a bunch of records from an application" on page 136 for step-by-step instructions.

- **Make Table query.** This kind of query (also called an Append query) selects records from a table and inserts them into another table. In QuickBase, you create a report ("Creating, Editing, and Printing Reports" on page 60) that shows the records you want. Display the report, and then click Other→"Export this Report to Another Table". In the dialog box that opens, choose the table into which you want to insert the records. Click OK and QuickBase exports the records to the table you chose.

- **Query parameters.** Access lets you set up query parameters so users can select which items to display from a list of criteria you define. So does QuickBase, with customizable reports. "Customizable Reports" on page 77 tells you how.

Creating Reports in QuickBase

In QuickBase, querying and reports go hand in hand, thanks to the Report Builder. Here's how Report Builder works (see "Creating a Report from Scratch" on page 61 for the specifics):

1. Choose the application and table whose data you want to query.

2. Choose the kind of report you want to create: Table, Grid Edit, Summary, Calendar, Chart, or Timeline.

3. Tell QuickBase which data you want and how you want it displayed.

4. View your report (admiring it is optional, as is saving it for future reference).

This is just a bare-bones overview of what you can do with QuickBase reports. For the full scoop, read Chapter 2—and spend some time playing around with Report Builder. Its power and flexibility let you find the info you need and display it in an effective, easy-to-understand graphic.

TIP

To get the most out of your QuickBase reports, check out "Tips for Creating Specific Report Types" on page 69.

The Missing Credits

About the Author

 Nancy Conner edits tech books from her home in upstate New York. She's also worked as a medievalist, an English teacher, and a corporate trainer. When she's not writing or messing around with someone else's prose, she likes to read mysteries, visit local wineries, and listen obsessively to opera.

About the Creative Team

Dawn Frausto (editor, copy editor, indexer) is assistant editor for the Missing Manual series. When not working, she rock climbs, plays soccer, and causes trouble. Email: *dawn@oreilly.com*.

Peter Meyers (editor) is the managing editor of O'Reilly Media's Missing Manual series. He lives with his wife, daughter, and cats in New York City. Email: *peter.meyers@gmail.com*.

Nan Barber (editor) has worked with the Missing Manual series since its inception—long enough to remember booting up her computer from a floppy disk. Email: *nanbarber@oreilly.com*.

Michele Filshie (copy editor) is coordinating editor in the Dynamic Media division of O'Reilly. Before turning to the world of computer-related books, Michele spent many happy years at Black Sparrow Press. She lives in Sebastopol and loves to get involved in local politics. Email: *mfilshie@oreilly.com*.

Jessica Mantaro (technical reviewer) is a member of Intuit's QuickBase team. She is also the author of *FrontPage 2003: The Missing Manual (http://www.oreilly.com/cata log/frontpagemm/)*.

Terri Glaze and **Preeti Singhal** (technical reviewers) were provided by Advantage Software, a leading QuickBase solutions provider and developer group. Advantage uses best practices and proprietary development to make QuickBase even more powerful and valuable to companies, helping them get the most out of the QuickBase platform.

See additional QuickBase resources, demos, and webinars at www.advantagesoftware.net (*http://www.advantagesoftware.net/*). Email: *sales@advantagesoftware.net*.

Index

Symbols

" (quotation marks)
  Find box and, 126
  placeholders and, 291
$ (dollar signs), variables and (formulas), 435
& (ampersands), as operators (formulas), 424
() (parentheses)
  functions and, 426
  in formulas, 425
* (asterisks), as operators (formulas), 424
, (commas), function arguments and, 419
/ (forward slashes), as operators (formulas),
      424
/n argument (formulas), 427
; (semicolons), in variable definitions, 434
= (equal signs)
  as operators (formulas), 424
  in variable definitions, 434
>/< (greater/less than), as operators (formulas),
      424
? (question mark) icon, 101, 301
[] (brackets), variables and, 259
^ (carets), as operators (formulas), 424
~ (tildes), in field codes, 478

A

absorbing tables, 321
accepting invitations, 6
access levels
  custom, 365–369
  for realms (Enterprise Edition), 335–336
  roles, 353
  vs. roles, 336
access, searching by, 14, 125
Access, switching from, 495–510
  querying tables, 508
  terminology, 498
  working with forms, 505
  working with tables, 500
account information, changing, 19
accounts, xv
  annual/monthly, 27
  billing, 7, 23–35
    cross-application relationships and, 390
  changing profile, 19
  creating, 2–6, 21
  default, 23
  invitations and, 6
  multiple for single user, 21
  realms, 27
  signing in, 7
  trial, 2
  unverified, 6
actions, 451
Add a New Table box, 227
Add buttons, adding to calendars, 86
Add Fields page, 220, 221
Add forms, 439
adding
  buttons, 272
  dependencies, 313
  documents, 121
  fields, 177, 219, 294, 304
    to relationships, 393
  records, 40, 100
    selecing forms for, 455
  relationships, 385
  sections to Dashboards, 275
  tables, 318

We'd like to hear your suggestions for improving our indexes. Send email to *index@oreilly.com*.

notification emails (see change notification emails)

Notify Whom option (change notification emails), 165

nouns, pluralizing (tables), 327

null values, 430

Numeric (field type), 237, 420

Nz function (formulas), 431

O

objectives, defining, 182

one-to-many relationships, 244, 384

online help, 47

Open permission type, 167

operators, 77, 418, 424

or (formula operator), 425

OR (search operator), 70, 126

Outlook, 179

Override permissions of sub-fields checkbox, 310

ownership of applications, transferring, 260

ownership of records, 356

P

padlock icon, 141

page banners, customizing, 216

Pages tab (Application page), 259

parentheses ()
    functions and, 426
    in formulas, 425

participant role, 353

passwords
    changing, 21
    Enterprise Edition and, 27
    forgotten, 4, 7
    policies for realms (Enterprise Edition), 337

pasting, 53
    importing data by, 104, 245–249
    paste special, 54

payments, requesting receipts for, 25

Percent (field type), 238

percent of series, total options (bar charts), 90

Permission Type option (change notification emails), 165–168

permissions, 7
    restricting, 309
    roles, 353

subfields and, 300, 310

Permissions property (fields), 300

Permissions tab (Manage Billing Account page), 31

Permissions tab (Tables page), 332

Personal Automated Emails page, 157

personal reports, 43
    exact forms and, 488

phone numbers, 238, 421

phrases, searching for, 126

Pick New User option, 293

pie charts, 57
    creating, 87

placeholders, 291

plain text format, 290

policies
    password (realms), 337
    sign-in (realms), 337

Policies tab (Enterprise Edition), 335, 337

prebuilt applications (see templates)

precedence (operators), 424

Predecessor (field type), 240

predecessors (dependencies), 313

preferences, user, 20

primary keys, 230, 242
    (see also key fields)

printing
    address labels, 153
    charts, 69
    exact forms, 488
    Print this page command, 68, 153
    records, 152
    reports, 68, 152

prioritizing roles, 358

problems, defining, 181

process excellence templates, 203

professional services templates, 199

profiles (user), editing, 19

Project (see Microsoft Project)

project management templates, 197
    Project Manager Plus, 208

prompting users (Report Builder), 77

properties
    application, 254
    field, 299
    table, 325

Properties page
    Revisions section, 145

provisional user status, 284

provisioning users, 26

Q

Q icon (QuickBase links), 273
query identifiers (quids), exact forms and, 487, 490
question mark (?) icon, 101, 301
Quick Find feature, 302, 325
Quick Share feature, 284
Quick Start Guide, 210
QuickBase Community Forum, 470
QuickBase Enterprise Edition (see Enterprise Edition)
QuickBase Support Center, 213, 418, 469
quotation marks (")
    Find box and, 126
    placeholders and, 291

R

ranges of cells, selecting, 53
Rating (field type), 238
reactivating users, 35
real estate templates, 202
    Manage Residential Property, 207
realms, 27, 333–346
    access levels, setting, 334–336
    controlling access to, 345–346
    creating, 334
    customizing, 340–342
    password policies, 337
    reports for monitoring, 342–346
    reports on, 342–345
    sign-in policies, 337
recategorizing applications, 13
receipts, requesting, 25
Recent list (Find function), 42
Recipient permission type, 167
Record ID #s, 102, 385
    (see also key fields)
Record Picker, 325
records, 21, 100
    adding, 40, 100
        selecting forms for, 455
    attaching fields to, 239
    change notification emails, 162
    changed, displaying only, 74
    copying, 100
        recursively, 413

defined, 230
deleting, 54, 136, 397
importing, 102–108
inserting, 54
labels, pluralizing, 327
master, 393
modifying, 41, 134
owners, 356
permissions and, 310
preventing multiple-record edits, 364
printing, 152
searching for, 42
undeleting, 54
viewing, 40
recursive copying, 413
recycling applications, 316
reference fields, 388
    deleting, 395
registering with QuickBase, 3–6
relationships, 383–412
    adding fields to, 393
    between tables, 243, 328
    creating, 385
    cross-application, 256, 389
    deleting, 395
    deleting fields from, 394
    deleting related records, 397
    details tables (one-to-many relationships), 384
    linking tables, 387
    lookup fields, 392, 399
    master tables (one-to-many relationships), 384
    one-to-many, 384
    Report Link fields, 410
    roles and, 390
    shared multiple-choice fields, 403
    snapshot fields, 401
    summary fields, 408
    table, 328
releasing reservations (documents), 142
reminders, 169–171
    limits on, 156
removing
    applications
        from My QuickBase page, 14
        vs. deleting, 15
    users from groups, 33
renaming

CPSIA information can be obtained at www.ICGtesting.com
Printed in the USA
BVOW080231030412

286721BV00006B/14/P